WAGNER

as Man and Artist

WAGNER

AS
MAN AND ARTIST

❦

❦

BY

Ernest Newman

GLOUCESTER, MASS.

PETER SMITH

1974

VINTAGE BOOKS

are published by Alfred A. Knopf, Inc.
and Random House, Inc.

FIRST VINTAGE EDITION

Originally published by Alfred A. Knopf, Inc., October 1924

Reprinted, 1974, by Permission of
Alfred A. Knopf, Inc.

ISBN: 0-8446-2653-8

TO

Vera

Preface to the Second [English] Edition

In the ten years that have elapsed since the publication of the first edition of this work a number of new letters and other documents relating to Wagner have become available. The text of the book has therefore been not only expanded but drastically revised at various points; the issue of Wagner's letters to Frau Julie Ritter, for example, has both cleared up one or two points in the Laussot episode which were formerly obscure, and added considerably to our understanding of the affair. This section of the book, accordingly, has been virtually rewritten. It will be seen also that a much fuller treatment is given of the old question of Wagner's parentage.

The vocal score of *Das Liebesverbot* has now been published, and the opera was performed publicly in Germany in the spring of 1923.

There may be people who will think it unnecessary to inquire as minutely as I have done into some of the details of Wagner's private life. Their point of view, no doubt, is that expressed by Frau Mathilde Wesendonck (then an old lady of sixty-four) in a letter to Mr. W. Ashton Ellis given in facsimile in the latter's edition of the Wagner-Wesendonck correspondence. I quote it with its own quaint spelling:

> It is a base and hateful beginning, that of Mr. Ferdinand Prager's, in writing and publishing a book, merely to darken the Meister's Memory to Mankind, by making "Gossip" on the Intimacy of his private Life, a Life, full of Conflikt, affliction and Suffering!—

What hath the Publik to do with it? Deed he not bequeath to him, his unequaled, unrivaled everlasting Work's? And is this holy Testament not above all Doubt and Calumny? Is it not sufficient to secure him vor ever, the grateful and tender Respect, the awe and the Consideration, due to his Greatness and his Genius?—

The "Episode" of Bordeaux has been related by the "Meister" himself, and is to be found in the Edition of: "Hinterlassene Schriften." May we not be content with what He tell's us about it? Need we know more?—

The truth is: that R. Wagner's affection and gratefulness to the "Wesendonck's" remained the same throughout his life, and that the "Wesendonck's" on theire Side, never ceased to belong to his most true and sincerest friend's until to Death!—

What shall I say More! Is it worth while, to speak in so serious a matter, from my owne personal Self?—

The tie that bound him to Mathilde Wesendonck, whome he than called his "Muse," was of so high, pure, nobel and ideal Nature that, alas, it will only be valued of those, that in their own Noble chest find the same elevation and selfishlessness of Mind!—

There would indeed be some reason for respecting the privacy of a great man's life if he and his family set us the example. But both Wagner and the Wagner family have gone to unheard-of lengths to make us sharers of that privacy. His letters have been published by the thousand: he himself left us a huge autobiography. It is a very natural desire in us, under these circumstances, to try to see him as he really was; and that means the careful comparison of one document with another in order to get at the truth. The letters have sometimes been garbled; the autobiography is often incomplete or disingenuous. Moreover, other reputations besides Wagner's are concerned. A man cannot expect to have his say about everyone with whom he came into contact without our trying to find out precisely

how much he was justified in saying some of the things
he did about them. Wagner was anxious to paint his own
portrait for posterity: it is for us to try to find out to what
extent the portrait is true or false.

E. N.

September 1923

Preface to the First [English] Edition

Some apology is perhaps needed from an author for writing three books on the same subject. I can only plead in extenuation that the subject of Wagner is inexhaustible; and I am defiant enough to refuse to pledge myself not to repeat the offense in another ten years or so. It is possible that readers who have done me the honor to make themselves familiar with my *Study of Wagner* (1899) may discover that in the present book I express myself differently upon one or two points. My defense is that even a musical critic may be allowed to learn something in the course of fifteen years; and I can only hope that if here and there I have changed sides since then, the side I am now on is that of the angels.

In spite of the size of this volume, many readers will no doubt feel that it either discusses inadequately several aspects of Wagner's work and personality, or that it passes them over altogether. Again I plead guilty; but to have followed Wagner up in every one of his many-sided activities—in all his political, ethical, economic, ethnical, sociological, and other speculations—would have necessitated not one book but four. I have tried to keep within the limits of my title—first of all to study Wagner as a man, and then his theory and practice as a musician. His operas are now so universally known that I could afford to dispense with detailed accounts of them; in any case the reader will find them fully described in a hundred books, and best of all in Mr. Runciman's admirable *Richard Wagner, Composer of Operas*—though I must dissent from Mr. Runciman's views on *Parsifal*. Nor could

I bring myself to attempt a biography of Wagner. A new biography, incorporating all the material that the last ten years have placed at our disposal, is urgently needed. The work of Glasenapp is copious enough and fairly accurate, but it is hopelessly uncritical of Wagner either as man or artist—to say nothing of its occasional lapses into the disingenuous. But even if I had felt that I were qualified for a new biography of Wagner I should have shrunk appalled from the magnitude of the task. I have preferred to give the reader a chronological digest of Wagner's life in the Synthetic Table at the conclusion of the present volume, and for the rest to try to reconstruct him as man and musician from his own letters, his autobiography, the letters and reminiscences of others, his prose works, and his music. As the book is going to press I learn that a new edition of his correspondence, containing some two thousand hitherto unpublished letters, is to appear under the editorship of that indefatigable Wagner researcher, Dr. Julius Kapp. But it ought to be possible to reconstruct the man from the 2,700 letters of his that we already have, though the picture will no doubt need some filling in and perhaps some corrections in detail when Dr. Kapp's edition is available. With the expiration of the Wagner copyrights, and the passing of the control of his letters out of the hands of Villa Wahnfried, we may hope for a higher standard of literary rectitude in these matters than we have been accustomed to in the past. The earlier, and even some of the later, editions of the letters have been so manipulated as to be thoroughly misleading. I have drawn attention to one or two of these manipulations in the following pages.

I have made all translations from the prose works, the letters, the autobiography, etc., direct from the originals. This has necessitated referring to them throughout in the German editions; but no one who has the current English versions will have any difficulty in tracing any particular passage by means of dates and indices. I cannot hope that with prose so involved as that of Wagner's I have always been able to achieve perfect accuracy; but I am consoled by the consciousness that native German scholars to whom I have referred a few passages have been as puzzled over them as myself.

I have used Wagner's prose works in the latest edition (the fifth) of the *Gesammelte Schriften und Dichtungen* (always referred to in the following pages as *G.S.*), the Wagner-Liszt correspondence in the new and expanded and more conscientiously edited third edition, and all the other letters in the latest editions available. The operas are always referred to in the new Breitkopf edition.

I have to express my thanks to several friends for help of one kind and another—to Mr. Bertram Dobell, the publisher of my earlier *Study of Wagner,* for allowing me to make whatever use I liked of that book for the present one; to Messrs. Breitkopf and Härtel for placing at my disposal a set of proofs of the full scores of Wagner's earliest unpublished operas, *Die Hochzeit* and *Die Feen,* and proofs of a number of other unpublished compositions of his; and, above all, for lending me the manuscript orchestral score of the still unpublished opera *Das Liebesverbot.* I am indebted also to Professor H. G. Fiedler, Mr. R. A. Streatfeild, and other friends for assistance of various sorts.

Some of the matter of the book has already appeared in the *Fortnightly Review,* the *Contemporary Review,* the *Nation,* the *New Music Review* (New York), the *International* (New York), the *Musical Times,* and the *Harvard Musical Review.* My thanks are due to the editors of these journals for permission to reproduce such portions of the articles as I desired to make use of here.

E. N.

1914

Contents

IV • *The Mature Artist:*

WAGNER

as Man and Artist

Introduction

While there is at present no really adequate Life of Wagner on a scale commensurate with the subject, there is probably more biographical material available in connection with him than with any other artist who has ever lived; and on the basis of this material it seems justifiable now to attempt—what was impossible until the publication of *Mein Leben* in 1911—a complete and impartial psychological estimate of him. There has probably never been a more complex artist, and certainly never anything like so complex a musician. A soul and a character so multiform are an unending joy to the student of human nature. It has been Wagner's peculiar misfortune to have been taken, willy-nilly, under the protection of a number of worthy people who combine the maximum of good intentions with the minimum of critical insight. They have painted for us a Wagner so impeccable in all his dealings with men and women—especially women—a Wagner so invariably wise of speech, a Wagner so brutally sinned against and so pathetically incapable of sinning, that one needs not to have read a line of his at first hand to know that the portrait is an absurdity—that no such figure could ever have existed outside a stained-glass window, or if it had, could ever have had the energy to im-

press itself upon the imagination of mankind even for a
day. The real Wagner may be hard enough to disentangle
from the complications and contradictions presented by
his life, his letters, his prose works, his music, his autobiography, and the testimonies of his friends and enemies;
but in the case of no man is the attempt better worth
making. For the enduring interest of his character, with
its perpetual challenge to constructive psychology, is in the
many-sidedness of it. The well-meaning thurifers who try
to impose him upon us in a single formula as one of the
greatest and best of mankind[1] do but raise him to their
own moral and reduce him to their own intellectual level,
making their god in their own image, as is the way of
primitive religious folk. The more authentic and more
interesting Wagner is the one who stands naked and unashamed before us in the documents of himself and others
—equally capable of great virtues and of great vices, of
heroic self-sacrifice and the meanest egoism, packed with
a vitality too superabundant for the moral sense always to
control it; now concentrating magnificently, now wasting
himself tragically, but always believing in himself with the
faith that moves mountains, and finally achieving a round-
ness and completeness of life and a mastery of mankind
that make his record read more like romance than reality.

It is in keeping with the whole character of the man
that he should have left us more copious documentary
material concerning himself than perhaps any other artist
has ever done. Publicity was as much a necessity to him
as food and air. The most interesting person in the universe to him was always himself; and he took good care
that the world should not suffer from any lack of knowledge of a phenomenon that he rightly held to be unique.
It would be a sign of unwisdom to despise him for this. It

[1] "From her [Frau Wesendonck] it was I earliest learnt a truth
which added years have simply verified; that in Richard Wagner
we have more than a great,—a profoundly good man." Mr.
Ashton Ellis's Introduction to his version of the *Wagner-Wesendonck Letters*, p. xl.

has to be recognized that whatever criticism the contemporary moralist might have had to pass upon this or that portion of Wagner's conduct with the outer world, he was always the soul of purity and steadfastness in the pursuit of his ideal. He believed he had come into the world to do a great and indispensable work; and if he occasionally sacrificed others to his ideal, it must be admitted that he never hesitated to sacrifice himself. Regarded purely as an artist, no man has ever kept his conscience more free from stain. And it is precisely this ever present burning sense of the inherent greatness of his mission that accounts primarily for his constant pouring out of himself, not only in music—his musical output, after all, was not a remarkably large one—but in twelve volumes of literary works and in innumerable letters. I say "primarily" because a second set of impulses obviously comes into play here and there. Wagner had the need that many men of immense vitality have felt—Mr. Gladstone was a notable example in our own day—of dominance for dominance' sake; there is something aquiline in them that makes it impossible for them to breathe anywhere but on the heights. Wagner felt the need of over-lordship as irresistibly as his own Wotan did. Had he been a soldier living in a time of warfare he would have become one of the world's despots, with Alexander, Julius Caesar, and Napoleon. Had he been a businessman he would have controlled the finance of a continent through the strength and the thoroughness of his organizations. Being an artist, a dealer in the things of the mind alone, his ends could be achieved only by example and argument. His voluminous letters and prose works are the outcome of the one great need of his life—to win the world to see everything as he saw it. The letters to Lizst, to Röckl, to Uhlig, and to others show how powerful was this desire in him; the least expression of disagreement, the least failure of comprehension would call forth a whole pamphlet of eager explanations. He yearned to hunt out misunderstanding with regard to himself as Calvin yearned to hunt out heresy. Always there was the inability to conceive himself, Wilhelm Richard Wagner, except as the central sun of his universe; ideas and persons had to revolve obsequiously around him or find orbits in another and smaller universe. Here again ethical commentary by way of either praise or blame would be the merest supererogation. One simply notes the phenomenon as one notes the color of his eyes or the shape of his head; it was one of the things that made Wagner Wagner, as the lion's mane is one of the things that make him a lion.

The need for mastery over everything and everybody that came within his orbit extended from art to life. All accounts agree that with people who loved and looked up to him he was the most charming of men;[2] while not only the testimony of his associates but his own words and conduct show with what difficulty he accommodated himself to the natural desire of others to take life in their own way. Read, for example, his naïve account of his anger with Tausig and Cornelius for not coming to him when he wanted them:

"Cornelius and Tausig had again been to see me. Both had first of all to bear the brunt of my real ill-temper for their behaviour during the previous summer [1862]. Having had the idea of bringing the Bülows and the Schnorrs to me at Biebrich, my cordial interest in these two young friends of mine decided me to invite them too. Cornelius accepted immediately, and so I was all the more astonished when one day I received a letter from him from Geneva, whither Tausig, who suddenly seemed to have money at his disposal, had taken him on a summer excursion—no doubt of a more important and more agreeable nature. Without the slightest expression of regret at not being able to meet me this summer, I was simply told that they had just gaily 'smoked a splendid cigar to my health.' When I met them again in Vienna, I could not refrain from pointing out to them the offensiveness of their conduct; but they did not seem to understand that I could have had any objection to their preferring the beautiful

[2] See, for example, the reminiscences of Judith Gautier, *Wagner at Home*, English translation by Effie D. Massie.

tour in French Switzerland to visiting me at Biebrich.
They obviously thought me a tyrant." [3]

In the winter of 1872–3 Nietzsche decided to spend his
brief holiday at home, partly in order that he might see
something of his mother, partly to work undisturbedly at
his book on Greek philosophy. Wagner, however, had
need of him, and sent him an urgent call to Bayreuth,
which Nietzsche felt himself compelled, under the circumstances, to disregard. Wagner was so vexed that he
would not even acknowledge the receipt of the privately
printed thesis that Nietzsche shortly afterward sent him.
It was not for some time after that Cosima was allowed to
write to him thus:

"Why did I not at once thank you, even if only in a
few lines, without even having read the manuscript [*sic*]
through . . . ? Why did I let the gift and the beginning
of the New Year go by without even sending you a tele-
gram to let you know I was thinking of you? This is precisely the point that I want to touch upon frankly with
you, since only such frankness seems to me worthy of
the joy you have given me, and that still refreshes me. The
Master was offended by your not coming, and by the way
in which you announced your intention to us." [4]

All through the correspondence and the autobiography
we see the same spirit of unconscious egoism. His conviction that he was always in the right naturally led to a
passionate desire that those who differed from him should
hear every word he had to say on his own behalf. Hence
the frequent and lengthy *plaidoyers* in the letters—hence
too the autobiography. His lust for dominance looked even
beyond the grave: thirty years after his death the world
should read a document that should be his final, and, he
hoped, successful effort at self-justification. We cannot, I
think, understand Wagner fully unless we recognize that

[3] *Mein Leben,* pp. 829, 830.
[4] Elisabeth Förster-Nietzsche: *Wagner und Nietzsche zur Zeit
ihrer Freundschaft,* pp. 137, 145. See also pp. 148, 149, where
Nietzsche tells his friend Gersdorff of the perplexity and pain
often caused him by Wagner's proneness to take offense.

however honest he may have been in intention, this consuming desire to prove himself always in the right should
make us chary of accepting everything he says at its face
value. No man is a perfectly unprejudiced witness on his
own behalf, in his own suit; and in Wagner's case the very
vehemence of his pleading lets us see how earnestly he
desired to impress his own reading of himself upon the
world, and is therefore a warning that he may often have
seen things as he desired them to be rather than as they
were. It is pretty clear that at an early age he realized that
he was destined to be a great man, and took care that the
world should not suffer from any lack of materials for the
writing of his life.[5] The autobiography is simply the last
and longest speech of a thousand long speeches for the
defense. We need not consider at present the particular
opinions upon his friends and associates and enemies that
Wagner expresses there. The only question for the moment is as to the general trustworthiness of the book. That
he has been exceedingly, even embarrassingly, candid on
some points all the world now knows. Whether he always
saw things from the correct angle is a different matter. It
is obviously impossible to check him throughout, even
where one suspects him to be unconsciously distorting the
truth;[6] but there are several instances in which he is obvi-

[5] In 1835 he was traveling about in search of singers for the
Magdeburg Opera. A temporary financial stringency—neither the
first nor the last in his life!—forced him to remain a week at
Frankfurt. "To kill time," he says, "I had recourse, among
other things, to a large red pocket-book which I carried about with
me in my valise; I wrote down in this, with exact details of dates,
some notes for my future biography." (He was twenty-two at
the time, and almost unknown outside his own little provincial
circle.) "It is the same book that is before me at this moment to
refresh my memory, and which I have kept up without any
breaks at various periods of my life." *Mein Leben*, p. 133.

[6] It would be unwise, for example, to believe without further
evidence his story (*Mein Leben*, p. 743) that the Paris press
during the *Tannhäuser* events of 1861 "was entirely in Meyerbeer's hands"; that (p. 723) Meyerbeer had some years before
bribed Fétis *père* to write articles against Wagner; or (p. 708)
that Berlioz was influenced against Wagner by the former's wife,

ously not telling quite the truth or all the truth, and in more than one instance he can certainly be convicted of manipulating the facts to suit his own purpose.

I shall try to show later that the account he gives of the episode with Madame Laussot in 1850 does not square at every point either with his letters to Minna or with those to Frau Ritter. He deliberately tries to mislead the reader with regard to his relations with Frau Wesendonck; everyone who has read Wagner's ardent letters to her must have gasped with astonishment to find him in *Mein Leben* glossing over that long and passionate love-dream, and actually speaking of "Minna's coarse misunderstanding of my real relations—friendly relations—with the young wife, who was continually concerned for my repose and my well-being." [7] That is not an actual untruth, but it is considerably less than the truth. In the preface to *Mein Leben* Wagner tells us that the only justification of the volumes was their "unadorned veracity." Perhaps he found "unadorned veracity" at this point a trifle embarrassing; perhaps he forgot his letters to Mathilde, or had never considered the possibility of their being published. But the fact remains that his own letters show the account he gives of his relations with Mathilde Wesendonck to be quite unreliable. What warrant have we, then, for believing him implicitly in other cases in which it may have been to his interest to suppress or distort the truth?

Let us take one of the most striking cases of this suppression and distortion. One of the friends of the middle period of Wagner's life was a certain Baron Robert von Hornstein. In 1862 Wagner—who was at that time in Paris—was, as frequently happened with him, looking for someone who would undertake the burden of keeping a home over his head. He tried two or three people, but without success; then he thought of the young Baron von

---

who had received a present of a valuable bracelet from Meyerbeer. Everyone who has mixed much with musicians knows how prone many of them are to believe that their colleagues—and still more their critics—are always "intriguing against them."

[7] *Mein Leben*, p. 667.

Hornstein. This is the account he gives of the matter in *Mein Leben:*

"Finally I bethought me of looking for a quiet abode in the neighbourhood of Mainz, under the financial protection of Schott. He had spoken to me of a pretty estate of the young Baron von Hornstein in that region. I thought I was really conferring an honour upon the latter when I wrote to him, at Munich, asking permission to seek shelter for a time at his place in the Rhine district; and I was greatly perplexed at receiving an answer that only expressed terror at my request." [8]

On the face of it this seems candid and credible enough. Von Hornstein's son, Ferdinand von Hornstein, has, however, thrown another light on the affair. When Baron Ferdinand published a memoir of his father in 1908 he omitted certain letters, he tells us, "out of consideration for Wagner and his family." The wounding allusions to Baron Robert in *Mein Leben* and the evident animus displayed against him there unlocked, however, the son's lips. He resents Wagner's description of his (Von Hornstein's) father—the friend of Schopenhauer, Paul Heyse, Hermann Lingg, and others—as a "young booby," [9] and proceeds to explain "why Wagner has misrepresented my father's character."

On an earlier page (627) of *Mein Leben* Wagner tells us that during their stay together at Zurich in the winter of 1855–6 Von Hornstein declared himself to be so "nervous" that he could not bear to touch the piano—that his mother had died insane, and that he himself was greatly afraid of losing his reason. "Although," says Wagner, "this made him to some extent interesting, there was blended so much weakness of character with all his intellectual gifts that we soon came to the conclusion that he was pretty hopeless, and were not inconsolable when he sud-

---

[8] *Mein Leben,* pp. 795, 796.
[9] *Mein Leben,* p. 602. On another page (626) he speaks of the "young booby" as being "agreeable [*anschmiegend*] and intelligent," apparently because he shared Wagner's views upon Schopenhauer.

denly left Zürich." [1] This impression conveyed—and obviously intended to be conveyed—is that the young man's departure was a piece of half-mad caprice.

As it happens, however, Von Hornstein, at his death, had left among his papers an account of the affair which puts a different complexion on it. Wagner's own eccentricities had been making the relations of the little circle none too pleasant.[2] And Von Hornstein, so far from leaving Zürich in obedience to a sudden impulse, had actually made arrangements at his lodging under which he could leave at any time when the "scenes" with Wagner became intolerable. He often expressed to Karl Ritter and the latter's mother[3] his regret that he was not in a position to "take his revenge" for the invitations he received to Wagner's table. Their reply always was: "Wagner does not at all expect this now. He knows your circumstances, and is sure to follow you up later. He is waiting for a more favourable moment." When he voiced his regret that there should be anything but ordinary friendly feeling to account for Wagner's attentions to him, his friends replied: "Oh, there is no doubt Wagner likes you and prizes your talents greatly; but these calculations [*Hintergedanken*] are too much second nature with him for him to be able to make an exception." "This," says Von Hornstein, "was to become still clearer to me." He learned that Wagner's guests were expected to bring bottles of wine with them —a point on which Von Hornstein, as a young man of breeding,[4] evidently felt some delicacy. On his birthday the great man entertained Von Hornstein and Baumgartner at dinner. "During the dessert, Wagner asked his sister-in-law—it came like a pistol shot—to bring him the wine list from a neighboring restaurant. She hesitatingly carried out this unexpected commission. The card comes.

[1] *Mein Leben*, p. 627.

[2] He admits, on the same page of *Mein Leben* (627), that he was very ill at this time, and prone to outbursts of irritability, during which his friends often had to suffer.

[3] Frau Ritter was at this time making a yearly allowance to Wagner.

[4] He was twenty-two at the time. Wagner was forty-two.

Wagner runs down the list of the champagnes and their prices, and orders a bottle of a medium quality to be brought. Everyone felt uncomfortable. The bottle having been emptied, Wagner turned to his two guests with a sneering smile, and said loudly: 'Shall I now present another thaler to each of these two gentlemen?' His wife and his sister-in-law fled in horror, like the ladies in the Wartburg scene in *Tannhäuser*. Baumgartner and I were stunned; we looked at one another, and each of us probably had an impulse to throw a glass at the head of our dear host." Instead of doing so, they burst into laughter, thanked him, and took their leave. Baumgartner declared to Von Hornstein that he would never accept another invitation from Wagner, "and I, for my part," says Von Hornstein, "*was firm in my resolve to leave Zürich as soon as possible.*" Afterward Wagner, as was no doubt his wont, came and excused himself to Von Hornstein and Karl Ritter.[5] He had not meant *them*, he said, but "the German Princes" who performed his operas and raved about him, but gave him nothing: "it does not occur to them to send me a hamper of wine"; and so on. The young men, however, were not to be so easily appeased, and Wagner "had to listen to many things that he would rather not have heard." An outward reconciliation was effected, but the sting remained; Von Hornstein delayed his departure for a few weeks, and still visited Wagner's house, though less frequently than before. "I had," he writes, "to tell this distressing story, as it gives the key to my later conduct when, soon after my father's death, Wagner tried to borrow so heavily from me. The correspondence connected with this attempt led to a permanent separation from Wagner."[6]

All this, it will be seen, puts the Zurich episode in a new light. There is not the least reason for doubting Von Hornstein's veracity. What he says is quite consistent with the accounts of Wagner's behavior that we get from other

[5] Von Hornstein had told the story to Karl, who was furious, and insisted on sending Wagner at once a hamper of champagne.
[6] There is not a word in *Mein Leben* as to these borrowings.

sources, private and public. Moreover, Von Hornstein's reminiscences simply take the form of a note left among his personal papers. He could not have anticipated the misleading version that was to appear in *Mein Leben* many years after his death,[7] and, as has been said, his own version would probably have remained unpublished forever but for the provocation given to his son by Wagner's autobiography.

Baron Ferdinand von Hornstein gives further evidence of the pettiness of Wagner's rancor against this young man from whom, notwithstanding his disparagement of him, he was willing to borrow money. For now comes the full record of the incident to which Wagner alludes so airily in the passage from *Mein Leben* quoted on page 10. Here is the actual letter, dated, "19, Quai Voltaire, Paris, 12th December 1861," in which Wagner, according to *his* account, merely asked permission to stay for a time at Von Hornstein's place in the Rhine district.

DEAR HORNSTEIN,—I hear that you have become rich. In what a wretched state I myself am you can easily guess from my failures.[8] I am trying to retrieve myself by seclusion and a new work. In order to make possible this way to my preservation—that is to say, to lift me above the most distressing obligations, cares, and needs that rob me of all freedom of mind —I require an immediate loan of ten thousand francs. With this I can again put my life in order, and again do productive work.

It will be rather hard for you to provide me with this sum; but it will be possible if you WISH it, and do not shrink from a sacrifice. This, however, I desire, and I ask it of you against my promise to endeavour to repay you in three years out of my receipts.

Now let me see whether you are the right sort of man!

[7] He died in 1890, twenty-one years before the publication of *Mein Leben*.
[8] In connection with the Paris production of *Tannhäuser*, etc.

If you prove to be such for me,—and why should not this be expected of some one some day?—the assistance you give me will bring you into very close touch with me, and next summer you must be pleased to let me come to you for three months at one of your estates, preferably in the Rhine district.

I will say no more just now. Only as regards the proposed loan I may say that it would be a great relief to me if you could place even six thousand francs at my disposal immediately; I hope then to be able to arrange to do without the other four thousand francs until March. But nothing but the immediate provision of the whole sum can give me the help which I so need in my present state of mind.

Let us see, then, and hope that the sun will for once shine a little on me. What I need now is a success; otherwise—I can probably do nothing more!— Yours,

Richard Wagner.

"I must confess," says Von Hornstein, "that the largeness of the amount and the tone of the letter made a refusal easier to me. What made it easier still was my knowledge that I had to do with a bottomless cask,—that while ten thousand francs were a great deal for me, they were simply nothing to him. I knew that Napoleon, Princess Metternich, Morny, and Erlanger had been bled of large sums that were simply like drops of water falling on a hot stone." Von Hornstein was particularly grieved at the remark that the loan would draw him nearer to Wagner. "Was I not near to him, then," he asks, "before I gave him money? Was the intimate intercourse with him at the Lake of Geneva, on the Seelisberg, in Zürich, intended only to prepare the way for the borrowings he had in view when my father should die?" [9] So he replied to Wagner in these terms:

DEAR HERR WAGNER,—You seem to have a false idea of my riches. I have a modest [*hübseh*] fortune

[9] This, it will be remembered, had been hinted by Karl Ritter.

on which I can live in plain and decent style with my wife and child. You must therefore turn to really rich people, of whom you have plenty among your patrons and patronesses all over Europe. I regret that I cannot be of service to you.

As for your long visit to "one of my estates," at present I cannot contrive a long visit; if it should become possible later I will let you know.

I have read in the papers with great regret that the production of *Tristan and Isolde* will not take place this winter. I hope that it is only a question of time, and that we shall yet hear the work. Greetings to you and your wife.—From yours,

Robert von Hornstein.

To which Wagner replied thus:

PARIS, 27*th December*, 1861.

DEAR HERR VON HORNSTEIN,—It would be wrong of me to pass over without censure an answer such as you have given me. Though it will probably not happen again that a man like me [*ein Mann meines Gleichen*] will apply to you, yet a perception of the impropriety of your letter ought of itself to be a good thing for you.

You should not have presumed to advise me in any way, even as to who is really rich; and you should have left it to myself to decide why I do not apply to the patrons and patronesses to whom you refer.

If you are not prepared to have me at one of your estates, you could have seized the signal opportunity I offered you of making the necessary arrangements for receiving me in some place of my choice. It is consequently offensive of you to say that you will let me know when you will be prepared to have me.

You should have omitted the wish you express with regard to my *Tristan*; your answer could only pass muster on the assumption that you are totally ignorant of my works.

Let this end the matter. I reckon on your discre-
tion, as you can on mine.—Yours obediently,

Richard Wagner.[1]

I have given this episode in such detail because, as
Ferdinand von Hornstein caustically remarks, it enables
us to test the value of Wagner's claim for the "unadorned
veracity" of his memoirs. He is plainly guilty of serious
sins both of omission and of commission in his account of
his dealings with Von Hornstein. What guarantee have
we that he was any more scrupulous in his record of other
matters in which his reputation or his *amour propre* were
concerned? Let us check him in one or two other cases.

How unreliable the autobiography is, with what caution
we have to accept Wagner's opinions of men in the
absence of confirmatory testimony, may be seen from a
survey of his dealings with Franz Lachner.[2]

The first reference to Lachner in *Mein Leben* is under
the date 1842. Wagner had written two articles in Paris
à propos of Halévy's opera, *La Reine de Chypre.*[3] In the

[1] See *Zwei unveröffentlichte Briefe Richard Wagners an Robert von Hornstein, zur Erklärung der auf Robert von Hornstein
bezüglichen Stellen in Wagners "Mein Leben"; herausgegeben
von Ferdinand Frh. von Hornstein.* Munich, 1911.

[2] Franz Lachner (1803–90) was successively conductor at
Vienna, Mannheim (1834), and Munich (1836). From 1852
to 1865 he was General Musical Director at Munich.

[3] One of these appeared in the Dresden *Abendzeitung* of January 26, 27, 28, and 29, 1842, under the title of *Bericht über eine
neue Pariser Oper.* The other was written for Schlesinger's *Gazette Musicale,* appearing in the February 27, March 13, April
24, and May 1, 1842, numbers of that journal. A translation of
this article is given by Mr. Ellis in volume viii of his English
version of the Prose Works. Wagner tells us in *Mein Leben*
(p. 248), however, that the editor of the *Gazette Musicale,*
Édouard Monnaie, had cut out a number of passages praising
Auber and belittling Rossini. The original German text of the
first half of the article has been preserved in the Wahnfried
archives. It was published for the first time by Julius Kapp in
Der junge Wagner, and is now to be had in volume xii of the
G.S. The first two portions of the article are given in German
on pp. 129 to 146. A comparison of this with Mr. Ellis's version
will show the passages that have been omitted. The remainder

article published in the Dresden *Abendzeitung*, he says:
"I made particularly merry over a mischance that had
befallen Kapellmeister Lachner." Küstner, the Munich
director, had commissioned a libretto for Lachner from
St. Georges, of Paris (the librettist of *La Reine de
Chypre*). After the production of the latter opera, it
turned out that this book and that of the Lachner opera
were virtually identical. In reply to Küstner's angry protests, St. Georges "expressed his astonishment that the
former should have imagined that for the paltry price
offered in the German commission he would supply a text
intended only for the German stage. As I had already
formed my own opinion as to this French opera-text-
business, and nothing in the world would have induced
me to set to music even the most effective piece of Scribe
or St. Georges, I was greatly delighted at this occurrence,
and in the best of spirits I let myself go on the subject for
the benefit of the readers of the *Abendzeitung*, who, it
is to be hoped, did not include my future 'friend' Lachner." [4] Evidently he did not love Lachner.

The next reference to him in *Mein Leben* is in 1855.
Wagner had returned to Zurich after his London concerts.
There he learned that Dingelstedt, at that time Intendant
of the Munich Court Theatre, wished to give *Tannhäuser*
there, "although," says Wagner, "thanks to Lachner's
influence," the place was not particularly well disposed
toward him.[5]

The third reference to Lachner is in 1858, just before

of the article exists only in French, as it appeared in the *Gazette
Musicale* of April 24 and May 21. It is given in G.S., xii,
404–11.

[4] *Mein Leben*, pp. 248, 249. The word "friend" is put in inverted commas by Wagner himself. The passage to which he
refers will be found in the *"Bericht über eine neue Pariser Oper,"*
in G.S., i, 244. He there mentions 1,500 francs as the sum paid
by the Munich director for the libretto. In the original article in
the *Abendzeitung*, according to Mr. Ashton Ellis, the amount
was given as 3,000 francs, and Lachner was referred to not as
Kapellmeister Lachner, but *"der brave Lachner."*

[5] *Mein Leben*, p. 626.

Wagner's departure from the "Asyl"; there was a "national vocal festival" at Zurich which seems to have irritated Wagner a good deal, depressed as he was at that time by the Minna-Mathilde catastrophe. Lachner was taking part in the festival. Wagner gave him the cold shoulder, and refused to return his call.[6]

Now let us see, from documents of the time, how matters really stood as regards Lachner. In 1854 Wagner was hoping to get *Tannhäuser* produced at Munich, where, as we have seen, Dingelstedt was Intendant and Lachner Kapellmeister. Lachner was a conductor and composer of the old school. Wagner had a poor opinion of him, and apparently thought him incompetent to do justice to *Tannhäuser*. "I don't at all know," he writes to Liszt on May 2, 1854,[7] "how to get Lachner out of the way. He is an utter ass and knave." In the summer of 1852 there had been some talk of giving *Tannhäuser* at Munich. Lachner thought it advisable first to familiarize the public with the style of the work by giving the overture at a concert on November 1. The success was doubtful. Wagner had previously sent Lachner a copy of the explanatory program of the overture that he had written in the preceding March for the Zurich orchestra. Perhaps this was thought too long for the Munich program; in any case, a much shorter "explanation" was given, which aroused Wagner's ire.[8] With his customary blind suspicion of people he did not like, he assumed that the concert production of the overture was a deliberate attempt to prejudice the public against the opera. This suspicion, as Sebastian Röckl says,[9] finds no support in the external facts. A fortnight after the Munich performance of the overture, *Tannhäuser* was given at Wiesbaden with great success, and soon became one of the favorite pieces in the repertory of the theater there. Dingelstedt at once sent his theater

[6] *Mein Leben*, p. 675.
[7] *Briefwechsel zwischen Wagner und Liszt*, ii, 25.
[8] See his letter to Uhlig of November 27, 1852.
[9] See the first chapter of his *Ludwig II und Richard Wagner: Erster Teil, die Jahre 1864 und 1865*. Munich, 1913.

inspector, Wilhelm Schmitt, to Zurich to arrange with
Wagner for a production at Munich. Unexpected difficulties arose, however; an outcry was raised against the proposed performance of a work by "the Red Republican,
Richard Wagner"; and there was opposition on the part
of the Bavarian Minister, Von der Pforten. By the spring
of 1854 all obstacles had been removed, and, as we have
already seen, Dingelstedt now arranged with Wagner for
the production, although the composer thought Munich
"not particularly well-disposed towards him, thanks to
Lachner's influence." Having heard that the singer destined for the part of *Tannhäuser* was incompetent, Wagner asked Dr. Härtinger, of the Munich Opera, to undertake it. Härtinger came to Zurich in May to study the
role with the composer, and seems to have deepened
Wagner's mistrust of and contempt for Lachner. The
performance did not take place, as was intended, in the
summer of 1854, but, as Röckl says, the cause of the post-
ponement was not Lachner but the cholera.

Later on, Dingelstedt found himself unable to fulfill
his promises to Wagner with regard to the honorarium.
"Thereupon," says Röckl, "Lachner, fearing that he might
be looked upon as answerable for the production having
fallen through a second time, wrote to his friend Kapellmeister G. Schmidt, of Frankfort, asking him to arrange
with the composer for more favourable conditions."[1]
In the end this was done. "And now," says Röckl,[2]
"Lachner, although in his innermost conscience an opponent of the 'musician of the future,' did all he could in
order to produce the work as excellently as was possible
to him. Rehearsal after rehearsal was held, though the
musicians were always moaning over the extraordinary

[1] Yet Glasenapp (*Das Leben Richard Wagners*, ii [2], 108)
speaks of Wagner having "forced his entry" into Munich with
Tannhäuser "in spite of the bitter opposition of Lachner." In
dealing with Wagner's Munich days, again, Glasenapp speaks of
Lachner as being "from of old an embittered opponent, whom
the most obliging and amiable behaviour could not reconcile"
(iv, 43).
[2] Op. cit., p. 8.

efforts they were called upon to make"—as is shown by reference to a Munich comic paper of the time. As the tenor was unmistakably incompetent, a singer who was already familiar with the work was engaged from another opera house. *Tannhäuser* was given on August 12, 1855, with extraordinary success. Lachner was called on the stage, whence he thanked the audience in Wagner's name. He communicated the evening's result to the composer, and received a letter, dated August 17, 1855, warmly thanking him for the trouble he had taken over the work and the sympathy he felt with it, and for the friendliness of his feelings toward Wagner; and he was asked to thank the singers and orchestra in the composer's name. "Finally accept the assurance of my great gratification at having been brought by this circumstance closer to yourself. I sincerely hope for a continuance of this approach to an understanding that is necessary for the artist and possible to him alone." [3]

The success of *Tannhäuser* emboldened Dingelstedt to venture upon *Lohengrin* for the winter of 1856, but various events conspired against the production. In February 1857 Dingelstedt resigned the Intendantship. *Lohengrin* was put in rehearsal by his successor, Von Frays, in November 1857, and produced on February 28, 1858, under Lachner. It was well received on the whole, but the opera found more antagonists than *Tannhäuser* had done.

From July 21 to August 2 there was held at Zurich the vocal festival at which, as we have seen, Wagner refused to return Lachner's call. What Röckl rightly calls the ambiguous words of Wagner in this connection in *Mein Leben* are explained by the following letter from the composer to Lachner, which is published for the first time in Röckl's book:

VENICE, *26th September* 1858.

HIGHLY HONOURED SIR AND FRIEND,—Now that, after a long and painful interruption of the way of living I have been accustomed to for many years, I

[3] Röckl, p. 12.

have again won a little repose, permit me to approach you with the remembrance of your so friendly advances to me last summer, in order in some degree to link myself again with the life on which you have imprinted a significantly agreeable memory. If you found something strange at our meeting, something on my part apparently not quite corresponding to your friendly intentions, I now permit myself, by way of exculpation, to say that at that time I was in a very agitated and embarrassed frame of mind; few people know what difficult resolutions were maturing in me at that time.[4] It may, however, suffice for me to tell you that only now, after leaving my friendly refuge by the Lake of Zürich, in order to compose my mind here, in the greatest seclusion, for the resumption of my work, has the pleasant and encouraging significance of your Zürich visit become quite clear to me. By my sincere regret to know that you were in some degree hurt through a mistake of my servant[5] you probably, nevertheless, understood even then how earnestly I realised the value of your visit; your friendly assurance that you were satisfied with my explanation of that misunderstanding was most tranquillising for me. Let me now say that I estimate highly the value of your advances, and with my whole heart I shall do my best to deserve your friendship—if you will favour me with it—and most sincerely to reciprocate it. On the occasion of another personal meeting, if you will be so good, I hope that you will learn, with some satisfaction, in what sense I give you this assurance. I chiefly remember with the greatest pleasure that you expressed to me the wish that perhaps the first performance of my latest work, *Tristan and Isolde*, might be entrusted to you. I have so agreeable a recollection of this wish, that I can only regret not being able to gratify it immedi-

[4] The reader will remember that the Wesendonck catastrophe was just then drawing to a head.

[5] In the light of Wagner's own account of the affair in *Mein Leben*, we can probably regard this as a piece of fiction.

ately. Unfortunately just at the time when we met I was so grievously interrupted in this very work that only now again, for the first time, can I cherish the hope of getting into the proper mood for continuing and completing it. Consequently this *opus* is not one as to the time of whose coming to the light I can decide anything definite—which is in every respect unpleasant for me.

The friendly wish you showed to occupy yourself with me once more soon, emboldens me, however, to approach you with regard to the granting of a very big request on my part. My *Rienzi* has again been given in Dresden with real success, and since I now no longer have any special reason for keeping back this effective work of my youth, I have been inviting the theatres that are friendly to me to take up this opera as quickly as possible; in so doing I am moved by the firm conviction that I am recommending to them a very good and remunerative work. Almost all whom I have approached have fallen in with my wishes. Would you therefore think it too bold of me if I were to request you also to get this score (which you have only to ask for, in my name, of Chorus-master Wilhelm Fischer, of Dresden), without much hesitation and delay, and to see what you can do with this tamed rebel [*mit dem gezähmten Unband*] for my consolation and benefit, while I am finishing *Tristan?*

I beg you to take this in good part. But in any case I owe you very great thanks, and if you are not angry with me on account of this request, I shall take this as a particularly good sign.

In any case I may probably hope to receive soon from you a friendly reply; console me also with the assurance that you have forgiven me, and accept in return the assurance of the sincerest devotion and esteem of your most indebted

Richard Wagner.[6]

[6] Röckl, pp. 17 *ff.*

Lachner at once got the score of *Rienzi* from Fischer, and wrote to Wagner (October 13) expressing his pleasure at the prospect of an early production of the opera. "In spite, however, of his sincere endeavours," says Röckl, "*Rienzi* was not put into rehearsal. The reading committee felt the subject to be inadmissible on religious grounds."

In July 1860 Von Frays had the idea of giving *The Flying Dutchman*, and wrote to Wagner on the matter. Wagner thought that Lachner had been the moving spirit in this, and thanked him warmly in a hitherto unpublished letter of August 20, 1860.[7] But again Wagner's malignant demon intervened. Von Frays had to resign the Intendantship on account of illness, and his successor abandoned *The Flying Dutchman* project owing to the expense of the new inscenation. It was taken up again in 1864, and produced on December 4, Wagner conducting. Lechner had taken most of the rehearsals, and, though not much in sympathy with the work, he plainly did his best with it.[8]

The reader is now in a position to estimate the true value of Wagner's disparaging references to Lachner in *Mein Leben*. He seems to have started out with a prejudice against him which nothing could alter. Lachner was admittedly by temperament and training, and both as conductor and composer, in the opposite camp to Wagner. This, however, only entitles him to the more commendation for the pains he took to establish Wagner in Munich, and for the care he expended upon the performances.[9]

[7] Röckl, pp. 21 *ff*.
[8] Röckl, p. 56.
[9] It is even doubtful whether his conducting was as detrimental to the operas as Wagner seems to have thought. The records show that both *Tannhäuser* and *Lohengrin* were very well received under his baton. Liszt heard a performance of *Tannhäuser* under Lachner at Munich in 1856, and writes thus to Wagner on December 12 of that year: "Lachner had certainly rehearsed the score with the utmost precision and care, for which we can only thank and praise him." He doubts whether Lachner understood the *drama* as Wagner meant it to be

Wagner nurses his imaginary grievance against the man, persists in believing that he is prejudicing all Munich against him, insults him, and denies him his door in Zurich; and then, when he has need of him, writes to him in the friendliest and most flattering way. Finally, when he pens his memoirs, he forgets all that Lachner had, on his own admission, done for him, forgets his own letters of thanks, and refers to him throughout in a tone of scarcely veiled contempt and dislike. What conclusion can we come to except that it would be imprudent of us to accept, without corroborative evidence, Wagner's disparaging record of anyone he detested? No doubt he found Lachner in his way when, under cover of King Ludwig's favor, he was trying to transform the musical life of Munich. But even if Lachner *did* intrigue against him then, as the Wagnerians always hold, he was simply acting in self-defense; and in any case Wagner, when he came to write his autobiography, should not have passed over Lachner's earlier services to him without a word, and still less have given the unsuspecting reader the impression that Lachner's opposition to him began several years before it actually did. Once more we feel that had Wagner only postponed the writing of *Mein Leben* for a few years, till he had quite got over the bitterness of his Munich failure, the book would have been both pleasanter in tone and more reliable in fact.

Let us now take another case—his treatment of Hanslick in *Mein Leben*. At one time these deadly enemies had been friends.[1] In the course of years Hanslick's antipathy to Wagner became more and more pronounced, and by the spring of 1861, when Wagner visited Vienna, the critic of the *Neue Freie Presse* was an opponent to be

---

understood; but granting that, the trouble that Lachner had evidently taken to do justice to the music is all the more creditable to him. That he was pretty free from prejudice toward Wagner is shown by his recommending him for the Maximilian Order in 1864, and again in 1873. The King granted Wagner the Order the second time. See Röckl, pp. 57, 234.

[1] They had met in Dresden in 1845.

feared. Wagner, as he more than once tells us, never troubled to be particularly polite to critics; but in Vienna he seems, by his own account, to have been gratuitously rude to Hanslick. The critic was introduced to him on the stage at a rehearsal of *Lohengrin*. "I greeted him curtly, and as if he were a total stranger; whereupon Ander, the tenor, introduced him to me a second time with the remark that Herr Hanslick was an old acquaintance of mine. I replied shortly that I remembered Herr Hanslick very well, and turned my attention to the stage again." [2] The opera singers did their best to smooth matters over, but Wagner was irreconcilable; and to his refusal to be friendly with Hanslick he attributes his subsequent failure to make headway in Vienna.

A little while after, they met again at a dinner party at Heinrich Laube's, where Wagner refused to speak to Hanslick.[3] They met a third time, at an evening party at Frau Dustmann's, who was to sing Isolde in the projected performance of *Tristan*. Wagner being, as he tells us, in a good temper, he treated the critic as "a superficial acquaintance." Hanslick, however, drew him aside, "and with tears and sobs assured me that he could no longer bear to be misjudged by me; whatever extraordinary there might be in his judgment of me was due not to any malicious intention, but solely to his limitations; and that to widen the boundaries of his knowledge he desired nothing more ardently than to learn from me. These explanations were made with such an explosion of feeling that I could do nothing but try to soothe his grief, and promise him my unreserved sympathy with his work in future. Shortly after my departure from Vienna I heard that Hanslick had praised me and my amiability in unmeasured terms." [4]

Whether Wagner's account of the interview is strictly accurate or not, we have no means of knowing; but the story, even as he tells it, indicates that Hanslick was not

[2] *Mein Leben*, p. 761.
[3] *Mein Leben*, p. 784.
[4] *Mein Leben*, pp. 818, 819.

at this time a hopelessly prejudiced or evil-natured antago-
nist. In November 1862 they met again at the house of Dr.
Standhartner in Vienna. Wagner read the *Mastersinger*
poem to the company. "As Dr. Hanslick was now supposed
to be reconciled with me, they thought they had done
the right thing in inviting him also. We noticed that
as the reading went on the dangerous critic became paler
and more and more out of humour; and it was noticed
that at the end he could not be persuaded to stay, but
took his leave at once with an unmistakable air of irritation. My friends all agreed that Hanslick regarded the
whole poem as a pasquinade against himself, and the
invitation to listen to it as an outrage. And truly from that
evening the critic's attitude towards me underwent a
striking change; it ended in an intensified enmity, of the
consequences of which we were soon made aware." [5]

The touching innocence of it, the air of perfect candor,
of conscious rectitude, of surprise that men should be
found so base as Hanslick proved himself to be! Would it
be believed from this ingenuous record that Wagner had
given Hanslick the most unmistakable cause of offense?
It may have occurred to more than one reader to ask *how*
Hanslick managed to recognize a caricature of himself in
Beckmesser. It is hardly likely that he could have done so
from the poem alone. We may be tolerably sure he had
something more to go upon.

We possess three prose sketches of the *Mastersinger*
libretto. The first was made in 1845, the second and
third—there is hardly any difference between the two—
in the winter of 1861. The actual libretto was written
in Paris in November 1861 and January 1862. In the

[5] *Mein Leben*, p. 829. Writing against Hanslick in the
Musikalisches Wochenblatt of 1877, Wilhelm Tappert gave an
account of these two episodes as he had received it from Wagner
himself. Wagner had presumably copied from *Mein Leben* the
two passages I have just cited, for they agree almost word for
word with the *Wochenblatt* article. See Glasenapp: *Das Leben
Richard Wagners*, iii, 352, 405, 483. Hanslick seems to have
denied the authenticity of Wagner's version of what happened
at Standhartner's.

second sketch the Marker is given the name of "Hanslich." [6] In the third he becomes "Veit Hanslich." In these
two later sketches the Marker is drawn with a perceptibly
harsher hand. That the conferring of this name on the
Marker was something more than a passing joke is shown
by its appearing in both sketches, and not merely in the
list of *dramatis personae*, but written out in full throughout. These two sketches were made, as we have seen, after
the first meeting of Wagner and Hanslick in Vienna in
1861. With an author so fond of reading his own works
to his friends as Wagner was, it is incredible that news
of Hanslick being satirized as the pedantic Marker in
the forthcoming opera should not have spread through
musical Vienna, and have reached the critic's ears. His
feeling, therefore, at the party in November 1862, that
the shaft was aimed at himself may safely be put down
not so much to his own intuition as to either a presuspicion
or a knowledge of the truth. He would be quite justified,
then, in regarding the invitation to be present at the
reading as an insult. But even if we allow no weight at
all to this theory, in spite of its inherent probability, what
are we to think of Wagner's later conduct? He tells us
more than once of Hanslick's enmity toward him; he
makes no mention of himself having treated Hanslick, in
the *Mastersinger* sketches, in a way that the critic and his
friends could only regard as insulting. Hanslick was of
course hopelessly wrong about Wagner the musician; but
after Wagner's brusque treatment of him whenever he
met him, and after the attempt to ridicule him in *Die
Meistersinger*, who will say that Hanslick was under any
obligation to be fond of Wagner the man? Yet it is only
Wagner's side of the case, as usual, that is given us in
Mein Leben.

The autobiography, then, has to be used with caution:
not that Wagner, I suppose, often consciously perverted
the truth, but that it was impossible for him to believe
he was ever in the wrong in his judgments of other people,

[6] The "h" is without significance. Wagner often spelled proper
names along the line of least resistance.

and that it would therefore be necessary to let the reader have the whole of the story in order that he might judge for himself. Nor can the careful student of his letters resist the feeling that Wagner was often writing with at least one eye on the possibility of the publication of his words at some time or other. His intense egoism—I use the term here in no condemnatory sense, but simply to denote the passion of vigorous temperaments like his for mastery— his intense egoism could probably not bear the thought that any estimate of his conduct but his own should obtain currency. Time after time we feel that his letters to and about Minna are speeches of the counsel for the defense, addressed to a larger audience than the letter's first recipient. Here again it is only a thick-fingered psychological analysis that would write him down as a deliberate trickster. Wagner was in some respects a selfish man, as numberless testimonies agree; but he was not a bad man in the sense that it ever gave him pleasure to inflict suffering. His heart no doubt bled for Minna, but it is probable that he merely pitied her out of the vast fund of aesthetic and ethical feeling that was in him, as in all artists, without being a motive part of his life. The commonest daily facts prove that a musician need not have a beautiful soul of his own in order to write beautiful music or to perform music beautifully. This implies no conscious insincerity; it is simply the actor's faculty for dramatization, for momentary self-hypnosis. And many of them can carry the exercise of this faculty beyond art into life itself. Wagner was apparently one of these. When he pitied Minna, it was in the abstract, detached way that we pity Desdemona or Cordelia on the stage—without feeling in the least impelled to rise from our seats and run any personal risk in order to save her. Nietzsche, who, for all his tendency to overwrite his subject, often saw to the secret center of Wagner's soul, was always laying it down that the instinct of the actor was uppermost in everything Wagner did. "Like Victor Hugo," he says, "he remained true to himself even in his autobiography—he remained

an actor." [7] An actor he certainly is in many of his letters
—an actor so consummate as to deceive not only his
audience but himself. And so, when we read the plentiful
and handsome certificates of good conduct he gives himself, in *Mein Leben* and the letters, with regard to Minna,[8]
we may be pretty sure that he believed every word he said,
and really regarded himself as a monumentally patient
and saintly sufferer of unmerited misfortunes. But the
Von Hornstein and other affairs have shown us that
Wagner is not always a perfectly veracious witness in his
own behalf; and we may reasonably decline to give him a
verdict in this or that episode of the Minna matter on his
unsupported testimony.

What I have called his passion for self-justification is
shown in nothing more clearly than in the device of post-
poning his autobiography for some thirty years after his
death, when the persons so liberally criticized in it would
all be tolerably certain to be no more. It is singular, indeed, how fortunate Wagner has been in having the
stage to himself throughout. This has materially helped to
create and sustain the Wagnerian legend. Most of the
people with whom he came into unfriendly or only par-
tially friendly relations in his youth or early middle age
died before it was realized what a world figure he was to
become; consequently they have left hardly any records
of their impressions of him. Meyerbeer, for example, died
in 1864. We need not take up any brief for Meyerbeer
as a whole; but will anyone contend that if we could get
his account of his dealings with Wagner, the current
story would not have to be modified at many points?
Wagner, it must be confessed, was often lacking in delicacy
of soul. Had Liszt and Von Bülow, Wesendonck and
Wille, Cornelius and Tausig been equally indelicate, and
written as frankly of Wagner the man as he has written

[7] Postscript to *The Wagner Case* (English translation), p. 37.
[8] See, for example, *Mein Leben*, pp. 158, 499, etc.; his letters
to Minna of April 17, 1850, January 25, 1859, May 18, 1859,
etc. etc.; and his letter of August 20, 1858, to his sister Clara.

of them, would not many features of Wagner's portraits of all of them need altering? And if Minna had had something of her husband's literary faculty and passion for special pleading, could she not have shown more alloy than *he* ever suspected in the golden image he loved to make of himself? Everywhere, in fact, in dealing with the memoirs and the letters, we have to remember that we are face to face with an artist who is as persuasive as he is powerful, with an overwhelming lust for mastery and for unfettered self-realization, and with a faith in himself that must have made other people's occasional scepticism a pure mystery to him. Wherever, then, his written words involve the interpretation of his own or other men's acts and motives, they are to be accepted with caution. For the rest, the psychologist can only be thankful that Wagner poured himself out in such profusion. Let us now try to trace from his own records his general development as a man.

· 1 ·

The Man

1 · *Childhood*

From the autobiography and the letters to Apel we can get an excellent idea of what he was in his boyhood. He came of a family of rather more than average ability. As a child he was nervous, excitable, and imaginative, impatient of control either at home or in school, but quick enough to assimilate life and knowledge in his own way. It is clear, both from what he says in *Mein Leben* and from scattered hints in that book and in his letters, that he was occasionally a source of great anxiety to his relations. Already he had a bias toward the theater, which would be increased by his frequent association with actors and singers.[1] For a time he haunted the smaller gambling dens of Leipzig—even going so far on one occasion as to stake his mother's pension—entered into the usual students' follies and dissipations, and generally must have seemed to the ordinary eye as complete a young wastrel as could be imagined. He himself tells us: "I bore, as if in a state of complete stupor, even the contempt of my sister Rosalie, who, like my mother, hardly vouchsafed a glance

---

[1] See *Mein Leben*, pp. 19, 20. Later on he speaks of "the importance the theatrical had assumed in his mind in comparison with the ordinary bourgeois life" (*Mein Leben*, p. 25).

at the incomprehensible young profligate (*Wüstling*), whose pale and troubled face they only rarely saw." [2] He picks up the rudiments of a general and of a musical education. Then he knocks about from one small theatrical troupe to another, his character inevitably coarsening and relaxing in the process. He was at this time extraordinarily sensitive to his environment; and as this was a rule of an intellectually superficial kind, he came to take the average actor's or singer's superficial view of life and art. And as from his boyhood he was hopelessly incapable of managing his financial affairs with any prudence, and soon acquired that habit of borrowing from friends and eluding tradespeople which clung to him for the greater part of his life, the iron was not long in entering into his soul. So rich a nature as his could of course afford to squander itself extravagantly, and in the end no doubt his art was all the better for his having eaten so freely of the tree of the knowledge of good and evil; but to the relations and companions who cared for him in those early years he must often have seemed to be wasting himself beyond all power of recovery. His life until long past his fiftieth year resembles a ship steering with incredible recklessness among every sort of shoal and rock. More than once it looked as if the vessel would founder; only a unique combination of courage and determination and extraordinary good fortune managed to keep it afloat and bring it finally into haven.

ii · *The Apel Correspondence*

The best picture of him in his adolescent years is given in the correspondence with Theodor Apel, the friend of 1832–6. There we have in epitome the whole Wagner of the later years, with his imprudence in all the practical affairs of life, the irrepressible vitality that enabled him to recover so quickly after each of the many crises he

[2] *Mein Leben*, p. 65.

went through,[3] his extravagance, his incurable tendency
to run up debts with tradesmen and to borrow money
from his friends, his Micawberish confidence in the speedy
turning of his luck. It is evident that at an early stage
of their friendship he had drawn upon the purse of Apel,
who had the dangerous gift—for a friend of Wagner's—of
riches. But the young Micawber has no doubts as the
future. In October 1834 he is quite convinced that he is
going to have a great success with *Die Feen,* which will
lead to a still greater success for *Das Liebesverbot*; he will
make a lot of money, and he and Apel will go and enjoy
themselves in Italy for a year or two. This desirable con-
summation is to come about in the spring of 1836. In
Italy he will write some Italian operas, and then they will
go to France, where he will write a French opera—and
so on.[4] We have some indication of the depth of the
draughts he was then taking of the physical joy of life
in a letter of June 6, 1835, in which he tells Apel to "enjoy
and be merry." "I have now resolved," he says, "to be a
complete Epicurean with regard to my art: nothing for
posterity, but everything for the present and the moment." [5]

But soon there comes an emotional crisis of the kind
that occurred so frequently in Wagner's life. The tearful,
almost hysterical, letter to Apel of August 21, 1835, is a
remarkable document. Wagner seems to have got heavily
into debt, to have done all sorts of foolish things, and to
have vexed and saddened his friends and relations. Even
Apel appears to have been estranged from him for a while.
Wagner beats his breast in agony. He has been mad;
the promised happiness of youth has fled from him; but
he will make a brighter future for himself. Note already,
in this letter, the passion for self-revelation and self-drama-

[3] "He had a temperament like a watch-spring, easily com-
pressed, but always flying back with redoubled energy," says
Pecht, who knew him during the time of his appalling misery in
Paris. Glasenapp: *Das Leben Richard Wagners,* i, 329.

[4] *Briefe an Apel,* p. 15.

[5] *Briefe an Apel,* p. 48.

tization which is evident in so much of his later correspondence. He was not a dramatist, said Nietzsche once: he merely loved the word "drama." He certainly loved the words "repentance" and "morality."

"I have sinned. Yet not so! Does a man sin when he is mad? I have fallen out with my family, and must regard our relations as at an end. . . . Till now I have managed my life very badly. Dearest, I was not wicked, I was mad; that is the only expression I can find for my conduct—it was a conventional madness [*ein konventioneller Wahnsinn*]. I see now only too well that money is not a chimera, not a despicable, worthless thing of no importance; I have formed the conviction that money is as much alive as the society in which we are placed. I was mad, I say, for I did not understand myself and my relation to the world. I knew that I had no surely-founded foothold and support at all, and yet I acted like one insane, went beyond my circumstances in every respect, and with the ignorance and inexperience of a man who has never any solid title to money; no one, not even a rich man, throws away money as I did. The result was a whirlpool of perplexity and misery, the entanglements of which I cannot contemplate without dismay. I cannot reckon up the details; it is unheard of and inexplicable into what an abyss I have fallen. Your enormous and incessant efforts to rescue me from it only made me more daring, and made me put my trust in a blind something of which, indeed, I could give no clear account to myself, but that blinded my eyes more and more completely. My life in Leipzig, the pitiable position I had there, were intolerable burdens; I was driven into so-called independent displays of strength; I broke out into extravagances which, combined with the still lasting consequences of my earlier follies, completely estranged my family from me, and at last brought about a rupture with all my surroundings." He is sure, however, that he has now learned wisdom. Then comes a passage of a type that we often meet with in his letters. "I cannot, however, go back to Magdeburg[6] until I have

[6] He is writing from Frankfurt.

got rid of the burden of a debt of 400 thalers. So I stand
—I am forsaken by, and separated from, everyone, everyone on whom I might otherwise reckon, and accompanied
only by the painful anxiety of my mother. She can give
me nothing. You are the only one left to whom I can
appeal"; and so on, and so on, in the customary profes-
sional borrower's style.

A few months later there is a similar wail. He has
recovered his elasticity of spirit; he is working incredibly
hard not only at his conducting but at the composition
of his new opera. "I am now at the focal point of my
talent; I do everything easily, and am pleased with it" he
writes to Apel on December 27, 1835. In another three
weeks the repentant sinner who had been so eloquent
about having learned wisdom is once more distracted at
the thought of his debts. "I must have money," he tells
Apel, "if I am not to go mad." [7]

III · *Dislike of Critics*

We can visualize him in these early years as a creature of
the strangest contradictions—charming enough with those
he liked, supercilious and insulting to people he disliked,
and always liable to some fit of the nerves which would
make him unaccountably irritable, perverse, tactless, and
ready to wound even friends; generous with his help where
his sympathies were engaged, and with a fine code of
honor for many of the relationships of life, but a sad lack
of delicacy and even of honor with regard to money matters. The full extent of his borrowings and his debts, even
at this early period of his life, will never be known; but
one feels a sort of terror at the hints as to the total of
them that are given here and there in *Mein Leben* and
his letters. It is easier to explain than to justify his conduct
in this regard. He was never too well paid, and he had an
ineradicable artistic inclination toward certain of the good
things of life that only money can buy. His incurable
optimism, too, was always painting the future the rosiest

[7] Letter of January 21, 1836.

of rose-pinks. One can understand his habit of borrowing, and even sympathize with him to some extent; what one finds it harder to explain or to condone is his evident callousness toward his creditors, especially his tradesmen, some of whom had to wait ten years or more for their money, and then only obtained it with much difficulty.

A man who, for all his fine qualities, had two or three grave defects of character of this kind was likely to make as many enemies as friends—perhaps more. The worshipping official type of biographer paints for us a sort of ineffable angel of a Wagner always in the right, always misunderstood and traduced. The untruthfulness of the portrait is evident to the most casual readers of the letters and the autobiography. Wagner's now notorious laxity of principle with respect to money matters must have been common knowledge in the small provincial towns in which he lived, and must have done a good deal to make him distrusted and disliked. In addition, his frequent irascibility and rudeness must have made many enemies for him. In *Mein Leben*—more candid and more critical in this respect than his incense-bearers—he makes several confessions on this score. His outbursts can no doubt be mostly explained by the irritability of his temperament and its swift transitions of mood, by his frequently bad health, or by the action of wine. But it is one thing to make allowances for a man's failings of temper or manners half a century or so after the event; it is another to make allowances at the time. We smile now at the stories that are told of Beethoven's grossness and ill-breeding; but had we experienced the effect of these at first hand we should certainly have voted him an impossible person to live with. Wagner was undoubtedly very trying to live with at times. In *Mein Leben* he occasionally gives us a glimpse of himself in his least likable moods. In 1834 he visits Prague, where he meets again some people whose acquaintance he had made on a previous visit there—the daughters of the recently deceased Count Pachta. With one or both of these girls the ever amorous young man had apparently been in love. "My behaviour," he says, "was wild and arrogant; in this way the bitter feelings with which I had formerly taken leave of this circle now found expression in a capricious passion for revenge." He does nothing but indulge in the maddest pranks. "They could not understand this astounding change in me; there was no longer in me any of the old love of intimacy, the mania for instructing, the zeal for converting,[8] that they had previously found so annoying. But at the same time no one could get a sensible word out of me, and the ladies, who were now disposed to discuss many things seriously, got no answer from me but the wildest buffoonery." [9]

Every now and then, in his account of the misunderstandings with Minna, he confesses to the coarseness of his language when he was angry, the "raging vehemence" of his insults, the "unrestrained violence" of his speech and behavior. Nietzsche has given us a hint of what Wagner could be in a mood of this kind.[1] In Dresden especially, in the years of his conductorship (1842-9), he appears to have made many enemies, particularly among the critics. These gentlemen were, of course, often wrong as against Wagner in matters of art. But though musical critics are frequently stupid, they are not, as a rule, all stupid at the same time and in the same way. It is possible, as many of the modern Wagnerians have shown, to be as stupid in approbation of Wagner as anyone could be in disapprobation of him. So that when we find the critics—in Dresden, for example—so uniformly opposed to Wagner, it is a fair supposition that there was more behind their words than mere disapproval of his art or his theories. They apparently pursued him with unusual rancor. Even in the absence of evidence, we should be entitled to assume that when a man becomes the object of such general and unrelenting hostility in his own town, it implies some

[8] He was twenty-one at this time, and evidently very like his later self.

[9] *Mein Leben*, p. 105.

[1] See the account of his quarrel with Wagner in Daniel Halévy's *Life of Friedrich Nietzsche* (English translation), p. 167.

defects in his own character as well as in those of his assailants. Evidence is not lacking that this was so. Wagner, we all know, loved most those who agreed with him, and had no use at all for men of opposite ways of thinking.[2] His constant craving for love in life had its counterpart in his desire to be approved and believed in as an artist. In *Mein Leben* he is always praising someone or other for his devotion to him, and speaking coolly or angrily of others for their indifference to his concerns. Alwine Frommann is "faithfully devoted" to him; he speaks of Von Bülow's "warm and heartfelt devotion"; the Laussots, the Ritters, Uhlig, and others are all lauded for their "devotion," their "fidelity." He speaks well of Meyerbeer so long as he believes his interests are being furthered by him, and turns on him and makes sundry unproved and unprovable charges against him when he thinks his aid is withdrawn. One does not censure him for this: rational criticism aims less at giving or withholding marks for conduct than at understanding the complexities of human nature. One merely notes the idiosyncrasy, not unsympathetically, and tries to see how it worked in the actualities of life. A nature of this kind was constitutionally incapable of taking criticism philosophically; the critic's sin would not be against the artist so much as against the art. And granting that many of his critics were not very intelligent men, it is clear that part at least of their enmity toward him as the result of his own tactless attitude toward them. "Though I was anxious to be obliging with everyone, yet I always felt an unconquerable aversion to showing special consideration towards any man because he was a critic. In the course of time I carried this to the point of almost studied rudeness, as a consequence of which I was my whole life long the victim of unheard-of persecution from the press." [3] It seems prob-

[2] This was true of him even as a boy of seventeen. He cared, he said, only for a companion who would accompany him on his excursions, "and to whom I could pour out my inmost being to my heart's content, without my caring what the effect might be on him" (*Mein Leben,* p. 50).

[3] *Mein Leben,* p. 282.

able that his studiously unconciliatory manners brought
him more ill-will than was ever necessary.

That the mere lack of intelligence of some of these
critics was not the reason for his rudeness to them is shown
by the warmth of his welcome to critics no more intelligent
who happened to bring with them butter instead of gall.
A certain Gaillard, of Berlin, happened to have written
an "entirely favorable" criticism of *The Flying Dutchman*.
"Although," he naïvely says, "I had already of necessity
accustomed myself to be indifferent as to the attitude of
the critics, this particular article impressed me greatly, and
I invited the unknown writer to Dresden to hear the first
performance of *Tannhäuser*." The young man comes to
Dresden, and Wagner is distressed to find that he is
threatened with consumption. "I saw from his knowledge
and capabilities that he would never attain to any great
influence; but his sincerity of soul and the receptivity of
his intelligence filled me with genuine regard for the poor
man." He dies in a few years, "having never swerved from
his fidelity to and thoughtfulness for me, even in the
most trying circumstances." [4] In other words, he was that
very common product, an enthusiastic admirer possessed
of only limited intelligence; but his "fidelity" was sufficient to make Wagner tolerate and even like him. It looks
as if the "systematic rudeness" was not for "the critics,"
but only for the critics who disagreed with Wagner.

How badly he could behave when irritated by the press
was shown by his incessant insinuations against the
honesty of the London critics during and after his conducting of the Philharmonic Concerts in 1855. There is
no proof forthcoming of their being bribed to oppose him.
Mr. Ashton Ellis, who has gone thoroughly into the
newspaper history of that period, and who will not be
suspected of any desire to smooth matters over for Wagner's antagonists, gives it as his opinion that "James
Davison bears the character of an unimpeachably honest
'gentleman.'" But Wagner could never imagine any
other motive for opposing him except (1) that the op-

[4] *Mein Leben*, p. 368.

ponent was paid to do so, or (2) that he was either a Jew or under the orders of the Jews.[5] In a letter to Otto Wesendonck of April 5 he vents his rancor against Davison and Chorley, and recklessly charges them with being corrupt: "they are paid to keep me down, and thus they earn their daily bread." [6] He throws out a hint to the same effect in *Mein Leben*.

[5] Mr. Ashton Ellis (*Life of Wagner*, v, 126 *ff.*) has pointed out how many difficulties might have been avoided had Wagner taken the advice of some of his friends and called upon Davison, the critic of the *Times*. Wagner would have cleared Davison's mind of many misconceptions that had become current as to the aims of "Wagnerism" and his own attitude toward the older composers and Mendelssohn. Wagner's temper and his dislike of critics made him refuse. He refers to them *en masse*, in a letter to Otto Wesendonck, as "blackguards," and again (to Liszt) as "this blackguard crew of journalists." Mr. Henry Davison, in his biography of his father, the former music critic of the *Times*, gives a reasonable enough explanation of the antipathy of the London press to Wagner in 1855. Berlioz was giving concerts in London at the same time. His music was as strange to English ears as Wagner's; but he was much more gently handled by the press. "The explanation," says Mr. Davison, "is not very difficult. . . . Berlioz had not written books in advertisement of his theories and himself. He had not attacked cherished composers—far otherwise. He had not studiously held aloof from the critics; on the contrary, he had courted and conciliated them. In fine, with all the peculiarities of an irritable, extraordinary, and self-conscious mind, Berlioz was polished, courteous and fascinating. Wagner was somewhat pedantic, harsh and uncouth" (Henry Davison: *From Mendelssohn to Wagner*, p. 180).

[6] The charge was indignantly repudiated by Davison when it came to his ears. See the quotation from the *Musical World* of May 12, 1855, in Ellis, v, 128 *n*. Davison replied to a letter of Wagner's to a Berlin paper (after the London concerts were over) in the *Musical World* of September 22, 1855. (See Mr. Henry Davison's *From Mendelssohn to Wagner*, p. 175.) Wagner's readiness to bring these unfounded charges must make us regard with suspicion his unsupported allegations against Meyerbeer and others.

iv · *Asperities of Temper*

Of his irritability and tactlessness we have several instances, some of them given us by himself. Take, for example, Meissner's account of the supper Wagner gave to Laube[7] after the performance at Dresden of the latter's play, the *Karlsschüler*. There were a number of people present, and the usual compliments passed. Meanwhile, however, "Wagner had been fidgeting about on his chair for some time, and finally he threw out the question: Whether, in order to put a Schiller into a play, one ought not to have something of Schiller's genius oneself? The question was first of all couched in general terms; some compromised, some disagreed. Then Wagner proceeded to a more positive criticism of the piece that had been produced: it was merely a well-constructed comedy of intrigue in the style of Scribe, with several very piquant scenes, and did not at all solve the problem of how to write a drama the hero of which was the most ideal poet of the German race. Not till the ice-bucket appeared with its champagne did he cease; and everything was to be put right again by a congratulatory toast. But nothing now could put matters right; people emptied their glasses, and dispersed all out of tune. I myself went off with Laube, and wandered about for some time with the dejected man in the dark, quiet streets by the river." [8] Mr. Ellis, in translating this passage, has to admit that "however exaggerated, there is a grain of truth in the little tale,[9] for Pecht also informs us: 'After the performance Wagner gave Laube a feast, at which he congratulated the poet very intelligently and to the point, but, to the minds of us enthusiasts, by far too insufficiently, the consciousness of his own superiority seeming to dominate it all.' Which-

[7] November 12, 1846.

[8] Glasenapp, ii, 171.

[9] It would be interesting to know how Mr. Ellis, who was *not* present at the supper, is able to decide that the account of a man who *was* present is "exaggerated," but still has "a grain of truth in it."

ever account we accept," Mr. Ellis goes on to say, "it was awkward for the guest of the evening, and scarcely more palatable because, as Meissner himself adds, 'Perhaps Wagner was right.' He had no intention of wounding his guest,[1] but he does appear to have had the unfortunate habit of thinking aloud; and his standards were so far above the heads of his company that his thoughts were bound to bruise when suddenly let fall on them." Plain people would probably sum it up in much simpler terms— that Wagner had been unnecessarily tactless and rude to a guest.

I have already cited Wagner's own confession of similar tactlessness and ill-breeding toward Count Pachta's daughters in Prague in 1834. He makes a similar confession with regard to his conduct to a certain Professor Osenbrück, whom he met at a party in Zurich about 1851. "I remember that I made a special exhibition of the immoderate excitement that was characteristic of me at that time, in a discussion with Professor Osenbrück. All through supper I irritated him with my obstinate paradoxes till he had such an absolute horror of me that for ever afterwards he anxiously avoided meeting me." [2]

The Von Hornstein episode in Zurich gave us an example of the bad manners into which his excited nerves sometimes betrayed him. In *Mein Leben* he frequently confesses that his irritability was very trying to his friends; and in 1858 he congratulated himself on now being able to argue with them without getting excited as of old.[3] Whether the improvement was permanent or not we cannot say; but certainly his temper stood in need of a curb. In March 1856 he says: "My illness and the strain of work [on *Die Walküre*] had reduced me to a state of unusual irritability. I remember the extreme ill humour with which I greeted our friends the Wesendoncks when they paid me a sort of congratulatory visit on the evening of my completion of the full score. I expressed myself

---

[1] How does Mr. Ellis know?
[2] *Mein Leben*, pp. 568, 569.
[3] See *Mein Leben*, pp. 627, 641, 656, 659, 662, etc.

with such extraordinary bitterness on this way of showing sympathy with my work that the poor distressed visitors departed at once in the utmost dismay; and it afterwards cost me many difficult explanations to atone for the mortification I had caused them." [4]

How tactless and lacking in ordinary *bonhomie* he could be even when his temper was not on edge was shown by his conduct to Gounod in Paris in the *Tannhäuser* time of 1861. "With Gounod alone did I preserve friendly relations. I was told that everywhere in society he championed my cause with enthusiasm; he is said to have remarked: '*Que Dieu me donne une pareille chute!*' To requite him for this I gave him a full score of *Tristan*,— for his conduct was all the more gratifying to me in that no consideration of friendship had been able to induce me to hear his *Faust*." [5]

Sufficient has been said to show that he must have been an exceedingly difficult person to get on with at times, and that of the many enemies he made, some of them must have had quite good reasons for disliking him.

As one studies him, indeed, the innocent, long-suffering angel of the sentimental biographers disappears from our view, and is replaced by a less perfect but more complex and more humanly interesting figure. Again let me repeat that we are not taking sides against him any more than for him, but simply showing him as he was. That he had some serious intellectual and moral defects, that he could at times be selfish and quarrelsome and unjust, can be disputed by no one who reads him with an open mind. The trouble was that with his immovable belief in himself it was impossible for him ever to doubt that he was wholly in the right. A tragedy of some sort is never far from the homes of men of this type. Wagner's greatest tragedy was Minna; and it will be as well to consider the history of his relationship with her in detail, some recent documents having thrown new light upon the old perplexing problem.

[4] *Mein Leben*, p. 631.
[5] *Mein Leben*, p. 755.

v · *Minna and the Wagnerians: The Case of Fips*

Minna has always been the subject of contumelious and
sometimes venomous remarks from the simpler-minded
Wagnerians, especially those who have apparently taken
their cue from Wahnfried. Their quick and easy way with
the problem has been to assume, as usual, that Wagner
was in all things the just man made perfect; his marriage
with a woman who was his intellectual inferior was a mistake, but his conduct was always that of an affectionate
husband and an honorable gentleman—his patience and
forbearance, indeed, with such a thorn in his side being
nothing less than angelic. The Wagnerians detest poor
Minna even more than they detest Meyerbeer or Nietzsche.
The climax of comic pettishness was reached a few years
ago in Mr. Ashton Ellis's remark that for the offense
of flicking a pellet of bread on to a manuscript that Wagner was reading to a young friend she should have been
put in a cab and taken to the nearest station, railway or
police.[6] Fortunately even the Wagnerians are not always
so comical as this; but by way of doing justice to the
memory of Wagner, they have showered their contempt or
their hatred in abundance upon poor Minna's head. How
grievously the recollection of the old unhappy days rankled
in Wagner's memory is shown by the meanness of some
of his revelations about her in *Mein Leben*. The fires
of fate, when he dictated these reminiscences, seemed to
have scorched rather than warmed him; he had learned
many things from life, but neither delicacy nor magnanimity. Nor, one regrets to say, was Cosima, vastly as
we must admire the power of her remarkable personality,
the woman to impose these virtues upon him. One can
recall nothing in literary history quite so unpleasant in its
moral shabbiness as this spectacle of the second wife taking
down from her husband's dictation the most damaging details he can remember of the conduct of his first wife—both
of them knowing that in the circumstances under which
these reminiscences would be published it was impossible

[6] See the *Fortnightly Review* for July 1905.

for either Minna or her friends to state her case for her as
she and they must have seen it. And all the world knows
that this second wife, when Wagner fell in love with her,
was herself wedded to another man, who divorced her on
July 18, 1869; that their son Siegfried was born on
June 6, 1869, and that she and Wagner were married
on August 25, 1870.[7] Plain people, used to putting things
in plain language, would say that this virtuous gentleman,
who was so severe a censor of Minna's matrimonial conduct, first of all stole the affections of a friend's wife—or at
any rate accepted them when they were offered to him[8]—
and afterward lived in adultery with her, to the anger of
her father and of many of Wagner's best friends.[9] It
strikes one, then, as rather a mean thing for a couple of
people with a far from immaculate record of their own
to be laying their heads together, day after day, to commit
to paper, for the benefit of the world half a century or so
later, a record of the failings of a poor creature who was

[7] It is less generally known that while Cosima was still the
wife of Von Bülow she bore Wagner two daughters—Isolde,
born in Munich on April 10, 1865, and Eva, born at Tribschen
on February 17, 1867.

[8] It was the third case of the kind, though the Madame Laussot
and Frau Wesendonck affairs apparently did not go so far.

[9] Wagner's candor about Minna contrasts strongly with the
concealments the worshipping Wagnerian biographers practice
with regard to the fact of his son Siegfried being born out of
wedlock. At the end of the first volume of the Glasenapp *Life*,
for example, is a genealogical table of the Wagner family from
1643. It ends thus:

WILHELM RICHARD WAGNER (1813-83)

Married (first) 1836, Christine Wilhelmine Planer (1814-66),
   secondly Cosima Wagner [sic], née Liszt (born 1837)
Helferich Siegfried Richard Wagner, born 6th June 1869.

It will be seen that the date of Wagner's marriage with Cosima,
which must have been perfectly well known to Glasenapp, is
deliberately omitted; nor is there any mention of the two
daughters Cosima bore Wagner while she was still Von Bülow's
wife, or indeed of the fact that she had previously been married
to Von Bülow. By the way, it is now known that Minna was
born in 1809, not 1814.

no worse than either of them—and a record, of course, colored throughout by their own prejudices. The disproportion between what Richard tells us about Cosima and Frau Wesendonck and what he tells us about Minna, and the vast difference in candor in his treatment of these episodes, is very remarkable in a book of which the sole value is alleged to reside in its "unadorned veracity." Of course in telling the story of how you took his wife from a friend, and deceived him day by day, the fact that the lady herself happens to be both your own wife and your amanuensis rather militates against "unadorned veracity"; but Wagner and Cosima might have reflected on this simple fact, and stayed their eager hands a little when dissecting the first wife. People so vitreously housed should be the last to commence stone-throwing.

Minnaphobia seems to be traditional in the circles that have chosen to regard Wagner as peculiarly their own. Apparently no tittle-tattle about her is too absurd for them to believe. Let us take, in illustration, the portentous case—it really deserves to become historic—of Mr. Ashton Ellis and the little dog Fips. Wagner and Minna were both animal lovers, and were virtually never without a dog or a bird. These beloved animals, as Wagner more than once tells us, counted for much in their childless home. Fips had been a present from Frau Wesendonck. He died somewhat suddenly and inexplicably in June 1861, during the sojourn of Wagner and Minna in Paris. Apparently a legend had grown up in certain quarters that as the dog was Frau Wesendonck's present to Wagner, Minna poisoned it to gratify her hatred and jealousy of that lady and of Wagner. Mr. Ellis, at any rate, propounded this theory in his English edition of the letters to Mathilde Wesendonck. Wagner's account of the death of the dog may here be quoted in Mr. Ellis's own translation:

"At the last there even died the little dog that you once sent me from your sick bed; mysteriously suddenly! It is presumed he had been struck by a cart wheel in the street, injuring one of the little pet's internal organs. After five

hours passed without a moan, quite gently and affectionately, but with progressive weakness, he silently expired"
[June 23].[1]

Mr. Ellis, in some "valedictory remarks" at the end of
the volume, asks why only fourteen of Frau Wesendonck's
letters to Wagner have been preserved, and of course finds
the explanation in the wickedness of Minna. "Looked at
from whichever side [sic], I am forced to the conclusion
that *Minna destroyed the whole bundle* just before laudanuming Mathilde's living present, Fips—a doing to death
so plainly hinted page 273." [2]

The reader is now invited to turn once more to the
above citation from Wagner's letter, and to discover, if
he can, where this "laudanuming" of Fips is "so plainly
hinted." We know that Minna used to take laudanum to
alleviate her heart trouble, but where in the letter is the
barest suggestion on Wagner's part of her having made
away with Fips by means of that poison? It is safe to say
that this theory that Mr. Ellis believes to be "so plainly
hinted" would never have occurred to a single reader of
the letter if it had not been put into his head by Mr.
Ellis.[3] Apart from this, it is interesting to see that *Mein
Leben* (which was published seven years after the Wesendonck letters) gives no support to this wild charge. But
though there is not a hint in *Mein Leben* of an insinuation
against Minna in connection with the dog's death, there

---

[1] *Richard Wagner to Mathilde Wesendonck*, p. 273.

[2] Ibid., p. 372. The italics are Mr. Ellis's own. He does not
offer any evidence in support of this charge. He merely remarks
loftily that "it is too long an argument to set forth here."

[3] Wagner writes thus to Otto Wesendonck on June 25, 1861,
seventeen days before the letter to Mathilde: "In this anxious
time [the Paris *Tannhäuser* fiasco had occurred three months
before, and his prospects were unusually black], when any resolution is impossible for me, and I am incapable of any mental
effort, everything conspires to grieve me. The dear little dog
that you once gave me died the day before yesterday, quite
suddenly and in an almost inexplicable way. I had become so
used to the gentle animal, and the manner of its death, everything, distressed me greatly." *Briefe Richard Wagners an Otto
Wesendonck*, pp. 99, 100.

is a curious discrepancy between the account given there
(English edition, p. 781; German edition, p. 765), and
that in Wagner's letter of July 12, 1861. In the latter, as
we have seen, he says that "it is presumed he had been
struck by a cart-wheel in the street." There is not the barest
hint here of the barest suspicion of poisoning. Mr. Ellis
conjectures that the *vermütlich* ("it is presumed") is really
vermeintlich ("allegedly") in the manuscript of the letter.
It is a wild conjecture, but let us accept it. It at least makes
it clear that Minna had "alleged" that the dog had been
struck by a cartwheel, and that Wagner accepted the
statement. But in the autobiography we get this surprising sentence: "According to Minna's account, we could
only think that the dog had swallowed some virulent
poison spread in the street." On Wagner's own showing,
this had *not* been "Minna's account"; and for a true
version of that account one would rather trust a letter
written within a few days of the event than an autobiography written some seven or eight years later. Does it
not look as if the laudanuming legend had grown up in
the interval, among people who made detestation and
denigration of Minna a fundamental article of the Wagnerian faith? But there is a further mystery to be solved.
"Though he" (Fips) "showed no marks of external injury," says the autobiography, "he was breathing so con-
vulsively that we concluded his lungs must be seriously
damaged." Why in the name of common sense *should* he
show any marks of *outward* injury, or should anyone look
for such marks, if it was suspected that the dog had been
poisoned? The curious thing is that if we omit the sentence
from the autobiography, quoted above, about the "virulent
poison," the account there agrees with that of the letter
of July 12, 1861, in attributing the accident to some external injury received in the street. It looks as if the
"poison" theory had been spatchcocked into the paragraph
later on, without its being observed how it clashed with
the context. In any case, it is satisfactory to see that not
only is there not a hint even in Wagner's later and fuller
account of any suspicion of Minna having caused the dog's

death, but it is clear that she was as grieved about it as he was. "In his first frantic pangs after the accident," [4] says Wagner, "he had bitten Minna violently in the mouth, so that I had sent for a doctor immediately, who, however, soon reassured us as to her not having been bitten by a mad dog." [5] The dog could not have bitten Minna in the mouth unless she had had her face very near his, probably against it, caressing and comforting it; and one leaves it to common sense to decide whether a woman who had been brutal enough to poison a dog out of hatred of her husband and another woman would have been foolish enough to put her face near the teeth of the writhing animal. And, by the way, would laudanum have brought on "frantic pangs"? Is it not pretty clear that the laudanum has only been suggested because it is known that Minna became addicted to that drug as her heart disease developed?

It only needs to be added that although Fips had been given to Richard and Minna by Frau Wesendonck, *it had always been Minna's dog rather than Wagner's.* "A special bond of understanding," he says, "had been formed between them [Minna and Mathilde] by the gift from the Wesendoncks of a very friendly little dog to be the successor of my good Peps. He was such a sweet and ingratiating animal that it very soon gained the tender affection of my wife: I too was always much attached to him. This time I left the choice of a name to my wife, and she invented—apparently as a pendant to the name Peps—the name Fips, which I was willing he should have. But he was always in reality my wife's friend, for . . . on the whole I never again established with them [i.e., any later animals] the intimate relations I had had with Peps [a previous dog] and Papo" [a parrot].[6]

On examination, then, of this theory that Frau Wesendonck had given Wagner a dog, which dog Minna had

---

[4] *"Nach dem Vorfalle,"* which may mean either "after the accident," or "after the occurrence."

[5] *Mein Leben,* pp. 765, 766.

[6] *Mein Leben,* p. 631.

poisoned in her fury against the pair, it turns out (1) that the dog had always been Minna's pet rather than Wagner's; (2) that while no reason is given for her suddenly becoming inflamed with hatred against it, Wagner himself makes it clear that she was distressed at its dying; (3) that Wagner's account of the affair in his letters (written from two to nineteen days after the event) agrees with that in *Mein Leben* (not written till some years after), with the exception of that one sentence, in the latter, as to Minna having said that the dog had swallowed poison in the street; (4) that this sentence obviously makes nonsense of the remainder of the account in *Mein Leben*; (5) that the inference is (*a*) that the poisoning theory was an afterthought on Wagner's or someone else's part; and (*b*) that the "plain hinting" of Minna's guilt that Mr. Ellis sees in the letter of July 12, 1861, but that no other human being can see there, was not suggested to him at all by that letter, but that he was indebted to some other source for it.[7]

VI · *Wagner and Minna*

The publication of *Mein Leben*, the Wesendonck letters, and the letters to Minna have made it possible to see both Wagner and Minna more in the round than we could do a few years ago. Not that any number of documents would ever bring reason into the writings of the more extreme Minnaphobes; their method in the future, as in the past, will no doubt be to insist that the composer

---

[7] *Mein Leben* had not been given to the world at the time Mr. Ellis wrote; but in the *Richard Wagner und die Tierwelt* of the well-known Wahnfried partisan Hans von Wolzogen occurs this passage: "but the little dog died suddenly in the confusion of Paris, *perhaps poisoned*." (Quoted in Glasenapp, iii, 330.) These last words are probably due either to a private reading of the then unpublished *Mein Leben*, or to conversations in the Wagner circle. Again there is no evidence: we are simply left with Wagner's own words in *Mein Leben* and the two Wesendonck letters.

was in every relation of his life as near impeccable as
mortal man could be, and that Minna was very bad or
very mad or a blend of both—to belittle all the evidence
that does not square with the demigod theory of Wagner,
to sneer at the character and the intellectual attainments
of everyone who seems to be a witness for the other side,
and to declare effusively that the kind of evidence that
does square with the demigod theory is "worth a hundred
times" the testimony that does not.[8] It may soothe these
good people—who always become infuriated at the mildest
refusal to see Wagner through their spectacles—if we assure them that to believe that Minna was not so black as
she is generally painted is not at all to hold that Wagner
was an unmitigated villain. As a rule, unmitigated villains
exist only in fiction; the tragedies of married life among
real human beings generally come not from deliberate and
conscious turpitude on one side or the other, but from
the mere friction of two quite normal characters who
happen to be ill-adapted to each other in a few more or
less trifling respects. Wagner was certainly no villain of the
melodramatic sort. He could be kind enough to Minna
at times; he certainly—when away from her—felt the
acutest pity for her as well as for himself; and he could
no more be consciously and intentionally cruel to her than
to any other suffering creature. Yet an unprejudiced reader
of the records can hardly doubt that he was often cruel
unconsciously and unintentionally. It was Minna's misfortune to be the greatest obstacle to the realization of
himself along certain lines. Everyone who has studied
Wagner knows how impossible it was for him to tolerate
frustration anywhere. There probably never was a man so
honest with himself in most ways. His art absorbed the
whole of his nature. He knew what he wanted to do, and
what he needed in order to do it; and for him to need
a thing and to insist on having it were mental processes
hardly separable from each other. At certain periods of

[8] See, for instance, Mr. Ashton Ellis's Introduction to the
English edition of the letters to Mathilde Wesendonck.

his life it became an imperative necessity for him to win
from other women the spiritual fervor, the idealistic glow,
that were denied him at home. He once found what he
wanted in Frau Wesendonck. To reach her he swept
aside with calm indifference both his own wife and Frau
Wesendonck's husband. With the blindness of perfect
honesty, he could not see how Minna could regard the
Mathilde Wesendonck affair from any other standpoint
than his own. It seemed unreasonable of Minna to make
such a pother over the matter after he had so carefully
and fully explained to her that his relations with Mathilde
were purely ideal. Why could not his wife keep home for
him and be happy in administering to his physical comfort, and leave his intellectual and emotional appetites
free to satisfy themselves where they would? As an abstract
logical proposition the theorem had a good deal in its
favor. It broke down through Minna declining to be
thrilled by the beauty or convinced by the abstract logic
of it. She saw herself simply as the wife neglected for
another woman; it did not pacify her in the least to be
told that so far as Wagner was concerned this other
woman was an ideal rather than a reality—that he sought
her society less for what she was in herself than for something in the finest soul of him that came into being only
when he talked to her. The average wife is not consoled
for her husband's obvious preference of another woman
by the assurance that his passion for the latter is free
from any physical implications.[9] That is simply equivalent
to telling the wife, in a roundabout way, that *she* has not
intelligence enough to be his spiritual companion. It
may be quite true that she has not; but the average woman
is not likely to be pleased at being told so. Minna was an
average woman, and she no doubt strongly objected to
what could only appear to her as a criticism and a slight.

[9] Especially when the wife does not believe the husband on
this point. As we shall shortly see, Minna had good reasons
for doubting the purely ideal attitude of Wagner toward other
women.

Wagner had to choose between her feelings and his own satisfaction. He chose the latter, as he always did in these cases. His letters to her place it beyond dispute that his heart bled for her in her misery; but the demon within him forbade him to terminate the acquaintanceship that was the cause of her misery. To have done that would have hindered the one thing in the universe that seemed to him to be worth any sacrifice of other people to further —the development of his personality and his art to their very richest possibilities.

This, I venture to think, is a fair statement of the case as it must have looked to any impartial friend of the pair in the later fifties and sixties who tried to do justice to the psychology of both of them. I would suggest, though, that there were hitherto unsuspected reasons for Minna's unrelenting bitterness toward her husband throughout the Wesendonck affair. Unfortunately we do not possess her letters to him; but from many of Wagner's letters to her in the fifties and sixties we can see that she was forever expressing suspicions of him—suspicions that he combats at great length and with all the epistolary skill he can command. Was there anything at the root of this attitude of Minna's toward him beyond a merely suspicious and jealous nature? Had she anything concrete to go upon? I think we can show that she had. The key to a good deal of the trouble, I imagine, is to be found in the Madame Laussot affair. And in that affair I am afraid we cannot acquit Wagner of a certain amount of disingenuousness both toward Minna and toward us.

vii · *The Jessie Laussot Episode*

He was always much more fond of women than of men, having seemingly found the former more sympathetic not only to his art but to himself. His great desire, as a thousand passages in his letters and his prose works show, was for love that knew no bounds in the way of trust and self-surrender. In his immediate circle he probably had more experiences of this kind among the women than among the men; the women probably had a subconscious quasi-maternal sympathy for the sufferings of the little man, and would no doubt be more likely to overlook the angularities of his everyday character—if indeed, which is doubtful, he showed those angularities as openly to them as he did to his male friends. The story of his life is studded with the names of devoted women, from the Minna of the earliest days to the Cosima of the latest. Madame Laussot never attained the sanctification of some of the later women who played a part in Wagner's life, for the episode in which she figures was brief, and the end of it was of a kind that admits of no going back; but for a while she certainly loomed larger in his thoughts than has hitherto been suspected.[1]

Jessie Laussot was a young Englishwoman who had married a wine merchant—Eugène Laussot—of Bordeaux, in which town the pair lived with Jessie's mother, Mrs. Taylor, the widow of an English lawyer.[2] Wagner's first

---

[1] Chamberlain actually tells us (*Richard Wagner*, Eng. trans., p. 65) that she was "personally unknown to Wagner." Glasenapp ignored the whole episode, though he must have known all about it.

[2] Wagner was introduced to her in Dresden in 1848 by his friend Karl Ritter, the son of that Frau Julie Ritter to whom he afterward owed so much in other senses besides the financial. The young girl was about twenty-one at the time, and Wagner about thirty-five. She was more than ordinarily intelligent, and Wagner himself testifies to her ability as musician and pianist. She had literary and philosophical as well as musical interests. Some years after the Wagner affair she separated from Laussot and married, in 1879, the celebrated historian Karl Hillebrand. She settled in Florence, where she founded and conducted an *a cappella* choir and took a leading part generally in the musical life of the town. Liszt dedicated twelve of his choral works to her. Under the pseudonym of Aldobrandini, she wrote in Italian a treatise on music; and she translated into English, in 1888, Schopenhauer's *Fourfold Root of the Principle of Sufficient Reason*. She died in 1905.

She and Von Bülow were fellow pupils, as children, of the piano teacher Fräulein Schmiedel. They corresponded regularly

account of his meeting with her is rather vague, but vague in that peculiar way that suggests to the careful student of him that he is deliberately saying less than he might. The young girl had shyly expressed her admiration for him "in a way," he says, "I had never experienced before." "It was with a strange, and, in its way, quite a new sensation," he goes on to say, "that I parted from this young friend; for the first time since my meeting with Alwine Frommann and Werder, in *The Flying Dutchman* days, I experienced again that sympathetic tone that came as it were out of an old familiar past, but never reached me from my immediate surroundings." [3] Knowing his susceptibility to feminine sympathy, we may probably assume already that Madame Laussot counted for rather more to him even in 1848 than he cared to put into words some twenty years later.

In Zurich, whither he had fled after the political troubles of May 1849, he received a letter from her in which she "assured him of her continued sympathy in kind and affecting terms." [4] In January 1850 he goes to Paris with the half-hope of getting an opera produced there. He is very depressed, and has a longing to escape to the East, where, he says, "I could live out my life in some sort of humanly-worthy fashion, without any concern with this modern world." [5] While in this mood he receives an invitation from Madame Laussot to spend a little time in her house. On March 13 he excuses himself to Minna for not returning at once. He simply *must* go to Bordeaux, so cordial and pressing has the Laussots' invitation been: they have even sent him his traveling expenses: and Madame Laussot[6] is joining Frau Ritter in paying him

in later life, and Von Bülow's letters of 1869 and 1870, when the Wagner-Cosima affair was coming to a climax, show that he often turned to her for consolation: they evidently felt themselves to be fellow victims of Wagner.

[3] *Mein Leben*, p. 429.
[4] *Mein Leben*, p. 510.
[5] *Mein Leben*, p. 515.
[6] Or rather Mrs. Taylor, who, as we learn from *Mein Leben*, p. 516, defrayed the expenses of the Bordeaux household.

an annuity that is to free him from the necessity of doing anything against his inclination as an artist. He will be back with Minna "in the first week in April." On March 17 (19?) he writes to Minna from Bordeaux, where he had arrived on the 16th. Reading between the lines, we gather that he has doubts about whether the little excursion will quite commend itself to her: he is awaiting a letter from her that may perhaps tell him she is cross with him.

He stays three or four weeks with the Laussots. In the letter of the 17th to Minna he is delighted with Eugène Laussot, who is "a most amiable and confiding young man," who has greeted him with "quite indescribable joy." From *Mein Leben*, however, we learn that husband and wife got on very badly together. Wagner and Jessie were alone a great deal. He found her exceedingly intelligent and sympathetic; he divines, indeed, that Jessie is the only human being who thoroughly understands him. An *entente* is established between them. "I soon discovered," he says, "the gulf which separated myself, as well as her, from her mother and her husband. While that handsome young man was attending to his business for the greater part of the day, and the mother's deafness generally excluded her from most of our conversations, our animated exchange of ideas upon many important matters soon led to great confidence between us." [7] He read her his poem of *Siegfrieds Tod* and his sketch of *Wieland der Schmied*, and they discussed these and other topics connected with his art. "It was inevitable," he goes on to say with the crude frankness into which he sometimes falls in *Mein Leben*,[8] "that we should soon feel the people around us irksome to us in our conversation." "The people around us" is Wagnerian for "the lady's husband and her mother."

The visit lasts three weeks or so, at the end of which time Minna, like a prudent and anxious wife, insists on

[7] *Mein Leben*, p. 516.
[8] One is reminded of his calm recitals of how he almost shouldered Otto Wesendonck and François Wille off their own hearths.

his returning to Paris in order to pursue his plans for a rehabilitation of the shattered finance of the home.[9] He evidently does not like her letter. At the same time he reads in the papers that his friends Röckl, Bakunin, and Heubner had been sentenced to death for their part in the Dresden rising. Out of tune with the world, he determines, he says, to break with everyone and everything. He will give Minna half of the income his friends intended to settle on him, and with the other half go to Greece or Asia Minor, to forget and be forgotten. He communicates this plan to Jessie, who, dissatisfied with her own life, is disposed to seek a similar salvation for herself. "This resolve expressed itself in hints and a brief word thrown out now and then. Without clearly knowing what this would lead to, and without having come to any arrangement, I left Bordeaux towards the end of April, more agitated than calmed, full of regret and anxiety. I went to Paris in a sort of stupor, quite uncertain what to do next." [1]

Wagner now begins to be a little disingenuous, and we catch a glimpse or two of him as the "actor" that Nietzsche said he was. The facts and the dates must be carefully borne in mind. Wagner says[2] that he went to Bordeaux on March 16, and that he stayed there more than three weeks.[3] That would make the date of his departure about April 7. In a letter of April 17 to Minna he speaks of having been "a fortnight again" in Paris—which would make the date of his return there about the 3rd. The precise date is of no importance; it is sufficient that it was somewhere between April 3 and 7.[4]

---

[9] One surmises that she may also have had an inkling of the state of affairs in Bordeaux.

[1] *Mein Leben*, p. 519.

[2] Letter of March 17, 1850, to Minna.

[3] *Mein Leben*, p. 518.

[4] In the passage just quoted from *Mein Leben* he says he returned "towards the end of April." This is demonstrably a slip of the pen for either "the end of March" or "the beginning of April." The true dates are clearly established by letters to Minna and to Liszt, and indeed by Wagner's own remark,

In this letter of April 17 he refers to Minna's letter as having caused "an irremediable" dissonance between them,[5] and he gives, at great length, the whole story of their married life, the thesis, of course, being that he had always been the loving and she the loveless and uncomprehending one. The *plaidoyer* is needlessly elaborate, and raises the suspicion that it was ultimately intended for more eyes than those of Minna; it reads like a plea to posterity to see him as he saw himself. But it is plainly insincere in part. "Your letters to Bordeaux," he says, "have startled me violently out of a last beautiful illusion about ourselves. I believed I had won you at last; I fancied I saw you softening before the might of true love,—and then realised with terrible grief, more deeply than ever, the inescapable certainty that we belonged to each other no more. I could bear it no longer after that: I could not talk to any one: I wanted to go away at once—to you: I left my friends in haste and hurried to Paris, thence to go with all speed back to Zürich. I have been here [Paris] again a fortnight: my old nerve-trouble got hold of me: like an incubus it lies on me: I must shake it off,— I must, for my sake,—and yours." How little truth there was in his remark that "I wished to go away at once—to you; I left my friends in haste," etc., can be seen now from his own account in *Mein Leben*. He plainly left Bordeaux with his head full of the scheme for going to Greece or Asia Minor with Madame Laussot. Of this scheme he of course does not breathe a word to Minna; the consummate, self-deluding actor tries to persuade her that it was to her his injured heart turned first.

Let us now take up the narrative again in *Mein Leben*. After his return to Paris, he says: "I was at length obliged to reply to my wife's urgent communication. I wrote her a copious letter, recapitulating in a friendly but frank

---

on the next page of *Mein Leben*, that "towards the middle of April" he left Paris for Montmorency.

[5] She was evidently more than usually angry with him, for in her letter she had asked him to address her in the future not with the intimate "*du*" but with the formal and distant "*Sie*."

way the whole story of our life together, *and explaining that I had firmly resolved to release her from any immediate participation in my lot, since I was quite incapable of ordering this in a way that would meet with her approval. She should always have half of whatever money I might have; she must fall in with this, and accept it as fact that the occasion had now arisen for parting from me again, as she had said she would do on our first meeting in Switzerland.* I brought myself to the point of breaking with her completely."

He then (still according to *Mein Leben*) writes to Jessie telling her what he had done, though, in view of his lack of means, he is unable to give her any definite information as to his plans for his "complete flight from the world." He receives from her the positive assurance that she had determined to take the same step as himself; she asks to be taken under his protection when she has completely freed herself. "Much alarmed," he tells her that it is one thing for a man in *his* woeful difficulties to resolve on flight, and another thing for a young woman in outwardly happy circumstances to do so, for reasons which probably no one but he would understand. This does not frighten her: she calmly tells him that her flight will be quietly effected—she will first of all pay a visit to her friends the Ritters in Dresden. Wagner is so upset by all this that he has to seek solitude at Montmorency, near Paris, in the middle of April.[6]

Now of all that I have italicized in the last paragraph but one, there is not a word in his letter of April 17 to Minna. The only passage remotely hinting at it is the final sentence of the letter: "Can I hope to attain that [i.e., to make her happy] by *living* with you?—Impossible." It may be thought that, writing his reminiscences of the affair twenty years or more after, his memory had played him false, and that he imagined he had actually written to Minna what he no doubt intended to say. But this explanation is negated by his next letter to her, dated May 4, in which he says: "I cannot help writing to you

[6] *Mein Leben*, pp. 519, 520.

once more before going far away from you. It has remained
unknown to me—as indeed I could have wished—how you
received *the decisive step on my part which I announced to
you in my last letter*. As you have long familiarised yourself
with the thought of living apart from me, and so regain-
ing your independence, I presume and hope that you were,
if perhaps surprised, at any rate not alarmed by my
decision."

Clearly, then, he *had* announced, in the letter of April
17, his intention of leaving Minna. We may be sure
that with his usual tendency to copiousness he must have
occupied considerable space in doing so. What has become
of this passage? Why is it not included in the printed
edition of the letters? If it has been intentionally omitted,
why has not someone conceived it to be his editorial
duty to advise the reader of the fact?[7] In any case the
omission of the passage does not strengthen our already
tottering confidence in the integrity of such Wagnerian
records as have come to us from Wahnfried.[8]

There is certainly something inaccurate in the sequence
of events as given in *Mein Leben*.[9] We have seen that,
apparently on April 17, he wrote to Minna announcing
his intention of leaving her. A few sentences after the
narration of this part of the episode in *Mein Leben*, he
says that he left Paris to seek repose from his worries in
Montmorency, "about the middle of April." We are left
to infer that in these few days the events happened that
are narrated in the sentences in *Mein Leben* describing
his alarm at Jessie's reply. He fixes this date, both for
himself and for us, by the fact that while resting at Mont-

[7] It is significant that the letter of April 17, as printed, termi-
nates with the utmost abruptness and bears no signature—suggesting a suppression of the final matter.

[8] The letters to Minna were given to the world in two volumes
in 1908, without any editor's name, and without a preface or a
single explanatory note. It appears, however, from the publisher's
preliminary announcement, that the editing was done by Baron
Hans von Wolzogen.

[9] It will be seen later that he was then deliberately trying to
minimize the importance of the affair.

morency he looks over the score of *Lohengrin* and decides
to send it to Liszt, with a request that his friend produce
it at Weimar. "Now that I had also got rid of this score
I felt as free as a bird, and a Diogenes-like unconcern as to
what might happen took possession of me. I even invited
Kietz to visit me in Montmorency and share the joys of
my retreat."

It is quite true that this happened "about the middle
of April." We have the actual letter to Liszt; it is dated
April 21. But this same letter makes it clear *that the project
of flight to the East is still in his mind*:

"Decisive events have just happened in my life: the
last fetters have fallen from me that bound me to a world
in which I should shortly have had to go under, not
only spiritually but physically. Through the endless constraint imposed upon me by those nearest to me,[1] my
health is gone, my nerves are shattered. Now I must live
almost entirely for my recovery. My livelihood is provided
for; you shall hear from me from time to time." [2]

Though there is here no specific mention of the East,
there can be little doubt that he is referring to his projected flight from Europe. It is hard to explain otherwise
the remark as to the last fetters that bound him to the
world having fallen from him, or his promise that Liszt
should hear from him from time to time; and there would
be no truth in his remark that his livelihood was provided
for in his new habitat, except in the sense that Madame
Laussot's purse was at his disposal.[3] Moreover, he writes to
Liszt some two months and a half later, when the whole

---

[1] *"Durch meine nächste Umgebung."* In the English version
of the Wagner-Liszt letters this is rendered "by my immediate
surroundings." Apparently Minna is meant.

[2] *Briefwechsel zwischen Wagner und Liszt*, i. 48.

[3] It will be remembered that he proposed to divide between
Minna and himself the annuity of 3,000 francs he was to receive
from Frau Ritter and Mrs. Taylor. We can hardly imagine Wagner maintaining life on sixty pounds per annum, even in Greece
or Asia Minor; and surely he could hardly expect that Mrs.
Taylor would continue the annuity after he had eloped with
her married daughter.

affair had blown over: "When we meet again I shall have much to tell you: for the present only this much, as regards my immediate past, that *my contemplated voyage to Greece* has been knocked on the head. There were too many doubts, all of which I could not overcome. I should have preferred to have gone out of the world altogether. Well, you shall hear later." [4]

It is evident, then, that Wagner, whether by accident or design, has got the sequence wrong in *Mein Leben.* He makes it appear as if he had worried during the first week or two of April over Madame Laussot's plan for leaving Europe with him, that he had sought retirement in Montmorency about the middle of April, and that there the burden had quickly been shifted from his mind. He says no more about Madame Laussot and her scheme, but tells us that while in Montmorency with Kietz he is startled by the news that Minna had come to Paris to look him up. Now the letter of April 21 to Liszt suggests a doubt as to the absolute correctness of all this; and that doubt is turned into certainty by Wagner's letter to Minna of May 4, in which he definitely announces his intention of leaving her. "The news I have to give you to-day gave me a special reason for writing to you again, since I have a feeling that it may soften for you all the possible bitterness of our separation. I am on the point of setting off to Marseilles, whence I shall go at once in an English ship to Malta, and thence to Greece and Asia Minor. I have always felt, and most strongly of all of late, the need of getting out of this mere life of books and ideas, that consumes me, and once more looking round me in the world. For the present the modern world is closed behind me, for I hate it and want nothing more to do either with it or what is nowadays called "art." Germany can only become a field of stimulus to me again when all its conditions shall be utterly changed. . . . So of late my longing has been again directed to distant travel, so as to get quite away for a time from our present-day con-

---

[4] Letter of July 2, 1850, *Briefwechsel,* i, 49.

ditions, and restore myself bodily and mentally by a change of sight and sound in other climes."

Not a word, it will be observed, of Madame Laussot's accompanying him! He has simply felt, as any tired and worried man might feel, the need of a change of scene.

He continues thus: "In these last decisive days, then, I conceived the plan of going to Greece and the East, and am lucky enough to find the means for carrying out this scheme placed at my disposal from London. For in London I have gained a new protector,—one of the most eminent English lawyers, who knows my works and will give me his support in return for the original manuscript of everything I may write."

Even Mr. Ashton Ellis, writing before the publication of *Mein Leben*, was constrained to conjecture, in a foot-note to this letter, that this "new protector" in London "strongly resembles a myth." Let us eschew more forcible language, and be content to call it a myth. *Mein Leben* puts it beyond dispute that the contemplated financier of the expedition was Madame Laussot.[5]

Wagner's account of the affair so far is, I venture to say, colored by his desire, twenty years later, to minimize the seriousness of the whole affair; and by telescoping, in *Mein Leben*, the two letters of April 17 and May 4 he has misled us as to the real sequence of events. He would have us believe that it was *after the date of the first* letter that he told Jessie of his own intention to flee from Europe, and received the reply, announcing her unexpected and unwelcome desire to co-operate in the plan, that so dismayed him. There can be no doubt whatever that it was his desire that she should go with him, and that everything was arranged for their flight. But the story of his disingenuousness or his inaccuracy is even yet not complete.

---

[5] Her father, by the way, *was* an English lawyer. But as he had been in the grave for some time he could hardly be said, with a strict regard for accuracy, to be interested in Wagner's music, and to be advancing money on phantom assignments of the copyright of unwritten works.

By his own account he now does a rather shabby thing. He apparently dreads meeting Minna; so he "bilks" the lady. He leaves Montmorency, goes to Paris, and instructs Kietz to tell Minna that he knew nothing more of her husband than that he had left the capital. The ruse succeeds. Wagner flies to Villeneuve, on the Lake of Geneva, where he puts up at the Hôtel Byron. There, in a little while, he is joined by Karl Ritter. He has not been long settled down at Villeneuve, however, before the Laussot affair begins to take on a very unpleasant tinge. Jessie had apparently told her mother, the mother had told the husband, and the husband had expressed the intention of putting a bullet through Wagner at the first convenient opportunity. According to *Mein Leben*, Wagner writes to Laussot "trying to make him see matters in their true light," but at the same time declaring, with characteristic impudence, that he "could not understand how a man could bring himself to keep a woman with him by force when she did not want to have anything to do with him." He is on his way to Bordeaux, he says, where he is at M. Laussot's service. He also writes to Jessie, advising her to be "calm and self-possessed." In three days he is at Bordeaux: he sends word to M. Laussot at nine o'clock in the morning. No reply is vouchsafed; but late in the afternoon he is summoned to the police station. He is requested to leave the town, ostensibly because his passport is not in order, but in reality, as the authorities admit, because they have had a communication from the Laussots. He obtains a respite of a couple of days, which he uses to indite a letter to Jessie, "in which I told her exactly what had occurred, and said that my contempt for the conduct of her husband, who had exposed his wife's honour by a denunciation to the police, was so great that I would have nothing more to do with her until she had released herself from this shameful situation." [6]

[6] The people in whose private affairs he was thus confidently meddling were, on his own showing, "utter strangers," to him a few weeks before this. It would be interesting to have Laussot's opinion of *him!*

The Laussots had left Bordeaux when he arrived; so he obtains admission to the flat,[7] goes from room to room till he comes to Jessie's boudoir, places his letter in her work basket, and returns. Still no reply is vouchsafed, and he makes his way back to Switzerland in quite a cheery frame of mind, evidently sure of having acted impeccably all through this affair.

In this, as in so many other episodes of Wagner's life, we have unfortunately only his version of what happened. He calls just the witnesses he wants, elicits just the evidence that suits him, and then complacently gives the verdict in his own favor. To the spectator it looks as if he had been extremely foolish with Madame Laussot and extremely arrogant with her husband; and we may reasonably suppose that if they could tell the story from their side they could make the case rather worse for Wagner than he has done for himself. The real facts will perhaps never be fully known: I say "the real facts," for no one who has studied the autobiography carefully, with a knowledge of such cases as those of Von Hornstein, Lachner, Hanslick, the Wesendoncks, and others, can believe that Wagner's account of the affair gives us the whole truth and nothing but the truth. But letting that pass, we may now observe how once more the story in *Mein Leben* fails to square with the evidence obtainable elsewhere.

That Madame Laussot had become disillusioned concerning him is plain from his own further account. One day Karl Ritter receives a letter from her which he hesitates to show to Wagner. The latter tears it out of his hand, and finds that "she had written to say she felt obliged to let my friend know that she had become sufficiently enlightened about me to make it necessary for her to drop my acquaintance." Afterward he discovers that her mother and her husband had taken steps to break off all

[7] According to his own account, which makes some demands on our credulity, he simply "rang the bell and the door sprang open: without meeting anyone I entered the open first floor, passed from room to room," etc. Julius Kapp suggests that he must have been wearing the Tarnhelm.

correspondence between her and Wagner; he gracefully refers to them now as "the two conspirators," and charges them with "calumniating" him. "Mrs. Taylor had written to my wife complaining of 'my intention to commit adultery,' expressing her sympathy with her, and offering her support; poor Minna, who now suddenly thought she had found a hitherto unsuspected reason for my resolve to live apart from her, in turn complained to Mrs. Taylor." There has been, in fact, "a curious misunderstanding" of a joking remark of his. He is very indignant over it all, but chiefly at the way Minna had been treated! While he is himself indifferent as to what the others might think of him, he accepts Karl Ritter's offer to go to Zurich and set Minna's mind at rest with a proper explanation.[8] Karl rejoins him, and tells him that Minna still contemplates settling down with him once more. He and Karl come to the conclusion that "nothing could be done with such a mad Englishwoman"; and with a smile Wagner dismisses from his mind the whole affair, in which, as usual, he had been so deeply wronged and so grievously misunderstood.

It was evidently both his desire and that of Cosima, when *Mein Leben* was being written, to say as little as possible about the Laussot affair of some twenty years earlier, and to affect to pooh-pooh the whole matter. So reticent were they on the subject that none of the earlier biographers knew anything about it. Glasenapp must have known some, at least, of the facts, but forebore to disclose them. He tells us that the Bordeaux project to pay Wagner an annuity suddenly fell through, owing to "peculiar and quite unexpected complications in the relations [between Wagner and his Bordeaux friends], to enter into which is not our business." Not even the name of Madame Laussot appears in Glasenapp's pages dealing with this period. Mr. Ashton Ellis also undoubtedly knew there was a story to be told, but refused to touch upon it: "If the veil of this mystery can never be completely lifted," he says, "in the absence of letters so private that they are

[8] *Mein Leben*, p. 528.

never likely to be given to the world . . ." He too achieves the feat of talking about the Bordeaux visit without mentioning even that certain people of the name of Laussot lived in the town. *Mein Leben* and the letters to Minna and Liszt combined create the impression that the account in the former falls somewhat short of perfect frankness; but the full extent of the disingenuousness of the account in *Mein Leben* could not be known until Wagner's letters to Frau Ritter were published in 1920.

We see at once from these that it was in a mood of anything but quiet amusement over the aberrations of a "mad Englishwoman" that he went with Karl on a trip through the Valais. His soul was sick almost unto death then and for some time after; he repeatedly speaks of himself as a man for whom everything in this world is finished. "Thoughts, wishes, hopes," he writes to Frau Ritter from Zermatt on June 9, "ah! what are all these as against reality!" By a mighty effort he has torn himself away from an old and painful life: but the new life hovers formless before him: "I am not dead and not living, tortured by memories," etc., etc. From the bottom of his soul he longs for death. He thinks with tenderness of poor Minna, who "lacked only one thing, without which all love is a delusion . . . the understanding of what it thinks it loves." He has been consoled by the visit of Frau Ritter and her daughter, whose hearts are full of love and sympathy and understanding. Then he breaks out into a wail: "In a year we can see each other again—in a year I shall hope to see Jessie also once more. *In a year!* [Jessie had promised her husband and her mother not to see Wagner for that period.] Good God! Are we not all experienced enough already to know what a year is? Are we children, that we are so free with years? Is our life so very abundant that we can wantonly let a year fall out of it? Do you know, dear Mother,[9] what a year must be to *me*, the unliving?"

Then comes the final blow. In the seventeen-page letter

[9] Frau Ritter was about twenty years older than himself. She would be fifty-six in 1850.

of June 26–7 he tells of the receipt by Karl, five days before, of a short letter from Jessie announcing that she has "broken with the past," and will throw future letters of Wagner into the fire unread; she has asked Karl to give him the gist of her letter and then burn it.

"I ought to meet so summarily curt a proceeding," he writes to Frau Ritter, "with a similar brevity towards her, and say that now I realise that I was unable to instil into Jessie love as I understand it; but I am grieved by the perception that I could not win from this woman even the most necessary *consideration* for myself. Nevertheless I herewith deposit in your hands the testament of a love of which I will never be ashamed, and which, even if bodily dead, will perhaps fill me to my dying day with the gladdest memories and an afterglow of happiness." He will tell Frau Ritter the whole story of the "catastrophe."

He recalls to her memory his state of mind when, at Geneva, he received the letter that decided him to go to Bordeaux. He saw that Jessie "had undertaken too much for her strength." She was not equal to her project. Love should dare all things, even if ruin befall in consequence. Jessie's sudden weakening, in face of the pressure put on her by her family, had at once completely altered his relations with her. He could not give her the strength she lacked. "What there was for me to do I did, however; and I confess to you that I faced with perfect indifference the danger of having a bullet put into my head by an offended husband. You will remember our conversations in Villeneuve, and how fully I agreed with your view that for Jessie little or nothing can now be done from the outside,—that only she herself can help herself, and that only by baffling . . . all the devices that now will be employed by those about her against her feeling for me. The only power that could help her she has abandoned and betrayed —the power of her love! She has lost herself, because— *she is weak!* The woman that would have brought me salvation has proved herself a child! . . . What foolish weakness, knowing as she did that she was dealing with the enemies of her love, to give these enemies a promise to prevent her beloved from communicating with her in any way!" The promise to refrain from writing to him for a year had evidently weighed heavily on his mind.

"I do not know," he continues, "what lies they have been telling her about me, or whether she herself suddenly became—forgive the word!—so stupid as to misunderstand certain passages in my letter to Madame Tailor [*sic*]. I wrote finally to this lady that, great as is my love for Jessie, of however immeasurable value its fulfilment must seem to me, yet in the pride of my soul I would renounce all hope of her if I saw that Jessie's love for me had not the unconquerable strength that alone could influence her [i.e., her mother] in its favour: for I would not woo her, but only receive her as an unhoped-for, highest happiness from herself. Could Jessie's love-sense all at once have become so blind as to misunderstand most coarsely the feeling I thus expressed? But just this was Jessie's unspeakable love-charm for me, that in everything she understood me so quickly, so clearly and so surely. . . . Or had they—and this is the conjecture that again gives me strength to go on—had they applied to my poor wife to learn whether I was really criminally separated from her by priests and lawyers? Could they have got from her the disclosure—so much desired by them—that I had not yet informed her that I was paying court to another, a rich woman, and consequently asking her to renounce her claim on me? Could they, with such testimonies in her hand, suddenly have given Jessie the idea that I cherished no 'solid, honourable views' towards her?" Jessie, it seems, knew well that he loved his "unfortunate wife," that a thousand sufferings in common bound them together, and that "only with a deep-bleeding heart could I tear myself loose from the poor creature, in order to separate her from a fate that was incomprehensible to her, and that could bring her only pain and grief without her understanding why. Who realised better than Jessie how wretched I was after this separation, since it was the candid testimony that I gave her of this misery that inspired her to the wonderful resolve to break with the whole world in order to come with me, to compensate me for everything, to heal every wound of my life, these last wounds as well? . . . She would go with me to the furthest ends of the world, so as to hide from the unhappy one [Minna] the spectacle, perhaps even the knowledge, of the happiness of our love! How I rejoiced never to find in her letters a trace of that horrible and unworthy bourgeois hypocrisy! She was wholly nothing but *love*: to the *god of love* we dedicated ourselves, and despised all the idols of this miserable world so deeply that we did not even think them worthy of mention. How then could Jessie have suddenly become so enslaved by one of these idols that she could swiftly and willingly sacrifice her god to it? . . ."

He can only assume that "my Jessie's" reason for breaking with him is to be found in those letters which he imagines his wife to have written to the family. "She suddenly recognised the happiness of decorous bourgeois love, and was so enraptured by it that she did not even think it necessary to seek for an explanation from me, but was all at once so angry over my supposed opinion on the matter that she lost all regard for me, and sent word to me through my young friend that 'henceforth letters from me would be burnt unread, etc., etc.' How was this possible? What power could so suddenly dethrone the most glorious love and turn it out of doors like an old dog?"

"And yet," he goes on, "how is the unhappy one to be pitied! My heart breaks with sorrow over the depth of her fall. O Mother, dear, faithful woman, had you seen the jubilation of love that broke forth from every nerve of the rich-souled woman as she not so much confessed as let me see, through herself, through the involuntary, clear and naked revelation of love, that she was mine!" . . . "No, we will not revile it, the dead one, the murdered one, for it was love! Never, dearest Mother, will I be ashamed of this love: if it has died, if I am convinced that it can never come to life again, yet was its kiss the richest delight of my life. Nor honour, nor splendour, nor fame will ever outweigh it for me. Farewell, thou fair one, thou blessed one! Thou wert dear above everything to me, and never will I forget thee! Farewell!"

He recurs to his suspicion that Madame Taylor had been corresponding with Minna, and no doubt making it appear that it was *he* who was seducing Jessie; whereas it was Jessie who "of her own accord offered me salvation." Then he gives Frau Ritter a full account of his late dealings with Minna: and this account does not quite square with that in *Mein Leben.*

He outlines first the letter of April 17, in which he had told Minna of his unalterable resolve to live apart from her in the future—a resolve so unalterable that he begged her not to try to communicate with him; he would leave it to her to decide whether, after this, she would take steps to make their separation a legal one. There is nothing to this last effect in the letter as we now have it; beyond all question it has been tampered with, the final passages, presumably, being omitted. He wrote her, he says, a second letter from Geneva "at the beginning of May": this is evidently the one dated May 4. The story he now tells Frau Ritter differs slightly from that in *Mein Leben.* In the latter, as we have seen, he says that while at Montmorency, near Paris, he was startled by the news that his wife had come to Paris; he told Kietz to tell Minna that he knew nothing more of him than that he had left Paris, and fled that same night to Geneva. In the letter to Frau Ritter he discloses first of all what he did not see fit to disclose in *Mein Leben*—that it was just then that Jessie had "opened her mind out to him unreservedly." [1] He heard, he says, that *friends from Zurich* were looking for him in Paris—friends who, he supposed, were informed as to the course of events. It was "almost physically impossible" for him to discuss circumstantially the "reasons for my last step" with any friends, however well-wishing. At all times he had been indisposed for this, but he was more than ever so now, in the state of agitation into which

[1] "*Zwar um genau dieselbe Zeit, als sich mir Jessie unumwunden eröffnete.*" See p. 35 of the Letters of Frau Ritter.

Jessie's letter had thrown him. Accordingly he left Mont-morency and Paris without saying good-by to anyone, and went to Geneva. Now either he knew at the time that it was Minna who had been searching for him in Paris—and who else, indeed, could it have been?—in which case he was deliberately deceiving Frau Ritter, or he is straying from the truth when, in *Mein Leben*, he tells us categori-cally that he knew it was Minna, and that his reason for not facing her was the decision, "after an hour's painful struggle with myself," that he must stand by his expressed determination to part from her. There can be no doubt that the *Mein Leben* version is the true one, and that he concealed the real facts from Frau Ritter, probably feeling that they hardly squared with the idealized portrait he was painting of himself for her benefit. It was only in Geneva, he tells her, that he learned from a friend in Paris that it was Minna who had pursued him. He assumes that she had come to try to explain away what she no doubt regarded as only one more of their many misunderstand-ings. He desires, of course, no explanation—for is he not on the point of eloping with Jessie? At the same time Minna's good feeling touches him: she evidently loves him in her own way, though her inability to understand him makes that love useless to him. Kietz, who kept in touch with him through the *poste restante* on his way to Geneva, has apparently told him what Minna has had to say: and he feels he must, for the last time, do what he can to soften the blow for her. So he writes her the letter of May 4, his summary of which to Frau Ritter is accurate enough. He tells Minna that he is going to Greece and the East, and that she can give his Zurich friends to understand that he is not separating from her, but merely cutting him-self adrift from a Europe that is distasteful to him. She is to settle down comfortably in Zurich with a little garden, a dog, and a bird, be as happy as she can, and not give up all hope of seeing him again someday.

He is, in fact, as he tells Frau Ritter, acting the good physician to Minna, and his conscience absolves him. But immediately before this he had written to Jessie "a holy, serious letter, decisive but difficult, wherein I told her pitilessly my whole situation, and laid before her, in the most solemn terms, the magnitude and the difficulty—a difficulty demanding the utmost strength and conviction —of the resolution she had communicated to me. I was not yet fully sure of her steadfastness, and so it would be the most ill-timed cruelty now—precisely now—when I felt irresistibly impelled to console her somehow, to deal my wife this last blow, that would be the death of all hope. Not because I wanted to keep in reserve the tasteless² choice, in case I did not win Jessie, of returning to my wife . . . but simply on the ground that I did not want, precisely now, to practise any unnecessary cruelty." If "the strength of Jessie's love" still held, his own resolution was unchanged to let Minna know through a friend at some later time, and from a distance, all that had happened, so that having now good grounds for obtaining a divorce from him she might do so. "But that I could bring myself to be cruel to my wife will convince you of the overwhelming strength of my love for Jessie. . . ."

He surmises that Minna may have sent his letter of May 4 to Madame Taylor, which would account for that lady's anger with him. He cannot account for Jessie's taking offense at the letter, however, except on the supposition that she *wanted* to be offended: "for she must have understood me, she must have recognised in this letter the man she loved,—or else she had never loved me, never understood me."

It would be interesting to know whether Minna really did send this letter to Bordeaux. If so, it would fully account for Jessie's sudden revulsion of feeling. Wagner, of course, does not tell Frau Ritter *all* that was in the letter. But we, who have it, know that it contained a gross fib about the "eminent English lawyer" who was going to maintain him in return for the assignment of future works; and, as we have seen, he held out to Minna the

² The *fade* in the original is only conjectural.

hope that they would come together again later. Jessie, if she ever read that letter, might well feel that there were depths of duplicity in her lover of which she had not hitherto been conscious. *Something* serious must have happened to make her turn against him so quickly and so completely; and her knowledge of this letter seems as likely an explanation as we can hit upon at present.

It is perhaps a not unreasonable assumption that Wagner was not wholly sorry that the affair with Jessie came so soon to so violent an end. That he was passionately in love with her and that he is thoroughly disingenuous in the account he gives of his feelings toward her in *Mein Leben* are proved conclusively by his long letter to Frau Ritter. At the same time it is probably true that he was seriously disturbed by her proposal that she should accompany him in his flight to the East; in spite of his temporary irritation with Europe he must have known that the artist in him could not be permanently submerged, and that only in Europe could this artist find expression. He probably drifted into *l'affaire* Jessie with his usual facile amorousness, and then found that it contained dangers of which he had not thought. Twenty years later, when writing *Mein Leben* under Cosima's eyes, he would be more conscious of the dangers he had escaped than of the love he had lost—after all, there had been plentiful compensations for this!—and in retrospect Jessie would appear to him only as the impulsive and inexperienced young woman whose rashness might have wrecked his life. Certain it is that at the very moment he realized that she was lost to him he began to contemplate the possibility of reunion with Minna, as appears from the concluding stages of the letter to Frau Ritter. He, of course, as usual, is the spotless, injured innocent. It must be Jessie's "bad conscience," he says, that made her write as she did to Karl, and especially made her withhold her change of address, so that neither Karl nor Wagner could write to her. He bids Karl find out just what Minna knows and how she feels about it. Minna forgives him and takes him back: his letter of July 10 to Frau Ritter shows that, egoist as he was, he had been deeply touched by her devotion.[3]

It will now be absolutely clear that the account given of the Laussot affair in *Mein Leben* is quite untrustworthy; and this experience alone should be sufficient to make us chary of believing anything whatever in the autobiography that is not supported by independent testimony.

One curious doubt remains after the chief obscurities of the affair have been cleared up. Did Minna know at the time that Wagner intended to elope with Jessie? And if she did know this, did she conceal the knowledge from her husband? According to *Mein Leben*, he gave Minna, through Karl, "the necessary explanations for her peace of mind." This is rather vague: it would be interesting to know precisely how much explanation Wagner thought "necessary." Our doubts are awakened by a curious passage in one of his letters to Minna of nine years later:

"Neither can I blame you for giving me that dear Bordeaux to smell at in return, especially as you have kept a secret from me, the hearing of which really astounds me. So someone wrote you at the time, that I went that second time to Bordeaux to abduct a young wife from her husband? Now let me assure you on my honour and most sacred conscience that such a shameless lie and calumny was never yet invented against any man. If it would conduce to your honour and peace of mind, I should be quite ready to give you the exact details of the whole of the episode, and you would then find that I doubtless acted

[3] Jessie Laussot's name appears only once in the later letters to Frau Ritter. In November 1856 Wagner hears from Liszt that Madame Laussot is about to make an independent existence for herself by opening an educational establishment. He asks if details can be procured for him. He is still in doubt as to the meaning of her unfortunate letter to Karl in 1850. "It would be a great consolation to me to be able to give my hand to Jessie as a friend, now that the passion of our relationship can no more trouble us. You will surely recognise in this request . . . only the honest wish of a man in need of peace, a man longing for reconciliation, who would like to have won a lasting friendship from the transient storm of passion." *Briefe an Frau Julie Ritter*, p. 104. As late as 1854 he was asking Von Bülow for news of Jessie. *Briefe Richard Wagner an Hans von Bülow*, p. 43.

very stupidly at that time, but certainly *not evilly* to anyone." [4]

I do not see what meaning we can attach to this except
that for nine years Wagner had been unaware that Minna
knew as much as she actually did of the Bordeaux affair.
The revelation evidently comes as a complete surprise to
him.

We have seen, not only from *Mein Leben*, but from
the letters to Frau Ritter, that he had the suspicion that
Minna and Madame Taylor had been in communication
with each other. Can it be that he never suspected that
Minna knew the *whole* story of his duplicity, and that she
magnanimously (or sagaciously) forebore to let him see
that she knew? And what are we to say of the quibble
in this letter of his of 1859? It may be quite true that his
second journey to Bordeaux was not with the object of
abducting Jessie; but it is no less true that he had seriously
contemplated an elopement with her. How much, one
wonders, did Minna really know?

At any rate we have here, I think, the explanation, or
partial explanation, of a good deal of Minna's jealous suspicion in the fifties and sixties, especially as regards Frau
Wesendonck. Knowing of Wagner's relations with Madame Laussot, knowing also that he had kept these relations a secret from her both when he was writing to her at
the time and in the years that followed, knowing at first
hand, too, as well as we know now through *Mein Leben* and
the letters, her husband's ineradicable tendency to *prendre
son bien où il le trouvait*, we can understand her frequent
uneasiness of mind. If we are to be fair to her we must get
away from the ideal historical standpoint, from which all
that is seen is the great musician blundering through life
and sacrificing everybody and everything in order to consummate his art; we must look at it also from the standpoint of Minna and the moment, putting the genius out
of the question and taking it purely as a case of any husband and any wife. And when this is done, though we may
still regret the tragedy of their union and admit that

[4] Letter of May 30, 1859: *Richard an Minna Wagner*, ii, 95.

Minna was not the best wife possible for such a man as he—that she had, indeed, almost as many faults as a wife as Wagner had as a husband—we shall at all events refuse to join in the venomous outcry of the extreme Wagner partisans against her.[5]

[5] The Laussot story as told in *Mein Leben* is another instance of the damage Wagner has done his own case by voluntarily going into the witness box to give evidence on his own behalf. The older biographers apparently know nothing of the Laussot affair. There is not a word of it even in the latest edition of Glasenapp, though it is hard to believe that Glasenapp had never heard of it. (His work as a whole, with its copiousness and its general accuracy as to facts, suggests access to *Mein Leben* before publication of the latter.) Reading his account of the Paris-Zurich excursion of 1850, indeed, in the light of our present knowledge, it is impossible to resist the conclusion that he knows more than he is telling.

It is interesting to recall the fact that Ferdinand Praeger, whose *Wagner as I Knew Him* is anathema to the Wagnerians —and to some extent rightly so—has a story that is evidently a muddled version of the Laussot affair. "At Bordeaux," says Praeger, "an episode occurred similar to one which happened later at Zurich [Frau Wesendonck?], about which the press of the day made a good deal of unnecessary commotion and ungenerous comment. I mention the incident to show the man as he was. The opposition have not spared his failings, and over the Zurich incident were hypercritically censorious. The Bordeaux story I am alluding to is, that the wife of a friend, Mrs. H——, having followed Wagner to the south, called on him at his hotel, and throwing herself at his feet, passionately told of her affection. Wagner's action in the matter was to telegraph to the husband to come and take his wife home. On telling me the story, Wagner jocosely remarked that poor Beethoven, so full of love never had his affection returned, and lived and died, so it is said, a hermit" (p. 196).

There is plainly an enormous admixture of fiction here; but equally plainly the basis of the story is the Laussot episode. Had there really been an affair of the kind narrated by Praeger, in which Wagner's virtue had shone so brilliantly, we may be sure we should have been told all about it in *Mein Leben*. Praeger apparently got his story from a hurried perusal of the privately printed autobiography, which, he says (p. 330), Wagner put in his hands one day before going out (at Triebschen). This seems to have been the case. Chamberlain (*Richard Wagner an Ferdinand Praeger*, p. 93) says that "according to a communication made to me [by Cosima?] Praeger's story of being left alone

VIII · *In Love with Minna*

That Minna was as much sinned against as sinning will hardly be disputed by any unprejudiced reader of *Mein Leben* and Wagner's correspondence. Let us throw as rapid a glance as possible over the various stages of their union.

Wagner himself sings the praises of the earlier Minna frequently enough. The picture we first get of her is that of a pretty bourgeoise, of no great intellectual capacity, but modest, sensible, and sympathetic. On the other hand, several of Wagner's self-revelations show him in his youth as the harum-scarum one might expect a genius of his dynamic temperament to be—not vicious, perhaps, in the style of more stupid men, but keen for pleasure, and anxious to taste every vintage that life could offer him. His early life probably differed from that of tens of thousands of highly strung young artists only in the degree of ardor with which he pursued his will-o'-the-wisps, and his quite abnormal imprudence in the affairs of daily life— financial affairs in particular. Throughout his career the protection, the solace, the domestic care of a woman were necessities to him. We may believe him when he says that he was the most home-loving of men; home and a devoted woman were haven and anchorage for him.[6] His longing for this haven would always be increased by the despair into which his vivacious nature, so keen for pleasure, was forever bringing him. His early twenties were undoubtedly

---

with the volumes is essentially true, except that it was not in Triebschen and not in 1871. Whatever may be the explanation, however, the fact remains that Praeger, whom it has become the fashion to despise as a mere Munchausen, did actually know of a "Bordeaux episode" of some sort; and that though he had hold of the wrong end of the stick, that there was a stick of some sort has now been proved by Wagner himself and by the letters to Frau Ritter.

[6] From his childhood he was extremely susceptible to women. His heart, he tells us, used to "beat wildly" at the touch of the contents of his sisters' theatrical wardrobe (*Mein Leben*, p. 21).

a very critical time for him mentally and morally. The debt-acquiring habit was already firmly rooted in him, and we get hints here and there of a certain hectic quality in his views of sex. In the *Autobiographical Sketch* (1842) he tells us how, under the impulse of these ideas, he dealt with Shakespeare's *Measure for Measure* in the act of metamorphosing it into his own *Das Liebesverbot*:

"Everything around me appeared to be in a state of ferment, and it seemed to me the most natural thing to give myself up to this fermentation. During a lovely summer's journey amongst the Bohemian watering places I drafted the plan of a new opera, *Das Liebesverbot*; I took the matter for it from Shakespeare's *Measure for Measure*, only with this difference, that I deprived it of its prevailing seriousness and cast it in the mould of *Das junge Europa*: free and uncloaked [*offene*] sensualism [*Sinnlichkeit*] won the victory, purely by its own strength, over Puritanical hypocrisy." [7]

In this mood even the froth of the lighter French and Italian operas became a pleasure to him:

"The fantastic dissoluteness of German student-life, after some violent excesses [*nach heftiger Ausschweifung*] had soon become distasteful to me: *Woman* had begun to be a reality for me.[8] The longing which could nowhere still itself in life found ideal nurture in the reading of Heinse's *Ardinghello*, as also the works of Heine and other members of the then 'Young-German' school of literature. The effect of the impressions thus received found utterance in my actual life in the only way in which Nature can express herself under the pressure of the moral bigotry of our social system." [9]

[7] "*Autobiographische Skizze*," in *G.S.*, i, 10.

[8] In the first edition (1852) there came after this a passage in which Wagner more than hints at sexual escapades in his youth. He deleted the passage from the second edition (1872), as also the following words after "moral bigotry of our social system": namely, "as what people call unfortunately to-be-tolerated vice." See Mr. Ellis's translation of the *Prose Works*, i, 396.

[9] "*Eine Mittheilung an meine Freunde*," in *G.S.*, iv, 253.

His own commentary on the libretto of *Das Liebesver-bot* is that it expressed a change in his moral nature of which he was fully conscious at the time:

"If one compares this subject with that of *Die Feen*, it becomes evident that there was a possibility of my developing along two diametrically opposite lines: confronting the religious [*heilige*] earnestness of my original sensibilities was a pert inclination to the wild frothing of the senses [*zu wildem sinnlichem Ungestüme*], to a defiant cheerfulness that seemed utterly at variance with the earlier mood. This becomes quite obvious to myself when I compare the musical working-out of these two operas. . . . The music to *Das Liebesverbot* had played its part in shaping both the matter and the manner; and this music was only the reflex of the influence of modern French and (as concerns the melody) even Italian opera upon my receptive faculties in their then state of violent physical excitation."

His libretto and his music were the reflection of his life:

"My path led me first of all straight to frivolity in my artistic views; this coincides with the epoch of my first practical experience as theatrical musical director. The rehearsing and conducting of the loose-jointed French operas that were then the mode, the knowingness and smartness [*Protzige*] of their orchestral effects, often filled me with childish delight when I could set the stuff going right and left from my conductor's desk. In life, which from this time consisted in the motley life of the theatre, I sought in distraction the satisfaction of an impulse which showed itself in more immediate things as sensualism [*Genussucht*], and in music as a flickering, tingling unrest." [1]

Mein Leben shows him as he must have been in the Magdeburg days—ardent, passionate, variable, lacking in self-control, eager for the joys of life, and in danger of being sucked down into the maelstrom of the minor theatrical world. His own version of the outcome of all this—in *"Eine Mittheilung an meine Freunde"*—runs thus:

[1] *"Eine Mittheilung an meine Freunde,"* in G.S., iv, 256.

"The modern retribution for modern levity, however, soon visited me. I was in love; married in impetuous haste; under the unpleasant impressions of a moneyless home harassed myself and others; and so fell into the misery whose nature it is to bring thousands upon thousands to the ground." [2]

One may be allowed to surmise, however, that his marriage was at the time a godsend to him: it probably steadied him at a critical moment and saved him from greater spiritual damage. His picture of Minna as she appeared to him at their first meeting must be given in his own words:

"Her appearance and bearing formed the most striking contrast to all the unpleasant impressions of the theatre which I had received on this fateful morning. The young actress looked very charming and fresh: I was struck by the remarkable seemliness [*Bemessenheit*] and grave assurance of her movements and her behaviour, which lent an agreeable and engaging dignity to the affability of her expression." [3] Her "unaffected sobriety of character and her dainty neatness" did something to reconcile him to the vulgar and superficial theatrical world in which his lot had been cast. She was exceedingly kind to the nervous and *maladif* young conductor, yet all that she did for him was done "with a friendly calm and composure that had something almost motherly about it, without a suspicion of frivolity or heartlessness." [4]

After a few weeks or months of acquaintance, in which he had shown a decided liking for her society, Minna begins to be more distant with him—apparently because there is a more serious lover in the field. "I now experienced for the first time," he says, "the cares and pains of a lover's jealousy." For a time they are estranged; but early in 1835 they return to their former friendly footing. And now we get the first symptom of that egoism in his attitude toward her that was afterward to be so fruitful in

[2] *"Eine Mittheilung an meine Freunde,"* in *G.S.,* iv, 256.
[3] *Mein Leben,* p. 109.
[4] *Mein Leben,* p. 110.

misfortune. Though he was not her accepted lover, he jealously objected to her receiving the attentions of other men—of whom there were plenty always dancing attendance on the pretty, engaging girl. He protests with "bitterness and quarrelsome temper" against her receiving other men's attentions, though he admits that "thanks to her grave and decorous behaviour, her reputation was unimpaired"; and while *she* remained as calm and sensible as ever, *he* cubbishly vents his rage in pretended dissipation, which had the effect of "filling her with the sincerest pity and anxiety" for him.

He gives a New Year's party to the opera company, which is evidently meant to be a lively affair, and asks Minna to it; everyone doubts whether she will come. She accepts, however, "with perfect ingenuousness." As the evening wears on and the liquor circulates—punch succeeding champagne—"all the shackles of petty conventionality were thrown off," and the conduct of the theatrical ladies and gentlemen drifted into what Wagner calls "universal amiability." One can imagine the scene.[5] Throughout it all Minna acts with a simplicity, modesty, and dignity that win Wagner's praise.

So far she appears much the more decent and likable human being of the two. Wagner's further account of her increases our respect for her:

"From that time onward my relations with Minna were of an intimately friendly kind. I do not believe that she ever felt for me an affection that came near passion—the genuine feeling of love—or indeed that she was capable of such a thing; I can only describe her feeling for me as one of heart-felt good-will, the most fervent wish for my success and well-being, the kindest sympathy and a genuine delight in my gifts, which often filled her with astonishment. All this became at last part and parcel of her ordinary existence" [*welches alles ihr endlich zu einer steten und behäglichen Gewohnheit wurde*].[6]

[5] He had been so certain in advance of the liveliness of the party that he had warned the landlord of possible damage to his furniture, for which he would be compensated.

[6] *Mein Leben*, p. 117.

The fact that, feeling no genuine passion for him, she should have been as kind to him as she was, and should have been willing to unite her life with his, simply increases our respect for her. To her he was simply a young wastrel of talent, who needed the care and protection of a sensible woman. She "mothered" him, as other women were destined to do in the course of his wild and wasteful life.

Then comes the—to Wagner—discreditable episode,[7] too long for narration here, that makes them avowed lovers. Still there is apparently nothing more on her side than kindliness and sympathy, while Wagner is madly in love. He shrinks from marriage in view of the difficulty and uncertainty of his position, while Minna too "declared that she was more anxious to see these [their finances] improved than for us to be married." But soon Minna leaves him to join a theatrical company in Berlin. This precipitates matters. "In passionate unrest I wrote to her urging her to return, and, in order to move her not to separate her fate from mine, spoke formally of an early marriage." He appears also to have threatened, in the same letter, that if she did not return, he would "take to drink and go to the devil as rapidly as possible." [8]

He persuades the Magdeburg theater authorities to renew her engagement, and sets off "in the depth of an awful winter's night" to meet her on her return, greets her "joyously, with tears from his heart," and leads her back "in triumph to her cosy Magdeburg home, that had become so dear to me." [9]

It is evident, however, that in *Mein Leben* he is not telling the reader the whole of the facts. Certain passages in the contemporary letters to Apel make it clear that in at any rate the latter part of the Magdeburg period he and

[7] See *Mein Leben*, p. 117 ff.

[8] This letter is not included in the published volume of Wagner's correspondence with Minna, which commences with 1842. I quote it from Julius Kapp's *Richard Wagner und die Frauen: eine erotische Biographie* (1912), p. 34. Kapp has had access to a large number of still unpublished Wagner letters.

[9] *Mein Leben*, p. 138.

Minna were husband and wife in everything but legal form. On October 27, 1835, he writes thus to Apel: "Don't get too many fancies in your head with regard to Minna. I leave everything to fate. She loves me,[1] and her love means a great deal to me now: she is now my central point; she gives me consistency and warmth: I cannot give her up. I only know that you, dear Theodor, do not yet know the sweetness of such a relationship; it has nothing common, unworthy or enervating in it; our epicureanism is pure and strong—not a miserable illicit liaison;—we love each other, and believe in each other, and the rest we leave to fate;—this you do not know, and only with an actress can one live thus; this superiority to the bourgeois can only be found where the whole field is fantastic caprice and poetic licence." [2]

Das Liebesverbot is given and fails; his career as musical director in Magdeburg is terminated, and hungry creditors, seeing the end of all his hopes and perhaps theirs, begin legal proceedings against him. Every time he comes home he finds a summons nailed to the door. "And now Minna, with her truly comforting assurance and steadfastness in all circumstances, proved the greatest possible support to me." [3] She gets an engagement in Königsberg, whither he follows her. Then he begins to doubt her. He is uneasy as to one Schwabe, who is "passionately interested" in her. He afterward learned that the pair had already been friendly; though he adds that he could not regard her rela-

---

[1] The bitterness of the later years seems to have affected Wagner's memory of the earlier ones. In *Mein Leben* his thesis is that Minna was kind enough to him, but without love, and perhaps without the capacity for loving. That was not his opinion at the time, however. "Minna was here," he writes to Apel on June 6, 1835, from Leipzig, "and stayed three days for my sake, in the most dreadful weather, and without knowing a single other person, and without going anywhere, simply to be with me. . . . It is remarkable what influence I have acquired over the girl. You should read her letters; they burn with fire, and we both know that fire is not native to her" (*Richard Wagner an Theodor Apel*, p. 48).

[2] *Richard Wagner an Theodor Apel*, p. 62.

[3] *Mein Leben*, p. 146.

tion with Schwabe as an infidelity to himself, as she had rejected the former in his favor. But he was made uneasy by the reflection that the episode had been concealed from him, and by the suspicion that Minna's comfortable circumstances were in part due to the friendship of this man. In fact, he, Wagner, the butterfly amorist, was jealous like any common person; and the desire grew upon him to hasten the marriage with Minna in order that he might find peace and quiet—a refuge from the storms of the miserable theatrical world in which his lot had been cast.

In Königsberg he obtains an appointment as conductor: and now we behold him drifting, like his own gods in the *Ring*, headlong to destruction. His reason warns him of the folly of a marriage with Minna, but his impulses drive him irresistibly into it:

"Minna made no objection, and all my past endeavours and resolutions seemed to show that, for my part, I was anxious for nothing so much as to enter into this haven of rest. Notwithstanding this, strange enough things were going on at this time in my inmost being. I had become sufficiently acquainted with Minna's life and character to be able to see, as clearly as this important step required, the great differences between our two natures, if only besides this perception I had had the needed ripeness of mind." [4] But blind lover as he had been, he goes into marriage with his eyes open:

"The peculiar power she exercised over me had no source in the ideal side of things, to which I had always been so susceptible; on the contrary she attracted me by

[4] *Mein Leben*, pp. 154, 155. At this point he digresses to give us the story of Minna's early life. From the age of ten she had had to help to maintain the family, her father having sustained misfortunes in business. She was a most charming girl, "and at an early age tracted the attention of men." At sixteen she was seduced; her child, Natalie, was always supposed during her lifetime to be her younger sister. Minna went on the stage. She had no particular talent for acting, and saw in the theater only a means of livelihood. According to Wagner she was "devoid of levity or coquetry," but used her powers of charm to make friends and obtain security of tenure in the theater.

the soberness and solidity of her character, which, in my wide wanderings in search of an ideal goal, gave me the needed support and completion." [5]

Always me! me! me! He used Minna as he used everyone else, as an instrument for his own happiness and comfort. And as he was the more intellectual of the two, and saw clearly the fatal differences of character between them,[6] one can only regard the unfortunate consequences of his marriage as an avengement of his own egoism and jealousy. On her part, though she "made no objection" to the marriage, she was plainly not anxious for it; she never seems to have concealed the fact that her feeling for him was mainly one of sympathy. He learns that her friendship with Schwabe had been more intimate than he had suspected:

"It ended in a very violent scene between us; it established the type of all the later similar scenes. I had gone too far in my outbursts, treating as if I had some real right over her a woman who was not tied to me by any sort of passionate love, but who had yielded to my importunities only out of kindness, and who, in the deepest sense, did not belong to me at all. To reduce me to utter confusion, Minna had only to remind me that from a worldly point of view she had refused really good offers, and had yielded out of sympathy and devotion to the impetuosity of a penniless and uncomfortable [*übel versorgt*] man, whose talent had not yet been proved to the satisfaction of the world. I did myself most harm by the raving violence of my speech, by which she was so deeply wounded that as soon as I became conscious of my extravagance I always had to appease her injured feelings by admitting my injustice and begging her forgiveness. So this, like all similar scenes in the future, ended, outwardly, in her favour. But

[5] *Mein Leben*, p. 157.
[6] He had soon accustomed himself, he says, not to talk of his ideal cravings before her. Uncertain of them himself as he was, he passed over this side of his life with a laugh and a joke. With the better part of him thus sealed up from her, it is no wonder they ultimately drifted apart.

peace was undermined for ever, and by frequent repetition of these affairs, Minna's character underwent a notable change. Just as in later times she was perplexed by the [to her] more and more incomprehensible nature of my conception of art and its relationships, which gave her a passionate uncertainty as to her judgments upon everything connected with it, so now she became increasingly confused by my opinion—so different from hers—with regard to delicacy in moral matters; this confusion—as in general there was so much freedom in my opinions which she could not understand or approve—gave to her easygoing temperament a passionateness that was originally foreign to it." [7]

The "delicacy in moral matters" is good. Minna would probably have said that she considered it neither moral nor delicate to run away without paying your tradespeople, and to sponge, and make your wife sponge, upon your friends. She was a bourgeoise, but at any rate she had the normal bourgeois scrupulosity in matters like these, in which Wagner's moral sense was anything but delicate. Posterity will credit him with very little in the way of moral delicacy. His failings in this respect were a source of sorrow to the friends who loved him most. Cornelius, for example, who adored him, sums him up thus in his Diary under the date February 3, 1863:

"Wagner! That is a leading chapter! Ah! I may not speak at large upon that subject. I say in a word: his morality is weak and without any true basis. His whole course of life, along with his egoistic bent, has ensnared him in ethical labyrinths. He makes use of people for himself alone, without having any real feeling towards them, without even paying them the tribute of pure piety. Within himself he has been too much bent on making his mental greatness cover all his moral weaknesses; and I am afraid that posterity will be more critical" [*die Nachwelt nimmt es genauer*].[8]

Yes, posterity sees the sharp division between the artis-

[7] *Mein Leben*, pp. 157, 158.
[8] Cornelius: *Ausgewählte Briefe*, i, 698.

tic greatness and the moral littleness of the man even more clearly than his contemporaries did; and it has learned to distrust the plausibility of his accounts of himself and others, and to distrust them most when they are most plausible. If only Minna could have survived to read *Mein Leben,* and to have given her own version of why the pair drifted so widely apart in the Dresden days—why she, who had endured untold sufferings for him in Paris, should in the course of four or five years have lost all respect for him and all belief in him!

So the breach widened between them. "The really painful feature of our later life together was the fact that owing to this passionateness of hers I lost the last support that Minna's peculiar nature had hitherto afforded me. At the time I was filled only with a dim foreboding of the fateful consequences of my marrying Minna. Her pleasant and soothing qualities still had such a salutary effect on me, that with the levity natural to me, as well as the obstinacy with which I met all attempts at dissuasion, I silenced the inner voice that prophesied dark disaster." [9]

Who, after that, will lay the blame wholly on Minna? He urges her into a marriage for which she has no great desire, forces her to abandon the career that had maintained her in decent comfort, hitches her to his fiery and erratic chariot and drags her through misery and privation unspeakable, quarrels with her from time to time, and insults her with the "raving violence" of his speech.[1]

[9] *Mein Leben,* p. 158.

[1] He pleads guilty more than once to an offensive manner of speech when he was angry. We can dimly imagine what he was like in moments such as these. Von Hornstein, Nietzsche, and others had experience of it. Nietzsche's account of *his* scene with Wagner has become classical. See Daniel Halévy's *Life of Friedrich Nietzsche,* Eng. trans., p. 167. The definitive version of the incident will be found in Frau Förster-Nietzsche's *Wagner und Nietzsche zur Zeit ihrer Freundschaft,* p. 202.

ix · *After Marriage*

In the end they marry (November 24, 1836); Wagner was twenty-three and a half, Minna twenty-seven. At the altar, he says, he had the clearest visions of his life being drawn in different directions by two crosscurrents; but he accounts for the levity with which he chased away these thoughts by the "really heart-felt affection" he had for this "truly exceptional girl," who "gave herself so unhesitatingly to a young man without any means of support."

Almost immediately after the marriage, whatever little idyll there had been in it is shattered. In a few months new financial troubles have accumulated. Minna cannot resign herself to them as easily as he does. The less he is able to provide for the necessities of the household, the more does she feel compelled to take upon herself the duty of supplying them. This she does, to his "unbearable shame," by "making the most of her personal popularity." He was unable to bring her to see the matter from his point of view; and, as usual, all attempts at an understanding were frustrated, as he admits, by the bitterness and violence of his words and manner.[2] What he means by "making the most of her personal popularity" it is not easy to say. On the surface it suggests infidelity to Wagner; but a letter of his to Minna on May 18, 1859, makes this hypothesis more than doubtful. Ultimately there appears on the scene one Dietrich, a rich merchant, of whom Wagner is obviously jealous. On May 31, 1837, Minna leaves her home while Wagner is at the theater. She has fled to Dresden, Dietrich accompanying her a small part of the way. Wagner half recognizes that she has done no more than flee from a desperate situation, and he reproaches himself for being the cause of her despair. He finds her on June 3 under her parents' roof in Dresden; there she confesses that she regarded herself as badly treated by him, and thought him "blind and deaf" to the misery of her position.

[a] *Mein Leben*, p. 166.

Matters grow brighter for a time, but Dietrich turns up once more, and Minna again disappears with him. In time she writes Wagner "a most affecting letter," in which she confesses her infidelity, but pleads that she had been driven to it by despair. She has been deceived in the character of her seducer; now, again in despair, ill and wretched, she begs Wagner's forgiveness, and assures him that she has only now become truly conscious of her love for him. He writes back, taking on himself the chief blame, and declares that there should never again be any mention between them of what happened—a pledge, he says, which he can pride himself on having carried out to the letter.

He was unquestionably generous on this occasion;[3] no doubt his conscience told him that he himself was largely answerable for the distracted state of Minna's mind. Her flight was no romantic love affair, but the mere willingness to accept any outstretched hand that would help her to escape from her husband and the disillusionment the marriage with him had brought her.

His own view of their early married life is further given in two later letters to Minna. They are both instructive. We have to bear in mind, in reading them, his inveterate tendency to dramatize and idealize himself, and his actor's gift of plausible expression. Making the necessary deductions on this account, the story in the letters agrees with that told here. He brings passion to the marriage, Minna brings merely sympathy—which only makes her sacrifice of herself the more remarkable. Both letters are much too long for quotation here, and extracts can give only an imperfect idea of them. They must be read in full. In the first letter, written, as we have already seen, as a sort of farewell to her before going to the East with Madame Laussot, he paints the picture of their early married life as *he* saw it—he all pure, unquestioning love, she pos-

[3] It must be remembered, however, that we have only his account of all this. It is possible that the accounts of the other actors in the episode might have given it a slightly different color here and there.

sessed merely with an ideal of duty. "It was duty that
bade you bear with me all the troubles we endured in
Paris." (It apparently did not strike him that it must have
been a remarkable sense of duty—hardly distinguishable
in its effects from love—that made his wife endure such
agonies for his sake.) The cue of the more inflexible of
the Wagner partisans has always been that Minna was
incapable of appreciating her husband's genius. She may
not have been able to follow the later flights of it; how
many even of his musical contemporaries could, for that
matter? But there is evidence enough that whatever doubts
she may have had about him as a man, she had a sincere
admiration for his gifts as a composer. After the Wesendonck catastrophe in 1858, when Minna was living apart
from her husband in Dresden, and had no reason to be
particularly well-disposed toward him, she wrote to a
friend: "*Lohengrin* was at last given on the 6th of this
month, at the Court Theatre in Dresden, for the first time.
I am very fond of this opera. . . . I have often to refresh
and strengthen myself with Richard's works, or else I
could not write to him in a friendly tone. He certainly has
in me an ardent worshipper of his earlier works. I have a
feeling as if I had created them with him, for during that
time I looked after him and took all the household cares
on my own shoulders alone. How different it has been
during the last few years of our union!" [4] And in the
grievous Paris days we find her writing to Apel for help
for her husband, and declaring her willingness to bear her
weary burdens cheerfully in order that his genius might
have a chance of coming into its own. "What to do now
is at the moment a chaos to me; but even if I had the
means of leaving Paris, I would never leave Richard in
this position, for I know he has not fallen into it through
levity, but the noblest and most natural aspiration of an
artist has brought him where unfortunately every man
perhaps must come without special help." And the poor
woman, whose great desire in life is to live with bourgeois

[4] Printed for the first time in Julius Kapp's *Richard Wagner
und die Frauen*, p. 143.

honesty, is reduced to making a piteous appeal to Apel to rescue her husband by a further loan of money. The same cry is wrung from her in a letter of three weeks later. "I am perhaps better fitted than Richard to plead with you to make a sacrifice on his behalf, as I speak for another rather than for myself. I can put myself in the same category as you, for I too have brought him sacrifices; I have given up my own peaceful, independent lot in order to bind myself to his, for it seems to be appointed that only through the most violent storms and trials will he reach his goal. Therefore I am fulfilling now a holy duty; perhaps, indeed, I sacrifice myself in writing to you again [for money, after Apel's declared unwillingness to give any more]. You say in your letter to Richard that it is impossible for you to do more for him than you have done. That you have given this much shows your good and noble will; and I must believe, since you assure me it is so, that without over-stepping your usual expenses it is impossible for you to make a greater sacrifice for him. Let me, however, with-out any desire to boast, tell you what I did as a girl for my brother, who perhaps in certain relationships stood less closely to me than Richard to you. He was to have studied in Leipzig, but my parents could not support him; so I undertook to do so, at a time when, owing to the wretched state of the finances of the theatre, I had not even four groschen for my dinner. I pawned my ear-rings and such things—which were often indispensable to me at the theatre—sent the money to my brother for his studies, and kept for myself only three pfennigs for a bit of bread which I ate for my dinner while out walking, having pretended to the hotel people that I was invited out to dinner somewhere. Now should it be only the poor and needy to make sacrifices of this kind? . . . In Rich-ard there is a fine talent to be rescued, that will be brought nigh to ruin, for already he has nearly lost heart, and if that happens his higher destiny is lost. . . ." [5]

Surely here was a character of which one who was a

[5] Minna's letters of October 28 and November 17, 1840, in Richard Wagner an Theodor Apel, pp. 80-7.

poorer composer but a better man might have made some-thing finer than Wagner did. In the light of these letters and the self-sacrifice they reveal, read now the sublimely egoistic lines in which Wagner speaks of these Parisian days in his letter to Minna on April 17, 1850:

"Since our reunion after the first disturbance of our married life [i.e., the Dietrich affair] it was really only duty that controlled your conduct towards me,—it was duty that made you bear with me all the miseries we suffered in Paris, and even in your last letter but one you only speak of duty in connection with those days,—not love. Had you had real love for me in your heart then, you would not be giving yourself credit now for enduring those miseries, but, in your firm belief in me and what I am, you would have recognised in them a necessity in which one acquiesces for the sake of something higher; when one thinks only of this higher thing, and is happy in the con-sciousness of it, he forgets lower sorrows."

This is the magnificent dominating spirit that created Bayreuth; but it is hardly the spirit for a happy married life, or the way in which to talk about the hunger your wife has endured for you, the trinkets she has pawned for you, and the lodger's boots she has cleaned for you.[6]

So the letter runs on. Wagner reviews their life in Dresden—always, as it seems to me, pleading his case for posterity as much as stating it to Minna, who probably listened to it with a melancholy curl of the lip; how often before had she not had to listen to these panegyrics of himself!

---

[6] See *Mein Leben*, pp. 212, 213, 232. His feeling toward her seems to have hardened during their later residence in Dresden. In the first sketch of *The Flying Dutchman* he gave the name of Minna to the redeeming heroine; and as late as 1845 he could speak warmly of her to Hanslick. When the latter praised Minna's good looks, Wagner said: "Ah, you can scarcely recog-nise her now. You should have seen her a few years ago. The poor woman has gone through much trouble and privation with me. In Paris we had a wretched time, and without Meyerbeer's help we might have starved" (Hanslick: *Aus meinem Leben*, i, 65, 66).

Let us be fair to him also, however. The business of criticism—at any rate a generation after the actors in the drama have become dust—is to try to see the case for each of them through his own eyes. Occasionally one's anger or contempt may be stirred at some particularly unpleasant manifestation of character; but on the whole, as Oscar Wilde says, "Nobody with the true historical sense ever dreams of blaming Nero, or scolding Tiberius or censuring Cæsar Borgia. These personages have become like the puppets of a play. . . . They have passed into the sphere of art and science, and neither art nor science knows anything of moral approval or disapproval." It is quite true, as Wagner goes on to say, that everything he did in Dresden was the inevitable outcome of his artistic nature; without being untrue to his faith as an artist he could not have acted otherwise. With her inartistic clearness of vision, Minna saw all along whither his idealism was leading them both—to poverty and a repetition of the distress of the Paris days. He admits that she gave him "bodily tending," but complains that what "a man of his inner excitability" needed most—"mental tending"—was withheld from him. But before we blame Minna for not fully understanding the Wagner of this period and seeing the future ruler of musical Europe in him, let us ask how many even of his musical associates were capable of that feat. After the Dresden catastrophe everyone must have been of her opinion—that he was an excitable, ill-balanced man of genius, with a fatal gift for making the worst of life, who had by his own folly sacrificed forever his chance of making an honorable livelihood. Nobody could judge him fairly, because no such man as he—no man so possessed with the idea that anything was permissible to the artist that was necessary for his self-realization—had ever come within the ken of any of them. To the careful housewife, who had endured so much for him only to see all the hardly won comfort of the last few years imperiled forever, he could only appear an impossible wastrel to whom life could never teach prudence. How deep was her anger with him is shown by her long-continued refusal to go to him after his flight. She wrote to him that "she would not join him till he could support her abroad by his earnings." Evidently she had not his gift for living complacently on charity and debts. It is impossible not to be moved by this letter of Wagner's, however conscious we may be that it is merely a dexterous piece of special pleading. The situation between them had evidently become hopeless, yet neither realized that it was so. Minna's hope was that he would again become the Wagner of the early Dresden days, working patiently to provide an honorable livelihood for them both. He had done with all this; henceforth nothing existed for him but his dreams. We can now see that as an artist, he was, as usual, right; but what wife, seeing her husband cease from musical composition for six years and apparently waste his time in writing argumentative books that few people read and fewer still understood, would have judged him and their position much otherwise than Minna did? It was his great grievance against her at this time that she insisted on his doing all he could to get a contract for a new opera for Paris[7]—a project that became every day more distasteful to him. "You stand before me implacable," he cries bitterly: "you seek honour where I almost see disgrace, and feel shame at what is to me most welcome." He apparently could not realize that to Minna the thought of living on other women's bounty and perpetually staving off hungry creditors was as horrible as the idea of sinking back into the filth of the ordinary operatic world was to him.

The same note of eager self-justification is sounded again in the interminable letter of May 18, 1859. There is the same inability to see the problem from any angle but his own. He once more admits that Minna has suffered greatly for him, especially in those ghastly years in Paris. But she should regard her sufferings as part of the game. *He* was a man of genius, who had to follow his star or die. If *her* path was not a happy one, she should regard it as "a necessity in which one acquiesces for the sake of something higher."

[7] Liszt also urged him to do this.

Let us look a moment at this second letter, in which the clever actor is even more apparent. Minna has taken offense at the passage in *"Eine Mittheilung an meine Freunde"* relating to their marriage; and he writes very sensibly and tactfully on this point, doing all he can to soothe the poor woman, who was by this time hopelessly ill both in body and in mind, and, as even her enemies admit, not to be held answerable for the suspicions by which she was obsessed. He discourses with his customary wordiness upon the nature of love; like Wotan and some of his other characters, he could never stop talking when once he had been wound up on the subject of his wrongs. Like Wotan, Lohengrin, and the rest of them, he always has a grievance, and is always misunderstood—hence the need for such lengthy explanations. But there is a touch of meanness in his unnecessary reminder to Minna of her flight from him in their early married days.[8] In *Mein Leben* he is candid enough, as we have seen, to admit that he was chiefly to blame for this lapse on her part.[9] His thesis now is that she did not love him then, or she would not have run away; whereas although he had behaved badly to her, it was all out of the greatness of his love! The sophistry of it all is too unconscious, too naïve, for us to do anything but smile at it; but we may doubt whether Minna, with her keen eye for facts and her impenetrability to words, admired the performance as much as he did.

Then he puts into her mouth a long imaginary description of her own conduct and psychology, and the sort of plea he was always making for himself and desirous that *she* should make for him. He reminds us irresistibly of his own Wotan:

---

[8] He had apparently forgotten his promise (*Mein Leben*, p. 177) never to mention the affair to her again; and when he said in *Mein Leben*: "I can pride myself on having kept this resolution to the letter," he had evidently forgotten his epistle of May 18, 1859.

[9] See above, p. 89.

Wouldst thou, oh wife,
In the castle confine me,
As god this boon thou must grant me,—
Though in the fortress fettered,
Yet to my rule the whole world I must win.
Ranging and changing
All love who live;
This sport I cannot desist from.

So says the self-justifying god to his wife in *Das Rhein-gold*. And again in *Die Walküre*:

Nought learnedst thou
When I would teach thee,
What ne'er thou canst comprehend
Till clear in daylight 'tis shown.
Only custom canst thou understand;
But what ne'er yet befell
Thereon fixed is my thought.

So would Wagner have poor Fricka-Minna regard him. He obligingly writes out for her at length the confession he would like to hear her recite:

"With Richard's individuality, that on the one hand qualified him for the production of such important works and in the end for such unusual successes, it was inevitable, on the other hand, that heavy shadows should thereby fall on our life. I am not thinking of the constant outward care and trouble, although they taxed my vital powers most severely; it could not be otherwise than that his original artistic nature, the peculiarly emotional and wildly moving quality of his works, should keep him in the same state of excitation as they created in others,— inevitably causing disturbances of my own repose. An artist so significant as Richard, one perpetually at work with such passionate artistic tools, retains all his life a certain youthfulness, which must no doubt often cause anxiety to the wife at his side; and whereas this wife remains close to him in the accustomed narrow circle of the household as an old possession, which one often does not notice any longer just because one is so sure of it and so intimate with it from of old, from without there may present themselves new figures, towards the effect of which the anxious wife will probably have to show forbearance." [1]

Wotan, in fact, was to do all the ranging and changing. For Fricka the cue was to be forbearance. Incidentally, I may observe that this was also to be the cue for the masculine heads of the households—those of Von Bülow, Wesendonck, and Laussot, for example—in which Wotan was to indulge freely in the sport he could not desist from.

It was a simple and lucid philosophy of married life, the premises being granted. Minna's misfortune was to dispute the premises. The egregious self-satisfaction of this letter and its pose of the wronged but forgiving husband apparently provoked her not only into reminding him of some of his own peccadilloes, but into letting him see, for the first time, that she knew a little more of his escapades than he had imagined; for it is in his next letter, date May 30, that we find him raising his eyebrows in astonishment at the news that she had known all along of that Laussot plans of nine years ago. He, good man, was no doubt honestly surprised at Minna's inability to see him just as he saw himself, idealized by a vivid imagination. No man ever had a higher ideal of duty—the duty of other people toward himself. Nothing is more remarkable, among the many remarkable features of *Mein Leben*, than the coolness of his references to the services that various people had done him, or the total omission, in some cases, of any such reference.[2] He took all sacrifices as a matter of course; he would have liked a world full of trusting Elsas and faithful Kurvenals. "You must let me have peace," he writes to Minna;[3] "take me as I am, and

---

[1] *Richard Wagner an Minna Wagner*, ii, 92.

[2] No one would guess, for example, from *Mein Leben* how much money had been put at his disposal and how much consideration had been shown him by Napoleon III and others during the Paris *Tannhäuser* period.

[3] November 9, 1851; *Briefe*, i, 88.

let me do what I have joy and pleasure in: don't worry
me into anything I cannot and will not do: rest assured,
on the other hand, that I shall always be doing something
that somehow gives joy to others and contents my inner
sense." This is apparently a justification of his refusal to
write an opera for Paris, or to do anything else that went
against his artistic conscience. For his determination not
to be shaken from his moral and artistic center in such
matters as this no one will blame him; the difficulty only
began when he imported the doctrine of his own infalli-
bility into domestic matters. Even his own Elsa, lymphatic
innocent as she was, had in the end to admit that there
was a limit to her capacity for trusting her husband
blindly. Minna's capacity for that kind of blind devotion
was less than Elsa's; yet nothing short of blind devotion
would satisfy him. One hardly knows which is the more
magnificent in some of his letters—his disregard for himself where his work and his destiny were concerned, or his
disregard for the humble being whom fate had flung upon
his troubled hearth. "See, poor wife," he writes from
Venice on September 1, 1858, "your destiny—which
surely ought to have been made easier and more uniform
for you—was knit up with the destiny of a man who,
greatly though he longed for quiet happiness, yet in every
respect was appointed to so extraordinary a development
that at last he believes himself bound to renounce even his
wishes simply to fulfill his life-task. All I now seek is inward self-collection, in order to be able to complete my
works: fame has no longer any effect on me: I even despair
of succeeding in producing my works [the *Ring*]: nothing
—nothing—but work, the act of creation itself, keeps me
alive. It is natural that so extraordinary a destiny should
also inspire extraordinary sympathy; there are many people
who have turned to me with deep and ardent feelings. If
you must suffer for it, those sufferings will some day be
accounted to you also, and your reward must be—my success, the success of my works." [4]

Who shall say that the artist's faith in himself was not

[4] *Richard Wagner an Minna Wagner,* i, 302.

a noble and a holy thing? The misfortune was that this faith had too often to be nourished in ways that the world cannot help calling ignoble. He saw himself as we see him now, with the eyes of the historical sense; but people who have no prospect of living in history and for whom the present is the only life they know may be excused for feeling that the ideals of other people are too dearly bought at the cost of their own poverty and shame. When all is said, it remains true that Minna would gladly have borne privation for him, as she did in Paris, in order to further his genius, but that she could not reconcile herself to her husband's easygoing attitude with regard to other people's money and other people's wives. It is one thing to love your neighbor as yourself; it is another thing to love your neighbor's wife as your own—or even a little more.

The toughness of the problem that fate had given her to solve is shown by Wagner's letters immediately after his flight from Dresden. The seven years in that town must have been, until near the end, the happiest of Minna's life. Here at last, it seemed, was a haven; her husband was secure for life in a Court Kapellmeister's post, and he had already made an enviable reputation as composer and conductor. She was wiser than he in many of the simpler things of life, and clearly foresaw the ruin to which his political activities were leading him. The unrelenting harshness of her attitude toward him during his flight, of which he makes so much in his letters and *Mein Leben*, was no doubt the result of sheer despair at the extent of his folly, and anger at this grown-up child who apparently could never be brought to listen to reason. A letter of Minna's, published for the first time by Julius Kapp, throws an interesting light on their relations at this time.

"You will know what Wagner was when I married him, —a forlorn, poor, unknown, unemployed musical director. As regards his intellectual success, I am happy to think that all his works were created only in my company: and that I understood him he proved to me by the fact that to me alone he first read or played all his poems, all his compositions, scene by scene as he sketched them and discussed them with me. Only I could not follow his political doings. With my simple understanding I saw that no good would come to him out of them, and the more he departed from the path of art, the deeper became the sorrowful feeling in me that he was breaking away from me also." [5]

His own view of their Dresden life may profitably be placed side by side with this of Minna's:

"After my appointment in Dresden your growing discord with me came just at the time and in the degree as, forgetting my personal advantage, I could no longer, in the interest of my art and of my independence as man and artist, accommodate myself to the deplorable managerial relations of that art-establishment, and consequently revolted against them." Anyone who loved him, he says, would have seen what was going on within his soul and would have sympathized with him; but "when I came home profoundly dispirited and agitated by some new annoyance, some new mortification, some new disappointment, what did my wife give me in lieu of consolation and uplifting sympathy? Reproaches, fresh reproaches, nothing but reproaches! Fond of home as I was, I remained in the house in spite of it all; but at last no longer able to express myself, to communicate what was in me and be strengthened, but to keep silence, let my grief eat into me, in order —to be *alone!*"

His makes, no doubt, the finer literary record now; but who would have said in 1848 that Minna was the more in the wrong?

How hopelessly immiscible were their ideals of living becomes fully apparent a very little while after their reunion in Switzerland in 1849. Incapable of his imaginative flights and his belief in the future, she could see nothing but the misery and the humiliations of the actual day. For him there was his star; with his eyes on that he could forget his daily cares, or leave them to others; some raven or other, he knew, would feed him. Nothing is more re-

[5] Kapp: *Richard Wagner und die Frauen*, p. 65.

markable in his letters of this period than the paradoxical
sense of relief he felt at being, so far as the everyday world
was concerned, a ruined man. "Never in all my life have
I felt so happy and gay as in the summer of 1849 in
glorious Switzerland. . . . I know that with the best I
can do—and must do, since I can—I cannot earn money,
but only love, and that from those who understand me, if
they want to. So I am without a care for money either,
since I know that love is caring for me. So let good Ottilie
[his sister] and all the rest of you be easy in your mind
about me and take it that a great piece of luck—aye, the
greatest that could befall a man—has come to me." [6]

We can well believe him. On the whole his position was
probably not so distressing as it is generally held to have
been. He was not rich, of course; but he seemed to be
assured of a livelihood, he had ample leisure for thought
and for quiet self-development[7] without the necessity of
wasting himself in inferior work—which is always the
greatest misery to artists who have to reconcile the claims
of art with those of life—and he was able to get a good
deal of enjoyment out of travel. On one point he was
quite firm; had no intention of ever again competing
in the arena with other men for a living. It was the world's
duty to provide him with food and shelter in return for his
work; how, as he pathetically put it, could he give the
world the best that was in him if he had to waste his
energies on futile things? Thousands of other artists, it
is needless to say, have felt the same difficulty; probably
nine brain workers out of ten have to squander two thirds
of their best mental powers on futilities in order to win
a little time in which to exercise the other third in the
way they like. One thinks of George Meredith, for example, feeling his bent to be mainly toward poetry, but

[6] Letter to Hermann Brockhaus of February 2, 1851, in
Familienbriefe, p. 165.

[7] Minna objected energetically to the time spent in writing
prose instead of music. Between August 1847, when he finished
Lohengrin, and the autumn of 1853 he seems to have written
no music at all, though he was occupied with the text of the
Ring.

compelled to boil the pot with novels, and to purchase the pot itself by "reading" for a publisher. But Wagner, in this as in every other relation of his life, was nothing if not thorough; it was the secret, indeed, of all his successes and all his failures. Other men might truckle to expediency, but not he. His experiences in various opera houses had taught him how difficult it was for a man like himself to reconcile his artistic ideals with the facts of the theater. There has probably never yet been a Kapellmeister with a soul who has not felt precisely as Wagner did;[8] but he makes the best of a bad bargain, is content with fifteen shillings if he cannot get a sovereign, and uses all the tact that he can command to smooth his relations with his colleagues and to bend them to his will without their suspecting their own compliance. Wagner had no tact where his susceptibilities were hurt, and compromise was always hateful to him. Like the singer who was out of tune with the orchestra and expected it to tune to him when he gave it his A, Wagner blandly took his own course in everything and called upon the world to follow him. The call was often heroic and the response magnificent, as in the case of Bayreuth. But occasionally the call was unreasonable, and the singer and someone in the orchestra inevitably came to blows.

We see, in a letter of Minna's of about 1851,[9] the clashing of his ideas and Minna's on the subject of whether it is more honorable to earn your living by work you do not like or to live—and compel your wife to live —on charity. "The director [of the Zurich theater] had offered Wagner 200 francs a month if he would accept the post of first Kapellmeister in the theatre; but he thinks it beneath his dignity to earn money, and prefers to live on charity or on borrowed money. You can understand, with one of my way of thinking, with what dis-

[8] See, for example, Weingartner's tragic-comic account of his experiences, in his *Akkorde*.

[9] It is quoted in Kapp's *Richard Wagner und die Frauen*, p. 90, but without date or name of addressee. It is simply given as "addressed to a lady friend."

esteem—to say nothing of what has already happened—I, as no doubt any other woman, must regard this. What will become of me—of us—on such principles as these? I often cry my eyes out, and am quite worn out with the worry my husband causes me."[1]

It is customary to censure Minna solemnly for not having a better insight into the genius of her husband, and for not having been willing to sacrifice the last vestige of her happiness and self-respect in order that he might be undisturbed in his inner world. It must be remembered, however, that in time a great many of the friends who had been most generous to him came round to something like Minna's point of view. Everyone knows the letter of June 25, 1870, to Frau Wille, in which Wagner speaks of his happiness in his retreat with Cosima who, he said, had showed that he "*could* be helped," and "that the axiom of so many of my friends, that I could not be helped, was false." [2] The last phrase hints at earlier disagreements between him and his friends on the question of finance. In *Mein Leben* he tells us how coldly some of them received his entreaties for help in the desperate days before King Ludwig came to his rescue. Perhaps they had not met with the gratitude they would have liked. When Madame Kalergis, in 1860, gives him 10,000 francs to wipe out the debt he had incurred in connection with his concerts in Paris, his only comment is: "I felt as if something were merely being fulfilled that I had always been entitled to expect." [3] It is hardly to be wondered at that ideas on finance so expansive as these did not always appeal with the same force to those who were expected to find the money as they did to him. Even the Wesendoncks declined to help him in his dire need in 1863.[4] Later on, a

----

[1] Wagner, however, conducted some concerts at Zurich for a fee.

[2] *Richard Wagner an Eliza Wille*, p. 123.

[3] *Mein Leben*, p. 731.

[4] "I left Baden to fill up my time with a little trip to Zürich, where I again tried to get a few days' rest in the Wesendoncks' house. The idea of helping me did not occur to my friends,

request to Otto Wesendonck to harbor him met with a point-blank refusal,[5] though Wesendonck knew that Wagner was fleeing from his Vienna creditors, and that he was in serious danger from the law. Von Hornstein, as we have seen, refused to open his purse to him; other people repulsed him still more roughly. At his wits' end to raise money, he thinks of divorcing Minna in order to marry some rich woman. "As everything seemed to me expedient and nothing inexpedient, I actually wrote to my sister Luise Brockhaus, asking her if she could not have a sensible talk with Minna, and persuade her to be satisfied in future with her yearly allowance, without making any claims on my person. In her reply she advised me, with deep feeling, first of all to think of establishing my good name and of obtaining undisputed credit by a new work, which would probably help me without my taking any eccentric step; in any case I should do well to apply for the vacant Kapellmeister's post in Darmstadt." [6]

Ultimately (March 23, 1864) he fled to Frau Wille at Mariafeld (Zurich). Wille himself had, as Wagner admits, become cool in his friendship. But at that time the master of the house was away in Constantinople. When he returned he was "uneasy" at the guest who had settled there in his absence. "He probably feared that I might count on his help also," says Wagner. He might well be alarmed, for Wagner, untaught by experience, was as convinced as ever that it was the world's duty to provide for him, and

though I told them frankly of the position I was in." *Mein Leben*, p. 857.

It was about this time that he wanted a number of friends to join in guaranteeing him a yearly subsidy. "Even Wesendonck," he wrote to Von Bülow on June 22, 1863, "should not be overlooked as a contributor." The "even" is significant: it indicates a slight sense on his part that after all that had happened Wesendonck could not be expected to go out of his way to serve him. See *Richard Wagner Briefe an Hans von Bülow*, p. 203.

[5] "Whereupon," he characteristically remarks, "I could not resist sending him a reply pointing out the wrongness of this." *Mein Leben*, p. 865.

[6] *Mein Leben*, pp. 866, 867.

as resolved as ever not to take up any work of the ordinary kind. Frau Wille has given us an interesting picture of him brooding over his wrongs and crying in the face of heaven against mankind:

"I had got together a number of books out my husband's library and placed them in Wagner's room—works on Napoleon, on Frederick the Great, works of the German mystics, who were of significance to Wagner, while he had turned his back on Feuerbach and Strauss as dry men of learning. What I could I gave him in happy impartiality for the best: but cheer him up I could not. I still see him sitting in his chair at my window (it is still there), and impatiently listening as I spoke to him one evening of the splendour of the future that would yet certainly be his. . . . Wagner said: 'What is the use of talking about the future, when my manuscripts are locked up in a drawer? Who can produce the art-work that I, only I, helped by good dæmons, can bring into being, that all the world may know *so* it is, *so* has the master conceived and willed his work?' He walked agitatedly up and down the room. Suddenly he stopped in front of me and said, 'I am differently organised; I have excitable nerves; I must have beauty, brilliancy, light! The world ought to give me what I need. I cannot live in a wretched organist's post like your Meister Bach. Is it an unheard-of demand if I hold that the little luxury I like is my due? I, who am procuring enjoyment to the world and to thousands?" [7]

It was this unshakable belief in the rightness of whatever ministered to his own comfort for the time being that

[7] *Richard Wagner an Eliza Wille*, pp. 74, 75.
Even in the first flush of his prosperity under King Ludwig's protection he could not suppress his rancor against the friends who, having done all they could for him, found themselves unable to achieve the impossible. "Believe me," he writes to Von Bülow on June 5, 1864, "only my friends pain me; of my enemies I take no notice. I have only to imagine the episode with the King never to have happened to find myself in a desert of misery —in spite of my friends, who would all have left me there; none would have helped me out." *Richard Wagner Briefe an Hans von Bülow*, p. 217.

accounts in large measure for the hopelessness of the mis-understanding between him and Minna on the question of Frau Wesendonck. As this romantic episode had the deepest bearing on his life and his art, and his attitude during it gives us the best possible illustration of the dual nature of the man, it is worth while studying it with some closeness.

As we have seen—as he himself indeed admits—he was always extremely susceptible to the charm of women. In October 1852 he writes from Zurich to his niece Franziska: "I cannot endure men, and would like to have nothing to do with them. No one is worth a toss unless he can really be loved by a woman. The stupid asses can't even love now: if they have any talent they tipple, or as a rule are satisfied with cigar-smoking. Only on the women do I count for anything now. If there were only more of them!" [8] His ideal of women then and before and for many a day after was the submissive, unquestioning Elsa. "Lohengrin," he says, "sought the woman who should *believe* in him; who should not ask who he was and whence he came, but love him as he was, and because he was just as he appeared to himself.[9] He sought the woman to whom there was no necessity to explain or justify him-self, but who would love him unconditionally." [1] In another place he gives us his notion of the ideal woman in still more explicit terms, this time *à propos* of Senta. "Like Ahasuerus, he [the Dutchman] longs for death to end his sufferings; but this redemption, denied to the undying Jew, the Dutchman can win through—*a woman*, who shall sacrifice herself for him for love. The longing for death drives him on to seek this woman; but she is no longer

[8] *Familienbriefe*, pp. 189, 190. He recurs to the same idea in a letter of December 30, 1852, to his sister Cäcilie Avenarius: *Familienbriefe*, p. 194. See also the letter of December 1849 to Uhlig, and other passages.

[9] "*Und weil er so sei, wie ihm erschiene.*" Mr. Ashton Ellis (*Wagner's Prose Works*, i, 341) translates this: "and because he was whate'er *she* deemed him," reading, perhaps rightly, "*ihr*" for "*ihm*."

[1] "*Eine Mittheilung an meine Freunde*," in G.S., iv, 295.

the home-tending Penelope, wooed by Odysseus of old, but woman in general [*das Weib überhaupt*]—the as yet non-existent, the longed-for, the dreamt-of, infinitely womanly woman,—in a word, *the Woman of the Future.*" [2] This was the kind of devotion he expected from men and women. I have already pointed out how, in *Mein Leben*, it is this or that person's "boundless devotion" to him that stirs his admiration. It is thus he writes of Cosima in a letter of 1870 to Clara Wolfram; she had shown him "an unexampled devotion and self-sacrifice." [3]

x · *The Mathilde Wesendonck Affair*

It was not very long after he had been disappointed in Jessie Laussot, and at a time when Minna had ceased to minister to his mental life, that he made the acquaintance of Mathilde Wesendonck. They first met in February 1852. The young wife was fascinated by the man of genius, and woman-wise pitied his evidently forlorn state. He, for his part, found in her the mental and moral sunlight his work needed at the time. Their affection for each other deepened month by month. Writing to his sister Clara on August 20, 1858, he speaks of having been "for six years supported, comforted and strengthened to remain by Minna's side, in spite of enormous differences between our characters and natures, by the love of that young woman, who drew close to me [*mir sich näherte*] at first and for a long time timidly, hesitatingly, and shyly, then more and more decidedly and surely." [4]

In the summer of 1854 he sketched the *Valkyrie* prelude, placing on the manuscript the letters "G . . . . s . . M . . . . . . ," which Frau Wesendonck afterward declared to represent "*Gesegnet sei Mathilde*" (Blest be Mathilde!). Von Hornstein, who saw a good deal of

[2] Ibid., p. 266.
[3] *Familienbriefe*, p. 279.
[4] *Familienbriefe*, pp. 217, 218. See also Wagner's letter to Mathilde in his diary of August 21, 1858: "What you have been and are to me these six years now."

Wagner and his household in 1855, speaks of him as having "long ceased to love his wife" and being "consumed with passion for another." [5] By September 1856 Mathilde is apparently sufficiently conscious of her love to be distressed at the idea of Wagner settling in Weimar; so she persuades her husband to lodge the composer in a house near them. He takes up his residence in the "Asyl," adjoining the Wesendonck's house, the "Green Hill," in April 1857.[6] Otto and Mathilde themselves move into their now completed villa on August 22. "Not one of Wagner's brief notes before that date suggests the faintest shadow of a passion shewn," says Mr. Ellis. On September 18, 1858, however—i.e., *after* the catastrophe that made it impossible for Wagner to accept Otto's hospitality any longer—he writes to Mathilde that exactly a year ago he had finished and brought to her the poem of *Tristan*. Then, he explicitly says, she confessed her love to him.[7] Are we to suppose, then, that their "passion" had grown up in three weeks—from August 22 to September 18? Mr. Ellis pontifically declares that "we may dismiss F. Praeger's observation 'during my stay I saw Minna's jealousy of another' . . . as on a par with his usual unreliability." Why? Is not Von Hornstein's evidence conclusive as to what was happening under everybody's eyes as early as 1855? [8] A

[5] Robert von Hornstein: *"Erinnerungen an Richard Wagner,"* in the *Neue Freie Presse* for September 23 and 24, 1904 (written in 1884; Von Hornstein died in 1890). I have been unable to procure a copy of the article. My quotation is from Mr. Ashton Ellis's preface to his translation of the Wesendonck correspondence, p. lv. Von Hornstein adds: "he [Wagner] would turn sulky, hasty, perverse, never coarse. With one little word he might have thrust a poniard in the woman [Minna]; he never breathed it."

[6] Earlier in the month a child had been born to Mathilde. Von Hornstein tells us that at the christening he stood by Wagner's side. "He was very moody; all at once he muttered to himself, 'It is like attending one's own execution.'" Ellis, p. lviii.

[7] *Richard Wagner an Mathilde Wesendonck*, pp. 44, 45.

[8] I do not know that Mr. Ashton Ellis is justified in assuming that "Wagner at last made his bosom friend [Liszt] a confidant and counsellor," on the basis of the letter to Liszt of November

letter of Wagner's own to his sister Clara, however (August 20, 1858), puts it beyond question that there was something going on in the Wesendonck household to which the friends of the pair could hardly be blind. "His wife's frankness could have no other effect than soon plunging Wesendonck in increasing jealousy. Her greatness consisted in this, that she constantly kept her husband informed of what was going on in her heart, and gradually brought him to the fullest resignation as regards herself. It can be imagined what sacrifices and combats it took to bring this about: her success was only rendered possible by the depth and grandeur of her attachment (in which there was no trace of self-seeking), which gave her the power to exhibit herself in such strength [*in solcher Bedeutung*] to her husband that the latter must stand

---

[5?] 1857 which he quotes: "Now take my hand, and take my kiss; a kiss such as you gave me a year ago, when you accompanied me home one night—you remember, after I had told my doleful tale to both of you. However much it may lose its impression on me,—what you were to me that night, the wondrous sympathy that lay in what you told me as we walked, —this heavenliness in your nature will follow with me, as my most splendid memory, to each future existence." (Op. cit., lvii.) What Mr. Ellis translates as "told my doleful tale to you both" is, in the German, "*nachdem ich Euch bei Dir meine traurige Geschichte von Bordeaux erzählt*" ("after I had told you both my mournful Bordeaux story"). *Briefwechsel zwischen Wagner und Liszt*, ii, 181. Wagner's confidence and Liszt's sympathy were apparently as much in connection with the Laussot affair as with the other. But the words "*von Bordeaux*" were suppressed in the first edition of the letters.

I find the "*von Bordeaux*" a little puzzling. If it is really in the original, then it indicates that as late as the end of 1856 Wagner was grieving over the tragic ending of his love for Jessie Laussot. If that were so, we get yet another light on his affectation of indifference in *Mein Leben*. He would hardly be likely to be opening out his heart to Liszt, six years afterward, on the subject of one whom, at the time, he had regarded merely as a "mad Englishwoman" who had forced her not very welcome affection on him.

It may be added that in a letter of January 16, 1854, he had hinted to Von Bülow that he would like news of Jessie. *Richard Wagner Briefe an Hans von Bülow*, p. 43.

aside from her even if she should threaten her own death, and prove his unshakeable love for her by upholding her in her care for me. It became a matter of preserving the mother of his children, and for their sakes—who, indeed, formed an insuperable barrier between us twain—he resigned himself to his rôle of renunciation. Thus, while he was consumed with jealousy, she succeeded in again interesting him in me to such an extent that he often came to my support; and when at length it became a question of providing me with the little house and garden I desired, it was she who, by dint of the most unheard-of struggles, persuaded him to buy for me the lovely piece of land adjoining his own estate. The most wonderful thing, however, is that I actually never had a notion of these combats that she endured for me: for her sake her husband had always to appear friendly and easy towards me: not a frown was to enlighten me, not a hair of my head was to be touched: serene and cloudless were the heavens to be above me, smooth and soft was my path to be. So unheard-of a success had this glorious love of the pure and noble wife." [9]

It all rings very false. Wagner is simply writing what the French contemptuously call "literature." He can see nobody in the universe but himself. He pours out his

[9] In *Mein Leben* Wagner tells the story of the purchase of the "Asyl" somewhat differently. There is not a word there of Wesendonck having been persuaded by his wife into buying the property for Wagner, or of the trouble in the Wesendonck household over him. See *Mein Leben*, p. 645.

The passage I have just quoted from Wagner's letter to his sister Clara has been suppressed in the German edition of the *Familienbriefe* (p. 218). Mr. Ashton Ellis, in his English version (*Family Letters of Richard Wagner*, p. 215), opines that Glasenapp, the German editor of the *Familienbriefe*, omitted the passage in compliance "with Wahnfried wishes." It is one more evidence of the utter untrustworthiness of the Wahnfried coterie. The letter was originally published in the *Deutsche Rundschau* in 1902. A complete English version of it will be found in the opening of Mr. Ellis's translation of the Wagner-Wesendonck correspondence. The German of the passage quoted above is given in Kapp's *Richard Wagner und die Frauen*, pp. 116, 117.

spurious commendations upon Wesendonck for his "renunciation"—a word that obsessed Wagner at that time:
but it never occurred to him to practice a little renunciation on his own side, and to refrain from driving a wedge
between the young husband and wife.[1] In any case, one
would have at least expected him to speak kindly of the
man who had made such unexampled sacrifices for him.
This is how he deals with Wesendonck in *Mein Leben:*

"I had often noticed that Wesendonck, in the honest
openness of his nature, was disturbed at my making myself so much at home in his house: in many things, such
as the heating, the lighting and the hours for meals, consideration was shown me which seemed to him to encroach
on his rights as master of the house." That is clear enough:
what follows is less clear. "It needed a few confidential
talks on the matter to establish a half-silent, half-expressed
agreement, which in the course of time assumed a doubtful significance in the eyes of others. Thus there arose
with regard to our now so close relations a certain circum-
spection [*Rücksicht*] which occasionally afforded amusement to the two initiated parties." This passage, with its
apparently designed obscurity, tells the practiced student
of Wagner nothing more than that he is deliberately concealing more than he is revealing. This suspicion is
strengthened by the sentence that follows: "Curiously
enough, the epoch of this close association with my neigh-
bours coincided with the beginning of the working out of
my poem *Tristan and Isolde.*"[2] The "curiously enough"
is a stroke of genius, the splendor of which will be appreci-
ated by everyone who had read his ardent correspondence
with Mathilde, and knows how inseparable she and the
new opera were in his mind. Only once again did he
achieve such a masterpiece of trail-covering—when he
spoke of Minna's "coarse misunderstanding of my *merely*

[1] I am aware that he filled his letters with moanings about
his "renunciation" and "resignation." But the words were little
more than resounding literary counters for him, helping him to
some of the best of his epistolary effects.

[2] *Mein Leben*, p. 654.

friendly relations" with Frau Wesendonck.[3] And *Mein Leben* really would have served to cover up his tracks in more than one critical place, had he not been imprudent enough to leave so many letters behind him.

How he repaid Otto's kindness to him, once he was settled in the "Asyl," may be guessed from other passages in *Mein Leben*. At the beginning of 1858 he was very melancholy. He attributes his condition to overwork on *Tristan:* but we may reasonably assume that his passion for Mathilde had something to do with it. "Even the immediate and apparently so agreeable proximity of the Wesendonck family only increased my discomfort, for it became really intolerable to me to give up whole evenings to conversations and entertainments in which my good friend Otto Wesendonck thought himself bound to take part at least as much as myself and others. His anxiety lest, as he imagined, everything in his house would soon go my way rather than his gave him moreover that peculiar burdensomeness [*Wucht*] with which a man who thinks himself slighted throws himself into every conversation in his presence, something like an extinguisher on a candle." [4] That, at any rate, is candid, and gives us a hint of the delicacy of his behavior to the husband who had shown him so many kindnesses, and with whose wife he was openly in love. But what a way to speak of the generous and unhappy man who had done and suffered so much for him! Wagner could remember everything, apparently, but the necessity for gratitude.

The crisis in his "merely friendly relations" with Mathilde had come, as we have seen, three or four months

---

[3] *Mein Leben*, p. 667. In his Venice diary of September 18, 1858 (after his flight from the Asyl), he reminds her of how she had placed her arm around him and declared that she loved him. See also under October 12. On January 1, 1859, he speaks with ardent recollection of her caresses. On November 1, 1858, he tells her how sweet it would be "to die in her arms." If we are to die in the arms of all the women with whom our relations have been "merely friendly" we shall all of us need more lives than a cat.

[4] *Mein Leben*, pp. 658, 659.

earlier—on that day in September 1857 when he had brought her the last act of the poem of *Tristan*, and she had placed her arms around him, and "dedicated herself to death that she might give him life." [5] Apparently there was trouble between Minna and Mathilde about this time. Kapp quotes from a letter of Minna's in which she says: "I had to say what was in my heart once more to young Frau Wesendonck. She all at once became very haughty and absurd, so that I refused her invitations, but she again asked my pardon, and now I am again friendly for Richard's sake." [6] Evidently the situation was an intolerable one for Minna—her husband openly calling Frau Wesendonck his "Muse," thinking of nobody but her, and running across the garden every few hours to sun himself in her presence. And it is equally evident that Wagner himself was in despair. We have seen him confessing, in *Mein Leben*, to being woefully out of tune in the winter of 1857–8, though he does not tell the reader the real cause. There is no reason to suppose that his relations with Mathilde had been anything else but ideal. At this juncture, however, he seems to have felt the impossibility of an indefinite continuance of these "merely friendly relations." Early in January 1858 he wrote a feverish, despairing letter to Liszt:

"You must come to me quickly. I am at the end of a conflict in which everything that can be holy to a man is involved. I must decide, and every choice that I see before me is so terrible that when I decide I must have by my side the friend who alone has given me heaven." [7] Liszt, however, is not to come to Zurich but to meet him in Paris. He follows this letter up by another on January 13,[8] in which he again speaks of his need of a temporary ab-

[5] *Richard Wagner an Mathilde Wesendonck*, p. 45. In the same winter he set to music the "Five Poems" of Mathilde.

[6] Kapp: *Richard Wagner und die Frauen*, p. 119.

[7] *Briefwechsel zwischen Wagner und Liszt*, ii, 184. This letter was omitted from the first issue of the Wagner-Liszt correspondence, and consequently will not be found in the English edition.

[8] Also published for the first time in the expanded edition (1910).

sence from Zurich. "I have not lost my head, and my heart
is still sound. Nothing will help me but patience and
endurance." [9] That Liszt understood is evident from his
reply of January 15: "Write me soon, saying what is in
your mind and what you intend to do. Does your wife
remain in Zürich? Are you thinking of returning later?
Where is Madame W——?" [1]

Wagner goes to Paris, and at a distance from Mathilde
becomes resigned to the impossibility of possessing her.
He sends Liszt a fantasia on his favorite theme of resignation.[2] He reads Calderon, finds supreme inward peace, and
asks Liszt for some more money.

The end, however, was nearer than he thought. He
returned to Zurich at the beginning of February, and apparently the unlucky pair drifted helplessly into the coils
of circumstance again. The crash came in April, when
Minna intercepted a letter from her husband to Mathilde.
The true story of the catastrophe and of the events that
led up to it has hitherto been only inperfectly known:
we have had to construct them as best we could out of the
incomplete Wesendonck correspondence and Wagner's
own letters: and needless to say, he is not to be accepted
as the most detached of witnesses when addressing the
court in his own defense. Further light has recently been
thrown on the history of this period by Kapp, who is able
to quote from a number of Minna's letters that had
hitherto been unknown.

"Madame Wesendonck," Minna writes, "visited my
husband secretly, as he did her, and forbade my servant,

[9] Ibid., ii, 186.

[1] Ibid., ii, 188. This passage was suppressed in the previous
editions of the Wagner-Liszt letters.

[2] Letter of January [24?] 1858, ii, 188 *ff.* That matters at
Zurich had been on the verge of a crisis we may guess from a
sentence in a previous letter (January [18–20?]); in which Wagner speaks of it being necessary for him to go away in order
to "give some appeasement to the sufferings of the good-natured
man [Otto Wesendonck]," and that this being done, he will
return in a few weeks. All this, again, and more was suppressed
in the first issue of the correspondence. Truly the way of
Wahnfried passeth understanding.

when he opened the door for her, to tell me that she was above. [Minna occupied the ground floor of the house, Wagner the first floor.] I let it all go on calmly. Men often have an affair; why should not I tolerate it in the case of my husband? I did not know jealousy. Only the meannesses, these humiliations, might have been spared me, and my ludicrously vain husband must conceal it from me." [3] In another letter, of April 30, 1858, she refers to the gossip of the place which had come to her ears, which at first she did not believe. But it struck her that Wagner "went over too often when the good man [Wesendonck] was not at home," and she was annoyed at the daily exchange of correspondence between the "Green Hill" and the "Asyl," and the secret visits. "On the 6th they were both with us. On the 7th I noticed that Richard was strangely restless:[4] at every ring he came out; he had a big roll of papers in his hand [sketches for Act I of *Tristan*], which he wanted to send to Frau Wesendonck; but he would not part with it when I wanted to look after it for him, and he hid it awkwardly. All this astonished me a little. When he could wait no longer, he called our servant. I was there by chance when the latter passed, and I asked him for the roll of music. I undid it, and took out the thick letter that was enclosed in it, opened it, and read the most jealous love letter, from which I will give you a couple of passages. After a wild night of love that he had had, he writes to her: 'Thus it went on the whole night through. In the morning I was rational again, and from the depth of my heart could pray to my angel, and this prayer is love! Love! Deepest soul's joy on this love, the source of my redemption. Then came the day with its evil weather, the joy of seeing you was denied me, my work would not go at all. Thus my whole day was a struggle between melancholy and longing for you,' etc. The letter ended in this way: 'Be good to me: the weather seems mild: to-day I will come again to your garden as soon as I see

---

[3] Kapp: *Richard Wagner und die Frauen*, p. 123.
[4] I have ventured, here and elsewhere, to improve upon Minna's rather illiterate system of punctuation.

you. I hope to find you undisturbed for a moment. Now my whole soul to the morning greeting. R.W.' What do you say to that? At mid-day I told my husband that I had opened and read his fine letter; he was rather alarmed, but I said I would not suffer this deception towards the poor man: I would go away, but he must call this woman his own for ever. Richard wanted to justify himself with his wonderful gift of the gab,[5] but I would not have it. . . . Richard tried to force me to be silent, and to persuade me of the purity of his relations. How ridiculous! I abide by my conviction." [6]

Now let us look at the letter in which Wagner gives his sister Clara *his* version of the catastrophe. After narrating the sacrifices Otto had made for him,[7] and declaring that although he and Mathilde loved each other they had been forced to recognize the necessity of resignation, he continues:

"My wife seemed, with shrewd feminine instinct, to understand what was going on: certainly she often showed jealousy, and was scoffing and disparaging: but she tolerated our intercourse, which never violated morals, but simply aimed at the possibility of knowledge of each other's presence. Therefore I assumed that Minna would be sensible and understand that there was really nothing for her to fear, since there could be no question of a union between us, and that therefore the most advisable and best thing for her to do was to be indulgent. I had to learn that I had probably deceived myself in that respect: chatter reached my ears, and she at last so far lost her senses as to intercept a letter of mine and—open it. This letter, if she had been at all able to understand it, would really have been able to give her all the pacification she could have desired, for the theme of it too was our resignation.

[5] "*Mit seiner vortrefflichen Suade.*"
[6] Kapp, pp. 124, 125. Mr. Ellis wrongly conjectures the intercepted note to be the one quoted as No. 36 in the German edition of the Wagner-Wesendonck correspondence (No. 49 in the English edition).
[7] See the quotation on p. 112, above.

However, she fastened simply on the intimate expressions in it, and lost her head. She came to me in a fury, and I was compelled to explain to her calmly and explicitly how things stood, that she had brought misfortune on herself by opening such a letter, and that if she did not know how to contain herself we must part. On this point we were agreed, I tranquilly, she passionately. Next day, however, I was sorry for her: I went to her and said, 'Minna, you are very ill.' [8] We arranged the plan of a cure [Kur] for her: she seemed to become composed again. The day for her departure to the Kurort drew near. At first she absolutely insisted on speaking to Frau Wesendonck. I firmly forbade her to do so. Everything depended on my gradually making Minna acquainted with the character of my relations with Frau Wesendonck, and thus convincing her that there was nothing at all to be feared for the continuance of our wedded life, wherefore she had only to be wise, prudent and noble, abjure all foolish ideas of vengeance, and avoid any sort of sensation. In the end she promised me this. She could not keep quiet, however. She went over [to the Green Hill] behind my back, and—no doubt without realising it herself—wounded the gentle lady most grossly. After she had told her: 'If I were an ordinary woman I should go to your husband with this letter,' there was nothing for Frau Wesendonck—who was conscious of never having had a secret from her husband (which a woman like Minna cannot understand!)—but to inform him at once of the scene and its cause.—Herewith, then, had the delicacy and purity of our relations been broken in upon in a coarse and vulgar way, and many things must now alter. Not till some time after did I make it clear to my friend [Mathilde] that it would never be possible to make a nature like my wife's comprehend relations so

[8] In Mr. Ellis's translation of the letter (preface to the English edition of the Wagner-Wesendonck correspondence, p. ix), this sentence is followed by "get well first, and let us have another talk then." I cannot find this sentence in the German edition of the Familienbriefe, p. 219.

lofty and unselfish as ours: for I had to endure her grave
and deep reproach that I had omitted this, whereas her
husband had always been her confidant."

Minna goes away to her cure, and returns unappeased.
There are violent scenes between her and Wagner: the
situation becomes quite impossible for everybody, and
there is nothing for it but for the Wagners to quit the
"Asyl." He can endure the bickering no longer, he tells
Clara, if he is to fulfill his life's task. "Whoever has observed me closely must have been surprised from of old
at my patience, kindness, aye, weakness; and if I am now
condemned by superficial judges, I have become insensitive
to that kind of thing. But never had Minna such an occasion to show herself worthy to be my wife as here, when
it was a question of preserving for me the highest and
dearest: it lay within her hand to prove if she really loved
me. But she does not even understand what such true love
is, and her rage runs away with her." He excuses her on
the score of her ill-health, but is resolved not to live with
her again. "She really is unfortunate: she would have been
happier with a lesser man. And so take pity on her with
me." [9]

Well might Minna be driven to distraction by his
"*vortreffliche Suade.*" Who, with no knowledge of the
facts beyond what he could derive from this letter, would
not think that Wagner had been at once the most perfect
and the most ill-used of men? Here we have the actor—
the self-deluding actor—marching and countermarching
across the stage in his full panoply. He is, as usual, dram-
atizing himself: he is painting the picture of himself that
he desires his friends and posterity to see. He is at work
on *Tristan*. Frau Wesendonck is necessary to him if he is
to maintain the artistic mood that the poem and the music
require. Everything and everybody must therefore give
way to his great need. He is utterly and honestly unable
to see the situation through either Otto's eyes or Minna's.
The former he dramatized also; of the grief the good

[9] *Familienbriefe*, pp. 218 ff.

man must have felt at seeing his wife's infatuation for a man who calmly took possession not only of the wife but of the whole household, he had plainly no conception. He allots Otto *his* part in the play: they are all playing parts, and the title of the tragi-comedy is "The Three Renunciators." Wagner and Mathilde may talk as they like about their "renunciation" and "resignation": these words are only literary symbols with them, a subtle self-flattery, an extra and rather delicious flavoring in their cup. But the cup itself was a sweet one. Poor Otto had *his* part thrust upon him willy-nilly: he was dragged on the scene, against his will, to act in a play for which he had no fancy, dressed up as Third Renunciator, and primed to speak the lines the author of the piece put in his mouth. But there was no delight in *his* cup: and probably he could not, like Wagner, drug himself with words. As for Minna, she was hardly in the play at all. Her business was mainly to attend to the costumes and sweep out the dressing room of the principal comedian, and generally to keep the stage clear for him and the leading lady. So colossal was Wagner's egoism that he could not realize the bare possibility of the affair taking on in other people's eyes any aspect but that it had in his own. He evidently thought in all sincerity that it was Otto's and Minna's duty to step aside in favor of himself and Mathilde, and that Minna in particular ought to prove that she really loved him by turning a blind eye to everything that wounded her as woman and as wife. And in the act of demanding these impossible renunciations from other people in order that *he* might have his way, he appealed volubly to God and man to witness the extent of *his* renunciation and to have compassion on him! It is easy enough to follow your star if other people will do the rough work of cutting out your path for you: it is easy enough to live in a world of ideal emotional freedom if the real people around you will be content to become mere feeders for your own inward life. The only weak spot in Wagner's position was his forgetfulness of the fact that Minna was a human being like himself. How he and Mathilde appeared in eyes that saw things as they were, without any haze of romance about them, may be guessed from Minna's description of Mathilde as "that cold woman spoilt by happiness," and Frau Herwegh's incisive description of Wagner as "this pocket edition of a man, this folio of vanity, heartlessness, and egoism." [1]

A comparison of Minna's letter with that of Wagner's concerning the incident that led to the rupture with the Wesendoncks will suggest how little he is ever to be relied upon for full and strict accuracy when he is stating his own case. We may acquit him, as a rule, of any willful intention to deceive; but he is so incapable of seeing the matter from any other angle than his own that he unconsciously distorts or rearranges the picture. Like the artist he is, he sees only the inside of the Mathilde affair. Minna sees only the outside of it: but precisely for that reason she is more likely to have given us the outward facts as they were. These facts could never be gathered from Wagner's letter alone. That letter shows us an angelic, patient, and greatly misunderstood man, worshipping his "Muse" as one might worship a saint in a shrine, and astonished and disgusted when coarser souls declined to see either a saint in her or an angel in him. As usual, he does not photograph the scene: he lets his imagination paint a fancy picture of it. It is from Minna's prosaic photograph that we get the facts and details—the secret visits on both sides, the deceptions and evasions, the trickery with the servants, and all the other petty irritations. Once more, sympathetic as we may feel toward him—and we are bound to sympathize with this eager, hungry, suffering soul, so wise in art, so foolish in life— can we deny that Minna merely acted as any other woman

---

[1] Kapp, op. cit., p. 102. The remainder of the letter shows that while Frau Herwegh had a good opinion of Minna, she was not blindly prejudiced in her favor; and she was quite conscious that intellectually Minna was unfitted to keep pace with her husband's development. Her testimony to the excellence of Minna's heart and the hardness of her lot with Wagner is therefore all the more valuable. Wagner, it is hardly necessary to say, did not like Frau Herwegh.

in the world would have done in the same circumstances? To be kept by his side for her value as a domestic animal,[2] yet be shut out from her husband's inner life while another woman was admitted to it under her very eyes, and to be living all the while in a home provided for them by this very rival—that was surely more than any woman with a spirit above that of a poodle could be expected to suffer quietly.

Leaving the psychology of the case, let us take up again the thread of the external facts. Minna's account of what happened during and after her interview with Mathilde runs thus:

"Frau Wesendonck was very grateful and friendly to me, accompanied me hand-in-hand to the steps, and everything was settled in a friendly way. Afterwards, however, she thought differently of it: she told her husband that I had insulted her frightfully, but without telling him the real truth as to the relations. She cried out to Richard how deeply and horribly I had offended her,—in spite of the fact that I had been delicate enough not to show her the fatal letter, which I had in my pocket. But this is the way with common little natures. They can do nothing but tittle-tattle and stir up mischief." [3]

Minna's heart trouble had been greatly aggravated by these emotional storms. To do Wagner justice, he was always making allowance in his correspondence for her conduct on the score of her ill-health,[4] but, needless to

[2] With all his sense of the intellectual and other divergencies between them, Wagner was not as a rule anxious to sever his life from Minna. He admits more than once that she was an excellent housewife, and specially expert in ministering to his comforts. After every dispute we find him setting up house with her again.

[3] Kapp, p. 127.

[4] See, for example, his letter of November 1, 1858, to the Dresden physician and friend Anton Pusinelli, to whose care he had entrusted Minna. *Bayreuther Blätter*, 1902, p. 98. "By periodical separations I have attained what I instinctively contemplate—namely, to place myself in a position to be able always to exert only a pacifying, conciliating influence upon her spirit. In view of the sad state of her health, this had been my only

say, it never occurred to him to help to restore her health by refraining from his pursuit of his "Muse" at the Green Hill, or by making any other "renunciation" of the things he liked.[5] "My good husband," writes Minna to Frau Herwegh on June 14, 1858, from Brestenberg, where she had been undergoing a "cure," "could be good and assuage my pains[6] if he would not let himself be dragged about by certain people: his heart is good but very weak! So it comes about that he often writes me really good, dear, comforting letters, but still more often throws the wickedest and vulgarest things at me in them, cracks other people up to the skies, and levels me to the earth. This, my dear Emma, eats away my heart. I can seldom weep over these vulgarities, and that is very bad for me: but the heart in my body chokes as if it were being twisted about. On Sunday, a week ago, I was at home, but only for twenty-three hours, so that I had no time to visit you. I wish I had not gone: the dear Richard vented his spleen on me till two in the morning"[7]—by way, presumably, of exercising himself in "renunciation" and "resignation."

She returns to the "Asyl," but every day the impossibility of an understanding between them becomes more evident. Their letters, read side by side, are pathetic. Wagner is convinced that the purity of his relations with Frau Wesendonck ought to absolve him in everyone's eyes, and reconcile Minna to a more accommodating at-

---

design during the time we lately lived together; but with a character as irritable as mine the agitation and excitement of the moment were too much for me now and then, as in general I too needs must truly suffer greatly during these eternal, useless and senseless vexations. Here, however, at a distance, I can choose the hour and the mood when I am fully master of myself, and have to achieve faithfully only my purpose, my duty." Letter of November 18 to Pusinelli; ibid., p. 100.

[5] He reminds us of Mr. Shaw's Prossy in *Candida*, who was only a beer teetotaler, not a champagne teetotaler.

[6] She has just given a distressing account of her sufferings from her heart disease.

[7] Kapp, pp. 129, 130.

titude toward him and his ways. (According to his own account, he invariably reasons with her patiently and from the serene height of his superior wisdom. This is not always borne out by Minna's testimony.) Minna, on the other hand, was resolved not to tolerate a situation that seemed to her to be beyond all reason.

"It grieves me," she writes to a lady friend on August 2, 1858,[8] "to hear you talk as if I alone were the cause of my separating from my husband. You know only too well, if you question yourself closely, how hard for me even a short separation has always been, especially now when it is uncertain whether and when I shall see him again. It is no small thing when a separation faces one after twenty-two years of marriage. I at any rate cannot take it lightly. If it rested with me, I assure you it would certainly not happen. As regards forbearance for men I am likewise enlightened, and have already overlooked a good many things, like other women. I have besides gone on being blind a good six years. It is simply impossible, for the sake of Richard's honour, to remain here, since her husband,—I don't know how—has also learned of the relation. When I returned I was violently assailed and threatened by my husband, with the object of getting me to associate again with that woman. I yielded, was willing to go this great length: that is really all that it is possible for a wife in my position to do: but the husband and in the end this woman herself will not: she is—so my husband himself shouted at me—raging, beside herself, at my being there, and out of jealousy will not suffer me to remain: only Richard shall live here, which, however, he cannot do. Richard has two natures; he is ensnared on the other side, and clings to me from habit, that is all. My resolve now is, since this woman will not endure my living with my husband, and he is weak enough to give way to her, that I will live by turns in Dresden, Berlin and Weimar, until either Richard or God calls me away. My health does not improve under these circumstances; all the

[8] Kapp (p. 134) wrongly gives the date as 1850.

waters in the world are no use when the mind is assailed by upsets of this kind." [9]

So, on August 17, 1858, Wagner leaves the "Asyl" and goes to Venice (via Geneva) with Karl Ritter, while Minna takes refuge with her friends in Dresden. Wagner continues to write to Mathilde, but his letters are returned to him unopened. Each of the lovers, however, makes a confidante of Frau Wille, and each of them keeps a diary. These diaries are exchanged in the autumn. That of Wagner is in the form of letters to Mathilde. These are full of the most ardent protestations of love. His declaration in *Mein Leben* that his relations with Frau Wesendonck were "merely friendly" reads rather curiously after such outbursts as these:

"When I have thought of you, never have parents or children or duties come into my mind; I only knew that you loved me, and that everything noble in this world must be unhappy." (Sept. 7.)

"That you loved me I know well: you are, as always, good, profound and sensible. . . . Our love is superior to all impediments, and every check to it makes us richer, brighter, nobler, and ever more intent upon the substance and the essence of our love, ever more indifferent towards the inessential." (Sept. 13.)

"It always remained clear to me that your love was my highest possession, and without it my existence must be a contradiction of itself." (Sept. 18.)

"The course of my life till the time when I found you, and you at last became mine, lies plain before you." (Oct. 12.)[1]

"Once more,—that you could plunge into every conceivable sorrow of the world, to say to me 'I love you,'— that has redeemed me, and was for me that holy hour of calm that has given my life another meaning." (Oct. 12.)

[9] Kapp, pp. 134, 135.
[1] Mr. Ashton Ellis, reading *"liegt deutlich vor mir,"* instead of *"vor dir,"* translates this "lies plain before *me*."

XI · *His Dual Nature*

Nothing shows more instructively the fundamental dualism of his nature than a comparison of these letters to Mathilde with those he was writing at the same time to Minna. Every thought of Mathilde is a dream, an intoxication; to Minna he is the practical man, discussing the ordinary little things of life in the most prosaic fashion. Their parting was not intended to be a permanent one: each of them was to "go his own way for a while in peace and reconciliation" in order to "win calmness and new strength for life." [2] As is often the case when he is away from her, he sees their relationship in something like its true aspect. He admits that she "has a hard time" with him, on account of his "indifference and recklessness towards the outer relations of life." She is to enjoy herself in Dresden, and to try to win self-control and strength to bear her trial. But an understanding was plainly impossible between two people one of whom persisted in regarding his extra-domestic love affairs as special dispensations of Providence to assist him in his work as an artist, while the other as persistently looked upon them as a selfish seeking of his own gratification at her expense. Wagner sums it all up very appositely in a letter of August 25, 1858: "Your letter showed me that it will probably be always impossible for you to see correctly and clearly. With you, a definite blame must always be attached to a definite person: you do not comprehend the nature of things and Fate, but simply think that if this person or that thing had never been, everything would have happened differently." [3] To his dual nature it did not seem in the least an impossible thing for him to retain Mathilde as his "Muse" and Minna as his housekeeper—a very competent housekeeper, as he frequently lets us see—if only Minna would be sensible enough to consent to this *ménage à trois.* On September 3 he tells Mathilde that he

[2] See his letter of August 19, 1858, *Richard Wagner an Minna Wagner,* i, 296.
[3] Ibid., i, 299.

hopes to get well for her sake. "To save you for me means to save myself for my art. With it,—to live to be your consolation, that is my mission, this accords with my nature, my fate, my will,—my love. Thus am I yours: you too shall get well through me. Here will *Tristan* be completed—a defiance to all the raging of the world. And with this work, if I may, I will return to see you, to comfort you, to make you happy. This is my holiest, loveliest wish." But while he intends returning to Mathilde he also counts on returning to Minna, to whom he writes on September 14, advising her to select carefully her future home; "thither I would come to you as often as I needed a home: and for the rest, quite apart from my personal need of habitation, it would be *your* peaceful retreat to which I also could withdraw when all the storms of life were weathered, there at last to find enduring repose beneath your care."

His whole spiritual life is centered in Mathilde: but his physical man also needs caring for, and who is so well qualified for this as Minna? A wandering life will not suit him in the long run, he tells his wife; at bottom he loves a permanent abode. He means to finish *Tristan*, and has hopes of being amnestied,[4] so that he can return to Germany and settle down in some town of his choice. "You can thus count with certainty on seeing me again next Easter, and—God willing—we shall then have no difficulty in finding the place where you can pitch the abiding tent for this wandering life of mine."

"How happy could I be with either," was the sigh of the old poet. "How happy could I be with both," says Wagner in effect. Even more than in most artists the inner and the outer life in him were separate and distinct. Into Mathilde's ear he could pour his dreams and his longings, while Minna's ear would be open to receive his less spiritual but equally sincere confidences upon the more material things of life. He looks at the stars over the Lido and thinks of Mathilde. "I have absolutely no hope, no fu-

[4] The warrant for his arrest for his supposed complicity in the Dresden rising of 1849 was still in force.

ture," he writes to her, as he had written to Frau Ritter a few years before. This is the genuine artist, amorous of his own sorrows, lapping luxuriously the bitter-sweet water of his dreams. For the real man we have to turn to his letter of the preceding day (September 28) to Minna, from which it appears that although he is absolutely without a future and without hope, he is trying all he can "to use the great success of *Rienzi* in Dresden" to "get profits out of the work elsewhere"; accordingly he has been inviting all the theaters with which he has friendly relations to acquire the opera quickly. He describes the material side of his life in Venice in detail. The world-weary and hopeless one seems to be enjoying his existence, working each day until four in the afternoon, crossing the canal, walking up the St. Mark Piazza, dining with Karl Ritter "well but dear (even without wine I can never get off under four to five francs)"; then in a gondola to the Public Garden, where he has a promenade; then a glass of ice at the pavilion on the Molo, and so home to bed. "So I have been living for four weeks now, and am not tired of it yet, even without real absorbing work. The secret of the enduring charm of it all is" so-and-so and so-and-so.

He keeps his dual psychological life going with perfect honesty and absolute unconsciousness. How easy it was for him to adopt a different attitude upon the same question, according to which of his correspondents he was addressing, is shown by his letters of September 28, 1858, to Minna and October 1 to Mathilde. In each of them he discusses the nature and attributes of joy and grief. He had witnessed the killing of a hen at a poulterer's stall a day or two before; the sufferings of the poor creature had stirred his sympathetic soul to its depths, and set him thinking of the general problem of suffering and pity. To Minna he writes thus:

"You are wrong to make light of compassion. Perhaps it is only because you have a false idea of it. All our relations with others have only one ground,—sympathy or decided antipathy. The essence of love consists in community of grief and of joy: but *community of joy is most illusory, for in this world there is little ground for joy, and our sympathy only has real durability when it is directed to another's grief."* [5]

To Mathilde he sings a different song. For her he can feel nothing but "community of joy, reverence, worship. . . . So do not contemn my pity where you see me exercise it, for to yourself I can now pour out nothing but community of joy. Oh, this is the sublimest: it can appear only in conjunction with the fullest sympathy. From the commoner nature to which I gave pity I must quickly turn away as soon as it demands community of joy of me. This was the cause of the last discord with my wife. The unhappy woman had understood in her own way my resolve not to enter your house again, and conceived it as a rupture with you: and she imagined that on her return, comfort and intimacy would necessarily be re-established between us. How fearfully I had to undeceive her!"

Yet it is to this "commoner nature" that he desires to return and settle down in some quiet corner of Germany for the rest of his life. "Only keep up your courage, my dear good Minna," he writes to her from Venice on November 14, 1858. "Overcome, and believe firmly in the perfect sincerity with which I now aspire to nothing—nothing on this earth—but to make up for what has been inflicted on you, to support and guard you, preserve you in loyalty and love, so that your suffering state may also improve, that you may once more feel joy in your life, and we may enjoy the evening of our days together as cheerfully and uncloudedly as possible"—with a break, presumably, to permit of his dying in Mathilde's arms. And again in a second letter on the evening of the same day: "Think of nothing but our reunion: and to make that thoroughly good and enduring and beneficial for both of us, simply attend to nothing now but your health. For this you can do nothing, nothing in the world, but—cultivate tranquillity of mind." To do this she is to forget the Wesendonck episode; he insists on her never saying a word about it again to

[5] Italics mine.

anyone. At Zurich "we were far too buried and thrown too much on our own resources; that was bound in time to be injurious and to set us bickering. When once we are in a large town again, where I can have performances to look after, and you can tend me when I am exhausted, and rejoice with me over their success,—it will be to you a dream that we were ever packed into a little den like that. . . . Well, well! All that will be altered, and a quite new life will begin, full of fame, honours and recognition, as much as I shall desire; so get in good trim to enjoy that harvest with me after a long and painful seed-time."

Thirteen days previously he had written thus to Mathilde:

"Help me to tend the unfortunate woman.⁶ Probably I can do it only from a distance, for I myself must regard remoteness from her as most apt for this purpose. When I am near her I become incapable of it: only from a distance can I tranquillise her, as then I can choose the time and the mood for my communications, so as to be always mindful of my task towards her.⁷ But I cannot do even that unless—you help me. I must not know that *your* heart is bleeding," etc., etc. "You know that I am yours, and that only you dispose of my actions, deeds, thoughts and resolutions." The night before he had stood on the balcony of his house, and while looking into the black waters of the canal below him, the thought of suicide had flashed upon him. But he withdrew his hand from the rail as he thought of Mathilde. "Now I know that it still is granted to me to die in your arms."

He talked to Minna, on his own showing, much as one talks to a child, without meaning all one says, one's only object being to comfort it in its grief. He meant to be kind, for Minna's sufferings undoubtedly rent his heart.

⁶ He had just had the Dresden physician's distressing report on Minna's health. In addition to her heart trouble and the nervous ravages made by laudanum, she was now said to be developing dropsy of the chest.

⁷ Compare his letter to Pusinelli on November 18, 1858, quoted on pp. 122–3 above.

He could be sympathetic with her at a distance. The difficulties always arose when they set up house again together, for then the impossibility of his giving up anything he really desired, even for an ailing wife's sake, became manifest. He was, as usual, hypnotized by his own eloquence. On paper he could easily settle every question that arose between Minna and himself: it was merely in practical domestic matters that he was a failure. It probably never occurred to him to ask how he was going to square the problem of living for the remainder of his days with Minna with the problem of dying in Mathilde's arms, or indeed the general problem of maintaining his passionate intercourse with his "Muse" and at the same time of resuming relations with the commonplace wife he had quarreled with so desperately over this very "Muse."

With this dualism of soul and this blindness in the face of facts it was inevitable that the catastrophe of 1858 should have befallen him—inevitable also that any renewal of his relations with Mathilde should lead to another catastrophe of the same kind. The renewal took place in April 1859, Wesendonck having once more invited Wagner to visit him, apparently in order to give a *démenti* to Zurich gossip. Later on, Wagner seems to have realized that Minna's stay in Dresden was doing her little good, either bodily or mentally: so he resolved to set up house with her once more in Paris.[8]

In *Mein Leben* he tells us that "under these circumstances [the difficulties he was finding in the way of his giving some concerts in Paris] I could only regard it as a most singular intervention of fate that Minna should announce her readiness to join me in Paris and that I was to expect her arrival shortly." But it is clear from letters of his to Minna on September 19 and 25, 1859, and to Dr. Anton Pusinelli on October 3,[9] that it was *his own suggestion* that she should come to Paris to take charge of

[8] Otto Wesendonck provided the funds, giving Wagner 24,000 francs for the rights of the still unfinished *Ring*.

[9] *Richard Wagner an Minna Wagner*, ii, 139 ff.; *Bayreuther Blätter*, 1902, p. 101.

his new household. He needed her, and he argued eagerly against the objections that Pusinelli had evidently put forward. He was going to live very quietly: Minna would be in ideal surroundings for her health of body and peace of mind; and all would again be for the best in the best of all possible worlds. "So I beg you not to advance any objections against her coming to Paris: have faith in my reasons! . . . A decided medical treatment was indispensable for my wife: finally, however, notwithstanding all the art and care of the physician, moral influences are the weightiest with patients of this kind; and in this respect —I know it—the life and death of my wife depend solely upon myself. I can destroy her or preserve her: consequently, since I know her fate to be given into my hands, my future conduct towards her is prescribed with the greatest certainty.[1] Trust me!"

No doubt he meant it all—on paper.

For a final light on it all, and more especially on his declaration in *Mein Leben* that his relations with Mathilde had been "merely friendly," and that he was, as usual, the victim of gross misunderstanding, let us look at another paragraph in this same letter of his to Von Bülow on October 7, 1859. He is in Paris. On his way there he had met the Wesendoncks once more. "In Zürich I stayed four days as guest in the Wesendonck house: the husband is very devoted to me, and in the truest sense to be admired. A beautiful and really uncommon [*seltenes*, singular] relationship has established itself here, and it has been proved what deep earnestness can achieve over even the least endowed natures. The husband stands between myself and his wife,—whom he had to renounce completely—as a mutual, I may say, indeed, the sincerest friend. I take the greatest pride in this development; only my most earnest longing to be able to maintain my proximity to the poor wife has guided me to it. Now is the almost unheard-of achieved. We visited each other

---

[1] He writes to the same effect, and in almost the words, to Von Bülow on October 7. See *Richard Wagner Briefe an Hans von Bülow*, p. 129.

several times between Lucerne and Zürich: I stayed continually at their house, and what I can do to help the faithful woman through her difficult life is done with the honest joy of the husband in my coming and staying."

xii · *Later Loves*

Minna joined him in Paris on November 17, 1859. Their relations were soon as embittered as usual. Wagner was playing for high stakes, living feverishly and expensively, entertaining largely, giving disastrous concerts, accumulating new and heavy debts. The clear-sighted and careful Minna was appalled at the prospect of the ruin that was threatening them once more: and Wagner made the mistake of not confiding in her. She felt herself shut out from his inner life. Apparently he was also giving her fresh cause for jealousy, the lady this time, it is said, being Liszt's eldest daughter, Blandine, the wife of the Paris lawyer Ollivier.[2]

After the disastrous *Tannhäuser* performances in March 1861, Wagner fluctuated for a while between Paris, Karlsruhe, and Vienna, at length settling down on August 14 in the last-named city, where it was proposed to produce *Tristan*. Minna had gone to Soden for a cure on July 10: from there she went on to Dresden once more.[3] In Vienna Wagner had the loan of Dr. Standhartner's house for some weeks during the physician's absence. His wants were attended to by a "pretty niece" of Standhartner's.[4] This pretty niece was one Seraphine Mauro. According to

[2] According to Kapp (p. 159), Wagner's relations with her were the subject of much comment in Paris at that time, and were the reason for the Princess Wittgenstein—Liszt's companion—breaking off all intercourse with him and refusing to visit him in Paris in 1860. "An anxious silence upon this affair," Kapp remarks, "has been maintained in the Wagnerian literature, which was the easier inasmuch as all the passages relating to it in Wagner's letters have been suppressed before publication. Later publications will bring to light much interesting material."

[3] Except for a few days, they never lived together again. They kept up their correspondence, however.

[4] *Mein Leben*, p. 779.

Kapp,[5] "Wagner was not insensible to so much beauty in his daily surroundings, and his 'dear little doll' [*Puppe*], as he always called Seraphine, did not let him sigh in vain. . . . The suffering in this affair of Wagner's fell upon his friend Peter Cornelius, who . . . had lost his heart to the beautiful Seraphine some time before."

Standhartner having returned to Vienna at the end of September, Wagner had to leave his comfortable quarters, and as there seemed no prospect of an early performance of *Tristan,* and life at a hotel was expensive, he accepted an invitation from the Wesendoncks to meet them in Venice. He remained there only four days—"four miserable days," he calls them.[6] How unbridgeable was the gulf made between him and Minna by the memory of the Mathilde affair of three years before may be estimated from his letters to his wife on October 19 and November 13, 1861. The first is sensible and tender; he is full of pity for the poor, suffering woman, and will gladly do anything in his power to alleviate her misery—anything, that is, but give up the Wesendonck acquaintance. He still has plans for a reunion, and a quiet old age to be spent together. But as a preliminary to any *rapprochement* he insists, as he had always done, on her consenting never again to mention the name of Mathilde, for whom, he declares, his passion has from beginning to end been absolutely pure. Of all the tragedies of Wagner's life this surely is the greatest, that his one noble love, the one that was so necessary to him as an artist, to which we owe *Tristan* and many of the finest moods of *Die Meistersinger* and *Parsifal,* should have been the one to embitter his existence and his wife's beyond all hope of remedy, while his less worthy attachments were either unknown to Minna or counted for little with her. With Wagner obstinately resolved not to give up the Wesendonck ac-

---

[5] *Richard Wagner und die Frauen,* p. 157.

[6] He seems to have taken it rather ill of his friends that they should have been prosperous and happy while he was poor and disappointed and up to his eyes in difficulties of all kinds. See his account of the visit in *Mein Leben,* pp. 787, 788.

quaintance, and Minna—blind to the true nature of the attachment, and seeing it, in all probability, merely as another Laussot affair[7]—as obstinately bent on making the cessation of this acquaintance a condition of a full reconciliation with her husband, it was impossible that the breach between the two tortured and self-torturing souls should ever be healed. That Wagner dreaded giving Minna any cause to be reminded of Mathilde's name is evident from the sophisticated version he gives her of his Venice excursion, in his letter of November 13, 1861: we can only regard as a piece of well-meant fiction his story that Dr. Standhartner, having been summoned in haste, as deputy physician in ordinary, to attend the Empress of Austria in Venice, had pressingly insisted upon Wagner accompanying him for his health's sake. "I returned early this morning. I hope it has done me good; at least I had no talking to do for several days, but only to go sight-seeing, which really benefited me." Not a word, it will be observed, as to having gone to Venice at the request of the Wesendoncks, or even as to their being in Venice at that time.

So matters drifted on in the old wav until Wagner had settled down in Biebrich (end of February 1862), after yet another visit to Paris. He took with him the furniture that had been in their Paris house. Minna came to help in the unpacking and arranging. She remained with him a week. According to the account he gives in *Mein Leben* "the old scenes were soon renewed," Minna being angry at his having removed from the custom house the articles he required for his new home, without awaiting her arrival.[8] The real reason of their quarrel, however—concealed from us, as usual, in *Mein Leben*—was once more Frau Wesendonck. By a most unlucky coincidence a letter and a box arrived from Mathilde on the second and third days

[7] Mathilde's character, like that of Wagner, has probably been slightly idealized for us by time. She had probably been less agreeable to the bourgeoise Minna than to her genius of a husband.

[8] *Mein Leben*, p. 798.

of Minna's visit. They were quite harmless,[9] but Minna would not listen to reason; she was more than ever convinced that her husband was carrying on another intrigue with Mathilde behind her back. It was enough, as poor Wagner says, to drive him out of his senses—the same scenes as four years before, the same invective, word for word. Yet in spite of it all, once more the wretched pair began making plans for a home in common, Minna's importunities among the Dresden government officials having made it possible for Wagner to obtain an amnesty by a formal petition to the King.

Biebrich remained his home until the autumn. He was working at the music of *Die Meistersinger*, and perhaps, on the whole, was not unhappy. He made several new friends, among them the actress Friederike Meyer—the sister of the Frau Dustmann who was to have "created" the part of Isolde in the Vienna production of *Tristan*—and a pretty and intelligent young girl, Mathilde Maier, the daughter of a deceased lawyer. The fire of his passion for Frau Wesendonck having already cooled, he fell in love with the gentle Mathilde Maier. Kapp conjectures that rumors of their "friendly relations" had come to Minna's ears, and that the renewed bitterness of her letters at this time decided Wagner to take the step that had long been urged upon him by his friends, and obtain a divorce from Minna. He commissioned his Dresden friend Dr. Pusinelli to sound Minna on the subject; she declined to oblige him.[1] His desire to marry Mathilde Maier, however, says Kapp, found a new and insurmountable obstacle. She was threatened with hereditary deafness; this, she thought, would unfit her to be the wife of a musician.

[9] Owing to his having ceased to correspond with the Wesendoncks, his changes of address were unknown to them. The box contained a present that Mathilde had sent him the preceding Christmas; after many journeyings it had been returned to her through the post. Having learned his Biebrich address, she sent it to him there. See his letter to Minna of June 12, 1862.

[1] *Mein Leben*, p. 806. See, however, his letter to Pusinelli of July 1, 1862, in *Bayreuther Blätter*, 1902, p. 103.

"The full significance of this tragic love in Wagner's life cannot be estimated yet," says Kapp, "since the autobiography preserves complete silence on this matter, out of consideration for Cosima, and the large and carefully guarded collection of intimate documents from Wagner's hands that Mathilde left behind her will not be published during Cosima's lifetime." [2]

[2] *Richard Wagner und die Frauen*, p. 182. In a letter to his sister Clara on July 11, 1862, Wagner denies that the idea of a divorce proceeded from him, "obvious as it is, and excusable as it might be for me to indulge the wish to utilise my remaining years for the benefit of my work, by the side of someone sympathetic to me" (*Familienbriefe*, pp. 247, 248), which last remark probably refers to Mathilde Maier. In this letter he makes clear that a reunion with Minna is out of the question. His idea was that she should have a small establishment of her own in Dresden, where he can visit her occasionally. In a letter to Minna of two days earlier he makes out that being unusually distressed as to her health—which was steadily worsening—he had sent Pusinelli to report upon her, but the physician had broached the question of divorce of his own accord (*Richard Wagner an Minna Wagner*, ii, 290). "Your believing that you were to understand the opinion he gave you on his own account as if I too entertained the idea of a divorce from you has greatly distressed me. Never has that entered *my* head, and it never will." Whether or not it had entered his head at that time, it certainly entered it later. In less than two years he had to fly from his Vienna creditors to Mariafeld, near Zurich. He was at the very end of his resources, and was apparently a ruined man had not King Ludwig come to his rescue. Discussing his prospects with his hostess, Frau Wille, "we touched, among other things, on the necessity of obtaining a divorce from my wife, in order that I might contract a rich marriage. As everything seemed to me expedient, and nothing inexpedient, I actually wrote to my sister Luise Brockhaus, asking her whether she could not, in a sensible talk with Minna, induce her to be satisfied with her settled yearly allowance, and abandon her claim to my person" (*Mein Leben*, p. 866). This letter is not to be found in the *Familienbriefe*. It would be interesting to know whether it is one of the letters that Glasenapp speaks of as being "lost beyond recall," or has simply been suppressed.

Minna was of course a hopeless wreck by this time. She died in Dresden on January 25, 1866. The last of Wagner's published letters to her is dated November 8, 1863.

Meanwhile his relations with Friederike Meyer—a lively actress temperament—had become more and more friendly. When he left Biebrich for Vienna in November 1862, he was accompanied by Friederike, who had surrendered her engagement at the Frankfurt theater for his sake.[3] He soon became involved, as he tells us, in disagreements with his Isolde, Frau Dustmann, Friederike's sister. "It was impossible," he says, "to make her see how matters really stood; she regarded her sister as being involved in a liaison, and cast out by her family,[4] so that Friederike's settling in Vienna was compromising for *her*."

We get a little light on the pair in an entry in the diary of Peter Cornelius under the date of November 20, 1862:

"We were at Wagner's. He gave a musical evening for his Fräulein Friederike M. . . . Her chambermaid was there as duenna. Friederike isn't so bad as they made out in Mainz; she isn't amiss as far as appearances go. She is intelligent, without making any attempt to thrust herself forward. She is not very pretty, but her face is animated. Wagner behaved very properly and decently in her presence. If he really must have a liaison of this sort, it looks as if he would get on quite tolerably with this one." [5]

The liaison seems to have been in one way at least a harmful one for Wagner. Frau Dustmann was so angered at Friederike's association with him and at her attempt to procure an engagement at the Burg theater that she cooled toward *Tristan*. This, says Kapp, was the real cause of the failure to produce the opera in Vienna, not, as has hitherto been supposed, the difficulty the singers found with the work.

Friederike, though there had been some question of her

[3] Kapp, op. cit., p. 187. See Wagner's own account in *Mein Leben*, p. 828.

[4] *Mein Leben*, p. 828. Later on he said that his relations with Friederike had involved her in serious trouble. Friederike had apparently already been the mistress of Von Guiata, the manager of the Frankfurt theater.

[5] Peter Cornelius: *Ausgewählte Briefe*, in *Literarische Werke*, i, 683.

coming to live with him in the summer of 1863,[6] soon passed out of his life. With his liking for women's society, however, it was impossible for him to live alone for long. We may believe him when he tells Minna (December 27, 1862): "I am living an utterly wretched life, daily, hourly —and am never, never happy." [7] He is busy with concerts and with the *Tristan* rehearsals; but he is getting no sleep, has palpitations of the heart, and is "completely knocked to pieces." After his Russian concert tour he settles in Penzing, a suburb of Vienna (May 12, 1863), in order to continue work at *Die Meistersinger*. He has apparently given up all idea of a reunion with Minna. He tells us that about this time he suffered a great deal of trouble on her account: "she reproached me bitterly for everything I did." [8] He kept, he says, to his resolution of the previous year; he wrote instead to Minna's daughter Nathalie, who was still living with her, and still under the impression that she was Minna's sister.[9] The idea occurred to him of getting Mathilde Maier to take charge of his Penzing household. Apparently the proposal created some commotion in the Maier circle. Mathilde, he had thought,

[6] *Richard Wagner Briefe an Hans von Bülow,* letter of June 22, 1863, pp. 201, 202. In *Mein Leben* he tries to make it appear that he (and Cosima) merely wanted to "bring order" into Friederike's "disorganised circumstances."

[7] "Keep that in mind," he continues, "and your own griefs will seem less to you. They simply add to mine." *Richard Wagner an Minna Wagner,* ii, 310, 311.

[8] *Mein Leben,* p. 848. What was the subject of these reproaches it is impossible to say, as Minna's letters to him have not been published.

[9] It is a little difficult to know what he means by a resolution made "in the previous year." He corresponded with her a good deal in 1862, and we have a few of his letters to her of 1863. In one of these, dated November 8, 1863, he tells her that there is a possibility of his conducting a concert in Dresden on November 25, and asks her if she can put him up. This letter is not included in the German edition. It was published in Adolf Kohut's *Der Meister von Bayreuth* (1905), and a translation of it will be found in Mr. Ellis's English version of the letters to Minna, p. 787.

"would be sensible enough to take my meaning correctly, without being shocked. No doubt I was right in that supposition; but I had not taken sufficient account of her mother and her bourgeois surroundings in general. She seemed to have been thrown into the utmost excitement by my invitation; and her friend Luise Wagner, with bourgeois sense and precision, gave me the good advice first of all to obtain a divorce from my wife, and then everything else would easily be arranged. Greatly shocked at this, I at once withdrew my invitation as having been made without proper consideration." [1] Perhaps he really was shocked, though we have to remember that these memoirs were dictated to Cosima, and he would probably be disposed to paint himself in the most favorable colors. But the whole passage, ambiguous as it is, in a way that the student of *Mein Leben* becomes accustomed to, points quite clearly to the belief in the Maier circle that his relations with Mathilde were very intimate.

Feminine society was an absolute necessity to him at all times, and now, perhaps, more than ever, for his life was a round of anxieties and his health was wretched. His lonely abode was brightened for a time by "a maiden of seventeen years, of an irreproachable family." According to his account,[2] she was bored and wanted to get back to the town again. He got rid of her with as much regard for her feelings as possible, and her place was taken by an elder sister. "She is more experienced," he tells Frau Wesendonck, "staid [*gemessen*], seems gentle, and is not unagreeable." "Eccentric as the episode may seem in itself," says Mr. Ashton Ellis,[3] "it disposes of the ridiculous legend— founded on a Viennese dressmaker's bills—that the writer used to dress himself in female garments. Long ago I had been struck by the 'we' in one of the crumbs of that correspondence flaunted by addle-brained purveyors of gossip, and felt more inclined to credit Hanslick's story of 'a pretty ballet-dancer'; but the amazing innocence of the

[1] *Mein Leben*, pp. 848, 849.
[2] See his letter to Frau Wesendonck of August 3, 1863.
[3] *Richard Wagner to Mathilde Wesendonck*, p. 318.

whole arrangement is proved alike by its narration to Elisabeth and her unrebuking answer."

Whether the purveyors of gossip were addle-brained or not, gossip there certainly was: and apparently there was some fire to account for the smoke. That this second serving maiden, says Kapp, "had a better understanding [than her sister] of the position she was intended for, and gave Wagner thorough satisfaction," is evident from the following letter, addressed to her after he had been away from Penzing some time on a concert tour:

DEAR LITTLE MARIE,—I shall be home again next Wednesday. I shall be at the Northern station in Vienna at half-past seven in the evening. Franz [his manservant] must be there punctually with the carriage, and he must also have what is necessary for the trunk. Now, my best sweetheart, have everything in the house very nice, so that I can get a cosy rest, which I very much need. Everything must be quite tidy, and—well warmed. See that everything is very nice in the lovely study; if it is hot, open it a little, so that the study may be warm; *and perfume it nicely: buy the best bottles of scent, so as to give it a nice odour.* Ach Gott! how delighted I am to be able to rest again with you there. (*I hope the rose-coloured pants are ready?*) Aye, aye! You must be very pretty and charming; I deserve to have a thoroughly good time once more. At Christmas I will arrange the Christmas tree: and then, my sweetheart, you will get all sorts of presents. My arrival need not be made known to everybody; but Franz must tell the barber and the hairdresser to come at half-past nine on Thursday morning. So: *Wednesday* evening at half-past seven in Vienna, and soon after in Penzing. I leave it wholly to yourself as to whether you will meet me at the station. Perhaps it will be nicer if you meet me first in the house, in the warm rooms. I shall probably need only the *coupée*. Kind greetings to Franz and Anna [Franz's wife]. Tell them to have everything thoroughly nice. Many kisses to my sweet-heart. *Au revoir!* [4]

This perhaps, is scarcely the sort of letter one writes to a servant who is no more than a servant.

In July 1863 he gives two concerts in Pesth, where he seems to have been smitten by the charms of a young Hungarian singer who greatly pleased him by her renderings of some of Elsa's music, and still more by her evident incandescence for himself. There is no mention of this young lady in *Mein Leben*, but Wagner tells Frau Wesendonck about her in the same letter (August 3, 1863) in which he speaks of the engagement of Marie as successor to her sister. "I was quite touched at meeting with some-thing so pure and unspoiled for my music; and the good child, on her side, seemed so moved by myself and my music that for the first time in her life she really felt. The expression of these feelings was indescribably charming and touching, and many might have thought that the maiden had conceived an ardent love for me:[5] so now I have to 'write' to her as well." He evidently takes a sort of impish pleasure in thus piquing the curiosity of his old love and "Muse." He adds: "See, I am telling you all the good I can; but I really don't know of anything more, and I am not even sure whether you will credit this last tale to me as something 'good.'"

XIII · *Cosima von Bülow*

All this while the understanding between himself and Von Bülow's wife had evidently been quietly ripening. Reading between the lines of his earlier accounts of Cosima, it is easy to see that there had been for some time a tentative if unavowed *rapprochement* between them. In 1861, when taking leave of Cosima at Reichenhall, she gave him, he

[4] Kapp: *Richard Wagner und die Frauen*, p. 194.
[5] "*Eine heftige Liebe.*" Mr. Ashton Ellis renders this "a sudden love."

says, "an almost timid look of enquiry" [6]—which strikes the old Wagnerian hand as one of those phrases in which the composer conceals more than he discloses.

By the following summer, matters had evidently matured a little. "The increasing and often excessive ill-humour of poor Hans, who seemed to be always in torment, had sometimes drawn a helpless sigh from me. On the other hand Cosima appeared to have lost the timidity [*Scheu*] towards me that I had noticed during my visit to Reichenhall in the previous year; she was now more friendly. One day, after I had sung 'Wotan's Farewell' to my friends in my own way, I noticed on Cosima's face the same expression that, to my astonishment, I had seen there when bidding her good-bye at Zürich; only now the ecstasy of it was raised to a serene transfiguration. There was silence and mystery over everything now; but the belief that she was mine took hold of me with such certainty, that in moments of more than normal excitement I behaved in the most extravagantly riotous way." [7]

He visits the Von Bülows both before and after his Russian concerts (March 1863), and again in November of the year, after the concerts at Budapest, Prague, and elsewhere. Von Bülow being busy on the latter occasion with preparations for a concert of his own, Wagner went for a drive with Cosima. "This time all our jocularity gave way to silence; we gazed into each other's eyes without speaking, and a passionate longing for an avowal of the truth overpowered us and brought us to a confession—which needed no words—of the infinite unhappiness that weighed upon us. It gave us relief. Profoundly appeased, we won sufficient cheerfulness to go to the concert without feeling oppressed. . . . After the concert we had to go to a supper at my friend Weitzmann's, the length of which reduced us, yearning as we were for the profoundest soul's peace, to almost frantic despair. But at last the day came

[6] *Mein Leben,* p. 777.
[7] *Mein Leben,* p. 816. This was in the summer of 1862, just a year before the Marie episode.

to an end, and after a night spent under Bülow's roof I resumed my journey. Our farewell so strongly reminded me of that first wonderfully affecting parting from Cosima at Zürich, that all the intervening years vanished from me like a wild dream between two days of the highest life's significance. If on that first occasion our presentiment of something not yet understood constrained us to silence, it was no less impossible to give voice to what we now recognised but did not utter." [8] Here again, anyone familiar with Wagner's literary manner must feel instinctively that there is a great deal more beneath these words than appears on the surface of them. This is the last reference to Cosima in *Mein Leben*: the further story of the pair has to be derived from other sources.

The Zurich leave-taking to which he refers can only be that of August 16, 1858, the day before he was compelled to leave the "Asyl" as a result of the Mathilde catastrophe. His account of the farewell in *Mein Leben*, however, does not suggest any special community of feeling between himself and Cosima; all that he says is that "on the 16th August the Bülows left; Hans was dissolved in tears, Cosima was gloomy and silent." If it were not for the tragedy of it, the situation would be decidedly piquant: Wagner, on the very eve of his severance from one man's wife, finding some consolation in the look that another man's wife gives him, and assuring us—or was it simply Cosima, his unofficial wife and amanuensis of the hour, that he was assuring?—that all the passion he poured out so eloquently to Mathilde in the days that followed the separation vanished from him, in 1863, "like a wild dream" at another look from Cosima. One could understand the elevated affection he felt for this remarkable woman ousting the smokier memories of Friederike Meyer and Blandine Ollivier and the maidservant Marie, but hardly the luminous figure of Mathilde Wesendonck. Could he really forget so easily, or did he only imagine he forgot, or did he simply wish Cosima to believe he had forgotten? But alas, he forgot Cosima too when she was away from him.

[8] *Mein Leben*, pp. 858, 859.

As we have seen, during his stay at Frau Wille's at Maria-feld, after his flight from his Vienna creditors (March 1864) he had it in his mind to restore his broken finances by means of a rich marriage.[9] Kapp conjectures that the lady he had in view was Henriette von Bissing, the sister of Frau Wille. (She had recently been left a widow, with a considerable fortune.) It is certain that Frau von Bissing and he had been drawn very close together at the end of 1863. When he went to Breslau in November, he tells us, she put up at the same hotel, listened sympathetically to his story of his woes and his financial difficulties, and dissuaded him from his projected Russian tour, promising to give him "the not inconsiderable sum necessary to maintain me in independence for some time to come." [1] But she found some difficulty in getting the needful funds from her family, "from whom she was meeting with the most violent opposition, apparently spiced with calumnies against myself." Plunged more and more deeply into debt, he at last appeals point blank to the lady for "a clear declaration not as to whether she *could* help me at once, but whether she *would*, as I could no longer stave off ruin." "She must," he says, "have been very deeply wounded by something that had been told her of which I knew nothing, for her to be able to bring herself to answer somewhat to this effect—'You want to know finally whether I will or will not? Well then, in God's name, No!' " He accounts for this answer afterward, as might be expected, by "the weakness of her not very independent character," particulars of which he had had from Frau Wille.[2]

Knowing him as well as we do, and knowing his trick of explaining every unpleasantness in other people's conduct toward him in a way that lays the blame with them rather than with himself, we can hardly accept his own

[9] King Ludwig gave him 15,000 gulden with which to pay his debts in Vienna. Röckl: *Ludwig II und Richard Wagner,* Erster Teil, p. 33.
[1] *Mein Leben,* p. 861.
[2] *Mein Leben,* p. 863.

account of the affair as the last possible word on the subject. It would be interesting to have Frau von Bissing's version of it. But if he has given us the events in their true sequence, Kapp's theory is untenable, for the rupture with Frau von Bissing must have taken place before the Mariafeld conversation on the subject of a divorce. It is not impossible, however, that he is anticipating the story of the severance from Frau von Bissing by a page or two.[3]

In May 1864 came his dramatic rescue by King Ludwig. His financial troubles were, for a time, at an end. And now the stage was clear for the last act of the drama in which he and Cosima were the principal actors. As the autobiography ends with the summons to Munich by King Ludwig, we are henceforth without any guidance from Wagner himself. We can imagine, however, that for a man of his temperament the necessity for feminine companionship soon became urgent. Minna was now out of the question; his other flames—Mathilde Wesendonck, Friederike Meyer, Mathilde Maier, Henriette von Bissing—had one by one died out. Only Cosima remained; and for the man who, with the turn of his fiftieth year, began to love with his reason as much as with his senses, the masterful Cosima was obviously the one woman in the world for him. She had apparently never loved Von Bülow, nor he her; we are told that his marriage with her was an act of chivalry on his part, due to the desire to legitimize in the eyes of the world the illegitimate daughter of the Liszt whom he so admired and loved. The truth seems to have slowly dawned on Cosima that it was her mission in life to tend the buffeted composer of genius. He must have admired her both for her insight and her indomitable will; and no admirer of Wagner would grudge him the splendid instrument for his purposes that came to him

---

[3] In a letter to Peter Cornelius of the end of March 1864, addressed from Frau Wille's house at Mariafeld, Wagner says that that lady, Frau Wesendonck, and Frau von Bissing "love him equally: only Frau von Bissing was lately so very jealous (I had a suspicion of it!), that her behaviour towards me is only now, through that discovery, intelligible to me." Peter Cornelius: *Ausgewählte Briefe* in *Literarische Werke*, i, 762.

in Cosima after so many years of delusion and disappointment. But it is tolerably clear that the pair, in the egoism of their devotion to each other, acted with a total lack of regard either for Von Bülow's feelings or for his position in the eyes of the world. In 1864 Von Bülow, at Wagner's request, sent Cosima and his own child to keep the lonely musician company in his Starnberg villa; and apparently at this time all barriers between the two were broken down, though their love for each other was still concealed from Von Bülow, who came to them in July at Wagner's request. Wagner persuaded the King to appoint Von Bülow his Court pianist—his avowed object being to rescue Hans from his unpleasant artistic surroundings in Berlin, the real object, as Kapp says, being "to keep the beloved woman near him."

In October, Wagner settled in the Munich house placed at his disposal by the King, and the Von Bülows took up their residence in the capital in the following month. Cosima constituted herself Wagner's secretary and general woman of affairs, two rooms being provided for her in his house, where she worked for several hours each day. On April 10, 1865, a daughter, Isolde, was born to Cosima. Von Bülow believed the child to be his own,[4] and Wagner

[4] See his letter of April 14, 1865, to Dr. Gille, in *Hans von Bülow: Briefe*, iv, 24.

In May 1914 Cosima appealed to the German courts to declare that Isolde (Frau Beidler) was Wagner's child, not Von Bülow's. (The family seems to have been quarreling over the division of the Wagner patrimony.) Glasenapp, whose partisan biography owes a great deal to first-hand information from Wahnfried, expressly states that Isolde, like the undisputed Eva, was Wagner's child. Isolde herself, according to the German newspapers, pleaded that Wagner wrote on the score of *Das Rheingold*: "finished on the day of the birth of my daughter, Isolde." There is also in existence a poem that he wrote for Isolde, on April 10, 1880, for her fifteenth birthday:

Vor fünfzehn Jahren wurdest Du geboren,
Da spitzte alle Welt die Ohren.
Man wollte "Tristan und Isolde"—
Doch was ich einzig wünscht und wollte,
Das war ein Töchterchen: Isolde.

became its godfather. In reality the child was Wagner's own. (A second child, Eva, was born to them February 17, 1867, at Triebschen; Siegfried was born on June 6, 1869.)

On January 25, 1866, Minna died in Dresden. As soon as Cosima heard of it, Cornelius tells us, she telegraphed to Wagner, who was in Geneva at the time, asking whether she should come at once to him; he advised her to wait. But while Von Bülow was on a concert tour in March she went to Geneva and stayed three weeks with Wagner.

> *Nun mag sie tausend Jahre leben,*
> *Und "Tristan und Isolde" auch daneben!*
> *Vivat hoch!*

["Fifteen years ago were you born: the whole world pricked up its ears. People wanted 'Tristan and Isolde'; but what *I* wanted was a little daughter, Isolde. May she live a thousand years, and 'Tristan and Isolde' with her!"]

At the trial, Frau Beidler's counsel put forward a mass of evidence pointing to the fact that she was Wagner's daughter; Cosima had declared that from June 12 to October 12, 1864, she had lived in intimate relations with no one but Wagner; Wagner had always treated Isolde as his daughter; she bore a physical resemblance to him; and so on. The Court, however, decided against her. The grounds for the judgment were not given; they were to be communicated to the parties concerned in private. Apparently the piece of evidence that weighed most heavily with the Court was that of Frau Anna Mrazek, the widow of Franz Mrazek, the one-time housekeeper of Wagner. This old lady died on June 11, 1914, at the age of eighty, shortly after having made a deposition to the effect that while Frau Cosima was living with Wagner at Starnberg she still occupied Von Bülow's room during his visits to them. In view of this it was evidently impossible for the Court to declare definitely in favor of Frau Beidler. But until its written reasons are given to the world, and unless these reasons are very cogent, most people will go on believing, in spite of the judgment, in the Wagnerian paternity of Frau Isolde. There were several points in the evidence that seemed fairly conclusive to the plain man, and it would be interesting to see how the Court managed to persuade itself that they ought not to count. The facial resemblance between Wagner and Frau Beidler, for instance—a resemblance that has struck many thousands of visitors to Bayreuth—on what grounds was this put aside?

His unpopularity in Munich had made it imperative for the King, however unwillingly, to request him to leave the city. He and Cosima now looked out for a Swiss refuge, and at the end of March found the ideal retreat in Triebschen, near Lucerne. There Cosima joined him, with her children, on May 12, 1866. A letter from Wagner to her arrived in Munich after she had left. "It was opened by Bülow, who thought it might contain something that it would be necessary to telegraph to his wife; it revealed to him the whole bitter truth." [5] His position was an unenviable one, Munich gossip already making very free with his name. He went to Triebschen, and learned that Cosima was resolved not to return to him. He agreed to a dissolution of the marriage, but stipulated that, out of regard for himself, and to give pause to the malice of the world, Cosima should not be united to Wagner for another two years, which time she was to spend with her father in Rome. She refused him this concession; and Von Bülow, after remaining in the house two months, in the hope of giving a *démenti* to Munich tittle-tattle, retired to Basle, leaving the children with Wagner.

In April 1867 King Ludwig appointed Von Bülow Court Kapellmeister. At the same time the King asked Wagner to superintend some projected performances of *Lohengrin* and *Tannhäuser*, which necessitated his frequent visits to Munich. Apparently to save appearances, Cosima took up her abode for a time with Von Bülow at his house in the Arcostrasse, where two rooms were always ready for Wagner's use. But gossip and calumny only raged all the more fiercely, both in the town and in the press. It was openly said of Von Bülow that he owed his appointment at the Court "to his complaisance as a husband"; and at the end there was nothing for it but for Wagner and Cosima to retire together to Tribschen, and cut the last traces that bound them to Munich and convention. Deeply wounded, Von Bülow found it impossible to continue his work in the town: he resigned

[5] Kapp: *Richard Wagner und die Frauen*, p. 222.

his appointment in June 1869, sent his own two children to Cosima, and went out alone into the world.[6]

The conduct of Wagner and Cosima led to a long estrangement between them and Liszt, and a cooling of other friendships; the King, too, pointedly showed his displeasure. Wagner, in his Tribschen retreat, turned his back angrily upon everyone who disapproved of him, and immersed himself in *Siegfried* and *The Twilight of the Gods*. On June 6, 1869, the birth of a son, Siegfried, sent him into the seventh heaven of delight. Cosima's marriage was dissolved, on Von Bülow's suit, on July 18, 1870; and on August 25 she was married to Wagner.

It is a thousand pities that Wagner himself has left us no account of the Von Bülow-Cosima affair. No one who has followed him thus far with me can doubt that he would have made himself, as usual, the suffering hero of the piece, that his intentions and his acts would have been strictly honorable from first to last, and that Von Bülow would somehow or other have been shown to be in the wrong, as all the other friends and enemies were who happened to cross his path. The interesting thing would have been to see how he managed the demonstration.

XIV · *Contrarieties of Character: Love of Luxury*

I have given the erotic history of Wagner in such detail not only because of the enormous part the erotic played in his life and in the shaping of his character, but because to know him thoroughly from this side is to have the key to his whole nature. Nowhere and at no time was a middle course possible for him. It was all or nothing. To that extent he was consistent: yet viewed in detail he was a bundle of inconsistencies—at once a voluptuary and an ascetic, a hero and a rogue, a saint and a sinner, always longing for death, yet always fighting lustily for his life, despising the public and pining for seclusion, yet unable

[6] He behaved afterward with the greatest nobility to Wagner, raising by his concerts £2,000 for the Bayreuth venture, though his presence at the Festival was of course impossible.

to live anywhere except in the very center of the stage and the full glare of the limelight. Frau Wesendonck once reproached him gravely and wisely with his inconsistency in this last regard. "The wretchedness of your state of mind froze my blood. I felt I could do nothing. I was to tell myself that all the gifts of nature, even the most glorious, are wasted if they are not crowned by empty external success; that they are futile in and for themselves, and he who has them above others possesses only the right to be more wretched than they! It made me almost bitter to think you would have me believe that. . . . It is quite incomprehensible to me how anyone can at once despise and seek mere success, *i.e.* applause. It seems to me that only the sage, who asks nothing of the world, may despise it; the man who uses it becomes its accomplice by mere contact with it, and can no longer be its judge. You are at once a knower [*Wissender*] and accomplice in the last degree. You hurriedly grasp at every new deception, apparently to wipe out from your breast the disappointment of previous deceptions; and yet no one knows better than yourself that it never can or will be. Friend, how is this to end? Are fifty years' experience not enough, and should the moment not come at last when you are wholly at one with yourself?" [7]

He knew no law of life except the full realization of himself at the moment. He was by turns Christian and Freethinker and Christian again, republican and royalist, lover of Germany and despiser of Germany, anti-Semite (in theory) and pro-Semite (in practice);[8] but in each of his many metamorphoses he was sincerely convinced that he was not only right as against all the world, but right as against the Wagner of earlier years. Feuerbach, Schopenhauer, Hafiz, and heaven knows who besides were in turn the one great philosopher the world has known. In later

[7] Letter of September 23, 1863: *Richard Wagner an Mathilde Wesendonck*, p. 355.

[8] He never had any objection to accepting money from Jews, or to calling on their assistance in the production of his operas. The first performance of *Parsifal* was conducted by Hermann Levi.

life he becomes a vegetarian: it therefore went without saying that all mankind should forthwith abjure meat. He has the sense to recognize that a flesh diet is imperative for most people in a climate like that of Northern Europe. But a little difficulty of this kind does not daunt him; all that European humanity has to do, he tells us, is to migrate into other parts of the world.[9] He gives us, in 1851 and 1856, two divergent interpretations of the philosophies that underlie *Tannhäuser* and the *Ring*. He of course explains it all by the fact that in his "intellectual ideas" he was at first working in opposition to his "intuitive ideal." The truth is that in 1851 he was still something of an optimist, while in 1856 he had become a pessimist with Schopenhauer.[1]

The many contradictions of his character have of course made him the easy butt of the satirists.[2] In 1877 there were published in the Vienna *Neue Freie Presse*[3] a series of letters of his to the milliner Bertha, who made him his wonderful lace shirts and satin trousers[4] and dressing

[9] "If the assumption be correct that a flesh diet is indispensable in Northern climates, what is to prevent us from carrying out a rationally conducted emigration into such countries of the globe as, by reason of their luxuriant fertility, are capable of sustaining the present population of the whole world,—as has been asserted of the South American peninsula itself? . . . The unions we have in mind would have to devote their activities and their care—perhaps not without success—to emigration; and according to the latest experiences it seems not impossible that these northern lands, in which a flesh food is said to be absolutely indispensable, will soon be wholly abandoned to hunters of boars and big game. . . ." "*Religion und Kunst*," in G.S., x, 243.

[1] See "*Eine Mittheilung an meine Freunde*," in G.S., iv, 279, and the letter to Röckl of August 23, 1856; also a general discussion of the subject in Henri Lichtenberger's *Wagner, Poète et Penseur*, pp. 109–16.

[2] See, for example, the very prejudiced and rather foolish book of Emil Ludwig, *Wagner, oder die Entzauberten* (1913).

[3] Afterward in book form as the *Briefe Richard Wagners an eine Putzmacherin*. Vienna, 1906.

[4] We must always remember that his extremely sensitive and irritable skin made coarse fabrics intolerable to him.

gowns, and decorated his Penzing rooms (and later his house at Triebschen) with the soft luxurious stuffs and colors he so loved. The witty editor of the Letters, Daniel Spitzer, twitted him on the inconsistency between his acts and his opinions, between his art and his life. Who would believe, he asks, that the man who indulged in these effeminacies was the same man who used to sneer in his books at the seductions of Paris: who, in his *Opera and Drama*, reproached Rossini with "living in the lap of luxury," called him the "luxurious son of Italy," and even, in a moment of towering virtue, styled him an "*ausgestochene Courtisane*"; or that the Wagner who, in the deplorable squib he wrote upon the French nation after its downfall in 1871, sneered at the French for their passion for bouquets, was himself ordering bouquets and rose garlands of the most extravagant kind from the *Putzmacherin?* [5]

[5] When the letters were republished in book form in 1906, Ludwig Karpath, who was at that time on the staff of the Vienna *Tagblatt*, accidentally discovered that an old man who had every day for the past thirty years brought the Stock Exchange price list to the financial editor was the brother of the *Putzmacherin*. Through him he discovered the old lady herself, whom everyone had thought long dead; in any case, no one could have known that Wagner's "Fräulein Bertha" was the former Bertha Goldwag, and now the retired Frau Maretschek. According to her, the letters had been stolen from her, though by whom or precisely when she did not know. When they were first published in the *Neue Freie Presse* in 1877, Wagner, of course, was still alive, and though she feared he would suspect her of having sold the letters, she did not write to him. (Herr Karpath informs me that he suspects the husband, Maretschek, who was always in financial difficulties, of having stolen and sold the letters. This, of course, he could not say in his book, Maretschek then being alive. He died soon after the publication of Herr Karpath's book. Bertha died some two years ago, aged over eighty).

She gave Karpath her reminiscences of Wagner. She fitted up for him a room in his Penzing (Vienna) house, with the usual silk decorations. He told her that he could work only when surrounded by luxury of this kind. He wore also silk trousers and a silk jacket, heavily wadded, as he was very susceptible to cold. When he fled from Vienna in 1864, hopelessly in debt

The man, in truth, who wrote with such a comic rage against the rich and their luxury, was himself the most luxurious of mankind. He may have admired the Spartan virtues of the poor, but he had not the least wish to practice them himself. He could not exist without a certain amount of pampering both of body and of soul, even in the days when, unable to make both ends meet, he was living on the charity of certain friends and borrowing at every opportunity from others. "It is with genuine desperation that I always pick up art again," he writes to Liszt on January 15, 1854; "if I am to do this, if I am once more to renounce reality,—if I am to plunge again into the woes of artistic fancy in order to find tranquillity in the world of imagination, my fancy must at least be helped, my imaginative faculty supported. I cannot live like a dog; I cannot sleep on straw and refresh myself with bad liquor. My excitable, delicate, ardently craving and uncommonly soft and tender sensibility must be coaxed in some ways if my mind is to accomplish the horribly difficult task of creating a non-existent world." [6] A few days after it is the same story; he must have money by hook or by crook. Liszt will understand him—though it will be "impossible for a Philistine to comprehend the exuberance[7] of my nature, which in these and those moods of my life drove me to satisfy a colossal inner desire by such external means as must seem to him questionable,[8]

---

to everyone, he owed Fräulein Bertha a large sum, which· he paid, however, when King Ludwig restored his fortunes. He sent for her to Munich to decorate his house there (she took with her silks, satins, etc., to the value of 10,000 gulden); and later she adorned his Triebschen house in similar style.

The final touch is the most piquant of all. After Spitzer had published the sixteen letters in 1877 he sold them to a Vienna manufacturer, Arthur Faber, who presented fifteen of them to —Brahms!

[6] *Briefwechsel zwischen Wagner und Liszt*, ii, 4, 5.

[7] *"Das Uberschwängliche meiner Natur."* In the English version of the Correspondence this is rendered "the transcendent part of my nature."

[8] *"Bedenklich"*—rendered in Hueffer's version "dangerous."

and at all events unsympathetic. No one knows the needs of men like us: I myself am often surprised at regarding so many 'useless' things as indispensable." [9]

He grew more and more luxurious in middle age. The scale of expenditure revealed in the *Putzmacherin* letters, and a stray piece of information or two from other quarters, give us a hint of his recklessness in the early sixties— a recklessness that brought him so near the verge of absolute ruin that it is terrible to think what might have happened to him had not King Ludwig come to his rescue. For the Christmas of 1863 he had, as is usual in Germany, a Christmas tree loaded with gifts for his friends. For a man without any income to speak of, very dubious prospects, and a grievous load of debt, his presents were magnificent. "The mad Wagner," says Cornelius in a letter to his sister Susanne (Vienna, January 11, 1864), "had a great Christmas tree, with a royally rich table beneath it for me. Just imagine: a marvellous heavy overcoat—an elegant grey dressing-gown—a red scarf, a blue cigar-case and tinder-box—lovely silk handkerchiefs, splendid gold shirt studs—the *Struwelpeter*—elegant pen-wipers with gold mottoes—fine cravats, a meerschaum cigar-holder with his initials—in short, all sorts of things that only an Oriental imagination could think of. It made my heart heavy, and the next day I gave away half of them, and only then was I happy,—to Seraphine the gold studs, to Ernestine a lovely purse with a silver thaler, to Gustav Schönaich a sash, to young Ruben the cigar-holder, to Fritz Porges the pen-wiper, something to each of my house people, a yellow handkerchief to Marie, a red one to Frau Müller, . . . to Herr Müller the tinder-box, to Karl Müller a new waistcoat from myself, in place of which I kept the one from Wagner." [1] All this was for Cornelius alone; no doubt his other guests were treated in equally generous fashion. We happen to have his own account of this affair; it is delightful. "Having very little ready money,

[9] *Briefwechsel zwischen Wagner und Liszt*, ii, 10.
[1] *Ausgewählte Briefe*, i, 748, 749.

but solid hopes,[2] I could now greet my few friends with tolerable good humour. . . . On Christmas Eve I invited them all to my house, had the Christmas tree lighted up, and gave each of them an appropriate trifle." [3]

With tastes and habits of this kind it is no wonder that he accumulated enormous debts, and came to be regarded by all his friends as perfectly hopeless on the financial side. King Ludwig gave him, as we have seen, 15,000 gulden with which to return to Vienna, to satisfy the more pressing of his creditors and to make arrangements with the others. He took up his Munich residence in the Briennerstrasse (No. 21), in October 1864, and sent for the *Putzmacherin* Bertha to drape and decorate it for him according to his liking, and to provide him with the satin dressing gowns, trousers, etc., etc., that he loved, paying her, of course, now and then when funds were more than usually plentiful.[4] His manner of living in Munich may be guessed from the fact that he was threatened with a writ on the day of the projected first performance of *Tristan* (May 15, 1865);[5] while in October of the same year he was compelled to borrow another 40,000 gulden of the King.[6] He soon earned in Munich the reputation of a reckless spendthrift, a reputation that has never left him. It is sometimes said that the standard of domestic comfort was so low among the good Müncheners of that epoch that a very modest expenditure upon fineries

[2] He had just returned from the meeting with Frau von Bissing, at which she had undertaken to provide for him.

[3] *Mein Leben*, p. 862.

[4] The *Putzmacherin* letters extended into the Lucerne period of 1866–87.

[5] Röckl: *Ludwig II und Richard Wagner*, Erster Theil, p. 151.

[6] The relations between Wagner and the King's ministers were already embittered at this time, and the King granted the loan against their wish. The Court Treasurer objecting to sending the money by a servant, Cosima had to call for it personally. He gave her the whole of the sum in silver coins, which she had to carry away in sacks, his object being to render the transport of it as public as possible, and so arouse popular feeling against the composer. The loan was repaid to the Munich Treasury by Wagner's heirs. See Röckl, op. cit., p. 197.

may have seemed to them a Capuan indulgence in luxury.[7]
But the details of the fitting up—evidently by Bertha—
of one of his rooms in the Briennerstrasse are proof enough
that he was giving full rein to his sybaritic tastes. "In the
middle of the first floor was a large room containing
Wagner's grand piano. On the right a door led into the
so-called Grail or Satin Room, which was about 3½ m.
high, 4½ broad, and 5 deep [roughly 11½ feet by 14½
feet by 16½ feet]. The walls were covered with fine yellow
satin, which was finished off above with yellow valances
of the same material. The two blunt corners of the long
wall that faced Count von Schack's house were broken by
iron galleries, making artificial recesses. These, about 70
cm. deep [about 28 inches], were covered with rose-
coloured satin in folds. Each of the iron galleries was
covered with two wings of white silk tulle, trimmed with
lace. The white curtains and the draperies were also
adorned with delicate artificial roses. The room was
lighted by a window at the small side at the left of the
entrance. The curtains of this window were of rose-coloured
satin, garnished with interlaced red and white satin draperies. . . . The top of the window curtain, the frame
of the mirror [on one of the walls], and that of the
picture [on another wall], were draped with rose-coloured
satin, tied back with white satin bows. The ceiling was
entirely covered with richly festooned white satin, then
divided diagonally from one corner to the other with
ruches of pearl grey satin of about 14 cm. wide [about 6
inches]. The ceiling was also bordered on all four sides
with similar pearl grey ruches; these were sown with artificial roses. The middle of the ceiling was decorated with
a rosette of white satin, about 30 cm. [12 inches] in cir-
cumference and 25 cm. [10 inches] deep, trimmed with
narrow silk lace and with roses like the others on the ceiling. The ground was covered with a soft Smyrna carpet.
In the middle of the room was a soft and elastically up-
holstered couch, covered with a white flowered moire." [8]

[7] See Ludwig Nohl: *Neues Skizzenbuch*, p. 146.
[8] Röckl, op. cit., pp. 245, 246.

Satin, I believe, was much more expensive in the sixties than it is now; but any lady reader will be able to make an approximate estimate of the expense of fitting up such a room. No one today, of course, will presume to pass moral censure upon him for his love of luxury. Every sensible man surrounds himself with all the luxury he can procure. The remarkable features in Wagner's case are the uncontrollable nature of the desires that urged him to their gratification at anyone's or everyone's expense, and the dualism of soul that permitted him equally to evoke hardy primeval heroes and to expound the doctrine of renunciation from the center of a bower of satin.

Von Bülow once confessed to Weissheimer that he could not make out how Wagner managed to get through so much money. The secret apparently was that he had to indulge himself liberally in order to put into practice his doctrine of renunciation. Here is an instance given us by Weissheimer himself from the dark days of 1862. Through the nonperformance of *Tristan* at Vienna, Wagner had been disappointed of the expected honorarium, which, as was usual with him, had been squandered in advance. He had been in the habit of giving splendid dinners after the concerts to his friends and the chief performers; and his hotel keeper had a two months' bill against him for food and lodging. "One evening when Tausig and I were with him, he bemoaned and lamented his wretched condition. We listened to him sympathetically, and sat miserably on the sofa, while he paced up and down in nervous haste. Suddenly he stopped and said, 'Here, I know what I need,' ran to the door, and rang vigorously. Tausig whispered to me, 'What's he up to? He looks just like Wotan after he has come to some great resolution.' The waiter came in sight slowly and hesitatingly—these people soon see how the wind is blowing—and was no less astonished than we when Wagner said, 'Bring me at once two bottles of champagne on ice!' 'Heavens above—in this state!' we said when the waiter had gone out. But Wagner gave us a fervid dissertation on the indispensability of champagne precisely when a situation was desperate: only *this* could help us over the painfulness of it." [9]

Glasenapp tells how in the very last years of his life he could not work unless surrounded by soft lines and colors and perfumes. His almost morbid sensitivity multiplied enormously the ordinary pleasant or unpleasant sensations of touch and of sight. When in a difficulty with his composition, he would stroke the folds of a soft curtain or table cover till the right mood came. Not only the fabrics but the lines about him had to be melting, indefinite: he could not endure even books in the room he was working in, or bear to let his eyes follow the garden paths; "they suggested the outer world too definitely and prevented concentration." Among scents, he particularly loved attar of roses, which he used to get direct from Paris—sent to him, however, under the fictitious name and address of "Mr. Bernard Schnappauf, Ochsengasse, Bayreuth," his barber obtaining delivery of it for him.[1] Such was the creator of the heroic, athletic boy Siegfried—this poor little sickly, supersensitive, self-indulgent neurotic who could hardly deny himself the smallest of his innocent little voluptuousnesses. The antinomy would be unresolvable did we not know from a hundred other cases that art is not life, and that the artist may be very different from his art. The Grand Duke of Baden once wounded Wagner deeply by declaring that he "could distinguish between the work and the man." [2] We have often to make that distinction with Wagner.

xv · *Egoism in Friendship*

At once a Spartan and a voluptuary in body, ready to endure many miseries rather than live any kind of life

[9] Weissheimer: *Erlebnisse mit Richard Wagner, Franz Liszt und vielen anderen Zeitgenossen.* Third edition (1898), pp. 229, 230. See Lilli Lehmann's *My Path Through Life*, p. 218, for an account of an expenditure of 25,000 marks on refreshments during the Bayreuth rehearsals of 1876.

[1] Glasenapp: *Das Leben Richard Wagners*, vi, 154, 155.

[2] *Mein Leben*, p. 811.

but the one he desired to live, yet unable to deny himself all sorts of luxuries even when he had not the money to pay for them, he was both a Spartan and a voluptuary in the things of the mind. He cut himself adrift uncompromisingly, even with rudeness, from people he disliked, even though they for their part were not ill-disposed toward him and might have been useful to him. But to his friends he clung with the same hungry passion as to his silks and satins and perfumes, and, it must be confessed, for the same reasons—because they warmed and refreshed and soothed him. He loved his friends sincerely, but for his own sake, not for theirs. This may seem a harsh judgment of him, but his letters and his record admit of no other reading. With his lust for domination, he could never endure independence in anyone around him. This was Nietzsche's great offense, that he dared to think his own way through life, instead of falling into the ranks and becoming simply the instrument of Wagner's will.[3] We have seen Wagner commending this person and that for their "devotion," their "fidelity" to himself, and becoming pettishly angry with Cornelius and Tausig and Nietzsche for not coming to him the moment he wanted them. In his old age he was as insistent as ever that no one in his circle should follow a desire of his own if it clashed with his. In the later Wahnfried days he used to go through Bach's preludes and fugues in the evenings, expatiating upon each of them to an admiring company. One night he was deeply displeased at young Kellermann for having absented himself from Wahnfried, having preferred to go to some concert in the town; Wagner "got violently excited over it, and regretted afterwards that he

[3] "Wagner has not the strength to make those around him free and great," he writes in his diary. "Wagner is not loyal; he is, on the contrary, suspicious and haughty." See Daniel Halévy: *Life of Friedrich Nietzsche* (Eng. trans.), p. 130.

Nietzsche was more than once hurt to find that Wagner's interest in his young friend's work began and ended where he thought this subserved *his* theories of music, the drama, European culture, etc. See Elisabeth Förster-Nietzsche's *Wagner und Nietzsche zur Zeit ihrer Freundschaft*, p. 72, etc.

could not 'give it to' anyone quietly and calmly, on which account he would rather avoid doing so altogether. On this day it was a long time before we could get to the 'Forty-eight.' " [4]

The unique correspondence with Liszt thrills us in its better moments even today; yet it can hardly be doubted that he loved Liszt selfishly, for the intellectual and emotional warmth his colleague brought into his life. He needs Liszt, we can see, in order that he may talk about and realize himself. After the Wesendonck rupture, in 1858, he goes to Venice. In September Liszt is in the Tyrol with the Princess von Wittgenstein and her daughter. Wagner writes him on September 12, asking him, as he is so near, to come to him at Venice, Liszt having been unable to accept a previous invitation to visit him at Zurich, owing to his having to attend the Jena University Jubilee celebrations. There had been some misunderstanding over another proposed meeting place, and Liszt did not go to Venice. Thereupon Wagner becomes very angry, as usual, and actually writes to this man, to whom he owed such infinite benefactions, in the same half-grieved, half-accusing tone that he adopted toward Tausig. "Your letter of 23rd ult. . . . awoke in me the hope that I should soon be able to see you and speak to you. But I doubt whether my letter to you to that effect, addressed to you at the Hôtel de Bavière, Munich, reached you in time, for I have neither seen you nor had an answer from you. I now fear that my desire to tell you of many things by word of mouth will not be realised; so I write, as I feel I owe you an explanation with regard to certain points that have not been clear to you. Although it cannot amount to much; in conversation it might have been more.

"I will not enlarge upon the moral necessities for my departure from Zürich; they must be known to you, and perhaps I may assume that Cosima or Hans has told you enough about them. To remain in Zürich under the previous conditions was not to be thought of; I had to carry out without any further delay a resolution made some

[4] Glasenapp, vi, 165.

months before. Each new day brought with it new and intolerable torments; only my departure could end them. From day to day I had to postpone this, however, for lack of the necessary means; I had to provide my wife with money, and make our definitive departure from Zürich possible by settling accounts, etc., that otherwise I should not have had to settle until the New Year. It was an unspeakable agony to go through day after day hoping in vain for money to arrive, and to see the troubles and torments that were the cause of my delay increasing. For you to have come to me suddenly at this time would have been a heavenly consolation for me and everyone involved in the conflict.

"You had to attend to University celebrations, etc., which, pardon me for saying so, appeared incredibly trivial to me in the mood I was in then. I did not press you any more, and was angry with Bülow for pressing you; but I must confess that when at last I received the news of your coming on the 20th, I had already become indifferent [unempfindlich] about it." [5]

In short, he was in trouble, thought that Liszt would be able to console him, and was angry with him for not coming to him at the instant he needed him. Liszt, always long-suffering and courteous, chides him gently in his reply of October 9.

"Another point in your letter, dearest Richard, has almost hurt me, though I can quite understand that you, in the midst of the griefs and agitations that embittered your last days in Zürich, should think the official impediments in the way of my coming to Zürich 'trivial,' and that you should not attach sufficient importance to the Jena University Jubilee and to the many considerations which I have to observe with regard to the Grand Duke,—were it

[5] *Briefwechsel*, ii, 216, 217. This and several other passages in the letter were suppressed in the first edition of the correspondence. The Countess d'Agoult—the mother of Liszt's daughter Cosima—was visiting Wagner at the same time as Cosima and Hans. Apparently there had been some gossip as to Wagner's behavior with her; and in this letter he indignantly protests against Liszt's "suspicions."

only in order that I may be useful to you now and then in small matters. In a calmer mood, however, you will easily understand that I cannot and ought not to leave Weimar at every moment, and you will certainly feel that the delay of my journey to Zürich was not motived by any sort of 'triviality.' When I wrote that I should be with you on the 20th August I took it for certain that even in case of your earlier departure from Zürich you would appoint some other place, Lucerne or Geneva, for our meeting. As this did not happen, I came to the conclusion which, however, I gladly put aside on your assurance; although, as I told you a little while ago, for years I have had to endure many incredible and deeply wounding things from the Countess d'Agoult.

"Enough of this, dearest Richard; we shall remain what we are,—inseparable, true friends, and such another pair will not be found soon." [6]

But Wagner was unappeasable. He does indeed write back to Liszt in cordial terms—"Thanks, dear friend! After the profoundest solace through the noblest, tenderest love that fell to my lot [i.e., Mathilde Wesendonck], your beautiful friendship alone can make any impression on me." [7] But that he still cherished some rancor against Liszt is evident from the account he gives of the episode in *Mein Leben*, written some years later. Liszt had carefully explained that he could not come to Zurich just at the time Wagner wanted him. That is not sufficient for Richard. Liszt had no right to have other engagements or other wishes when *he* had need of his society; when *he* was

---

[6] *Briefwechsel*, ii, 222. The passage relating to the Countess d'Agoult was at first suppressed.

[7] *Briefwechsel*, ii, 294. The first part of the sentence, as far as "fell to my lot," was suppressed in the first edition of the letters, as well as the succeeding sentences,—"The love of a tender woman has made me happy: she can throw herself into a sea of sorrows and torments in order to say to me 'I love you,'" etc. etc. This was the lady with whom his relations were "merely friendly." The first edition of the Wagner-Liszt correspondence was systemically manipulated so as to keep from the reader all knowledge of the Wesendonck affair.

in tears, was it not the duty of the heavens themselves to weep with him? "It seemed to me that there must be one human being specially qualified to bring light and solace, or at all events tolerable order, into the confusion that enveloped us all. Liszt had promised us a visit; he stood so fortunately outside these dreadful relations and conditions, knew the world so well, and had in such a high degree what is called '*aplomb*' of personality, that I could not help feeling he was just the man to approach these discords in a rational spirit.[8] I was almost inclined to make my last resolutions depend on the effect of his expected visit. In vain we urged him to hasten his journey: he gave me a rendezvous for a month later at the Lake of Geneva!"[9] It is clear that he still thought Liszt in the wrong in not setting everything aside in order to fly to *him* at once.

A year later he is sending Liszt congratulations on his birthday, and talking very beautifully about friendship. It soon becomes clear, however, that he is using the word in a sense of his own. "Your friendship is an absolute necessity for me; I hold on to it with my last vital strength. When shall I see you at last? Have you any idea of the position I am in,—what miracles of love and fidelity I need in order to win ever new courage and patience? Ponder upon this yourself, so that I need not say it to you! You *must* know me sufficiently now to be able to say it to yourself, although we have not lived much together."[1]

To this Liszt evidently replied that he could not come to Paris just then for any length of time, but that he would be glad to meet Wagner in Strassburg for a couple of days. This proposal Wagner curtly rejects. "What will be the use, to me, of these Strassburg days? I have nothing hurried to say to you, nothing that makes a discussion necessary. I want to enjoy you, to live with you for a while, as we have hitherto lived so little with each other. . . .

[8] The English version (p. 687) makes nonsense of this passage.
[9] *Mein Leben*, p. 674.
[1] Letter of October 20, 1859 (Paris), in *Briefwechsel*, ii, 275.

My poor deserted life makes me incapable of understanding an existence that has the whole world in view at every step. You must pardon me, but I decline the Strassburg meeting, greatly as I value the sacrifice you thereby offer me; it is just this sacrifice that seems to me too great at the price of a few hurried days in a Strassburg hotel." [2]

That is to say, he loved Liszt, and valued his friendship above everything else in the world; but he must have Liszt on his own terms and at his own time or not at all. He claimed the right to live his own life in his own way, while his friends were to stand by with their sympathies, their purses, their wives and daughters ready. Always hungering for the love and self-sacrifice of others, he never sacrificed for their sakes a single desire of his heart. And always there was the same honest, childlike inability to comprehend how people could be so cruel as to refuse him whatever he wanted. He was generous and honorable enough in his own way; he supported Minna's parents, for instance, and would never let Minna be without money if he could provide it. But his good qualities were those of a benevolent despot. He could be kind where kindness was compatible with power; but he could never be just to a personality too independent to be drawn into his orbit, nor could he ever understand other people's desire for independence as against himself. With a nature so self-centered as his, it was inevitable that at one time or other friend after friend should find it necessary to part company from him. No man ever had such friends; no man ever lost such friends; and he lost them all by placing too great a strain on their friendship, their purses, their rights or their independence. Cornelius once cut him to the quick with the remark that "he let his old friends drop"—"whereas," says the faithful Glasenapp with unconscious humor, "he himself had the sad consciousness that *they* had given *him* up as soon as he had tried to lift them above the narrow confines of their 'independence,' and demanded of them more than they were capable of performing,—Herwegh, for example, and

[2] Letter of November 23, 1859, in *Briefwechsel*, ii, 276, 277.

Baumgartner, and Cornelius, and Weissheimer, and Karl Ritter and others." [3] But these were not all—there were also Liszt, King Ludwig, Von Bülow, the Wesendoncks, Wille, Madame Laussot, and many another besides from whom he was estranged permanently or for a time. All his life through he insisted on being the center of his own universe. He saw and felt himself with exaggerated sensibilities; whatever happened to him was either a bliss or a woe above anything that could happen to ordinary mortals. Like Strindberg, he imagines at one time that the whole world exists simply to hurt him; at another, it is a portent of happiness for the whole world because *he* is happy. He cannot go through so simple an experience as becoming a father without feeling that an event of this kind happening to him is a vastly different thing from the superficially similar events that happen to ordinary people. He must call the child "Siegfried,"—the name of the ideal hero of his life's work. He must write a serenade for the wife who has conferred this dazzling wonder upon an astonished cosmos. Even the serenade is not enough; it must be accompanied by a poem in which the importance of the event for him and for music shall be made clear to everyone.[4] He dropped into verse at the slightest provocation; never could he repress his inborn impulse to pour himself out copiously upon any and every subject under the sun. Our old English poets used to write "Poems Upon Several Occasions." Wagner wrote poems upon every occasion. He could not even build himself a house without conferring a portentously symbolical title on it, and engraving a couple of lines of pompous doggerel over the lintel.

That this interpretation of his conduct and his psychology is not a strained one will be evident when the story of his dealings with Peter Cornelius is put beside the Liszt episode I have lately narrated. In the mad Paris and Vienna time of the early sixties he had become deeply attached to Cornelius; Liszt, the generous, kind Liszt, had

[3] Glasenapp, vi, 139.
[4] See the poem *Siegfried-Idyl*, in the *G.S.*, xii, 372.

apparently passed out of his life. He writes to Cornelius from Paris on January 9, 1862, in the strain that is now so familiar to us: he is tired of his wanderings and his buffetings; he must settle in some cozy nest if he is to go on with his work. But he needs a sympathetic friend near him. "Heavens! how glad I should be to have the poor 'Doll' [*Puppe*][5] with me as well! In these matters my moral sense is incurably naïve. I would see nothing at all in it if the maiden were also to come to me, and were to be to me just what, with her pretty little nature, she can be. But how to find the 'terminus socialis' for this? Ach Himmel! It amuses me and it grieves me!" However, if Seraphine could not come, Cornelius was to come alone; and they two were henceforth to be inseparable.[6]

When Wagner is settled at Starnberg under the protection of King Ludwig, Cornelius is again to come live with him and be his love. They are to live in the same house— Cornelius can bring his piano, and there is a box of cigars awaiting him—yet each is to maintain his own independence. "Exactly two years ago I ardently expected you in Biebrich: for a long time I had no news of you, and then I suddenly learned from a third person that you had let Tausig take you off to Geneva. You have never fully known how deeply this put me out of humour. Nothing of that sort must happen this time; but we must be open with each other, like men." He knew that Cornelius was working at his opera *Le Cid*, and doubted whether he could do this as well in Wagner's proximity as apart from him.[7] Wagner will have it that Cornelius can work at *Le Cid* and he at *Die Meistersinger* in their common home; he is willing and anxious, indeed, to advise his friend about his opera. "Either you accept my invitation immediately,"

[5] Seraphine Mauro. See above, pp. 133–4.
[6] Cornelius: *Ausgewählte Briefe*, i, 640 ff.
[7] The gentle and honorable Cornelius—whom it obviously pains to have to say a word in disparagement of Wagner—knew that his only chance of developing his artistic nature along its own lines was to avoid coming too much under the influence of the much stronger personality of the older man; he should, he says, "hatch only Wagnerian eggs."

he concludes, "and settle yourself for your whole life in the same house with me, or—you disdain me, and expressly abjure all desire to unite yourself with me. In the latter case I abjure you also root and branch [*ganz und vollständig*], and never admit you again in any way into my life. . . . From this you can guess one thing,—how sorely I need *peace*. And this makes it necessary for me to know definitely where I stand: my present connection with you tortures me horribly. It must either become complete, or be utterly severed!" [8]

Cornelius hesitated, as well he might, to give himself up body and soul to this devouring flame of a man; he knew Wagner, and knew what sacrifices a friendship of *his* kind meant for the friend. Wagner was very angry with him for not accepting the invitation at once. He came to Vienna to liquidate his debts with the 15,000 gulden placed at his disposal for that purpose by the King, and generally to put his affairs in order. Asked by Seraphine Mauro the object of his visit to the city, he curtly replied: "To quarrel with my friends." Heinrich Porges and his brother had called upon Wagner, but Cornelius did not go. "There were such scenes," he writes to his brother Carl on June 15, "and tears of rage and despair over my conduct: no answer to his letter—my *Cid* had 'miscarried,'—he could put everything in order, go through it all cordially and calmly with me—at Starnberg, etc., etc., pianoforte ready—a box full of cigars—Peter as man and artist, etc., etc." He saw Standhartner, who advised him, in case he did not mean to accept Wagner's invitation, not to go near him just then, as it would probably lead to a complete rupture. So Cornelius writes to Wagner between one and three in the morning, telling him that he could not settle in Munich now with anyone but his brother, but that when he has finished *Le Cid* he will be willing to live there in merry companionship with Carl and Wagner. No answer was vouchsafed to this letter. "Standhartner speaks

[8] Letter of May 31, 1864, in Peter Cornelius's *Ausgewählte Briefe*, i, 767.

to him again in my interest. Heinrich Porges writes him—
'Reconciliation with Peter: otherwise—Egoist!' Thereupon
he writes at once to Porges: 'do not visit me to-day,' and
to Standhartner: 'do not come till to-morrow,' etc., etc.,
etc., and when they come next day he is gone! So that one
can truly say that he has treated his best friends in Vienna
like so many shoe-blacks. . . . He came in May 1861. This
is the upshot of these three years!" [9]

Cornelius writes at the same time to Reinhold Köhler
on June 24: "A row with Wagner. . . . I was simply to
be a Kurvenal. Wagner does not understand that though
I have many qualifications for that,—even to a dog-like
fidelity,—I have unfortunately just a little too much *independence* of character and talent to be this cipher behind
his unit." And on the same day to his sister Susanne: "Unfortunately we have separated, perhaps for ever. He wrote
me: Come to Starnberg—come for ever—or I will have
absolutely nothing more to do with you.—I could not
consent to that,—for the *Cid* has haunted me all the time
since February, and is now coming to life,—*and if I were
with Wagner I should not write a note*. . . . I should be
no more than a piece of spiritual furniture for him, as it
were, without influence on his deeper life. I send you his
letter. Tell me if any man ought to put such an 'Or' to a
friend: either everything, skin and hair,—or nothing at
all. I have never forced myself on Wagner. I rejoiced
sincerely in his friendship, and was truly devoted to him
in word and deed. But to share his life,—that entices me
not." [1]

Wagner apparently got over his petulance, and still had
hopes of inducing Cornelius to come to Munich, where he
could have a post either at the Conservatoire or under the
King. "But if he is really well disposed towards me,"
Cornelius writes to his brother on September 4, 1864,
"let him interest himself actively in the *Cid*. Everything
depends on that now. But salvation will not come to me

[9] *Ausgewählte Briefe*, i, 770, 771.
[1] Ibid, i, 774.

the way; Wagner never for a moment thinks seriously of anyone but himself." [2]

That is the conclusion to which the study of Wagner's life and letters so often lead us.

XVI · *General Characteristics*

In *Mein Leben* he half humorously admits another little failing of his—a passion for reading his own works to his friends.[3] With the production of each new work he feels that here is something that the whole world of thinking men must be hungry to see and hear; so he either has it printed at his own expense—little as he can afford such a luxury—or he calls his friends and acquaintances together and remorselessly reads it to them. In 1851 he read the whole of *Opera and Drama* to his Zurich circle on twelve consecutive evenings! We have seen him reading the *Mastersinger* poem in Vienna.[4] As soon as he has finished the poem of the *Ring* (1853) he cannot rest until

[2] *Ausgewählte Briefe*, i, 784. At a later time Cornelius did yield to Wagner's solicitations and take up his abode for a time in Munich.

[3] All testimonies agree as to the extraordinary expressiveness and dramatic vivacity of his reading—as indeed of his conversation also. See Cornelius: *Ausgewählte Briefe*, i, 623; Weissheimer: *Erlebnisse*, pp. 89, 90; and Liszt's letter to the Princess Wittgenstein, in *Briefe*, iv, 145. His tumultuous conversation used to give King Ludwig a headache.

[4] He writes thus to Cornelius from Paris, at the end of January 1862: "Listen! On Wednesday evening, the 5th February, I am to read the *Meistersinger* at Schott's house, in Mainz. You have no idea what it is, what it means for me, and what it will be to my friends! You must be there that evening! Get Standhartner at once to give you, on my account, the necessary money for the journey [from Vienna]. In Mainz I will reimburse you this, and whatever may be necessary for the return journey." See the letter in Cornelius's *Augewählte Briefe*, i, 643.
The completion of the *Mastersinger* poem seems to have put him in an exceptional fever. Two or three weeks after this letter to Cornelius he writes to Von Bülow from Biebrich: "It was a peculiar grief to me not to be able to read my new poem to someone: I almost came to Berlin [to Von Bülow] to do so." On March 9 the Grand Duke and others had to go through it.

he has "tried it on the dog"; so he "decides," he tells us, to pay the Willes a visit and read it to the company there. He arrives in the evening, begins at once on *Das Rheingold*, continues with *Die Walküre* till after midnight, polishes off *Siegfried* the next morning, and finishes with *Götterdämmerung* at night. The ladies "ventured no comment"; he attributes their silence to their having been deeply moved. But the effort had worked him up to such a pitch of excitement that he could not sleep, and the next morning he left in a hurry, to the mystification of the company. A few weeks afterward he reads the tetralogy on four successive evenings to a number of people in the Hôtel Baur. He publishes the poem privately in February 1853—twenty-three years before the performance of the whole work—so anxious is this artist who despises our modern world, and shrinks from appealing to it, to keep in the very center of that world's eye.

This mania for reading to his friends increased as he grew older; in the last years at Bayreuth he would read not only his own works, but anything he was interested in at the moment. But at Wahnfried he had a carefully selected audience of worshippers, who indulged him to the full in his little vanities and weaknesses. The *Erinnerungen* of Hans von Wolzogen and the sixth volume of Glasenapp are full of his *obiter dicta* on these occasions. Like the bulk of the philosophizing in his prose works, they do not strike us as showing any particular insight into the problems he is handling; but he dearly loved the sound of his own voice. In 1879 he makes everyone listen night after night to a reading of the thirty-year old *Opera and Drama*; while to his little daughters he reads, on successive evenings, "A Pilgrimage to Beethoven" and "The End of a Musician in Paris."[5] Only the most devoted admirers could have stood this kind of thing night after night; did any one of them dare to rebel, he no doubt met with the same fate as the audacious and irreverent Kellermann.[6]

His nature was all extremes; he either loved intensely

[5] Glasenapp, vi, 161.
[6] See above, pp. 160–1.

or hated furiously, was either delirious with happiness or in the darkest depths of woe. His checkered life, so full of dazzling fortunes and incredible misfortunes, of dramatic changes from intoxicating hope to blind despair, had bred in him the conviction that he was born under a peculiarly powerful and maleficent star. "Each man has his dæmon," he said to Edouard Schuré one day in 1865, when he was still crushed by the news of the tragic death of his great singer Schnorr von Carolsfeld, "and mine is a frightful monster. When he is hovering about me a catastrophe is in the air. The only time I have been on the sea I was very nearly shipwrecked; and if I were to go to America, I am certain that the Atlantic would greet me with a cyclone." [7] He himself was either all cyclone or all zephyr: intermediate weathers were impossible for him. In 1865 he spent the happiest days of his life rehearsing *Tristan* in Munich. "He would listen with closed eyes to the artists singing to Bülow's pianoforte accompaniment. If a difficult passage went particularly well, he would spring up, embrace or kiss the singer warmly, or out of pure joy stand on his head on the sofa, creep under the piano, jump up on to it, run into the garden and scramble joyously up a tree, or make caricatures, or recite, with improvised disfigurements, a poem that had been dedicated to him." [8]

Edouard Schuré also saw something of him in those *Tristan* days. To him too Wagner exhibited both poles of his temperament. "To look at him was to see turn by turn in the same visage the front face of Faust and the profile of Mephistopheles. . . . His manner was no less surprising than his physiognomy. It varied between absolute reserve, absolute coldness, and complete familiarity and *sansgêne.* . . . When he showed himself he broke out as a whole, like a torrent bursting its dikes. One stood dazzled before that exuberant and protean nature, ardent, personal, excessive in everything, yet marvellously equilibrated by the predominance of a devouring intellect. The frankness and extreme audacity with which he showed his

[7] Edouard Schuré: *Souvenirs sur Richard Wagner*, p. 76.
[8] Röckl, op. cit., p. 133.

nature, the qualities and defects of which were exhibited without concealment, acted on some people like a charm, while others were repelled by it. . . . His gaiety flowed over in a joyous foam of facetious fancies and extravagant pleasantries; but the least contradiction provoked him to incredible anger. Then he would leap like a tiger, roar like a stag. He paced the room like a caged lion, his voice became hoarse and the words came out like screams; his speech slashed about at random. He seemed at these times like some elemental force unchained, like a volcano in eruption. Everything in him was gigantic, excessive." [9]

Liszt describes him thus to the Princess Wittgenstein in 1853: "Wagner has sometimes in his voice a sort of shriek of a young eagle. When he saw me he wept, laughed and ranted for joy for at least a quarter of an hour. . . . A great and overwhelming nature, a sort of Vesuvius, which, when it is in eruption, scatters sheaves of fire and at the same time bunches of rose and elder. . . . It is his habit to look down on people from the heights, even on those who are eager to show themselves submissive to him. He decidedly has the style and the ways of a ruler, and he has no consideration for anyone, or at least only the most obvious. He makes a complete exception, however, in my case." [1]

Turn where we will, we find the same testimony. "He talked incredibly much and rapidly," says Hanslick. . . . "He talked continuously, and always of himself, of his works, his reforms, his plans. If he happened to mention the name of another composer, it was certain to be in a tone of disdain." [2] And again: "He was egoism personified, restlessly energetic for himself, unsympathetic towards and regardless of others." [3]

He apparently could not even accommodate himself to such small courtesies of life as a sympathetic interest in other men's music. We have seen how chilled Cornelius

[9] Schuré, op. cit., pp. 54, 57.
[1] Liszt: *Briefe*, iv, 140, 145.
[2] Hanslick: *Aus meinem Leben*, ii, 11.
[3] Ibid., p. 12.

was by his attitude toward *Le Cid*. Weissheimer tells us that Von Bülow once played a composition of his own to Wagner, and was much hurt by the older man's reception of it. He said to Weissheimer afterward: "It is really astonishing how little interest he takes in other people; I shall never play him anything of my own again." [4]

Weissheimer tells us of an experience of his own of the same kind. "Once when I began to play my opera to Bülow alone at his wish (without Wagner), the servant came immediately to say that we were to stop our music, as the Meister wanted to sleep! It was then eleven in the morning! Bülow banged the lid of the piano down, and sprang up in agitation with the words, "It is a high honour for me to live with the great Master,—but it is often beyond bearing." [5]

It would be interesting to know precisely how much sincerity there was in his eulogies of Liszt's music in the earlier days, and how much of them we should put down to diplomacy, or to the feeling that Liszt's symphonic poems were somehow helping to make the path of his own art easier. In his article *On Franz Liszt's Symphonic Poems* (1857) he mostly discusses the new problems of form and spirit which Liszt was trying to solve: he does not discuss the music of the symphonic poems in detail, though at one point he speaks of "the uncommon richness of the inventive power that confronts us in these great works." We generally get the impression that he would not have been so profuse in his admiration had this music been the work of some composer to whom he was not so deeply indebted in more ways than one. Liszt undoubtedly influenced him, but he was unwilling to admit it publicly. In 1859 we find him complaining to Von Bülow of an indiscretion on the part of his admirer Pohl. "There are many things that we willingly acknowledge among ourselves—for example, that since I became acquainted with Liszt's compositions I have become quite a different fellow as a harmonist from what I was before; but when friend

[4] Weissheimer: *Erlebnisse*, p. 128.
[5] Weissheimer: *Erlebnisse*, p. 392.

Pohl, *à la tête* of a discussion of the *Tristan* prelude, blabs this secret before the whole world, it is at least somewhat indiscreet, and I cannot suppose that he was authorised to commit such an indiscretion." [6]

In later life he seems more than once to have been frankly contemptuous of Liszt as a composer. Lilli Lehmann tells us that once she was singing Liszt's *Mignon* for Cosima at Bayreuth, when she saw Wagner enter and listen to the end. "Then, with his head thrown back, a bearing that gave him the appearance of great self-consciousness, he strode rather stiffly through the drawing-room with a bundle of music under his arm, and turned, before leaving, to Frau Cosima. 'Really, my dear,' he said, 'I did not know that your father had written such pretty songs. I thought he had rendered service only in fingering for piano playing. On the whole, the poem about the blooming lemon trees always reminds me of a funeral messenger.' Whereupon he imitated the gestures of a funeral attendant carrying lemons. Frau Cosima had to receive, with a laugh, what was not pleasant for either her or me to hear." [7]

So he goes through life, luxuriant, petulant, egoistic, improvident, in everything extreme, roaring, shrieking, weeping, laughing, never doubting himself, never doubting that whoever opposed him, or did not do all for him that he expected, was a monster of iniquity—*Wagner contra mundum*, he always right, the world always wrong. He ended his stormy course with hardly a single friend of the old type; followers he had in the last days, parasites he had in plenty, but no friends whose names rang through Europe as the old names had done. One by one he had used them all for his own purposes; one by one he had lost them by his unreasonableness and his egoism. Even where they maintained the semblance of friendship with

[6] *Richard Wagner Briefe an Hans von Bülow*, p. 125.
[7] Lilli Lehmann: *My Path Through Life*, pp. 211, 212. The great singer hints that his manners were often bad, but that one had to excuse him, as it was not easy to "educate" him at the age of sixty-two.

him, as Liszt did, the old bloom had vanished, the old fire had died out. Yet it is impossible not to be thrilled by this life, by the superb vitality that radiates from that little body at every stage of its career, by the dazzling light that emanates from him and gives a brief noontide glory to the smallest person who comes within its range. There was not one of his friends who did not sorrowfully recognize, at some time or other, how much there was of clay in this idol to which they all had made sacrifice after sacrifice. Turn by turn they left him or were driven away from him, hopelessly disillusioned. Yet none of them could escape the magnetic attraction of the man, even after he had wounded and disappointed them. Von Bülow, as we have seen, worked nobly for him and for Bayreuth after the cruel Munich experiences. Nietzsche, after pouring out his sparkling malice upon the man and the musician who had once been for him a very beacon light of civilization and culture, sings his praises in the end in a passage that is full of a strange lyricism and a disturbing pathos. "As I am speaking here of the recreations of my life, I feel I must express a word or two of gratitude for that which has refreshed me by far the most heartily and most profoundly. This, without the slightest doubt, was my relationship with Richard Wagner. All my other relationships with men I treat quite lightly; but I would not have the days I spent at Tribschen—those days of confidence, of cheerfulness, of sublime flashes, and of profound moments— blotted from my life at any price. I know not what Wagner may have been for others; but no cloud ever darkened *our* sky." And again: "I suppose I know better than anyone the prodigious feats of which Wagner was capable, the fifty worlds of strange ecstasies to which no one else had wings to soar; and as I am alive to-day and strong enough to turn even the most suspicious and most dangerous things to my own advantage, and thus to grow stronger, I declare Wagner to have been the greatest benefactor of my life. The bond which unites us is the fact that we have suffered greater agony, even at each other's

hands, than most men are able to bear nowadays, and this
will always keep our names associated in the minds of
men." "I have loved Wagner," he says in another place;
and in another he speaks of "the hallowed hour when
Richard Wagner gave up the ghost in Venice." [8]

There is something titanic in the man who can inspire
such hatred and such love, and such love to overpower the
hatred in the end. Into whatever man's life he came, he
rang through it forever after like a strain of great wild
music. With his passionate need for feeling himself always
in the right, it was hard for him to bow that proud and
obstinate head of his even when he must have felt, in his
inmost heart, that some at least of the blame of parting
lay with him. But when he did unbend, how graciously
and nobly human he could be! There is no finer letter in
the whole of his correspondence than the one he wrote to
Liszt to beg his old friend and benefactor to end their
long estrangement by coming to him at Bayreuth in the
hour of his triumph, for the laying of the foundation stone
of the new theater on his fifty-ninth birthday.

MY GREAT AND DEAR FRIEND,—Cosima maintains
that you would not come even if I were to invite you.
We should have to endure that, as we have had to
endure so many things! But I cannot forbear to invite
you. And what is it I cry to you when I say 'Come'?
You came into my life as the greatest man whom I
could ever address as an intimate friend; you gradually
went apart from me, perhaps because I had become
less close to you than you were to me. In place of you
there came to me your deepest new-born being, and
completed my longing to know you very close to me.
So you live in full beauty before me and in me, and
we are one beyond the grave itself. You were the first
to ennoble me by his love; to a second, higher life
am I now wedded in *her*, and can accomplish what I

[8] *Ecce Homo* (Eng. trans.), pp. 41, 44, 97, 122.

should never have been able to accomplish alone. Thus you could become everything to me, while I could remain so little to you: how immeasurably greater is my gain!

If now I say to you "Come," I thereby say to you "Come to yourself!" For it is yourself that you will find. Blessings and love to you, whatever decision you may come to!—Your old friend,

Richard.[9]

The old egoistic note is there—it is he of course who has borne most and suffered most and is prepared to be most forgiving—but his heart must have been more than usually full when he wrote this. It must have cost his proud soul many an inward struggle to bring himself to take this first steps toward a *rapprochement*.

But the stupendous power and the inexhaustible vitality of the man are shown in nothing more clearly than in the sacrifices everyone made for him and the tyrannies they endured from him. Even those who rebelled against him were nonetheless conscious of a unique quality in him that made it inevitable that he should rule and others obey. "He exercised," says his enemy Hanslick, "an incomprehensible magic in order to make friends, and to retain them; friends who sacrificed themselves for him, and, three

[9] Liszt's reply of May 20, 1872, runs thus:

DEAR AND NOBLE FRIEND,—I am too deeply moved by your letter to be able to thank you in words. But from the depths of my heart I hope that every shadow of a circumstance that could hold me fettered may disappear, and that soon we may see each other again. Then shall you see in perfect clearness how inseparable is my soul from *you both*, and how intimately I live again in that "second" and higher life of yours in which you are able to accomplish what you could never have accomplished alone. Herein is heaven's pardon for me: God's blessing on you both, and all my love.

These are the first letters that appear in the correspondence between the two since July 7, 1861. *Briefwechsel*, ii, 307–8. The two letters are given in a slightly different form in Liszt's *Briefe*, vi, 350.

times offended, came three times back to him again. The more ingratitude they received from Wagner, the more zealously they thought it their duty to work for him. The hypnotic power that he everywhere exerted, not merely by his music but by his personality, overbearing all opposition and bending everyone to his will, is enough to stamp him as one of the most remarkable of phenomena, a marvel of energy and endowment." [1]

A remark of Draeseke's to Weissheimer gives us another hint of the same imperious fascination. "At present it is not exactly agreeable to have relations with him. Later, however, in another thirty or forty years, we [who knew him] shall be envied by all the world, for a phenomenon like him is something so gigantic that after his death it will become ever greater and greater, particularly as then the great image of the man will no longer be disfigured by any unpleasant traits" [*durch nichts Widerhaariges*].[2]

He was indeed, in the mixture of elements he contained, like nothing else that has been seen on earth. His life itself is a romance. In constant danger of shipwreck as he was, it seems to us now as if some ironic but kindly Fate were deliberately putting him to every kind of trial, but with the certain promise of haven at the end. The most wonderful thing in all his career, to me, is not his rescue by King Ludwig, not even the creation of Bayreuth, but his ceasing work upon the second act of *Siegfried* in 1857 and not resuming it till 1869. Here was a gigantic drama upon which he had been engaged since 1848; no theater in Europe, he knew, was fit to produce it—for that he would have to realize his dream of a theater of his own. After incredible vicissitudes he had completed two of the great sections of the work and half of the third. The writing of the remainder, and the production of it, one would have thought, would have been sufficient for the further life energies of any man. To anyone else, the thought of

---

[1] *Aus meinem Leben,* ii, 12.
[2] Weissheimer: *Erlebnisse,* p. 391.

dying with such a work unfinished would have been an intolerable, maddening agony. It would have been to him, had the possibility of such a happening ever seriously occurred to him. But he knew it was impossible—impossible that he, Richard Wagner, ill and poor and homeless and disappointed as he was, should die before his time, before his whole work was done. He gambled superbly with life, and he won. In those twelve hazardous years he wrote two of the world's masterpieces in music. He played for great stakes in city after city, losing ruinously time after time, but in the end winning beyond his wildest dreams. He saw *Tristan* and *Die Meistersinger* produced; he dictated his memoirs. And then he turns calmly again to the great work that had been so long put aside, takes it up as if only a day, instead of twelve years, had gone by since he locked it in his drawer, thinks himself back in a moment into that world from which he had been so long banished, and, still without haste, adds stone upon stone till, five years later, the whole mighty building is complete. What a man! one exclaims in amazement. What belief in himself, in his strength, in his destiny, in his ability to wait! what a sublime confidence that Time would wait for him! And then, after that, the toil of the creation of Bayreuth, and the bringing to birth of the masterpiece, twenty-eight years after the vision of it had first dawned upon the eager young spirit that had just completed *Lohengrin!* Was there ever anything like it outside fiction?

He lived, indeed, to see himself victor everywhere, in possession of everything for which he had struggled his whole feverish life through. He completed, and saw upon the stage, every one of the great works he had planned. He found the one woman in the world who was fitted to share his throne with him when alive and to govern his kingdom after his death with something of his own overbearing, inconsiderate strength. He achieved the miracle of building in a tiny Bavarian town a theater to which, for more than a generation after his death, musicians

would still flock from all the ends of the earth. After all
its perils and its buffetings, the great ship at last sailed into
haven with every timber sound, and with what a score of
incomparable merchandise within!

· 2 ·

The Artist in Theory

❧

1 · *His Early Italianism*

For so great a revolutionary, Wagner was curiously long
in coming to consciousness of himself. The record of his
youth and early manhood is one of constant fluctuation
between one ideal or influence and another. The most remarkable feature of him in these days, indeed, is his
mental malleability. In his later years he is the center of a
solar system of his own; everything else in his orbit is a
mere planet that must revolve around him or be cast out.
In his younger days, on the contrary, he is extraordinarily
sensitive to the changing currents of men and circumstances. One of the earliest writers to influence him was
E. T. A. Hoffmann, under whose sway he fell apparently
as early as 1827. It was about the same time that he first
heard, at a Gewandhaus concert, some of Beethoven's
music. During the early thirties he was deeply absorbed in
Beethoven, especially in the Ninth Symphony—a work
that, he tells us, was at that time regarded in Leipzig as
the raving of a semi-madman. Wagner's knowledge of it
was at first derived solely from copying the score; it was
without having heard a performance of the work that he
made in 1830 the two-hands pianoforte arrangement of it
which he vainly tried to induce Schott to publish. His own

Overture in D minor (1831), his *King Enzio* Overture, and his Symphony in C major (1832) were, as he admits, all inspired by Beethoven, the first of them being more particularly influenced by the *Coriolan* Overture. He heard the Ninth Symphony for the first time at a Gewandhaus concert in the winter of 1831–2; the performance, under Pohlenz, seems to have been a very unintelligent one, and it left Wagner in considerable doubt as to the value of the work. "There arose in me," he says, "the mortifying doubt whether I had really understood this strange piece of music[1] or not. For a long time I gave up racking my brains about it, and unaffectedly turned my attention to a clearer and less disturbing sort of music." [2]

Weber's *Freischütz* had also powerfully affected the boy's imagination; no doubt Weber struck him even then as a musician peculiarly German. In his own *Die Feen* (1833), he tells us, he tried to write "in German style." [3] Nevertheless, in spite of all these influences, he turned for a while against German music, which he criticizes with some frankness in an article entitled *"Die deutsche Oper,"* [4] published anonymously in the *Zeitung für die elegante Welt* in June 1834. The Germans have no German opera, he says, for the same reason that they have no national drama. "We are too intellectual and much too learned to be able to create warm human figures." Mozart could do this in the Italian melodic style; but with their contempt for that style the modern Germans have got further from the path that Mozart opened out for dramatic music. "Weber did not understand how to handle Song; Spohr is hardly any better"; yet it is through Song that a man expresses himself musically. Here the Italians have the advantage over the Germans. It is true that the Italians have abused the organ of late—"yet I shall never forget the impression that a Bellini opera lately made on

[1] He seems to be referring more particularly to the fourth movement.
[2] *Mein Leben*, p. 73.
[3] *Mein Leben*, p. 94.
[4] *G.S.*, xii, 1 *ff.*

me, after I had become heartily sick of the eternally alle-
gorising orchestral bustle, and a simple and noble Song
made its appearance again." Weber was too purely lyrical
and Spohr is too elegiac for the drama. Weber's best work
is consequently the romantic *Der Freischütz;* as for *Euryanthe*, "what paltry refinements of declamation, what a
finikin use of this instrument or that for bringing out the
expression of some word or other!" His style is not broad
enough; it dissipates itself in mincing details. His *ensembles* are almost without life. And as the audience do not
understand a note of it, they console themselves by calling
it amazingly *learned*, and respecting it accordingly. "O this
fatal learnedness," he cries, "this source of all the evils
that afflict us Germans!" In Bach's time music was regarded only from the learned side. The forms were then
limited, but the composers full of learning. Now the forms
are freer, but the composers have less learning, though
they make a pretense of it. The public also wants to appear
learned, affects to despise the simple, and is ashamed to
admit that it enjoys a lively French opera. We must not
be hypocritical, but must admit there is a good deal that
is good in both French and Italian opera; we must throw
over a lot of our affected science, and become natural men.
No real German opera composer has appeared for some
time, because no one has known how to "gain the voice
of the people"—no one has grasped life in its real truth
and warmth. We must find a form suited to the needs of
our own days. "We must seize upon the epoch, and
honestly try to perfect its new forms; and he will be the
master who writes neither Italian nor French—nor even
German."

The youthful essayist repeats a good deal of this, with
additions, in an article entitled *"Pasticcio,"* published in
the *Neue Zeitschrift für Musik* in November of the same
year, under the pseudonym of "Canto Spianato." [5] He is
greatly concerned at the deplorable fact that there are
hardly a couple of dozen well-trained singers in Germany.

[5] *G.S.,* xii, 5 *ff.*

"Nowadays one hardly ever hears a really beautiful and technically perfect *trillo*; very rarely flawless mordents; very seldom a rounded *coloratura*, a genuine, unaffected, soul-moving *portamento*, a perfect equalisation of the registers, and absolute maintenance of the intonation through all the various nuances of crescendo and diminuendo. Most singers, as soon as they attempt the noble art of *portamento*, get out of tune; and the public, accustomed to imperfect execution, overlooks the defects of the singer if only he is a capable actor and knows the routine of the stage."

Nor do our German composers know how to write for the voice; they are like bunglers who presume to orchestrate without having studied the peculiarities of the clarinet, say, as distinct from those of the pianoforte. "Most of our modern German vocal composers appear to regard the voice as merely a part of the instrumental mass, and misapprehend the true nature of Song. Our worthy opera-composers," in fact, "must take lessons in the good Italian cantabile style, taking care to steer clear of its modern excrescences, and, with their superior artistic capacity, give us something good in a good style. Then will vocal art bloom anew; then some day will a man come who in this good style shall re-establish on the stage the broken unity of Poetry and Song." He argues with portentous seriousness for ornate as well as simple Song; and ends with a claim that poetry is the only basis of opera—poetry, of which words and tones are merely expression. "The majority of our operas are merely a string of musical numbers without any psychological connection; our singers have been degraded into musical-boxes, set to a certain number of tunes, brought on to the stage, and started by a wave of the conductor's baton." Once more he lays it down that "he will be the master who writes neither Italian nor French—nor even German," and concludes thus: "But would you inspire, purify, and train yourselves by models, would you create living shapes in music, then combine, for example, Gluck's masterly declamation and dramatic power with Mozart's varied art of melody, *ensemble* and orchestration, and you will produce dramatic works that will satisfy the strictest criticism." [6]

This enthusiasm for the Italian style was largely due to the overwhelming impression made on Wagner by the great singer and actress Wilhelmine Schröder-Devrient, whom he heard as Romeo in Bellini's *Montecchi e Capuleti* in March 1834.[7] Her performance, however, magical as it must have been, would not have affected him so deeply had he not already been brought by other influences to a turning in the road. What these influences were he has himself told us in *Mein Leben*. Heinse's *Ardinghello* and Laube's *Young Europe* had inflamed the imagination of most of the young men of the day. Wagner was caught up by and carried along in a current of generous enthusiasm for a supposedly new spirit in art and literature; the older men were mercilessly ridiculed as pedants, and a newer and more sprightly art was to hustle the ponderous old one off the stage. Wagner's boyish life had been, in spite of an occasional wildness, one of almost morbid seriousness, culminating in what he calls "pathetic mysticism." The truth seems to have been that he was moving about in intellectual worlds too subtle for his spirit then to realize; he was mysteriously drawn to the greatest things in Beethoven and Weber, but when brought into actual contact with them, he had to admit that they spoke a language he could hardly understand. The magnetic personality of Schröder-Devrient dissipated the clouds that had formed around him. He could hardly have been so much his own dupe as his confessions would lead us to believe. He knew that the performance of Weber's *Euryanthe* he had recently heard was as superlatively bad as the performance of Bellini's opera was superlatively good;

[6] "*Pasticcio*," in G.S., xii, 5 ff.

[7] Mr. Dannreuther, in his article on Wagner in *Grove's Dictionary of Music* (v, 391), thinks that the young enthusiast for Beethoven perceived the weakness of Bellini's music clearly enough, yet the impression Mme Devrient made upon him was powerful and artistic. The first statement hardly squares with all the facts as we now know them.

and he would have been a much worse reasoner than we know him to have been, had he not been able to see that from these facts no valid conclusion could be drawn as to the worth of the two works. We may reasonably assume that his volatile nature was ripe for another change of front—there were plenty more of a similar kind even in his mature life—and that these outer experiences only marked the moment of the turning. He as good as admits this, indeed, in *Mein Leben*. He was disposed, he says, to take as lightly as possible the problem[8] that had arisen before him, and to show his determination to get rid of all prejudice by writing the article on *Euryanthe* in which he "simply jeered" at that work. "Just as I had passed in my student-time through my 'Flegeljahr,' I now boldly entered upon a similar development in my artistic taste." [9]

ii · *Coming to Himself*

That the articles praising the Italians at the expense of the Germans were the products of more than the mere impression of Schröder-Devrient's singing and acting—that they came from the depths of a real change in his intellectual and emotional nature—is shown by the length of time he remained at the same standpoint. The text of *Das Liebesverbot* was written in a mood of fiery youthful protest against what he held to be the cramping puritanism of the moralists. He deliberately transforms Shakespeare's *Measure for Measure*. "*Young Europe* and *Ardinghello*, helped by the strange antipathy I had conceived towards classical operatic music, gave me the keynote for my conception, which was especially directed against puritanical hypocrisy, and consequently led to the bold glorification of unfettered sensualism [*freien Sinnlichkeit*]. I took care to understand the serious Shakespearean subject only in this sense; I saw only the gloomy strait-laced viceroy, himself burning with love for the beautiful novice,

[8] I.e., as to why the poorer opera had impressed him more than the better one.
[9] *Mein Leben*, p. 102.

who, while she implores him to pardon her brother condemned to death for illicit love, kindles a ruinous fire in
the rigid Puritan's breast by the lovely warmth of her own
human emotion. The fact that these powerful motives are
so richly developed by Shakespeare only in order that in
the end they may be all the more seriously weighed in the
scales of justice, did not concern me in the least; all I had
in mind was to expose the sinfulness of hypocrisy and the
unnaturalness of harsh moral judgments." [1] He adds that
he was probably influenced by Auber's *Masaniello* and the
Sicilian Vespers.

The composition of *Das Liebesverbot* carries us from
1834 to the spring of 1836, and still the Southern fever
has not abated. In 1837 he carries the same enthusiasm
about him in Königsberg and Riga; we can imagine that
the more serious side of him had some difficulty in developing in such an environment as a fourth-rate operatic
and theatrical troupe. While in Magdeburg he writes a
short article on "Dramatic Song," in which he returns to
the thesis of three years before, though with more wisdom.
"Why," he asks, "cannot we Germans see that we are not
the possessors of everything; why cannot we openly and
freely admit that the Italian is superior to the German in
Song, and the Frenchman superior to him in the light
and animated treatment of operatic music? Can he not
oppose to these his deeper science, his more thorough culture, and above all the happy faculty that makes it possible
for him easily to make the advantages of the Italians and
the French his own, whereas they will never be able to
acquire ours? The Italians are singers by nature. The less
richly-endowed German can hope to emulate the Italian
only by hard study." Wagner rightly points out that no
artist can hope to achieve full expression of himself without a technique that has become second nature to him.
It was the acquirement by Mozart of this technique in his
childhood that gave his mature music its incomparable
ease and finish, while there was always a certain awkward-

[1] *Mein Leben*, p. 104.

ness about Weber, owing to his having begun late and learned his technique during the years when he was actually practicing his art. Without perfect vocal technique, the highest kind of dramatic expression is impossible. The great Schröder-Devrient, the finest operatic artist in Germany, was at one time within an ace of giving up her career as a singer, so great was the strain on her voice through a faulty production; but she studied hard on the right Italian lines, with the result that she can now sing the most trying parts without the slightest fatigue.[2] All this is sensible enough—so sensible, indeed, that Wagner could repeat it thirty years later in his "Report upon a proposed German School of Music for Munich." But that the nimble and relatively superficial Italian music still exercised something of its old fascination upon him is shown by another article of the same year on Bellini. Here, while admitting that a good deal of Italian music is poor stuff, and that the forms and tricks of the Bellinian opera are things only too easy to imitate, he yet lauds Bellini's melody at the expense of that of the Germans, and his simplicity at the expense of their clumsy erudition. "The German connoisseur of music," he says, "listens to one of Bellini's operas with the spectacles off his tired-out eyes," giving himself wholly up for once to "delight in lovely Song";[3] he evidently feels "a deep and ardent longing for a full deep breath, to win ease of being at one stroke, to get rid of all the stew of prejudice and pedantry that has so long compelled him to be a German connoisseur of music—to become instead a man at last, glad, free, and endowed with every glorious organ for perceiving beauty of every kind, no matter in what form it reveals itself." He has been enchanted by "the limpid melody, the simple, noble, lovely Song of Bellini. It is surely no sin to confess this and to believe in it; perhaps even it would not be a sin if before we went to sleep we were to pray

[2] See the article "*Der dramatische Gesang*," in G.S., xii, 15.
[3] The German "*Gesang*" is perhaps best translated here and elsewhere by this general capitalized term.

Heaven that some day German composers might achieve such melodies and such an art of handling song. Song, Song, and yet again Song, ye Germans!"

We see again his temporary lack of sympathy with the richer German style in a passage like the following, which reads like one of the less intelligent criticisms of his own later music:

"When we consider the boundless disorder, the medley of forms, periods and modulations of so many of the new German opera composers, by which we are prevented from enjoying many an isolated piece of beauty, we often might wish to see this ravelled skein put in order by means of that stable Italian form.[4] As a matter of fact, the instantaneous clear apprehension of a whole dramatic passion is made much easier when, along with all its connected feelings and emotions, it is cast into one lucid intelligent melody at a single stroke, than when it is muddled up with a hundred little commentaries, with this and that harmonic nuance, this and that instrumental interpolation, till in the end it is subtilised out of existence." [5]

It was his "zeal and fervour for modern Italian and French opera," in fact, that procured for him the conductorship at Riga, where the director, Holtei, was all for the lighter and more frivolous music.[6] At Riga, Wagner met his old Leipzig mentor, Heinrich Dorn, who was, he says, surprised to see his former pupil, "the eccentric Beethoven worshipper, transformed into a partisan of Bellini

[4] I.e., the conventional forms of Italian opera.

[5] See the article "Bellini, ein Wort zu seiner Zeit," in G.S., xii, 19. It must be remembered that this article, which was published anonymously, was intended to stimulate the interest of the Riga public in Bellini's Norma, which opera Wagner had selected for his benefit in December 1837. It is possible, therefore, that the impecunious young musician may have said a trifle more than he really thought. It is significant that Wagner omitted all these articles—"Die deutsche Oper," "Pasticcio," "Der dramatische Gesang," and "Bellini"—from the collected edition of his works.

[6] Mein Leben, p. 174.

and Adam." [7] The reaction, however, was coming fast. At Riga he seems to have passed through one of those spiritual crises that are not uncommon with artists of his many sided temperament. The loneliness of Riga, he says, gave him an anxious feeling of homelessness, which developed into a passionate longing to escape from the turbid whirl of theatrical life. "The levity with which in Magdeburg I had both let my musical taste degenerate and had allowed myself to take pleasure in the most frivolous theatrical society, gradually faded away under the influence of this longing." [8] A bass aria that he interpolated into Winter's *Schweizerfamilie* was "of a devotional character," and "bore witness to the great transformation that was taking place in my musical development." [9] In the winter of 1838 he derived much benefit from the study of Méhul's *Joseph in Egypt* for the theater. "Its noble and simple style, along with the moving effect of the music, contributed not a little to the favourable turn in my taste, which had been sadly debauched by my theatrical work." [1] At the same time he grew weary of the Bohemianism that had attracted him so strongly at Magdeburg, and consequently he got more and more out of touch with the actors and the management.

His weariness of it all culminated in a secret resolve to be quit of this kind of life as soon as possible. The deliverance was to be effected by his new opera, *Rienzi*.[2] He deliberately planned the opera on a scale so large that he would necessarily have to seek a bigger stage than that of Riga for its production. Everything conspired at the time to deepen his sense of the seriousness of things, and to make him loathe himself for having so long worshipped

[7] *Mein Leben*, p. 175.
[8] *Mein Leben*, p. 175.
[9] *Mein Leben*, p. 175.
[1] *Mein Leben*, p. 179.
[2] He had put aside his comic opera *Die glückliche Bärenfamilie*, as the performing of this *"Musik à la Adam"* would only have still further tightened his connection with the frivolous theatrical world about him.

false gods both in art and in life. Matrimonial troubles crowded thick and fast upon him, and he lost his favorite sister, Rosalie, by death. In March 1839 he was dismissed from his post at the Riga theater. Penniless as he was, he welcomed the discharge as the first step toward his redemption. To Paris he would go, and in Paris make his fortune: of that he had no doubt.

III · *The Awakening in Paris*

The miseries of his two years and a half in Paris are known to every reader of his life. Penury, deceptions, degradations, however, could not break him either intellectually or morally. A temperament so elastic as his could never be crushed, and least of all when it was young. He himself has told us of the amazement his associates expressed at the toughness and resilience of his spirit. But the fire he passed through in those dreadful days purified him as an artist. It was not alone the failure to get *Rienzi* accepted at the Paris Opéra which caused him to turn away in disgust from the hollow world of make-believe around him; visions were coming to him of shining deeds to be done, of untried possibilities in music. As usual with him, an external event brought all his faculties and desires swiftly into the one focus. In the winter of 1839 he heard a number of rehearsals and a performance of the Ninth Symphony at the Conservatoire, under Habeneck. The interpretation, he says, was so perfect that "in a stroke the picture I had had of the wonderful work in the days of my youthful enthusiasm, and that had been effaced by the murderous performance of it given by the Leipzig Orchestra under the worthy Pohlenz, now rose up again before me in such clearness that it seemed as if I could grasp it with my hands. Where formerly I had seen nothing but mystic constellations and soundless magical shapes, there was now poured out, as from innumerable springs, a stream of inexhaustible and heart-compelling melody. The whole period of the degradation of my taste, which really began with my confusion as to the expression in Beethoven's later works, and had been so aggravated by my numbing association with the dreadful theatre, now fell away from me as into an abyss of shame and remorse. If this inner change had been preparing in me for some years—more particularly as a consequence of my painful experiences— it was the inexpressible effect of the Ninth Symphony, performed in a way I had hitherto had no notion of, that gave real life to my new-won old spirit; and so I compare this—for me—important event with the similarly decisive impression made on me, when I was a boy of sixteen, by the Fidelio of Schröder-Devrient." [3]

The "Autobiographical Sketch" he wrote for Laube's *Zeitung für die elegante Welt* in 1842, after his settling in Dresden, ends with these words: "As regards Paris itself I was now without prospects there for some years: so I left it in the spring of 1842. For the first time I saw the Rhine: with great tears in his eyes the poor artist swore eternal fidelity to his German fatherland." It was indeed the prodigal's return: the service that Paris did him was to make him a better German, and so a better artist. Seen from a distance, Paris had once glittered before his dazzled eyes as a symbol of liberalism and freedom. Seen at too close quarters, Germany had laid itself bare to him in all its littlenesses, its stuffy provinciality. Now he saw them both from another angle. Paris was about him in all the cold brutality it can show to the stranger, the helpless, the penniless: its heart seemed to the eager young musician as hard as the stones of its streets. And he saw his native country as all exiles see theirs, with its asperities toned down, its little parochialisms veiled from view, and a certain kindly haze of idealism over all. It is with German affairs that he occupies himself as far as he can in the articles he writes at this time to keep the domestic pot boiling. The essay "On German Music" (1840) is very touching in its wistful little vision of tiny, cozy German towns, each with its circle of humble musicians roughly but lovingly wooing their art in their own simple, honest way. The lonely and homesick German artist has his quiet

[3] *Mein Leben*, pp. 210, 211.

revenge upon Paris in the delightfully humorous and satiri-
cal article upon the ludicrous French perversion of *Der
Freischütz* at the Opéra.[4] Beethoven is much in his mind:
he begins the attempt to fathom the secret of Beethoven's
power, to grasp the profoundly logical workings of his
music, and to take his own bearings with regard to sundry
aesthetic questions, such as "painting" in music, the reading of poetical ideas into purely instrumental works, the
relations between vocal and instrumental music, and so
on. His views upon Beethoven were far ahead of those
of his contemporaries, to whom, indeed, they must have
been in large part unintelligible. He was beginning to
realize dimly that out of the Beethovenian melody he
could himself beget a new art work. In "A Pilgrimage to
Beethoven" he puts his own views of opera into the mouth
of his predecessor. He has apparently already conceived
the idea that instrumental music had come to the end of
its resources with Beethoven, that music could in the future renew its vitality only by being "fertilised by poetry,"
and that the ideal music drama will be continuous in
tissue. "Were I to make an opera after my own heart," he
makes Beethoven say, "people would run away from it:
for it would have no arias, duets, trios, or any of the other
stuff with which operas are patched up to-day: and what I
would put in the place of these no singer would sing and
no audience would listen to. They all know nothing but
glittering lies, brilliant nonsense and sugared tedium.
Anyone who should write a real music drama would be
taken for a fool." And the old composer proceeds to outline the theory of the relation between words and music
which is made so familiar to us in Wagner's later writings.
"The instruments represent the primal organs of Creation
and Nature: what they express can never be clearly defined
and settled, for they reproduce the primal feelings themselves as they emerged from the chaos of the first creation,
when probably there was not one human being to take them
up into his heart. It is quite otherwise with the genius of
the human voice: this represents man's heart and its defi-

[4] "*Le Freischütz*," in *G.S.*, i, 220 *ff*.

nite [*abgeschlossen*] individual emotion. Its character is therefore restricted, but definite and clear. Now bring these two elements together, unite them! Set against the wild-wandering, illimitable primal feeling, represented by the instruments, the clear definite emotion of the human heart, represented by the voice. The incoming of this second element will smooth and soothe the conflict of the primal feelings, will turn their flood into a definite, united course: while the human heart itself, taking up into itself those primal feelings, will be infinitely strengthened and expanded, and capable of feeling clearly its earlier indefinite presage of the Highest now transformed into god-like consciousness." [5]

IV · *Aesthetic Principles*

It has often been pointed out that the subjects of all Wagner's dramas were conceived by him before his fortieth year. It is equally true that virtually the whole of the aesthetic theories of his later life were immanent in him from the days of his Parisian sojourn, and needed only to be brought into clearer outline by the thought and the practice of the forties and fifties. In the essay on Beethoven (1870) he insists that it is the human character of the voice, rather than the mere sentiment the voice is used to express, that gives the choral ending of the Ninth Symphony its tremendous significance. "Thus," he says, "with even what we have just called the ordaining will that led him to this melody" [i.e., the great melody of the final movement] "we see the master steadily remaining in music,—the Idea of the world:[6] for in truth it is not the meaning of the Word that engages us at this entry of the human voice, but the character of the voice itself. Nor is it the thought expressed in Schiller's verses that henceforth occupies us, but the intimate timbre of the choral

[5] "*Eine Pilgerfahrt zu Beethoven*," G.S., i, 90 ff.
[6] The reader may be reminded that Wagner has been expounding the Schopenhauerian theory of music as the Idea of the world.

song, in which we feel ourselves invited to join, and so take part as a kind of congregation in an ideal divine service, as was the case at the entry of the chorale in the 'Passions' of Bach. It is quite evident, especially with regard to the main melody, that Schiller's words have been tacked on arbitrarily [*nothdürftig*] and with little skill: for this melody had first of all unfolded itself in all its breadth before us as a thing in itself, given to the instruments alone, and there had filled us with a nameless feeling of joy in a paradise regained." [7]

The same idea is seen in embryo in "A Pilgrimage to Beethoven." "If men are to sing," says Beethoven, "they must have words. Yet who is capable of expressing in words the poetry that should form the basis of such a union of all the elements? The poem must of necessity be something inferior [*zurückstehen*], for words are too weak an organ for such a task.—You will soon meet with a new composition of mine, which will remind you of what I have just been descanting upon. It is a symphony with choruses. I ask you to observe how difficult it was for me to get over the inadequacy of the poetical art that I had called in to my aid. I have fully resolved to make use of our Schiller's beautiful hymn 'To Joy'; it is in any case a noble and uplifting poem, even if far from giving voice to what, in sooth, in this connection, no verses in the world could say." [8]

Here we light upon one of the fundamental principles of the Wagnerian aesthetic. Wagner did not set words to music: the words were merely the projection of an already conceived musical emotion into the sphere of speech.[9] There is in most musicians a certain amount of correspondence and interplay between the poetic and musical factors. With some composers the musical thought, having begun and completed itself along its own lines and according to its own laws, turns half appealingly, half con-

[7] "Beethoven," in *G.S.*, ix, 101.

[8] *G.S.*, i, 111.

[9] This explains why he was so unapt at setting anyone's poetry but his own.

descendingly, to words for a title or an elucidation, as was often the case with Schumann. With others, as with Bach and Hugo Wolf and Strauss, the word, written or implied, is the generator of the musical idea. It would be the very midsummer madness of aesthetics to attempt to decide which is the more purely "musical" of these two types of mind. Neither of them is "the" musical mind, any more than Shakespeare's or Milton's or Browning's or Blake's or Pope's or Swinburne's is "the" poetical mind. It is only the most superficial of psychologists and aestheticians who can regard any human faculty as wholly cut off from the rest. Our perceptions of sight, of taste, of touch, of hearing, are inextricably interblended, as is shown by our constantly expressing one set of sensations in terms of another, as when we speak of the color of music, the height, or depth, or thickness, or clarity, or muddiness of musical tone. In every poet there is something of the painter and the musician: in every musician, something of the poet and painter: in every painter, something of the musician and poet.[1] The character of the man's work will depend upon the strength or weakness of the tinge that is given to his own special art by the relative strength or weakness of the infusion of one or more of the other arts. In composers like Bach, Wagner, Berlioz, Schubert, Wolf, and Strauss the eye is constantly transmitting very definite impressions to the brain, with the result that their music readily leans to realistic suggestion: on a composer like Brahms the actualities of the visible, mobile world make comparatively little impression.[2] No one of these types is per se any better than the rest, or has any more right that his fellows to arrogate to himself the title of "pure" musician. We must just accept them all as branches of the one great tree.

It is no paradox to say that though Wagner was irresistibly impelled to express himself in the form of opera, he

[1] On this point see Albert Schweitzer's *J. S. Bach* (Eng. trans.), chap. xx.

[2] And of course the quality of the mixture of these factors may vary in different works of the same composer.

was by nature an instrumental composer of the line of Bach and Beethoven. It is the orchestra that always bears the main burden of expression in his later works. His ideal was a stream of endless melody in the orchestra, to the moods of which the words give a definiteness unattainable by music alone. And just as he did not "set words to music" in the ordinary way, so he did not set poetic ideas to music in the ordinary way. No man was ever more prompt to interpret great musical works in terms of poetry or life, as anyone may see by reading his elucidations of the Beethoven symphonies or the great C sharp minor quartet. But it is important to remember, if we are not to misunderstand him utterly, that he never supposed that the music was developed consciously out of any such poetic scheme as his or our fantasy may read into it. The music grew out of the spirit of music, and only rouses a poetic vision in us because it is the generalized expression of many particular visions of the kind. This conception of music was rooted in him from his earliest days of maturity, as we may see from the article "A Happy Evening," which he wrote in Paris in 1841. The narrator of the story is discussing with a friend—evidently intended for Wagner himself—a concert at which they have just heard performances of Mozart's Symphony in E flat and Beethoven's in A. The question arises as to what it is that Beethoven has expressed. The friend, who is designated R., objects energetically to an arbitrary romance being foisted upon the symphony:

"It is unfortunate that so many people give themselves useless trouble to confuse musical speech with poetical speech, and to make one of them supplement or replace the other where, in their limited view, this is incomplete. It remains true once for all that music begins where speech leaves off. Nothing is more intolerable than the preposterous pictures and stories that people imagine to be at the basis of those instrumental works. What quality of mind and feeling is displayed when the hearer of a Beethoven symphony can only keep his interest in it alive by imagining that the musical flood is the reproduction of the plot of some romance? These people in consequence often grumble at the great master when some unexpected stroke disturbs the even tenour of the little tale they have foisted on the work: they reproach the composer with unclearness and disconnectedness, and lament his lack of coherency. Oh the ninnies!"

R. is afterward careful to explain that he has no objection to each hearer associating the music, as he hears it, with any moods or episodes he likes out of his own experience. All he objects to is the audience having the terms of the poetic association dictated to them by the musical journalists. "I should like to tear the hair from their silly heads when they stuff this stupid nonsense into honest people, and so rob them of all the ingenuousness with which they would have otherwise have given themselves up to hearing Beethoven's symphony. Instead of abandoning themselves to their natural feelings, the poor deluded people of full heart but feeble head think themselves obliged to follow the course of some village wedding, a thing of which they probably know nothing at first hand, and in place of which they would certainly have been much more likely to imagine something quite different, something from the circle of their own experience. . . . I hold that no one stereotyped interpretation is admissible. Definitely as the purely musical edifice stands complete and rounded in the artistic proportions of a Beethoven symphony, perfect and indivisible as it appears to the higher sense, just so is it impossible to reduce the effects of the work on the human heart to one authoritative symbol. This is more or less the case with the creations of the other arts: how diversely will one and the same picture, one and the same drama, affect diverse individuals, and even the same individual at different times! And yet how much more definitely and positively the painter or the poet must draw his figures than the instrumental composer, who is not bound, like them, to model his form by the appearances of the everyday world, but who has at his disposal and immeasurable realm in a super-terrestrial kingdom, and to whose hand is given the most spiritual of substances—tone! But it is degrading to this high office of the musician to force him to make him fit his inspiration to the appearances of the everyday world; and still more would the instrumental composer deny his mission, or expose his own weakness, who should try to carry the restricted proportions of merely worldly things into the realm of his own art." [3]

"In instrumental music," he said in later life, "I am a *Réactionnaire*, a conservative. I dislike everything that requires a verbal explanation beyond the actual sounds." [4] In the light of this declaration, and of the aesthetic doctrines he expounded in the article "On Franz Liszt's Symphonic Poems" and elsewhere, it is interesting to see him setting forth the same doctrine of music as early as 1840. In "A Happy Evening" R. lays it down that he rejects all tone painting, except when it is used in jest or to reproduce purely musical phenomena.[5] He further dissents from his friend's theory that whereas Mozart's symphonies came from nothing but a purely inward musical source, Beethoven may have "first of all conceived and worked out the plan of a symphony according to a certain philosophical idea, before he left it to his imagination to invent the musical themes." The friend adduces the *Eroica* Symphony in support of this contention. "You know that it was at first intended that this symphony should bear the title 'Bonaparte.' Can you deny, then, that Beethoven was inspired to this gigantic work, and the plan of it decided, by an idea outside the realm of music?"

R. sweeps his friend off his feet with the vehemence of his reply. The *Eroica* Symphony, he contends, is not a translation into music of the petty details of Napoleon's first Italian campaign. Nowhere does the work suggest that the composer has had his eye on any special episode in the general's career. No realistic explanation of this kind

[3] *"Ein glücklicher Abend,"* in *G.S.,* i, 143, 144.
[4] See Mr. E. Dannreuther's article on Wagner in the new edition of *Grove's Dictionary of Music and Musicians,* v, 414.
[5] Like all musicians of that time, Wagner had no suspicion of the enormous amount of tone painting there is in Bach.

can be made to square with the Funeral March, the Scherzo with its hunting horns, or the Finale with its soft, emotional Andante. "Where is the bridge of Lodi, where the battle of Arcola, where the march to Leoben, where the victory under the Pyramids, where the 18th Brumaire? Are these not incidents which no composer of our day would have passed by had he been writing a biographical symphony on Bonaparte?" Then R. gives his own theory of the genesis of such a work as the *Eroica*. What stimulates the musician to composition in the first place is a purely musical mood: it may have come from either an inner or an outer experience, but it is wholly musical in essence and in its manner of expression. "But the grand passions and enduring emotions that dominate the current of our feelings and ideas for months or for half a year, it is these that urge the musician to those ampler, more comprehensive concepts to which we owe, among others, the origin of a *Sinfonia eroica*. These great moods, as deep suffering of soul or mighty exaltation, may derive from outer events, for we are human beings and our fate is ruled by external circumstances: but when they impel the musician to production these great moods have already turned to music within him, so that in the moment of creative inspiration it is no longer the outer events that guide and govern the composition, but the musicial emotion that this event has generated." We may imagine that the republican Beethoven's emotional nature had been fired by the career and character of Napoleon. "He was no general,—he was a musician: and in his own domain he saw the spirit in which he could accomplish the equivalent of what Bonaparte had accomplished on the plains of Italy." The product of this passionate yearning for self-realization was the *Eroica* Symphony, "and as he knew well to whom he owed the impulse to this gigantic work, he inscribed the name of Bonaparte on the title-page. Yet not a single feature of the development of the symphony can be said to have an immediate outer connection with the fate of the hero." [6]

[6] "*Ein glücklicher Abend*," in *G.S.*, i, 147, 148.

v · Essay on the Overture

Of even more importance than the article "A Happy Evening" in the story of Wagner's development is the essay "The Overture," which appeared in the *Gazette Musicale* in January 1841—that is to say, a couple of months after the completion of *Rienzi*, and nearly six months before the commencement of *The Flying Dutchman*. Here he anticipates some of the aesthetic he was afterward to expound so eloquently and so convincingly in the great article on Beethoven, and elsewhere. He begins with a survey of the early history of the overture. There had always been, apparently, a reluctance to plunging the spectator forthwith into the opera, just as in earlier times a prologue had always preceded the play. The prologue, however, had this at any rate to be said for it, that it summarized the action of the coming play, and in this and other ways prepared the spectator to listen more intelligently. The early overture, however, could not do this, for at that time the psychological powers of music were not sufficiently developed to permit of the summarizing in a few minutes of the actions and the motives of an opera. It became a conventional, not a characteristic, prelude. Later on, a regular "overture form" was elaborated, but even this was psychologically impotent. What connection has the overture to the *Messiah*, for example, with the oratorio itself? Would it not serve equally well as prelude to a hundred others of the old oratorios or operas? Practically the only method of musical development these composers had at their service was the fugal: it was impossible for them to work out an extended musical piece by means of ever widening circles of pure feeling.

Next came a tripartite form of overture—an opening and closing movement in quicker time, with an intermediate section in slower time and of softer character. This gave a certain amount of opportunity for the presentation of one or two of the main moods or episodes or characters of the opera: and in the "symphony" that introduces the

Seraglio, Mozart has given us a little masterpiece in this genre. But there was a certain helplessness in the division of the "symphony" into three sections, and in the predetermined nature of their contents: and in course of time there was evolved the operatic overture proper—a continuous musical piece, making a sort of dramatic play with the main motives of the opera. This was the form with which Gluck and Mozart worked such wonders. Gluck's masterpiece is the overture to *Iphigenia in Aulis:* Mozart's, those to *The Magic Flute, Figaro,* and *Titus.* According to Wagner, Mozart's merit was that he did not attempt to express in his overture all the details of the plot, but "fastened with his poet's eye on the leading idea of the drama, divested it of all its inessentials and material accidentiæ, and set it forth as a musically transfigured creation, a passion personified in tones, and presented it to the main idea as the justificatory counterpart of this, —a something through which the idea, and even the dramatic action itself, became intelligible to the spectator's feeling." At the same time the overture became a self-contained tone piece—this being true even of an overture like that to *Don Giovanni,* which runs without any formal close into the first scene of the opera. This form of overture became the property of Cherubini and Beethoven. The former remained mostly faithful to the transmitted type, which Beethoven also used in the E major overture to *Fidelio.* But Beethoven in time broke through the cramping limitations of this form. His "prodigious dramatic instinct," having never found the opera into which it could pour the whole of itself, turned for an outlet to instrumental music pure and simple—to the field in which he could "shape in his own way the drama of his desire out of pure tone-images," a drama "set free from the petty trimmings of the timorous playwright." The result of this effort was the great *Leonora* Overture, which, "far from giving us a musical introduction to the drama, really sets that drama before us more completely and more affectingly than the ensuing broken action does. This work is no longer an overture, but itself the mightiest of dramas." [7]

Weber, too, is commended for making his overtures dramatic "without losing and wasting himself in a painful depiction of insignificant accessories of the plot." Even when his rich fantasy led him to incorporate more subsidiary musical motives than the form transmitted to him could conveniently carry, he always managed to preserve the dramatic unity of his conception. He invented a new form, that of the "dramatic fantasia," of which the *Oberon* Overture is one of the finest examples. "Nevertheless," says Wagner—and here again we see his rooted antipathy to anything in the nature of excessive detail painting in music[8]—"it is not to be denied that the independence of purely musical production must suffer by subordination to a dramatic thought, if this thought is not seized in one broad trait consistent with the spirit of music,—for the composer who tries to depict the details of the action itself cannot develop his dramatic theme without breaking his musical work to fragments." The inevitable ending of this style of overture is the *potpourri*—a form of which Spontini's overture to the *Vestale* may be said to have been the beginning. The public liked this kind of thing because it dished up for them again the most effective snatches of melody from the operas.

The summing up is that the ideal form and ideal

[7] He expresses the same idea nearly thirty years later in his essay on Beethoven. "What is the dramatic action of the *Leonora* opera-text but an almost disagreeable watering down of the drama we have lived through in the overture,—as it were a tedious explanatory commentary by Gervinus on a scene by Shakespeare?" "Beethoven," in *G.S.*, ix, 105.

[8] This was the explanation of his dislike for much of Berlioz's music. See his remarks on Berlioz in the article "On Liszt's Symphonic Poems" (*G.S.*, v, 193, 194), and a similar passage in the conversation quoted by Mr. Dannreuther (*Grove's Dictionary*, v, 414): "The middle of Berlioz's touching *scène d'amour* in his *Romeo and Juliet* is meant by him to reproduce in musical phrases the lines about the lark and the nightingale in Shakespeare's balcony scene, but it does nothing of the sort—it is not intelligible as music."

achievement are those of the *Don Giovanni* and *Leonora No. 3* overtures. In the former no attempt is made to reproduce the course of the drama itself step by step: the drama is freshly conceived as the contest between two broad principles—the arrogance of Don Giovanni and the anger of a higher power—and "the invention, as well as the conduct," of these symbolic motives "belongs quite unmistakably to no other province than that of music." Beethoven's method in the *Leonora* Overture, on the other hand, is "to concentrate in all its noble unity the *one* sublime action which, in the drama itself, is weakened and impeded by the necessity of padding it out with trivial details,—to show this action in its ideal new motion, nourished only by its inner impulses." This "ideal action" is, of course, the loving self-sacrifice of Leonora. But by reason of its very greatness and its intense dramatic quality, the *Leonora* Overture ceases to be an *overture* in the proper sense of the word. It anticipates too fully the completed drama: if it is *not* understood by the hearer, because of his lack of knowledge of the opera, it conveys only a fragment of its real message to him: if it *is* wholly understood, it weakens his subsequent enjoyment of the drama itself.

Wagner therefore returns to the overture to *Don Giovanni* as the ideal, because here "the leading thought of the drama is worked out in a purely musical, not a dramatic, form." In this way the musician "most surely attains the general artistic aim of the overture, which is simply an ideal prologue, transporting us into that higher sphere in which to prepare our mind for the drama." The musical conception of the main idea of the drama can still be distinctly worked out and brought to a definite close; in fact "the overture should form a musical art-work complete in itself." No better model could be had than Gluck's overture to *Iphigenia in Aulis*. In a word, though the overture must not attempt to reproduce stage by stage all the episodes of the story, it can suggest in its own way the dramatic contest of two main principles by a contest between two symbolic musical ideas: only the working out of these musical ideas must follow from the nature of the themes themselves. It must be always borne in mind—and the frequency with which Wagner returns to this point shows the importance he attached to it— that "the working-out must always take its rise from the purely musical significance of the themes: never should it take account of the course of events in the drama itself, for this would at once destroy the sole effective character of a piece of music."

As I have already pointed out, this and one or two of the other articles of the Paris time are interesting because they show us the mature aesthetics of the sixties and seventies trying to find expression in the young Wagner of 1840. To most of the principles here laid down he remained faithful, as we shall see, to the end of his days. But it is interesting also to note that though theoretically he always remained constant to the guiding principles he here lays down for the overture, his practice by no means always conformed to them. His ideal overture, as we have just seen, was one of the type of that to *Don Giovanni* or that to *Iphigenia in Aulis*—i.e., one that either made no use at all of thematic material from the opera itself, or the minimum use of it, the dramatic conflict of the stage action being fought out ideally, as it were, in the overture, in the persons of two symbolic musical themes. "In this conception of the overture," he says, "the highest task would be to reproduce the characteristic idea of the drama by means pure and simple [*mit den eigentlichen Mitteln*] of self-subsistent [*selbstständigen*] music, and to conduct it to a conclusion which should correspond, by anticipation, with the solution of the problem in the scenic play."

It is difficult to square his practice in some of his own overtures with the theoretical principles he here lays down. Not one of his overtures corresponds with the form he so greatly admired in the overtures to *Don Giovanni* and *Iphigenia in Aulis*—a pre-presentation of the coming dramatic conflict in terms of a musical piece that made no drafts at all, or practically none, upon the thematic material of the opera itself. The brief Prelude to *Lohengrin* comes under no suspicion of being a mere *potpourri* of motives from the opera; but then it achieves its concision and its singular air of detachment from anything in the nature of mere storytelling in music by failing to do just what Mozart and Gluck are commended for doing—summing up the ensuing dramatic conflict by the opposition of two main musical moods and their final resolution. The *Lohengrin* Prelude tells us nothing of any dramatic contest—not even that which rages in the heart of Elsa. It shows us only Lohengrin, the representative of the Grail, coming to earth and leaving it again. There is no hint of the reason for his return to Monsalvat: there is no hint even that his stay on earth has been in any degree troubled by enemies or evil. Beautiful as it is, therefore, and eloquently as it sings of Lohengrin himself, the Prelude is not in the full sense of the word a real prelude to the drama. On the other hand, when Wagner *does* make his overture a genuine introduction to, and an instrumental summary of, the opera, he inevitably approaches the *potpourri*. It is true that his fine sense of form mostly saves him from attempting to reproduce in the overture *all* the dramatic or thematic motives of the opera. In *The Flying Dutchman* Overture, for example, there is no reference to Erik: so far as the overture itself is concerned, no such person might have ever come into the lives of Senta and the Dutchman. There is no hint of Daland, and no reference to the spinning scene—the latter a musical motive that, it is safe to say, none of the French or Italian writers of overtures, or perhaps even Weber himself, would have had the heart to set aside. On the whole, *The Flying Dutchman* Overture is concerned simply with the Dutchman, his curse and his grief, with Senta, and with the sea that forms the imaginative background to their drama:[9] and though of course the

[9] The only other element introduced is the song of the Norwegian sailors from the last act, which, however good in itself, is perhaps a superfluity in the overture—a slight concession to that passion for reproducing the details of the drama that Wagner

overture is entirely built up of thematic material derived from the opera, this is all so freshly and imaginatively treated, and made into so coherent and organic a piece of instrumental music, that, though the overture is by no means of the type of those to *Don Giovanni* and *Iphigenia in Aulis*, which Wagner praised as models, nothing could be further removed from the old-style *potpourri*. The overtures to *Tannhäuser* and *Die Meistersinger*, however, must frankly be called *potpourris*—though *potpourris* of genius. In the *Tannhäuser* Overture we are given not merely an instrumental symbol of the drama, but the drama itself compressed into a sort of *feuilleton*. The ground covered is so vast, and the expression so intense, that at the end of the overture we are inclined to ask ourselves whether it has not, like the great *Leonora* Overture, made a good deal of the ensuing drama almost superfluous, a mere padding out or watering down of the emotions and the spiritual oppositions set before us with such drastic power in the overture itself. One is inclined to say that an overture lasting nearly a quarter of an hour is not so much the door to a mansion as a cottage in itself. A work like the *Tannhäuser* Overture has its justification as a kind of symphonic poem for the concert room; it has little justification as a prelude to a drama in the theater.

In any case, a piece of prolonged storytelling of this kind is not what Wagner had in his mind as his ideal when he wrote the article "The Overture": it is not too much to say, indeed, that it is the very type of musical introduction he expressly wished to bar. It is true that he advises the composer who wishes to make his overture "reproduce the characteristic idea of the drama by means pure and simple of self-subsistent music, and to conduct it to a conclusion which shall correspond, by anticipation, with the solution of the problem in the scenic play," to give the introductory instrumental piece some thematic

---

reprobated in others. The true symbolic conflict of the governing desires and principles of the opera can and should be all suggested in the music of Senta and the Dutchman.

connection with the opera. But not, be it observed, by utilizing long stretches of this material, as is done in the *Tannhäuser* Overture. Wagner's advice to the composer is "to introduce into the characteristic motives of his overture certain melismic or rhythmic features that are of importance in the dramatic action itself—not features, however, strewn accidentally among the action, but such as play a decisively weighty part in it, characteristics that determine, as it were, the orientation of a human action on a specific *terrain*, and so give an individual stamp to the overture. These features must of course be purely musical in their nature, i.e., such motives from the world of tone as have a relation to human life. I would cite as excellent examples the trombone blasts of the Priests in *The Magic Flute*, the trumpet signal in the *Leonora*, and the call of the magic horn in *Oberon*. These musical motives from the opera, employed in advance in the overture, serve, when introduced there at the decisive moment, as veritable points of contact of the dramatic with the musical motion, and effect a happy individualisation of the tone-piece, which is intended to be a mood-defining introduction to a particular dramatic subject." [1] The ideal overture that Wagner had in his mind at this time was evidently something very different from the one he subsequently wrote for *Tannhäuser*: but the discrepancy between his theory and his practice is still more strikingly shown by a sentence that appears in the French version of the article but not in the German. In the French, the passage quoted above, commencing with the words "these features must of course be purely musical in their nature," was prefaced by the following: "But one should never forget that they [i.e., "the melismic or rhythmical features" from the opera which were to be interwoven into the tissue of the overture] should be entirely musical in their source, and not borrow their significance from the words that accompany them in the opera. The composer would in this case commit the error of sacrificing both himself and

[1] Loc. cit., i, 204, 205.

the independence of his art to the intervention of an alien art. These elements, I say, must be in their nature purely musical, and I would cite as examples," etc.

It is at once evident that this bars out whole passages such as the Pilgrims' Chorus, the Sirens' Chorus, and Tannhäuser's Hymn to Venus, and, in the *Mastersinger* Overture, such passages as Sachs's final address, the phrases in which the populace jeer at Beckmesser, etc. Strictly speaking, indeed, neither of these overtures can be made to square with Wagner's theoretical principles. The question of the overture was one of those on which he never attained to complete consistency. In *Tristan*, as in *Lohengrin*, he devotes himself simply to working out in a broad form one great emotional motive of the drama. The overtures to *Tannhäuser* and *Die Meistersinger*, and, in a lesser degree, that to *The Flying Dutchman*, are a mixture of the *potpourri* and the symphonic poem. The Prelude to *Parsifal* is again a sort of *potpourri*, though here, of course, there is no attempt at storytelling in detail, the Prelude setting before us, as Wagner himself said, the three motives of "Love, Faith and Hope," and showing, as it were, the emotional outcome of them. To *Das Rheingold* there is no overture, or even a Prelude in the formal sense of that word: the long-drawn chord of E flat is merely the oral counterpart of the visible sensation given the spectator by the Rhine. Similarly the preludial bars to *Die Walküre* only paint the storm in which Siegmund is flying from his enemies.

Even the greatest men and the boldest revolutionaries are fettered in their thinking by the age in which they live. Only in this way can we account for Wagner's failure to see that the true solution of the problem of the overture was to abolish the overture. It had never any real aesthetic justification. As he himself points out, it had its origin simply in the fact that at one stage of the development of opera the composer saw the necessity of keeping the audience occupied in some way for a few minutes before it would be safe to raise the curtain on the play. It is one more of the many illustrations that may be cited of what may be called the dead hand in art—the survival in a new art of some method of procedure that had its origin under quite other conditions. Pottery, for instance, continued for long to be decorated with lines that were merely imitations in clay—unnecessary imitations—of the designs and colors of the interlaced osiers out of which the primitive vessel was made. The symphony developed out of the custom of stringing certain dance movements into a suite: and in spite of the clearly recognized fact that there is no logical justification either in art or in life for casting the modern symphony into this arbitrary four-movement form, composers still weakly adhere to it. Wagner was fond of pointing out, again, how Beethoven's congenital inability to break away from the sonata form of his day led to a clash between this form and the purely dramatic, onward-urging impulse of the great *Leonora* Overture. It is little wonder, therefore, that Wagner was so far the slave of his epoch that it never occurred to him, and least of all in 1841, to question the necessity of having an overture at all. The freer thought of the present day has been able either to reduce the overture to a few bars of prelude, simply attuning the mind of the spectator to the coming scene, as in Debussy's *Pelléas et Mélisande*, or to dispense altogether with an instrumental introduction, as in *Salome* and *Elektra*.

vi · *Fermentation in Dresden*

After the Paris articles of 1841, Wagner wrote little or nothing upon the aesthetics of his art for some ten years. For a time, indeed, he wrote practically no prose of any kind. He left Paris for Dresden in April 1842. At the end of that year he wrote his "Autobiographical Sketch" for Laube's *Zeitung für die elegante Welt*. His pen was then silent until 1844, in which year we have the "Account of the Bringing Home of Weber's Remains from London to Dresden," and the "Speech at Weber's Grave." To 1846

belongs the program he wrote for the performance of Beethoven's choral symphony on Palm Sunday at Dresden.[2]
No doubt his duties at the Dresden Opera, which he seems
to have fulfilled with great thoroughness and conscienti-
ousness, left him little time for anything else but these
and the composition of *Tannhäuser* and *Lohengrin*. When
he at length took up the pen again, it was not to expound
a system of musical aesthetics, but to preach a social
evangel, and to come to the first grips with the new dramatic ideas that had been slowly maturing in him. In
May 1848 he submits to the Minister his "Project for the
Organisation of a German National Theatre for the Kingdom of Saxony." In September he sketches two operatic
poems, "Siegfried's Death" and "Friedrich Barbarossa,"
the former of which he works out in detail by November.
Early in January the religious drama *Jesus of Nazareth*
is sketched. In the summer of 1848 he writes the essay
"The *Wibelungen*."

During these years his discontent with the social and
political conditions of the times had been slowly rising.
Though it would be unfair to Wagner to attribute this
discontent solely to the miserable circumstances of his
own life, it is certain that his poverty, his debts, and his
disappointments had a good deal to do with making him
a rebel against the established order of things. Mr. H. S.
Chamberlain holds that Wagner was already a "revolutionist against the artistic world of the present" in Paris in
1840. It is quite possible, for Wagner was even poorer in
Paris at that time than he was a few years later in Dresden.
Gustav Levy agrees with Mr. Chamberlain, but even his
own sympathetic summary of the case unconsciously makes
it clear that Wagner's personal experiences and circumstances had something to do with making a revolutionary
of him. "Beginning of November [1847], Wagner returns
[from Berlin][3] in a state of discouragement. The inces-

[2] The "Report" that accompanies this program in the Prose
Works is an extract from the (at that time) unpublished *Mein
Leben*.

[3] He had gone there to produce *Rienzi*, and to try to arrange
for a performance of *Lohengrin*. *Rienzi* was a failure.

sant difficulties in the way of winning appreciation for his works, and his consequently ever-increasing financial embarrassments, as well as the persistent enmity of the press, the lack of support he received from Meyerbeer, and the refusal of Lüttichau[4] to take up his reform of the Opera, bring on an illness: he thinks of suicide. Everything in him presses powerfully towards the *spiritual* revolution, to the freeing of art from the fetters of un-German feeling and conventional, deeply-rooted ignorance" [*Unverstand*].[5]

VII · *Political and Artistic Ideals*

The years 1848 to 1852 were for Wagner a long spell of intellectual and spiritual indigestion: his too receptive brain was taking into itself more impressions of all kinds than it could assimilate. Art and life, opera and politics, called clamorously to him, and all at the same time, deafening and confusing him. With *Lohengrin* his second great creative epoch, which had commenced with *The Flying Dutchman*, had come to its perfect end. New ideas of music and drama were ripening in him, but as yet he had no clear conception of their drift. He had gradually become profoundly disgusted with the theater, yet saw no possible reformation of it except by way of a reformation of man and society as a whole. So he became a revolutionist—not for politics' sake, but for art's sake. To cooler heads than his own he seemed to be drifting toward destruction. Minna saw clearly enough that his views on politics were too idealistic to have any real bearing on the practicalities of the day; and other sympathizers no doubt regretted that the artist in him should be in danger of being ruined by the politician.[6]

[4] The Intendant of the Dresden Opera.
[5] Gustav Levy: *Richard Wagners Lebensgang in tabellarischer Darstellung*, p. 32.
[6] Liszt writes thus in June or July 1849, i.e. a month or six weeks after Wagner's flight from Dresden: "Forgive me if I suggest that you should manage so that you are not of necessity brought into enmity with things and men who bar your road to success and glory. A truce therefore to political commonplaces,

At first he thought it possible to reform the theater from the inside: and apparently nothing could surpass the zeal he showed in his work at the Dresden opera house, or the sincerity of his desire to raise the music of the town to the highest possible efficiency. In February 1846 he drafted a scheme for the improvement of the orchestra, that runs to nearly sixty pages of close print in the *Gesammelte Schriften*, and leaves not the smallest practical detail untouched.[7] Two years later he worked out his admirable scheme for the organization of a German National Theatre for the Kingdom of Saxony. Here again one is struck by the practical nature of his genius.[8] But once more his appeal fell on deaf ears.

His failure to interest the theater authorities in his schemes for the regeneration of the drama and music drove him deeper into politics. Only from a new humanity, a new relationship between man and the State, could come a clean and healthy and art-loving civilization. In June 1848 he made his famous *"Vaterlands-Verein"* speech, which created so many new enemies for him at the Court.[9] In February 1849 he wrote an article entitled "Man and Existing Society"[1] for Röckl's *Volksblätter*,

---

socialistic balderdash, and personal hatreds. On the other hand, good courage, strong patience, and plenty of fire, which will not be difficult for you with the volcanoes you have in your brain." *Briefwechsel zwischen Wagner und Liszt*, i, 24.

[7] *"Die Königliche Kapelle betreffend,"* in G.S., xii, 149 ff. No notice was taken of the Report by the authorities for a year; then they refused to act upon it.

[8] The essay—*"Entwurf zur Organisation eines Deutschen National-Theaters für das Königreich Sachsen,"* in G.S., ii, 233 ff. —must be read in full. "My plan," he says, "was not merely to rescue the theatre, but at the same time to conduct it, under the shelter and inspection of the State, to a noble significance and efficacy." His main thesis was that "the Theatre should have no other purpose than the ennoblement of taste and manners." See Wagner's own account of the affair in *Mein Leben*, pp. 444 ff.

[9] See *Mein Leben*, pp. 434 ff.

[1] G.S., xii, 238 ff.

and in April one on "The Revolution" for the same journal.[2] Each of these is a passionate cry of welcome to the new era that he thought was dawning. "In the year 1848 began the war of man's fight against existing society." For society as at present constituted "is an attack on man: the ordering of existing society is inimical to the destiny, the right of man. . . . Man's destiny is, through the ever higher perfecting of his mental, moral, and bodily faculties, to attain an ever higher, purer happiness. Man's right is, through the ever higher perfecting of his mental, moral and bodily faculties, to achieve the enjoyment of a constantly increasing, purer happiness." But this can only be done by the union of all, not by the unit. "Men therefore are not only entitled but bound to demand of society that it shall lead them to ever higher, purer happiness through the perfecting of their mental, moral and bodily faculties." The second of the essays chants a dithyramb to the coming revolution. Volcano rumblings are to be heard beneath the soil of all Europe; soon the great upheaval will come. "The old world is crumbling to ruin; a new world will be born from it." The artist burns with sympathy for the poor, the suffering, the oppressed, and looks forward to a new civilization, in which man will be free and have joy of his labor. It is impossible not to be moved to this day by the eloquence and passionate sincerity of his cry, and the purity of his hopes.

But the end was near—a very different end from the one anticipated by this ardent soul. All hope of success faded before the Prussian rifles, and on May 9 the disillusioned idealist was in flight.

It was long, however, before the hopes and dreams of 1848 and 1849 finally forsook him. From his Swiss and Parisian exile he sent forth two treatises—"Art and Revolution" (written in June 1849), and "The Art-Work of the Future" (written in October of the same year)—in which he voices once more his aspirations for a new humanity and a new art.

[2] G.S., xii, 243 *ff.*

VIII · "Art and Revolution"

In an interesting introduction that he wrote to "Art and Revolution" when reprinting the essay in his collective works in 1872, Wagner speaks of the influence of Feuerbach upon him at this time: in Feuerbach's conception of art he thought he recognized his own artistic ideal. What that ideal was is painted for us in full in the heated pages of "Art and Revolution."

His central point is the one to which he remained true his whole life long—that art should be the pure expression of a free community's joy in itself; it should be accessible to all, and placed beyond the necessity of maintaining itself by commercial means. He paints a fancy picture of "the free Greek"—a mythical being evolved by Wagner out of his own inner consciousness—and elaborates the theory that the community as a whole creates great art. "The tragedies of Æschylus and Sophocles were the work of Athens." "The public art of the Greeks, which reached its highest point in tragedy, was the expression of the deepest and noblest consciousness of the people: with *us* the deepest and noblest consciousness is the direct antithesis of this,—the denial of our public art." The Greek tragedy was witnessed by the whole populace: in our superior theaters only the well-to-do can watch the play. Among the Greeks the production of a tragedy was a religious festival: in the modern State art is only an amusement or a distraction for tired people in the evening. The Greek was educated to make an artistic whole of his body and his spirit; we are trained merely for industrial gain. "Whereas the Greek artist found his reward in his own enjoyment of the work of art, in its success, and in the public approval, the modern artist is maintained— and *paid*. Thus we attain the clear definition of the essential distinction between the two. Greek public art was really *Art*; with us it is artistic *handicraft*." He admits that the Greek freedom was the result of the State being founded on slavery; but today *all* are slaves together.

"Our god is gold, our religion the pursuit of wealth." With the Greeks, art lived in the public conscience: with us it lives only in the conscience of private individuals. "Greek art was therefore *conservative*, because it was a worthy and adequate expression of the public conscience: with us, true art is *revolutionary*, because it exists only in opposition to the community in general." "This is art," he cries, "as it now fills the whole civilised world. Its real essence is industry; its ethical aim the gaining of gold; its æsthetic pretext the entertainment of bored minds."

In "Art and Revolution" we get the first hint of that "united art-work" that was to occupy his mind so much during the succeeding year.[3] He holds that "with the Greeks the perfect work of art, the drama, was the sum and substance of all that could be expressed in the Greek nature; it was—in intimate connection with its history— the nation itself that stood facing itself in the art-work, that became conscious of itself, and, during a few hours, rapturously devoured, as it were, its own essence." With the later downfall of tragedy, "art became less and less the expression of the public conscience: the drama split up into its component parts,—rhetoric, sculpture, painting, opera, etc., forsook the ranks in which they had formerly moved together, and now went each its own way and pursued its own development, self-sufficing, indeed, but lonely and egoistic." The great "unified art-work" has been lost for us; only the dissevered arts exist now. In each of them wonders have been wrought; "but the one true art has never been born again, either in the Renaissance or since." And only "the great revolution of mankind" can restore to us this art work. "If the Greek art-work comprehended the spirit of a beautiful nation, the art-work of the future must comprehend the spirit of a

[3] In the "*Entwurf zur Organisation eines Deutschen National-Theaters für das Königreich Sachsen*" (G.S., ii, 248) he speaks of "demanding the fullest and most active interest of the whole nation in an artistic establishment that, conjointly with all the other arts, has for its object the ennobling of taste and manners." He does not develop the idea, however.

free humanity soaring above all barriers of race." The new art demands a new mankind, and, as a preliminary, a return to nature. Man has been destroyed by culture. The goal both of art and of the social impulse must be "the strong and beautiful man, to whom *revolution* shall give his *strength*, and *art* his *beauty*."

He looks forward to the time when man shall be free from care for the material things of life, with which the collective wisdom of the community will supply him; and "then will man's enfranchised energy manifest itself only in artistic impulse." Every man will become an artist, and the expression of the artistic emotion of the whole community will be the drama. But art will not be practiced for gain. The theater too must be freed from the greed of industrial speculation. The care of the theater will be the first concern of an emancipated and enlightened community; it must be managed by "the whole body of the artists themselves, who unite in the art-work and ensure the success of their common efforts by proper co-operation." Admission to the theater must be free, the community recompensing the dramatists and the performers.

The essay is written at a white heat throughout. His dreams are unrealizable in any world that we can think of at present: but he evidently believed in not only the possible but the speedy realization of them. In Dresden, in the days before the rising, he expounded them enthusiastically to everyone he met. And he clung to them long after his flight from Dresden. Though he thought nothing was now to be achieved by working for reform, and that only by revolution could a new heaven and a new earth be brought into being,[4] in the possibility of this new heaven and earth he continued to believe. To Sulzer, in Zurich, he "insisted in attaching to the artistic destiny of mankind an importance far above that of any concern of the State."[5] Even in 1851 he had not given up hope

---

[4] See the important letter of September 1850, in the Uhlig correspondence.

[5] *Mein Leben*, p. 546.

that the social revolution that would bring with it the artistic revolution was near at hand. "I assumed that there would soon come a huge revulsion with regard to the public and indeed our whole social life; for the new resulting state of affairs and its real needs I believed that the right material for a quite new and instantaneous relationship of art to the public lay in the work I had sketched so boldly." He saw that the political movement had been crippled, but hoped all the more from the social movement, especially in France. He counted on a great blow for freedom being struck in the French presidential election of 1852. "The condition of the other European States, in which every aspiration was suppressed with stupid brutality, justified one in thinking that this state of affairs also could not last very long anywhere, and everything seemed to be looking towards the great decision that was to be taken in the following year." Uhlig, as he says, argued against him: but nothing could shake Wagner's faith. "Whenever we had to complain of any baseness, I always pointed him to this hopeful and fateful year, my opinion being that we should calmly wait for the expected upheaval, so that when no one else should know what to do, we could make a start. I cannot measure how deeply this hope had taken root in me; I soon, however, was forced to recognise that the confident pride of my assumptions and affirmations was largely due to the greatly increased excitement of my nerves. The news of the *coup d'état* of the 2nd December in Paris seemed to me absolutely incredible: I was certain the world was coming to an end. When the news was confirmed, and it became clear that events no one had thought possible had happened and seemed likely to endure, I turned away from the investigation of this enigmatic world, as one turns from a mystery the fathoming of which no longer seems to be worth while." So deep was his disappointment at the triumph of reaction that for a little while his health was affected.[6]

[6] *Mein Leben*, pp. 566 ff.

IX · *"The Art-Work of the Future"*

It was while he was still panting in the mists of idealism
that he wrote "The Art-Work of the Future," in which
the aesthetic ideas that had been maturing in him during
the latter part of the Dresden period found their first
full expression.

The basis of his theory is again the belief that we shall
not have a real art until we have a new and free humanity.
"Man will never be what he can and should be, until
his life is a true mirror of nature, a conscious following of
the only real necessity, *the inner natural necessity*, and not
subjected to an *outer*, imaginary, and so not a necessary
but an arbitrary power." He is still vibrating with anger
against the politicians of the day, to whom he attributes
all the evils under the sun; and of course he idealizes that
mysterious abstraction "the Folk," to whom he sings a
rapturous paean.[7] It is the Folk alone that acts as Necessity
dictates—the Folk being defined as "the sum of all those
who feel a common need"; while opposed to the Folk are
all those "who feel no want," whose motive force is an
artificial and egoistic need, satisfaction for which they seek
in luxury—"which can only be generated and maintained
in opposition to and at the cost of the sacrifices of the
needy." These were not the views he held upon luxury in
later years, when he, one of the most luxurious-souled of
men, had the opportunity to satisfy his cravings for silk
dressing gowns and lace shirts and other vanities of this
world. His fulminations against luxury are simply the
eternal cry of the Have-nots against the Haves.

He is, as always, discontented with the life and the art
of his day, both of which seem to him fundamentally false
and artificial.

"The spirit, in its artistic striving for reunion with nature
in the art-work, must either look forward with hope to the

[7] See the passionate and almost hysterical passage commencing
"Not ye wise ones, therefore, are the inventors, but the Folk,
for Need drove the Folk to invention." *"Das Kunstwerk der
Zukunft,"* in G.S., iii, 53.

future, or mournfully practise resignation." He recognizes that we can find redemption only in the art work that is physically present to the senses (*nur im sinnlich gegenwärtigen Kunstwerke*), "thus only in a truly art-needing, *i.e.* art-conditioning Present that shall bring forth art from its own natural truth and beauty": that is to say, he has faith in the power of Necessity, for which this work of the Future is reserved. . . . "The great united art-work, that must embrace all the *genres* of art and in some degree undo [*verbrauchen*] each of them in order to use it as a means to an end, to annul it in order to attain the common aim of *all*, namely, the unconditioned, immediate representation of perfected human nature,—this great united art-work we cannot recognise as the arbitrary need of the individual, but only as the inevitable [*nothwendig denkbare*] associated work of the humanity of the future." [8]

He proceeds to elaborate his idea of this united art work, though the full exposition of it is to be found only in *Opera and Drama*. With his Teutonic passion for categorization, he divides man up into neat mental parcels. The intellect has for its organ speech; the organ of feeling is tone. Speech gives determination to the otherwise indeterminate vocal tone: it is "the condensed element of the voice, and the word is the consolidated measure of tone." The whole man is the man of intellect (speech), heart (tone), and body (gesture). Thus the three primeval intertwining sisters of art are Dance, Tone, and Poetry: and true art is a union of the three. Such an art expresses all the faculties of man, whereas the separate arts—the "art varieties," as he calls them—only issue from and express this or that faculty. Art must appeal to the eye. "Unless it communicates itself to the eye, all art remains unsatisfying, and thus itself unsatisfied, unfree. No matter how fully it may express itself to the ear, or merely to the combining and immediately compensating faculty of thought [*das kombinierende, mittelbar ersetzende Denkvermögen*], until it communicates itself intelligibly to the eye it remains only a thing that *wills*, and not yet fully

[8] G.S., iii, 60.

can. Art, however, must *can*—it is from *können* that art, in our language, has acquired the appropriate name of *Die Kunst*." [9]

Each of the dissevered arts longs for reunion with the others. "Dance longs to pass over into Tone, there to find herself again and know herself; Tone in turn receives the marrowy frame of its structure from the rhythm of Dance. . . . But Tone's most living flesh is the human voice; the Word again is as it were the bony, muscular rhythm of the human voice." Thus the emotion that overflowed from Dance into Tone finds definition and certainty in the Word, and so is able to reveal itself clearly. The union of these three is "the united lyric art-work," of which the perfected form is the drama. Both the music and the poetry of today are impotent. He looks forward to "the overwhelming blow of fate that shall make an end of all this unwieldy musical trash, to make room for the art-work of the future." Nor can poetry alone create the genuine art work, for no genuine art work is possible without an appeal to the eye. Poetry should be written to be acted, not read. "The whole impenetrable medley of stored-up literature is in truth—in spite of its million phrases—nothing but the toilsome stammering of speech-impotent thought that longs to pass over into natural immediacy,—a stammering that has been going on for centuries, in verse and prose, without achieving the living Word." Shakespeare was to the art work of the future no more than Thespis was to the perfected Greek drama. "The deed of the unique Shakespeare, which made a universal man, a very god of him, is yet only the deed of the solitary Beethoven, that revealed to him the language of the artistic manhood of the future. Only where these two Prometheus,—Shakespeare and Beethoven—shall reach out

[9] Had he been a trifle less Teutonic, less given to the national failing of imagining that a new truth has been established when all that has happened is that a new word has been manufactured or a mystic meaning perceived in an old one, he might have reflected that in other languages there is no etymological connection between art and the capacity for "canning."

hands to one another; where the marble creations of Phidias shall become living, moving flesh and blood; where Nature, instead of being represented on a narrow canvas on the chamber walls of the egoist, shall unfold herself luxuriantly on the ample stage of the future, swept by the warm breath of life,—only then, in the fellowship of his fellow artists, will the poet find redemption."

It is evident throughout that his theory is the product of his own aesthetic bias. *He* can express himself only in terms of poetry and music on the stage; it is therefore illegitimate for any other artist to adopt any other medium of expression. Poetry without music, music without poetry, cannot satisfy *him;* therefore no one else has any right to be satisfied with either of these arts separately. The truth is that he was utterly insensitive to the peculiar qualities in each of the separate arts which constitute its special charm for those who practice it exclusively. When he was in Milan in 1859 he suddenly realized, he tells us, that he was "no good as a judge of pictures, because the subject, when once it had made a clear and sympathetic appeal to me, at once and completely decided me." [1] The confession is quite superfluous. It is writ large over all his prose works that he had nothing of the painter's delight in painting, or any real understanding of its aesthetic effect. He seems to have been equally blind or deaf to the peculiar appeal of the other arts. If it were not so, he would hardly have laid it down, in all seriousness, that "literature poetry," as the "mere organ of the intellect," should be dissolved, self-abrogated, into the "unified art-work of the future," or that architecture decays when it passes from the service of the State and religion into the service of the "egoistic individual," or that sculpture too has become a merely "egoistic" art, only to be "redeemed" by being taken up into the "united art-work," [2] or that painting too must seek a similar "redemption."

[1] *Mein Leben,* pp. 691, 692.
[2] He plainly knew nothing of the sculpture of the Middle Ages, and regarded all modern sculpture as an imitation of the antique.

His notions that the landscape painter will find his impulses satisfied in the painting of scenery or a background for the living man of drama, and that the gestures of the mime will amply compensate us for the cessation of sculpture, are indeed not to be taken seriously; they are possible only to a man without the least understanding of the plastic arts. It is of course quite untrue that in such a union of the arts as he suggests "the highest faculty of each is unfolded to the fullest." Even in the Wagnerian opera none of the contributing arts receives anything like its full unfolding except music. The truth is that Wagner had still not rid his artistic ideas of their political encumbrances. He was poor, and unable to realize himself in the world as it was then. He naturally supposed there must be something fundamentally wrong with a world of that kind, and he looked forward to a speedy dissolution of it, and the rising of a new civilization from its ashes. He saw the rich buying pictures and sculptures and building houses for themselves, and the ordinary people reading poetry or prose, instead of them all flocking to the opera. People had a reprehensible passion for being what he called "units," each of them enjoying his own art in his own way. "True" art, therefore, would be possible only in a society in which the unit had lost consciousness of himself in the community. The communal art, the art enjoyed by great masses of people in the same place and at the same time, is the drama. The "units" who could not quite stifle their liking for painting and sculpture must therefore be satisfied with so much of these as could be given them in the theater. It was a very logical and symmetrical piece of pleading: the only defect in it was that it left just one thing out of account—human nature.

His political speculations have the triple disadvantage that they are rarely true in themselves, they are too obviously the product merely of the circumstances of Wagner's own time and place, and they have no practical bearing upon art. The angry idealist overshoots his mark when he tells us that our modern States are the most unnatural associations of men, inasmuch as they arose solely out of a "mere external caprice, *i.e.* dynastic family interests," and that "they yoke together once for all a certain number of men for an aim that either never correspond to a need they had in common, or, owing to the changes wrought by time, is certainly no longer common to them now." Even if it were true, it would be without any practical significance either for politics or art—for politics, because there is no one art that can be said to possess the imagination of a complex modern State, no one "need" for the satisfaction of which it is possible to induce all the citizens to labor: and for art, because art's business is to display to us the endless beauty and interest of things, not to argue us into the adoption of this or that view of this infinite, incomprehensible world. Too much of Wagner's political theorizing is the mere outcome of affairs as they happened to be in Germany at the latter end of the first half of the nineteenth century. He idealized the "Folk" because that unfixable abstraction was the natural antithesis of the rich governing class whom he held in abhorrence. It is right that the artist should have his dreams of life as well as of art, and if he chooses to find his ideal in an abstraction, no one can say him nay. But when he proceeds to endow that abstraction with all the impossible virtues under the sun, when he tells us that "the artist of the future" will be, not the poet, the actor, the musician, or the plastician, but the "Folk"—"to whom alone we owe all Art itself"—we can only decline to keep company with him until he shall be able to use words with some meaning in them. There is, in fact, a sort of nonsense prose as there is a nonsense verse. Wagner's dithyrambs upon the Folk—and upon many another topic —are simply the prose counterpart of Lear and Carroll.

x · *Opera and Drama*

Wagner was the most many sided of musicians, as a glance at the titles of his prose works will show. He benefited greatly by his versatility: no one can doubt that his music is all the richer for the stimuli his nature received from so many quarters. But if he gained something by it, it is probable that the world lost as much. There are few of us who would not give three fourths of the prose works for another opera from his pen; and he would have had time to write half a dozen if he had abstained from all this prose. But the prose was a necessity to him; it was a needed purgation of the intellect, without which the emotion could not function fully and freely. The most striking illustration of this is *Opera and Drama*. Wagner had already poured out his ideas upon man and art at great length in "Art and Revolution" and "The Art-Work of the Future." His mind was now brooding upon the great dramatic subject that was to occupy the bulk of his thinking for the next twenty years or more of his life. It was only for the realization of this dream that he now clung to existence. Yet the daemon within him drove him to postpone the composition of this poem until he had produced yet another huge theoretical treatise. The reasons for this were twofold. In the first place he had a despairing sense of the futility of bringing so new and vast a work into being until he had educated the artistic public of that day to comprehend his novel aims and style. In the second place, he felt an imperative need of coming to an understanding with himself. He probably saw the whole plan and technique of *Siegfried's Death*[3] more or less vaguely—too vaguely for him to be willing to trust himself all at once on that huge uncharted sea. It would clarify his own ideas, as well as prepare the public, if he were to draw out the

---

[3] This was the first form of the drama that ultimately became the *Ring*. It virtually corresponded with the present *The Twilight of the Gods*. He afterward saw the necessity of setting visibly before the audience a good deal that was only implied or narrated in *Siegfried's Death*. Accordingly a prefatory drama was written and called *Young Siegfried*. The same process was twice repeated, *Die Walküre* and *Das Rheingold* being added in turn. *Young Siegfried* was then entitled *Siegfried*, and *Siegfried's Death* became *The Twilight of the Gods*.

ground plan, as it were, of the music drama of the future. This he accordingly did in *Opera and Drama*. "My literary works," he wrote to Röckl, "were testimonies to my want of freedom as an artist; it was dire compulsion alone that wrung them from me." [4]

Opera and Drama was written in the winter of 1850–1. As it is the most thorough and the most comprehensive statement that Wagner has given us of his theory of drama and music, it will be as well to summarize its arguments and conclusions for the reader.

I. Until the present time, men have indeed felt that the opera was a monument of the corruption of artistic taste, but criticism has not fully fathomed the matter: and it therefore becomes the task of the creative artist to practice criticism, in order at once to "annihilate error and uplift criticism." The writer of an article on modern opera in Brockhaus's Lexicon[5] has pointed out the defects of this form of art, showing its artificialities and conventions; but when he comes to the practical problem "How is all this to be remedied?" he can only regret that Mendelssohn's too early death should have "prevented the solution of the riddle." But this is still proceeding on the wrong track. Had Mendelssohn any musical gift that Mozart, for example, did not possess? Could anything, from the standpoint of music, be more perfect than each individual number of *Don Giovanni*? Plainly the critic cannot wish for better music than this. It is evident, then, that what he wants in opera is the power and force of *drama*. But he is blind enough still to expect this from the *musician*; that is, wanting a house built for him, he applies, not to the architect, but to the upholsterer. And by the very failure of the critic's effort to solve the problem in this way, there is driven home the conclusion that *this way* the problem is really insoluble. Yet the true solution, so far from

[4] Letter of September 12, 1852, in *Briefe an Röckl*, p. 10.
[5] See Wagner's further account of this article in *Mein Leben*, p. 545.

being difficult of attainment, simply stares one in the face; and the formula for it is:

> The error in the art-genre of Opera consists in the fact that *a Means of Expression (Music) has been made the object, while the Object of Expression (the Drama) has been made a means.*

The truth of this formula can be attested by an appeal to the history of the opera. It arose, not from the folk plays of the Middle Ages, in which there were the rudiments of a natural co-operation of music and drama, but at the luxurious courts of Italy, where the aristocrats engaged singers to entertain them with arias, that is, with "folk-tunes stripped of their *naïveté* and natural truth," embroidered on a story whose only *raison d'être* was the occasional advent of these arias.[6] Music, in fact, was the all-in-all of opera, as is clearly shown by the old-time domination of the singer: while all the poet had to do was to stand as little as possible in the way of the musician. The great merit of Metastasio,[7] according to the standard of the practice of his own day, was that he almost effaced his own art in favor of music—"never embarrassed the musician in the least, never advanced any unusual claim upon him from the dramatic standpoint." Nor has the situation changed, in its main features, down even to the present day. It still is held to be necessary for the poet to shape his material according to the necessities of the musician from first to last. The whole aim of the opera is simply *music*, the dramatic story being only utilized to serve music as a means for its own display. The anomaly has finally become so fundamental a part of men's lives that they no longer realize that it *is* an anomaly: and accordingly they still have hopes of erecting the genuine drama on the basis of absolute music—that is, of achieving

---

[6] This and other statements as to the genesis of opera are not historically correct.

[7] The most admired of libretto writers of the eighteenth century.

the impossible. The object of *Opera and Drama* is to prove that great artistic results can follow from the collaboration of music with dramatic poetry, while from the unnatural position that music bears toward opera in our present system nothing but sterility can result.

Let us, then, in the first place, consider "Opera and the Nature of Music."

Music has been betrayed into a position where she has lost sight of her own limitations; although in herself she is simply an "organ of expression," she has fallen into "the error of desiring to define with perfect clearness the thing to be expressed." The musical basis of the opera was the aria, that is, the folk song deprived of its own original words, and adapted at once to the vanity of the singer and the luxurious tastes of the world of rank. Aria and dance tune, with an admixture of recitative, made up an opera, into the musical domain of which the poet was only allowed to enter in order to supply a little narrative cohesion. The significance of the so-called reformation of Gluck has been greatly exaggerated. All he did was to curtail the arrogant pretensions of the singer, while leaving the texture and plan of opera untouched. His was a revolt of the composer fighting merely for his own hand, not for the ends of *drama*: and every means by which he increased the power of music in opera was necessarily a further shackle on the limbs of the poet. Méhul, Cherubini, and Spontini in their turn broadened the old musical forms of opera, and made the musical expression more consonant with that of the words, but did nothing for opera except from the standpoint of music. The poet may now have had to provide a slightly better and firmer groundwork for the musician, but it was to the musician, and to him alone, that he still owed his existence in opera. People failed to see that the source of regenerative power could be nowhere but in the drama: and the trouble was that music tried by itself to perform the functions of drama, to be a "content" instead of mere "expression."

Mozart, again, was so entirely a musician that his work throws the clearest light on the relations of musician and poet; and we find him unable to write at his best where the poem was flat and meaningless. He could not write music for *Tito* like that of *Don Giovanni*, or for *Cosi Fan Tutte* like that of *Figaro*. He, the most absolute of all musicians, would long ago have solved the operatic problem had he met the proper poet. This poet he was never fortunate enough to meet: all his "poets" did was to give him a medley of arias, duets, and *ensembles* to set to music. But the flood of beauty and expression which Mozart poured into opera was too great for that narrow bed; the stream overflowed into wider and freer channels, until it became a mighty sea in the symphonies of Beethoven.

The aria was a degeneration of the folk song, in which poetry and music had been spontaneously one. The operatic aria was the music of the folk song, arbitrarily wrested from the words, and made to serve the indolent pleasure of the man of luxury. In course of time people forgot that a word stave should by rights go with the melody. It was Rossini who took this artificial flower, drenched it with manufactured perfume, and gave it the semblance of life. Rossini saw that the life blood of ordinary opera was melody—"naked, ear-tickling, absolute-melodic melody." Spontini erred in imagining the "dramatic tendency" to be the essence of opera: the real essence, as Rossini showed, and as the future history of opera proves, was simply absolute melody.

Earnest composers, however, while by no means denying the claims of melody, held that Rossini's melody was cheap and superficial, and endeavored to derive theirs more directly from the fountains of expression of the Folk. This was the course taken by Weber, who gave opera aria the deep and genuine feeling of the folk song—though the flower, thus torn from its native meadow, could not thrive in the salons of modern luxury and artificiality. And Weber, no less than Rossini, made his melody the main factor of opera, though of course it was far worthier and more honest than the melody of the Italian composer. Weber directed and constrained the poet of *Der Frei-*

schütz as emphatically as Rossini did the poet of *Tancredi*. And Weber's failure proves afresh the assertion that instead of the drama being taken up into the being of music, music must be taken up into the drama.

Weber's success in harking back to the Folk was envied by the composers of other nationalities, and a number of operas were produced which tried to proceed on similar lines—such as *Masaniello and William Tell*. The Folk, in fact, was exploited, but its real inspiration could not, from the very nature of the case, be embodied in opera. In the epic and the drama the Folk celebrated the deeds of the Hero, and in true drama the action and the character are recognized as necessary; but under the influence of the modern State, dramatic characters lose their personality and become mere masks. This was particularly the case in opera, where the folk song has degenerated into the aria, and the Folk itself has become the Mass, the Chorus. "Historic" opera became the fashion, and even Religion was dragged upon the stage, as in the operas of Meyerbeer. But the outlandishness thus imported into opera led in its turn to worse degeneration: and the "historic" mania became "hysteric" mania—in other words, Neo-romanticism.

Up to this time, every influence that had shaped the course of opera had come from the domain of absolute music alone. After Rossini, operatic melody was varied by the introduction of instrumental melody. People had not perceived that instrumental music was also unfruitful, by reason of its not expressing the purely human in the form of definite, individual feelings.

That the expression of an absolutely definite and clearly-understandable individual Content was in truth impossible in this language that was capable only of generalised emotional expression, could not be demonstrated until the coming of that instrumental composer in whom the longing to express such a Content became the burning, consuming motive-force of all artistic conception.

It was the function of Beethoven to show what music can do if it confines itself to its true sphere, that of expression. In his later works Beethoven, having his mind filled with a definite content, burst the bounds of many of the old absolute forms, and stammered through tentative new ones. Future symphonists followed him from this point, without seeing what it was in Beethoven that made him act in this way; they consequently misapplied his forms, copying the externals only. Hence the vogue of program music, of which the great representative is Berlioz. Then there came an influx of the wealth of instrumental music (developed independently of vocal music) into operatic melody. This is modern *characteristic*, of which Meyerbeer, the cosmopolitan Jew, is the great exploiter, and which differs from that of Gluck and Mozart in that the poet is infinitely more degraded, and absolute melody more exalted. This held good even in Paris, where the poet had hitherto always had *some* rights; but now Meyerbeer forced Scribe, his librettist, to run wherever he chose to drive him. The secret of his music is "Effect without Cause." Yet even Meyerbeer wrote fine music where he allowed the poet to guide him—as in parts of the great love scene in the fourth act of *Les Huguenots*.

To sum up, then, Music has tried to be the drama, and the attempt has ended in impotence. The only salvation for it lies in sensible co-operation with the poet. This may be seen by a glance at the nature of our present music. The most perfect expression of the inner being of music is melody; it is to harmony and rhythm what the external side of the organism is to the internal. Now the Folk's melodies were a revelation of the nature of things. Christianity, however, with its anxiety to lay bare the soul, found itself face to face not with life but death; and the folk song, the indivorcible union of poetry and music, almost died out. In the ages of human mechanism the longing of things was to produce the real man, which man "was really none other than Melody, *i.e.* the moment of most definite, most convincing manifestation of Music's

actual, living organism." The struggle of Beethoven's
great works is the struggle of mechanism to become a
man, an organism, uttering itself in melody. Thus, while
other composers merely took melody, ready made, from
the mouth of the Folk, and applied it to their own purposes, Beethoven's melody was the spontaneous effort
of Music's inner organism to find expression. But it is only
in the verbal outburst of the Ninth Symphony that Beethoven brings melody to true life; music was sterile until
fertilized by the poet. The error had always been that
operatic melody, coming as it did from the folk song, ran
on certain rhythmical and structural lines, beyond which
the musician could not stray; so that melody had no
chance to be born spontaneously out of poetry, for the
poet had simply to adapt his words to the one invariable
musical scaffolding. "Every musical organism is by its
nature a womanly; it is merely a bearer, not a begetter;
the begetting force lies outside it, and without fecundation
by this force it cannot bear." In the Choral Symphony
Beethoven had to call in the poet to fertilize absolute
music; and the folly of the latter is seen in its attempts
not only to bear but also to beget. "*Music is a woman,*"
whose nature is to surrender in love. Who now is to be the
Man to whom this surrender is to be made? Let us look at
the Poet.

II. When Lessing tries to mark out the boundaries of
poetry and painting in the *Laocöon*, he has in his eye
merely descriptive, literary poetry, not "the dramatic
art-work brought immediately into view by physical performance." Now the literary poem is an artificial art, appealing to the imagination instead of to the senses. All
the egoistically severed arts, indeed, appeal only to the
force of imagination. They "*merely suggest; an actual
presentation* would be possible to them only if they could
address themselves to the totality of man's artistic receptivity, communicate with his entire perceptive organism,
instead of merely his faculty of imagination; for the real

art-work only comes into being when it passes from imagination into actuality, *i.e.* physical presentation." There should be no *arts*, there should be *one veritable Art*. It is an error to look upon Drama as merely a *branch of literature*; although it is true that our drama is no more true Drama than a single musical instrument is an orchestra.

The modern drama has a twofold origin—in Romance, and in the Greek drama; the flower of the former being Shakespeare—of the latter, Racine. Our dramatic literature hovers undecidedly between these two extremes. The romance was not the portrayal of the complete man; this only became possible in drama, which actualized life, presented it visibly to the senses. Shakespeare "condensed the narrative romance into the drama"—made it, that is, suitable for stage representation. The great characteristic of his art was that human actions did not come before us merely in descriptive poetry, but by the actors addressing themselves directly to the actual eye, and the poet had to narrow down the diversity of the old Folk stage to suit the scenic and other demands of the theater. The action and the characters had to be made more definite, more individual, more circumstantial, in order to give the spectators the impression of an artistic whole. The appeal, in short, was no longer to fancy but to sense, the only domain left to fancy being *the imagining the scene itself*—for the stage craft of those days fell short of actually *representing* reality. This mixture of fancy and sense presentation in the drama was the source of endless future confusion in dramatic art; the giving up to fancy of the representation of the scene left an open door in drama through which romance and history might pass in and out at pleasure.

In the French drama, outward unity of scene determined the whole structure of the play, diminishing the part played by action, and increasing the function of "mere delivery of speeches." For the same reason, the French dramatists could not choose for representation the romance, with its bewildering multiplicity of incident; they had to fall back on the already condensed plots that they found in Greek mythology. Instead of dealing with his own people's life, then, as Shakespeare had tried to do, the French tragedian merely imitated the finished Greek drama. This unnatural, artificial world was reproduced in French opera, and most saliently in the French opera of Gluck.

Opera was thus the premature bloom on an unripe fruit grown from an unnatural,[8] artificial soil. The outer form, with which the Italian and French drama *began*, must be attained by the new drama by organic evolution from within, on the path of the Shakespearean drama; then first will ripen, also, the natural fruit of musical drama.

German dramatic art found itself between the Shakespearean play on the one side and the scenic Southern opera on the other—between the appeal to hearing, aided slightly by fancy in the representation of the scene, and the appeal to the eye alone. There were two final courses open: either, as Tieck suggested, to act Shakespeare with no more scenery than was employed in Shakespeare's own theater, or to represent each change of scene in the plays —that is, employ the gigantic apparatus of scenic opera. The result to the modern poet was perplexity and disillusion. The play was neither literature—as it was when men merely read it, allowing their imagination to represent the scene—nor actual, visualized drama. Hence the poet either wrote plays simply to be read, not acted, or, if he wrote for the stage, he employed the reflective type of drama, the modern origin of which may be traced to the pseudo-antique drama, constructed according to Aristotle's rules of unity. These results and tendencies are exhibited in Goethe and Schiller. Goethe, after various experiments, found his full expression in *Faust*, which makes no pretense

[8] The latest edition of the *Gesammelte Schriften* (which contains more than one regrettable error) has *"auf natürlichem, künstlichem Boden gewachsen,"* instead of *"unnatürlichem"* as in the earlier editions. See *G.S.*, iv, 15.

of stage representation, and is therefore really neither romance nor drama. *Faust* is "the point of separation between the mediæval *romance* . . . and the real *dramatic matter* of the future." Schiller was always perplexed by the contradiction between history and drama.

The whole dilemma is this. On the one side are romance and history, with all their multiplicity of character and action: on the other is the ideal dramatic form, presenting a simple, definite action and real moving characters visibly to the eye; and a compromise has to be effected between these two. The plain truth is "that we have no drama, and can have no drama; that our literary-drama is as far removed from the genuine drama as the pianoforte from the symphonic song of human voices; that in the modern drama we can arrive at the production of poetry only by the most calculated devices of literary mechanism, just as on the pianoforte we only arrive at the production of music by means of the most complicated devices of technical mechanism—that is to say, a soulless poetry, a toneless music." With *this* drama, true music can have nothing to do.

Man, conceiving the external world, is impelled to reproduce his conceptions in art in a mode that shall be intelligible to others. This has only once been done thoroughly—in the expression of the Greek world view in the Greek drama. The material of this drama was the myth—the Folk's mode of condensation of the phenomena of life—"the poem of a life-view in common." The Christian myth was concerned with death where the Greek had been concerned with life. It could therefore be painted or described, but not *represented* in drama. The Germanic myth, like the Greek, was in its essence a religious intuition, a life view in common; but Christianity laid hold of it and dispersed it into fragments of fable and legend—the Romance of the Middle Ages. What the artist had to do was to find *Man* under all this *débris*. Now whereas the drama selects an action from a mass of actions, and limits the surroundings to just so much as will illuminate and justify this action, the romance has to enter circumstantially and at great length into the surrounding circumstances, in order to make the action and the character artistically convincing. The drama goes from within outward, the romance from without inward; the drama lays bare the organism of mankind, the romance shows us merely the mechanism of history; the art procedure in drama is organic, in romance merely mechanical; the drama gives us the man, the romance the citizen; the drama exhibits the fullness of human nature, the romance the penury of the State. In the evolution that has gone on since the Middle Ages, Burgher society has come uppermost; but it offers nothing to romance but unloveliness. Everything in life is being disintegrated past the capacity of art to reunite it; the poet's art has turned to politics, and until we have no more politics, the poet cannot come to light again. As Napoleon said, the role of Fate in the ancient world is filled in the modern by politics; and this is what we shall have to comprehend before we can discover the true content and form of drama.

Now the myth is true for all time, and its content forever inexhaustible. Understanding it well, we see in it "an intelligible picture of the whole history of mankind, from the beginnings of society to the necessary downfall of the State." The political State lives on the vices of society; salvation and art are only to be found in the free, purely human individual. The essence of the State is *caprice*, of the free individual, *necessity*. It is then essential for us to annul the State and create afresh the free individual. The poet who tried to portray this individual found that he was face to face with him *only as he had been shaped by the State*; he could not then portray him, but only imagine him; could only represent him to thought, not to feeling. Our drama, in consequence, has been forced to make its appeal to the *understanding* instead of the *feeling*. Out of the mass of man's modern surroundings the poet has to reconstruct the individual, and present him to feeling, to sense, instead of to understanding. But this the poet cannot do; he can only address the understanding, and that through the organ of understanding—"abstract and conditioned word-speech." "The course to be taken by the drama of the future will be a return from understanding to feeling, in so far as we advance from the mentally-conceived individuality to an actual individuality." By the annihilation of the State, society will realize its purely human essence, and determine the free individual. And it is only in the most perfect art work, the drama, that the poet's insight into life can find complete expression, because this drama will address not the understanding, but the feeling, through the senses. It will present the poet's view of life physically to the eye; it will be a true *emotionalization of the intellect*. It must present things to us in such a manner that we cannot help realizing their necessity. This can only be done by avoiding the by paths of the intellect, and by appealing directly to the feeling. The *action*, then, must be so chosen as to make this appeal instinctively. Now a historic action, or one "which can only be justified from the standpoint of the State," is only representable to the understanding, not to the feeling; that is, by its very multiplicity and lack of warmth it cannot be seized definitely and quickly by the senses, but needs the combining function of thought. The true dramatic "action" must be seen at once to be the essential center of the periphery of circumstance. Man and nature, as cognized by the understanding, are split up into fragments; it is the *feeling* that grasps the organic unity of things, and it is from this point *outward* that the true drama must work. In other words, it must be generated from the *myth*.

Up to a certain point the intellect can work in the selection of material, and express itself through its own organ, word speech; but for the full *realization* of the action and the motives to the feeling, the organ of feeling— tone speech—has to be called in. "Tone-speech is the beginning and end of word-speech, as the feeling is beginning and end of the understanding, as myth is beginning and end of history, as lyric is beginning and end of poetry." The lyric "holds within itself all the germs of the essential art of poetry, which in the end can only be the justification of the lyric; and the work that accomplishes this justification is nothing but the highest human art-work, the *complete drama.*"

The primal organ of utterance of the inner man is tone speech, the fundamental nature of which may be seen by removing the consonants from our word speech. The latter is the result of the addition of prefixes and suffixes to the open sound, as distinguishing and delimiting signs of objects. In this way speech roots were formed from the primal melody of tone speech. In alliteration, or *Stabreim*, speech, by combining these roots according to similarity and kinship, "made equally plain to the feeling both the impression of the object and its corresponding expression, through an increased strengthening of that expression"—showed, that is, the unity in multiplicity of the object. *Stabreim's* similarity of syllabic sounds brings a collective image to the feeling. The *Stabreim* and the word verse were fundamentally conditioned by that melody which is the expression of primal human feeling, because the breathing conditions of man's organism determined the duration and segmentation of the utterance.[9] When poetry developed along the line of the understanding instead of that of the feeling, word speech became dissociated from its sister, tone speech; and having lost the instinctive sense of this bond, it tried to find "another bond of union with the melodic breathing-pauses." This was done in the *end rhyme*, which was the sign that the natural bond of tone speech and word speech in the *Stabreim* had been forgotten. This line of degeneration ended in "the dreary turmoil of prose"; and the separation from the feeling was complete. We now go upon convention instead of upon conviction. We cannot properly express our emotions in our present language, for it allows us to speak only to the understanding, not to the feeling; which is why the feeling "has tried to escape from absolute intellectual-speech into absolute tone-speech—our music of to-day."

The poet, then, cannot realize his aim in modern

[9] The reader may be reminded that when this was written, Wagner was working at the text of *Young Siegfried*, in which he uses *Stabreim*.

speech, because he cannot speak directly to the feeling. Yet he must not simply work out his drama on the lines of the understanding, and then try to add expression to it by means of music. *This was the error of opera.* The emotional expression itself must *also* be governed by the poetical aim. "A *tone-speech to be struck-into from the outset* is therefore the organ of expression by means of which the poet must make himself intelligible by turning from the understanding to the feeling, and for this purpose he has to take his stand upon a soil on which he can have intercourse with feeling alone." We must go back, in fact, to the primal *melodic* faculty, to which is given the expression of the purely human; the drama must utter itself in a form that shall be the marriage of understanding and feeling, of word speech and tone speech.

III. Until now the poet has tried in two ways to attune the organ of the understanding—word speech—to an emotional expression that would find its way to the feeling; through *rhyme* and through *melody*. It was a mistake to try to import the rhythms of Greek verse into modern poetry, for these rhythms were conditioned by the gestures of the dance, and the dislocation of the speaking accents was atoned for by melody. Our modern languages not being adapted to this ruling into longs and shorts, Greek prosody is impossible for us. Our iambic verse, for example, hobbles along mechanically, "putting grievous constraint upon the live accent of speech for the sake of this monotonous rhythm." "Longs" become "shorts," and "shorts" become "longs," simply to get the requisite number of feet into the line. On the other hand, where, as among the Romanic peoples, this kind of rhythm is not in vogue, the *end rhyme* has been imported into poetry, and has become indispensable. The whole line is built up with reference to this end rhyme, as the up stroke to the down stroke. The result is that the attention of the ear is only momentarily won, and the poet does not reach the *feeling*, for all he does is to make understanding speak to understanding.

We have seen that word speech and melody have traveled along divergent lines of development, and now neither can be properly applied to the other. Even where, as in Gluck's music, the composer tries to find a bond of union in the speaking accent of the word speech, his selection of this mere rhetorical accent leads to a disintegration of the rest of the line as *poetry*; it becomes dissolved into prose, and the melody itself becomes merely musical prose. The usual course is for the melody to do what it likes with the verse—to dislocate its rhythm, ignore its accents, and drown its end rhyme, according to its own pleasure. The poet ought really "so to employ the speaking accent as the only determinative 'moment' for his verse, that in its symmetrical return it should clearly define a wholesome rhythm, as necessary to the verse itself as to the melody." [1] Instead of this, we find on the one hand that many of Goethe's verses are declared too beautiful to be set to music, while on the other hand Mendelssohn writes *Songs without Words*.

We shall have to deal with speech as we dealt with action and the content of the drama. Just as we took away from the action all that was extraneous and accidental; just as we took away from the content all that savored of the State or of history, in order to reach simply the purely human; so we must "cut away from the verbal expression all that springs from and answers to these disfigurements of the purely-human and emotionally necessary," so that only the purely human core shall remain. Thus we shall arrive "at the natural basis of rhythm in the spoken verse, as revealed in the *liftings* and *lowerings* of the accent," which in turn can only find full expression when intensified into musical rhythm. The strong and weak accents must correspond to the "good" and "bad" halves of the musical bar. We must reach back through the understanding and its organ to "the sensuous substance of our *roots of speech*"; we must breathe the breath

---

[1] Again we are reminded of the *Ring*, with its perfect fitting of the melodic and the poetic accents, and its strict coincidence of melodic line length and poetic line length.

of life into the defunct organism of speech. This breath is music. The roots of words were brought into being by the Folk's primal emotional stress; the essence of these roots is the open vowel sound, which finds its fullest sensuous uplifting in music; while the function of the consonants is to determine the general expression to a particular one. The *Stabreim* indicates to the feeling the unity of sensation underlying the roots—shows their emotional kinship. It appeals, as it were, to the "eye" of hearing, while the vowel is addressed to the "ear" of hearing. And as a man only reveals himself fully to us by addressing both eye and ear at once, so "the communicating-organ of the inner man only completely convinces our hearing when it addresses itself with equal persuasiveness to both 'eye and ear' of this hearing. But this is possible only in *word-tone-speech*. Poet and musician have hitherto each addressed no more than half the man: the poet turned towards this hearing's eye alone, the musician only to its ear." The musician will take the vowel sounds of the poet, and display their fundamental kinship by giving them their full emotional value by means of musical tone. Here, then, the word poet ends, and the tone poet begins. The melody of the musician is "the redemption of the endlessly-conditioned poetic thought into a deep-felt consciousness of the highest emotional freedom." This was the melody that rose from Beethoven's Ninth Symphony to the light of day.

When Beethoven wrote the simple melody with which he accompanies the *"Freude, schöner Götterfunken,"* he was writing as an absolute musician. This melody "did not arise out of the poem of Schiller, but rather was invented outside the word-verse and merely spread above it." But in the *"Seid umschlungen, Millionen,"* and the *"Ahnest du den Schöpfer, Welt?"* he obeys the dictates of the poetic aim, and the broadening of the key kinship leads the feeling back to the purely human.

The kinship of feeling which the poet can only approximately express by *Stabreim*, the musician can bring to full expression by key modulation. Take, for example, the line "*Liebe giebt Lust zum Leben.*" The one emotion being expressed throughout, the musician would keep in one key. When setting "*Die Liebe bringt Lust und Leid,*" however, the change of feeling at the end of the line would be expressed by a modulation; while if this line were followed by "*Doch in ihr Weh auch webt sie Wonnen,*" [2] at the *webt* a modulation would be effected back into the original key. It is from this poetico-musical "*period*" that the true art work, the perfected drama, must take its rise.

Melody is the horizontal surface of harmony; and in harmony "the ear . . . obtains an entire fulfilling—and thus a satisfying—of its capacity for sensuous impression, and consequently can devote itself with the necessary composure to the apt emotional expression of the melody." But harmony in absolute music has existed solely for and in itself: whereas the melody ought to be conditioned by the speaking verse, and the concurrent harmony be used for making this obvious to the feeling.

In the drama of the future, there must be no characters whose only function is to swell the harmonic volume of sound; there must only be such characters as are essential in themselves to the plot. The chorus, then, "as hitherto employed in opera, . . . will have to disappear from our drama." Neither the chorus nor the main characters "are to be used by the poet as a musical symphonic tone-body for making the underlying harmonic conditions of the melody perceptible." The musician, however, possesses an organ that can make plain the harmony and characterize the melody in a far superior way to that of the vocal mass. This organ is the orchestra, which is an immense aid in the realization of the poetic aim. Until now the error has consisted in writing *absolute* melody in opera—melody, that is, which was conditioned by the orchestra itself, not

[2] I borrow Mr. Edwin Evans's (Senior) alliterative rendering of these three lines—"Life's delight is love"; "True love doth lighten loss"; "For 'tis from woe she weaves her wonders." See his translation of *Opera and Drama*, ii, 520 *ff.*

by the word verse, and which was therefore only "vocal" melody in the sense that it was given to the voice. It ought really to come from "an announcement of the purely emotional content of the verse, through a dissolution of the vowel into the musical tone"—the verse melody in this way becoming the mediator and bond of union between word speech and tone speech, the offspring of the marriage of poetry and music.

The great value of the orchestra is its power of uttering the *unspeakable*, i.e., that which is unutterable through the organ of the understanding. It may do this in three ways—by its organic alliance with *gesture*, by bringing up the *remembrance* of an emotion, when the singer is not giving voice to it, and by giving a *foreboding* of moods as yet unspoken.

All the constituents of drama have now been enumerated. It only remains to consider how they are to be knit together into a single form corresponding to the single substance. Just as the poet obtained his action by compressing all the motives into an easily comprehended content, so, for the realization of this action, must he proceed with the composition on the same principles. The expression, like the action, must be free from the accidental, the contingent, the superfluous.

We approach the drama in a mood of expectancy, which is ministered to by the orchestra in its quality of a producer of foreboding—although this preliminary utterance of the orchestra must by no means be interpreted to mean the ordinary "overture." This expectancy is afterward satisfied by the word speech of the performer, lifted into the higher emotional sphere of tone speech. The unity of content in the drama must be made evident in a unity of artistic expression; that is, the expression "must convey to the feeling the most comprehensive aim of the poetic understanding." Wherever the word speech approaches the language of ordinary life—the organ of understanding—the orchestra must keep the expression still on the higher plane, by means of its faculty of conveying foreboding or remembrance. Yet it must assume this function not through the mere caprice of the musician, but in obedience only to the poet's aim. Unity of content and unity of expression must go hand in hand. These melodic moments of the orchestra will take their rise only from the *weightiest motives of the drama,* which are the pillars of the edifice. In this way a binding principle of musical form may be obtained which springs directly from the poetic aim, and far surpasses the arbitrary, *merely musical* form of the old opera, which was loose, uncentralized, and inorganic.

Finally let us ask: "Has the poet to *restrict* himself in presence of the musician, and the musician in presence of the poet?" The answer is that they ought not to restrict each other, but raise each other to higher potency, in order thus to generate the true drama. If both the poet's aim and the musician's expression are visible, the necessary inspiration of each by each has not been effected. We must not be reminded of either aim or expression, "but the content must instinctively take possession of us as a human action fully justified to our feeling." In every moment of the musician's expression the poetic aim must be contained; and this poetic aim must always find complete realization in the musician's expression. Whereas Voltaire said: "When a thing is too silly to be said, one sings it," we now may say: "What is not worth being sung is not worth the poet's pains to tell."

There is no need to assume that poet and musician must necessarily be one person. Only in the present egoistic relations of these two—who are types of the egoism of the modern State—does it seem necessary for one man to become the unit of creation.

Three nations—the Italian, French, and German—have contributed to the evolution of opera; but the German language alone "still coheres directly and unmistakably with its roots," and therefore is alone adapted for the new art work. But the practice of singing operas with German words merely translated from the French or

Italian, and therefore not coinciding in meaning and accent with the music, has miseducated and demoralized German singers. In the new drama, the melody will always be conditioned by the word verse, and singers must learn to render it intelligently, bringing out not merely the melodic sequence but the *verbal sense* of the melody. And gesture must be employed with intelligent understanding, in order to make the orchestral moments of foreboding and remembrance[3] in their turn intelligible. But the primary condition for this new drama is a new public, which shall look at it seriously, as at an organism—a public that wants an art work, not a mere evening's distraction. We are less fortunate than the older artists, whose audience, whatever its social faults may have been, had at least delicacy and high breeding; whereas we are ruled by the vulgar and ignorant Philistine, the characteristic product of our commercial civilization. Yet even under the *débris* of modern life the artist can see the primal source of things, can reach to the *human being*, to whom the future belongs.

XI · *His Insensitiveness to the Other Arts*

It will be seen from this summary that Wagner, though now mainly occupied with purely aesthetic ideas, was still unable to refrain from mixing these up with political and other considerations that were quite alien to them. He still believes in the "Folk" as "always . . . the fructifying source of all art." [4] He is still angry—almost comically angry at times—with the richer classes who, in the Wagnerian philosophy of that period, are always to the Folk what the aristocratic villain of the melodrama is to the poor but virtuous hero. He might have forgiven Meyerbeer for writing poor music; but he could never forgive him for being a rich banker. The State too is still the most persistent of bees in his bonnet. He solemnly assures us that the reason for the decline in dramatic character draw-

---

[3] I.e., in modern phrase, the "leading motives."
[4] G.S., iii, 267.

ing since Shakespeare is "the influence of the State, with its perpetual tendency to make everything uniform, and to suppress, with more and more and more deadly power, the might of free personality." [5] This wicked "political State," indeed, "lives entirely on the vices of Society, the virtues of which are the product of the human individuality exclusively. . . . The State is the oppressor of Society, in proportion as the latter turns its vicious side to the individual"; though it is a comfort to know that "the downfall of the State" is "necessary." [6]

And he is as insensitive as ever to the appeal of the other arts. All the arts except drama "merely indicate." The "only real kind of art" is the drama, because there the thing portrayed is not left to the imagination, but is presented bodily to the eye. So blind is he to the characteristic essence and charm of painting and sculpture—for painters and sculptors—that he can speak of the new drama as not only "uniting within itself all the features of plastic art," but even "carrying these to higher perfections otherwise unattainable." A "literary poem" is merely a "miserable shadow" of the real art work. [7] In one of his letters to Uhlig he goes even further than this, actually laying it down that "plastic art must cease entirely in the future." [8] The poor practitioners of these "egoistically severed arts" are majestically swept aside: "only a true artist,—an artistic man, in fact, can understand this matter; but no other, even though he has the best will in the world to do so. Who, for instance, amongst our art-egoistic handicraft-copying, can comprehend the natural

[5] G.S., iii, 269.
[6] G.S., iv, 65, 66.
[7] G.S., iv, 2.
[8] "But if I wish to show that plastic art, being only an artificial art, one abstracted from real art, must cease entirely in the future; if consequently to this plastic art—painting and sculpture —that to-day claims to be the principal art, I utterly deny a life in the future, you will admit that this should not and could not be done with two strokes of the pen." (Letter of January 12, 1850; *Briefe an Uhlig*, etc., p. 26.)

attitude of plastic art to the direct, purely-human art?
I altogether set aside what a statue sculptor or a historical
painter would say to this." [9]

In the "Communication to My Friends," which followed *Opera and Drama* at an interval of a few months, he
once more insists on the impossibility of the dissevered arts
continuing to exist after the way to the one true art has
been pointed out. "Together with the historico-political
subject I also of necessity rejected that dramatic *art-reform*
in which alone it could have been embodied; for I recognised that this form had only issued from that subject, and
by it alone could be justified, and that it was utterly
incapable of convincingly communicating to the feeling
the purely human subject that alone I had in my eye; and
therefore, with the disappearance of the historico-political
subject there must necessarily also vanish, in the future,
the spoken play [*die Schauspielform*], as inadequate for
the novel subject, unwieldy and defective." [1]

Everywhere, as usual with him, he not only sees everything from his own angle, but is quite incapable of
understanding how anyone else can have a different view-
point. Just as he had nothing of the painter's or sculptor's
feeling for painting or sculpture, so he had little of the
poet's feeling for poetry. Apparently all that he assimilated
from poetry was the idea; the characteristic charm of
poetry—the subtle interblending of idea and expression—
did not exist for him. To what may be called the poetic
atmosphere or aroma of words he was quite insensitive.
For the poet the bare idea is next to nothing: the value
of the idea, for him as for us, lies in the imaginative heat
it engenders, the imaginative odors it diffuses. It is doubt-

[9] Letter 14 to Uhlig (undated), in *Briefe*, p. 46. Mr. Shedlock,
in his admirable English version of these letters, translates "art-
egoistic" (*künstlerisch-egoistischen*) in the second sentence
as "artificial egoistic," having apparently read *"künstlerisch"* as
"künstlich."

[1] *"Eine Mittheilung an meine Freunde,"* in G.S., iv, 315. He
is discussing the reasons that led him to give up the idea of a
play on the subject of Friedrich Barbarossa.

ful, indeed, whether there is anything either original or striking in nine poetical ideas out of ten; the poet's traffic must of necessity be for the most part with sentiments that, taken in themselves, have been the merest commonplaces for thousands of years. What difference is there, purely in idea, between "we are here to-day and gone to-morrow" and Shakespeare's

> We are such stuff
> As dreams are made on; and our little life
> Is rounded with a sleep?

Shakespeare's magic is in the phrasing—not, be it remembered, a merely extraneous, artificial grace added to the idea, a mere clothing that can be put on or off it at will, but a subtle interaction and mutual enkindlement of idea and expression. For the musician that enkindlement comes from the adding of music to the words: the music does for the idea what the style does for it in the case of the poet—raises it to a higher emotional power, gives it color, odor, incandescence, wings. Brünnhilde comes to tell Siegfried that he must die. The mere announcement of the fact is next to nothing; the infinities and the solemn silences only gather about it when the orchestra gives out the wonderful theme:

The pure poet, working in his own material alone, would give us this sense of illimitable sadness by the infusion into the mere idea of some remote, unanalyzable wizardry of words and rhythms, as in Clough's

Ah, that I were far away from the crowd and the
    streets of the city,
Under the vine-trellis laid, O my beloved, with thee!

or Arnold's

Hear it from thy broad lucent Arno-vale
    (For there thine earth-forgetting eyelids keep
    The morningless and unawakening sleep
Under the flowery oleanders pale).

Wagner was blind to this superintellectual quality in
words because for him that quality was most naturally
added to them by music. Speech was with him always "the
organ of the intellect"; our modern speech was "utterly
feelingless": the poet cannot communicate feeling because
"articulate language" is capable only of "description and
indication." [2] He himself was, strictly speaking, hardly
a poet at all: he was simply a writer of words for music—
words to which the music had to add the emotional beauty
that the genuine poet would have conveyed by speech
alone. We are therefore not in the least surprised to learn
that Wagner first of all wrote his "poems" in prose, which
he then turned into rhyme or rhythm at his leisure. We
possess, in "Wieland the Smith," [3] an intended operatic
libretto of his that never got past the prose stage. Having
decided not to set it to music himself, he offered it to
Liszt. "The poem," he writes to the Princess Wittgenstein,
"is fully worked out; nothing remains to be done [sic]
but the simple versification, which any tolerably skilful
verse-maker could do. Liszt will easily find one. In the most
important places I have written the verses myself." [4]
Hence all this elaborate analysis of vowels and consonant

----

[2] "In modern speech, poetical creation is impossible; that is to
say, a poetic purpose cannot be *realised* in it, but only suggested"
(*sondern eben nur als solche ausgesprochen werden*). *Opera and
Drama*, in G.S., iv, 98. There are many other passages of the
same tenor.
[3] G.S., iii, 178 ff.
[4] *Briefwechsel zwischen Wagner und Liszt*, i, 324.

sounds is quite beside the mark. He imagines "the feeling" of a word to reside in the "root-syllable" of it—"which was invented or discovered by the primitive emotional need of humanity" [*die aus der Nothwendigkeit des ursprünglich-sten Empfindungszwanges des Menschen erfunden oder gefunden ward*]. And the fountain of that emotional force in the root is the vowel sound, which is "the inner feeling incarnate" [*das verkörperte innere Gefühl*].[5] Portentous attributes are also ascribed to the consonants, and the initial consonant is pronounced to be of more significance than the terminal. Most of this is merely fantastic. Words, especially in the hands of a poet, are not simply clothed vowel sounds; they are entities with a marvelous life of their own. The appeal of Keats's

> The same that ofttimes hath
> Charmed magic casements, opening on the foam
> Of perilous seas in faery lands forlorn,

has nothing whatever to do with vowels and consonants: we no more think of these than we think of vibration numbers when we listen to a succession of musical harmonies. The beauty of the lines is in the totality and the rareness of the imaginative picture they flash upon our vision; and to attempt to explain the secret of this in terms of vowels and consonants is as futile as to try to explain the beauty and the scent of a flower by its physical particles.

XII · *The Musician Dominating the Poet*

One is sometimes amazed, in reading *Opera and Drama*, at the persistence with which Wagner pursues the obvious, hunting it down, as Oscar Wilde said of James Payn, with the enthusiasm of a short-sighted detective. He is almost as elaborately absurd over his vowels and consonants as M. Jourdain. The explanation is to be sought partly in the tendency to long-windedness, the passion for pursuing every idea to the death, which was always characteristic

[5] *G.S.*, iv, 128, 129.

of him—it derived ultimately from the inexorably logical nature of his mind—and partly from the fact that he had a very stupid public and a very stupid set of artists to educate. *Opera and Drama* has been made both more lucid and somewhat obvious for us today by Wagner's own operas. If there is less need today to labor certain points as he does, it is because they are now such universally accepted truths that it is hard for us to imagine a time when people needed to have them driven into them at the point of a pen. Here and there his letters give us an inkling of the difficulties with which he had to contend. Few people in the middle of the nineteenth century, apparently, had any idea of real drama in opera.[6] Even the singers—with the exception of a born genius here and there like Schröder-Devrient—had little notion that their parts consisted of anything but so many words to be sung as brilliantly as possible. In one of his letters to Liszt, Wagner describes his horror at seeing, in the Dresden opera house, the Tannhäuser, in the "Hall of Song" scene, shouting his declaration of unholy love for Venus straight into the face of the chaste Elisabeth!—and this in spite of the composer having taken particular care to have all directions copied in full in the separate vocal parts. "What result was possible but that the public should be confused and not know in the least what to make of it? Indeed, I discovered in Dresden that the public became acquainted with the dramatic contents of the opera only by reading the text-book; that is, they only came to understand the performance by abstracting their minds from the actual performance and filling-in from their own imagination." [7] And as he hints, if these things could be done in a first-class opera house like Dresden, what hair-raising horrors must go on in the smaller theaters?

[6] In the scene of the Contest of Song in the second act of *Tannhäuser* he says: "My real object was, if possible, to compel the hearer, for the first time in the history of opera, to take an interest in a poetic idea, and to follow it up in all its necessary developments." *Mein Leben*, p. 364. See his letter to Lilli Lehmann (L. L.: *My Path Through Life*, p. 41), March 1876.

[7] Letter of September 8, 1850; *Briefwechsel*, i, 75.

A good deal of *Opera and Drama*, then, took its rise in the immediate circumstances of the German operatic life of the early nineteenth century and has no particular validity for the world in general today.[8] Other portions of it relate only or mainly to the *Ring*. For all his insistence on the necessity of alliterative verse (*Stabreim*), he virtually discarded it when he had finished with the *Ring*. *Die Meistersinger* is written throughout in rhymed verse. In *Tristan* he employs in turn alliteration, rhyme, and unrhymed verse; *Parsifal* fluctuates between a sort of *vers libre* that is often as near as possible to prose, and a rhymed stanza form for the more pronouncedly lyric portions. *Opera and Drama*, in fact, was in large part the reduction to theory of the principles of structure that were slowly taking shape within him as he pondered on the Siegfried legend. As with all great artistic creators, each subject was seen so vividly, took such complete possession of him, that it unconsciously made for itself its own inevitable form. He himself knew that it was in the *Ring* that the theories of *Opera and Drama* had their origin. "Even now," he writes to Uhlig, "must I learn that I should not have discovered the most important conditions for the conformation of the drama of the future had I not, as artist, lighted quite unconsciously upon them in my *Siegfried*." [9] And working backward, as it were, from the completed work as we have it now, it is easy enough to see how the subject led him of itself to a new theory of opera. He had a gigantic saga to condense into the dimensions of a normal stage action; the most drastic economy of words was therefore necessary. As the burden of the emotional expression was to be undertaken by the

[8] Much of his laborious insistence of the proper relation between word and tone was due to the disregard of any coincidence between verbal and musical accents in most of the German opera texts and translations of his time, and to the bad enunciation of so many of the singers. He was still complaining of this latter —"the chaotic vocal style of our singers"—in 1879. See "*Uber das Opern-Dichten und Komponieren im Besonderen*," in *G.S.*, x, 166.

[9] Letter 21 (beginning of February 1851), p. 80.

music, the purely verbal portion would have to be reduced to the barest essentials consistent with making the conduct of the drama and the motives of the characters clear. And as every word had to be vital to the drama, and the musical phrase was to fit the verbal phrase as if the two had been predestined for each other from the beginning of time, each line, short as it might be, had to be packed with accents as salient as those of the music itself. This condition seemed to be most perfectly fulfilled in *Stabreim*, because there the vowel or consonant that gave definition to the word was thrown into the highest possible relief at the very moment of the incidence of the musical accent. The following quotations from *Die Walküre* will make this clear:

A
Die Be - trog' - ne lass auch zer - tre - ten.
Let them tramp - le on the be - trayed one.

B
Dass mit Zwang ich hal - te, was dir nicht haft - et.
That by force I hold what de - nies thee hom - age.

C
Wer bist du, sag', die so schön und ernst mir er - scheint?
Who art thou, say, who dost stand so beau - teous and stern?

It was therefore, as usual, the musician in him control- ling the poet, although he always strenuously denied this, and indeed his complaint against the old-time opera was that the poet was held in servitude to the musician. In each case the poet was the serf, but the terms of slavery were different. In the older opera he had to work within the limits of a set scheme that gave him little or no scope for character drawing or for the natural evolution of a great dramatic action. In the Wagnerian opera the poet was indeed allowed to make his portion of the work worthy and consistent, but he was permitted no further scope than was consistent with the necessities of the music. If it be true that Wagner restored the poet to liberty by making the drama the end and the music the means, it was only in the sense that he first of all made the drama of the dimensions and the pattern that music required. Beyond these dimensions, away from that pattern, it could not be allowed to go.

That the musician in Wagner ruled the poet is plain enough to us now, but the perception of this truth was always denied to Wagner himself. In the "Communication to my Friends," which elucidates so gratefully for us so many dark passages in *Opera and Drama,* he is persistently blind to the fact that is obvious enough to everyone else. As far as *Rienzi,* he tells us, he has taken his operatic subjects from ready made stories, while with *The Flying Dutchman* he struck out a new path, framing his own libretto out of the simple unpolished outlines of a folk saga. "Henceforward," he goes on to say, "with regard to all my dramatic works I was in the first instance *Poet,* and only in the complete working-out of the poem did I become once more *Musician.* Only," he rather naïvely continues, "*I was a poet who was conscious in advance of the power of musical expression for the working out of his poems.*" [1] Quite so: when a subject took possession of him, he would see it all in terms of musical expression and development; and unconsciously the poem would be so planned as to provide the needful framework, and no more, for the musical emotion. Later on, after arguing that music is the emotional expression per se, but that it can only ally itself with words that contain the possibility of emotion, he once more lets us see that it was the musician in him that determined his choice of subject and the manner of its treatment. "What I perceived, I now looked at solely with the eyes of music [*nur aus dem Geiste der Musik*]; though not," he rightly points out, "*that* music whose formal rules might still have embarrassed my expression, but the music that was complete within me,

[1] *"Eine Mittheilung an meine Freunde,"* in G.S., iv, 316.

and in which I could express myself as in a mother tongue." [2] Granting that the musical world from the center of which he wished to pour himself out upon poetry was not that of the stereotyped operatic composer, the fact remains that it was from the center of music itself that the outpouring was to come. And we may further grant that "it was precisely by the facility of musical expression" he had acquired that "he became a poet." What had happened in the interval between *Rienzi* and *The Flying Dutchman,* and still more in the interval between *The Flying Dutchman* and the *Ring,* was that his musical sense had so enormously expanded that it was now capable of weaving a continuous emotional tissue of its own—a tissue, however, that required the framework of poetry to make it definite. He was right; it was of the musician in him that the poet was born. And it was the musician insisting on the dramatic "stuff" being reduced to its pure essentials that led him to reject the wide-spreading romance and history, and to seize upon the myth, in which a human content was presented in the simplest possible form.

XIII · *Wagner and Beethoven*

The musician, then, being at the basis of all his aesthetics, all his theories of opera and drama, the question arises: what sort of a musician was he? He was the spiritual son of Beethoven; a remoter ancestor was Bach. This is the cardinal fact in the psychology of Wagner; and it will need to be examined in all its bearings.

Wagner was one of those dynamically charged personalities after whose passing the world can never be the same as it was before he came—one of the tiny group of men to whom it is given to bestride an old world and a new, but to sunder them by a gulf that becomes ever more and more impassable; one of the very few who are able so to fill the veins of a whole civilization with a new

[2] G.S., iv, 318, 319.

principle of vitality that the tingle of it is felt not only by the rarer but by the commonest spirits—some new principle from which, whether a man likes it or not, he will find it impossible to escape. Wagner is probably the only figure in the whole history of music of whom this can be said. Bach created no such upheaval. He counts for next to nothing in the music of his own day and that of the two generations that followed him. He did not make a new world in music: rather had a new world to be made before men's eyes were competent to take the measure of that towering stature, or men's hearts quick enough with life to respond to the profound humanism of that great soul. We were not fit for Bach until Beethoven and Wagner— and Wagner, perhaps, even more than Beethoven—made us so. Beethoven, again, had it not been for Wagner, would probably not have meant as much to us as he does now, or become the fertilizing force he is in modern music; and even that fertilization is effected through Wagner's work rather than along lines in continuation of Beethoven's own. If anyone doubts this, let him ask himself what new spirit of enduring vitality and power of propagation has come out of the classical symphony pure and simple. Not Brahms, assuredly, great as he is: "arrested development" is written large upon the forms and the ideas of all the music that has come out of Brahms's symphonies as clearly as upon those symphonies themselves. So far as modern instrumental music has developed in humanity of utterance or in breadth of structure, it is from assimilating from Beethoven, through Wagner, just the urgent poetic spirit that Brahms passed by in Beethoven— the spirit of which Beethoven was himself only dimly conscious, but which Wagner from the beginning saw to be inherent in him, and which he distilled from the general tissue of Beethoven's work and used in a new form for magical results of his own. The only explosive force in music at all comparable in general to Wagner was Monteverdi. But Monteverdi came a couple of hundred years too soon. The world was not ready for him—it is hardly a paradox to say that he was not ready for himself —and his explosion mostly spent itself in a desert. Wagner had first-rate luck in this as in everything else in his life that really mattered to him as an artist; not only had he the right dynamic spark within him, but he was born into an atmosphere made electrically ready by the passionate soul's cry of Beethoven. The explosion came—a cataclysmic upheaval, leading to a new geological formation, as it were, in music, new geographical delimitations, a new fauna and flora.

He had access to Beethoven's heart: and from the blood in Beethoven's veins he won the strength both for his own new expression and his new freedom of form. It is one of the things we should be constantly thanking Providence for that the natural man in him insisted on making its own world in its own way. Busoni, in his suggestive *Entwurf einer neuen Aesthetik der Tonkunst*, has remarked upon the curious formalism of most music, even the greatest. Here is an art fortunate enough to be free from all material factors: it is, as Busoni says, simply "sounding air," and is therefore presumably capable of a freedom of handling that should be the despair of workers in the other arts. Perfect freedom has yet to come; looked at from the heights, even giants like Bach and Beethoven and Mozart are seen to be loaded with chains of their own and their fellows' forging, and to be performing the same timid evolutions again and again in one small corner of a field, while glorious leagues of unexplored country unroll themselves all around them. Bach and Beethoven enriched music by a sort of intensive culture of an inherited estate. Wagner was really the first to leap the fences and break down the gates and send his plowshare deep into the bowels of a new earth. Almost from his earliest years he had an instinctive sense of the great force of emotional liberation that was struggling for an outlet in Beethoven's music. He was probably the only man in Europe to be aware of it and its tremendous significance for the future. There were plenty of men who felt the greatness of Beethoven; but not one of them, apparently, saw him as Wagner did. It is evident that people like Mendelssohn and Robert and Clara Schumann, for example, with whom he talked much in the forties, had no inkling that out of the spume of this eager, restless mind the future of music was to be born. To them his far-darting talk about Beethoven was apparently no more than the interesting speculations of a clever but slightly eccentric visionary. From the first he fastened upon the seminal essence of Beethoven's later work—the attempt of a great soul, hampered somewhat by a transmitted form, to pour out an endless fund of quasi-dramatic emotion in music. The problem that lay before Wagner was how to release this fund of emotion, to give it wings that would carry it over the whole field of human life, to give it a new and more wonderful articulation. After years of struggling he found his way to the light. It was one of the extremely lucky "throws" of Nature—a throw she will probably not achieve again for generations—that within the musician who had this unique vision of a music infinitely human and perfectly free there was a dramatist capable of providing the definite framework upon which the indefinite musical emotion could be woven into firm, coherent shapes. His theory that purely instrumental music had shot its last bolt with Beethoven, and that the choral ending to the Ninth Symphony is the unconscious, instinctive cry of the musician for the redemption of music by poetry, is the soundest of aesthetics if only we do not take it too literally. Music *did* need this fertilization by poetry if it was to win a new procreative power. Agreeable music has been made, and will continue to be made, by the passionless, disinterested weaving for its own sake of beautiful strands of tone. But great music must go deeper than this, and the deeper it goes, the closer it comes to the heart; and our name for the necessities of the heart is poetry.

XIV · *Beethoven a Tone-poet*

Having thus summarized the attitude of Wagner to Beethoven and to poetic music in general, let us proceed to
fill in the details of the theory, allowing Wagner, wherever
possible, to speak for himself.

He has set forth his views upon Beethoven with the
greatest positiveness in his letters to Uhlig, and much more
lucidly there than in *Opera and Drama*.[3] He saw in Beethoven's music the struggle to express a definite poetic
idea in an abstract form that necessarily made the communication of the nature of the idea itself impossible. He
always protested against the current fashion of performing
Beethoven's symphonies as if they were nothing more than
agreeable or exciting musical patterns. They were tone
poems, and could mean nothing to the hearer unless the
poetry at the core of them was made clear. "The essence
of the great works of Beethoven," he writes to Uhlig, "is
that they are only in the last place *Music*, but contain in
the first place a poetic subject. Or shall we be told that
this *subject* is only taken from music itself? Would not
this be like saying that the poet takes his subject from
speech, and the painter his from colour? The musical
conductor who sees in one of Beethoven's tone works
nothing but the music, is exactly like a reciter who should
hold only by the language of a poem, or the explainer
of a picture who could not get beyond its colour. This,
however, is the case with our conductors, even in the best
instances—for many do not even so much as understand
the music; they understand the key, the themes, the
working of the parts, the instrumentation, and so on, and
think that with these they understand the whole of the
content of the tone work."[4] And again: "The character-

[3] It must always be remembered that the Beethoven of whom
Wagner speaks is the Beethoven of the later symphonies, sonatas,
and quartets.

[4] Letter 57 (February 15, 1852) in *Briefe an Uhlig*, p. 160.
It was his complaint against Mendelssohn's conducting of the
Beethoven symphonies that it brought out "merely their purely

istic of the great compositions of Beethoven is that they are veritable poems, in which it is sought to bring a real subject to representation. The obstacle to their comprehension lies in the difficulty of finding with certainty the subject that is represented. Beethoven was completely possessed by a subject: his most significant tone pictures are indebted almost solely to the individuality of the subject that filled him; the consciousness of this made it seem to him superfluous to indicate his subject otherwise than in the tone picture itself. Just as our literary poets really address themselves only to other literary poets, so Beethoven, in these works, involuntarily addressed himself only to tone poets. The absolute musician, that is to say the manipulator of absolute music, could not understand Beethoven, because this absolute musician fastens only on the 'How,' and not the 'What.' The layman, on the other hand, could but be completely confused by these tone pictures, and at best only receive pleasure from *that* which to the tone poet was merely the material means of expression." [5]

Wagner recognized, however, the difficulty of grasping a poetic subject that had not been revealed by the composer, and held that it could only be divined by a poetic musician of the same kind. "If no special poetic subject is expressed in the tone speech, it may undoubtedly pass as easily understandable; for there can here be no question of *real* understanding. If, however, the expression of the tone speech is conditioned by a poetic subject, this speech at once becomes the most incomprehensible of all, unless the poetic subject be at the same time defined by some other means of expression than those of absolute music.

---

musical side," not their poetical content. Not understanding the spirit of them, Mendelssohn kept to the letter. His inability to understand the inner meaning of the music caused him to fall into the grossest errors of *tempo*. He took the first movement of the Ninth Symphony, for example, so fast that "the whole thing became the direct opposite of what it really is" (Letter 56 to Uhlig, February 15, 1852, p. 162).

[5] Letter 56 to Uhlig (February 15, 1852), p. 157.

"The poetic subject of a tone piece by Beethoven is thus only to be divined by a tone poet; for, as I remarked before, Beethoven involuntarily appealed only to such, to those who were of like feelings, like culture, aye, well-nigh like capability with himself. Only a man like this can make these compositions intelligible to the laity, and above all by making the subject of the tone poem clear both to the executants and to the audience, and thus making good an involuntary error in the technique of the tone poet, who omitted this indication. Any other sort of performance of one of Beethoven's veritable tone poems, however technically perfect it may be, must remain incomprehensible in proportion as the understanding is not facilitated in the way I have suggested." [6]

This indeed, he held, was Beethoven's error—an error forced upon him by the conditions of his time—that he should endeavor to make his music truly human without giving the hearer the clue to the emotions upon which it was based. Beethoven's mistake, he says, in one of the happiest and most famous of his analogies, was the same as that of Columbus, who, though merely trying to find the way to the India that was already known, actually discovered thereby a new world.[7] His vain effort to "achieve the artistically necessary in the artistically impossible" has, however, revealed to the modern world the infinitely expressive capacity of music. But though it is only by being fertilized by poetry that music can attain to the full expression of the truly human, Wagner, as was to be expected from one who allowed so little liberty to the imagination in art, was against this fertilization taking the form of program music. The poetic content must be communicated immediately and visibly to the hearer by presentation on the stage. In all this, of course, he was once more merely expressing an individual bias, and one that is not in the least binding upon musicians in general. When the

[6] Letter 55 to Uhlig (February 15, 1852), pp. 158, 159.
[7] *Opera and Drama*, in G.S., iii, 278. The whole of this section should be read carefully.

musician, he tells us, tries to paint by means of the orchestra alone, what he produces is neither music nor a painting.[8] He failed to perceive not only that instrumental music offers numberless instances of quite successful tone painting, but that a good deal of the pictorialism of his own music has to justify itself by means of the imagination alone. Every time the *Feuerzauber*, for example, is played in the concert room, the imagination supplies, quite successfully, the spectacle of the flames; and even in the theater it is left to the imagination to picture to itself the waves of the Rhine in the opening scene of *Das Rheingold*, for while the wave music is going on from the commencement, the curtain does not rise until the 126th bar. There is no need to elaborate the point. Hundreds of composers, from Bach to the present day, have "painted" in music, time without number, without the assistance of a stage setting, the subject of the painting being quite sufficiently indicated either by the words of the poem—the spinning wheel in Schubert's *Gretchen am Spinnrade*, for example—or by means of an explanatory note or title, as with the modern symphonic poem.

Without pursuing this side issue further now, let us follow up the more essential lines of the Wagnerian theory. We have seen him first of all frame his dramatic action in such a way that while making itself fully intelligible to the spectator, it supplies the music with endless opportunities for the outpouring of feeling. Romance and "historical" drama have both been rejected because of their containing so much that, according to Wagner, appeals less to the feeling than to the intellect. It was in the myth that he found the condensation he desired. Upon the myth the composer was to pour out the full flood of his emotion. The form and quality of the musical utterance are to be determined by the poem. Lyricism must no longer be imposed upon the drama from without, as in the older opera, but must grow out of the drama as a necessary

[8] *Opera and Drama*, in G.S., iv, 3.

consequence. It follows that neither the chorus nor any of the characters is to be employed purely for the purposes of concerted music. In the orchestra the musician has at his disposal an instrument of unlimited expressiveness. The orchestra, as Wagner says, has a capacity of its own for speech. In the Beethoven symphony this capacity was developed to such a height as to urge the orchestra to make the vain attempt to deliver a message which from its very nature it was impossible for it to deliver clearly. That message, however, can be *précisé* by the Word: and the true function of the orchestra is to announce what cannot be conveyed by speech.[9] Its specific meaning can be still further *précisé* by means of gesture—not the ordinary gesture of the older opera, which derived solely from the dance pantomime, but gesture that is the visible counterpart of the auditory sensation communicated by the orchestra. The range of this kind of gesture is as wide as human emotion itself. Moreover, the orchestra can carry on the action even after speech and gesture have ceased; it can use themes in such a way as to create presentiment, and it can recall the past. The orchestra, in fact, is to the drama of the future what the chorus was to the Greek drama—a totalized individuality apart from, yet intimately bound up with, the separate individualities on the stage. The musical expression will vary in intensity according to the intensity of the situations. The form of the music drama will therefore be a unified one, but one containing the possibility of an infinite variety of expressions; but it will not be permissible to introduce any expression for the mere sake of musical effect; everything must grow spontaneously out of the emotions and situations presented by the poet. The drama can be thoroughly unified by the employment of salient "leading motives";[1] whereas the

[9] *Opera and Drama*, in G.S., iv, 173.

[1] This term, it must be remembered, is not Wagner's own. It has come into such general use, however, and is so thoroughly expressive, that it is better to employ it than to adopt Wagner's rather circumlocuitous way of expressing the same thing.

older opera had no unity at all, but was a mere con-
glomeration of arias, duets, *ensembles*, and so on.[2]

xv · Symphonic and Dramatic Form

It must be clear to almost every reader, after this exposition
of Wagner's own views upon music in general and dramatic
music in particular, that, paradoxical as it may seem, he
was under a life-long illusion as to the nature of his own
genius and the origin and significance of his reforms. So
far from the poet in him shaping and controlling the
musician, it was the musician who led the poet where he
would have him go; so far from drama being with him
the end and the music the means, it was music that was
more than ever the end, to which the drama only served
as means; and so far from Wagner being first and last a
dramatist, the whole significance of his work lay precisely
in the fact that he was a great symphonist. This last
conclusion too may seem a paradox; but on a broad survey
it will, I think, be seen to be true. It was not for nothing
that Wagner always claimed descent from Beethoven
rather than from even the greatest of opera writers, such
as Gluck and Mozart and Weber. His instinct was a sound
one; it was Beethoven's work that he was really carrying
on. The whole of his productivity is given us, in essence,
in the later stages of the *Ring*, in *Tristan*, and in *Die
Meistersinger*. It was to achieve such an expression, such
a tissue, as this that he had been laboring and experiment-
ing and thinking for nearly thirty years; and what are
these works, seen with the historical eye of the twentieth
century, but stupendous symphonies for orchestra and
voices? He himself always proudly pointed to *Tristan* as
the supremely successful realization of all his theories as

[2] The reader who is unable to follow Wagner's exposition in
Opera and Drama should turn to "A Communication to My
Friends," in which practically the same ground is covered, but
in a much more luminous style.

to the expressive capacity and the formal possibilities of music. Very well; *Tristan* is of all his works the most symphonic, the one that least needs the apparatus of the stage, the one in which the actors could most easily be dispensed with for long stretches of time with the minimum of loss.

I have already pointed out that he was probably the only musician in Europe in the thirties and forties with an intuition of all that the achievements of the later Beethoven meant for music.[3] All through Wagner's theoretical writings runs the same simile of music as a vast sea, on which Beethoven alone had so far been able to trust himself with any freedom. While the other composers of his day—and indeed of a later day, as the case of Brahms shows—had little idea beyond cruising in Beethoven's track with more or less varied merchandise, Wagner even as a boy saw the infinite wonders that were awaiting the first mariner who should have the courage to leave the shelter of the great bay and adventure out into the unknown main. He knew all that Beethoven had added to German music, the new emotions he had poured into it, the new logic of form with which he had endowed it. He knew also that as much could still be superadded to Beethoven as Beethoven had added to Mozart and Haydn; and the story of his evolution, both as dramatist and musician, is the story of this gradual extension of the borders of the Beethoven territory.

He had in abundance what has hitherto been almost the exclusive possession of the German school of music— the sense of a far-sweeping logic of form. He had the rigorous, clean-cutting intellect that instinctively makes straight for what is the very essence of form—the spontaneous shaping of an idea, by itself, for itself, into the lines and colors most natural to it. "Swords without

[3] E. T. A. Hoffmann before him had been very enthusiastic over Beethoven, and no doubt Wagner had been stimulated by Hoffmann in this as in so many other matters. See in particular Hoffmann's *Fantasiestücke*.

blades" was his contemptuous description of the empty rules of "form" which they sell in schools and textbooks, much as the chemist sells the dried leaves of flowers. The true artist, he says, is always creating forms without knowing it.[4] *His* problem was to find the new form that should be as valid for what he had to say as Beethoven's form was for him. No such form was then in existence. In this respect he was far less fortunate than any of his great predecessors or successors; each of them had found his work all the easier in that he began with an inherited form, of opera or of instrumental music, which he simply exploited or expanded according to his necessities. Wagner's glance round upon the music of his day showed him that there was no form that *he* could take up and patch or hammer into a serviceable instrument. The symphony was not, nor indeed is it yet, a truly logical form. Its divisions, the number of its divisions, the order of its divisions, are all in large part arbitrary and conventional. Within each of the frames made by these divisions it had to submit itself to a more or less formalistic method of procedure which was often at variance with the very nature of the idea. Even Beethoven, giant as he was, could not quite burst the bonds of custom and prescription. Wagner's favorite illustration of the clash that sometimes occurred between the traditional form and a new artistic purpose was the repeat in the *Leonora No. 3* Overture. The controlling influence in the evolution of symphonic form had been the dance; the business of music had primarily been to make what variable play it could with certain given thematic figures. But bit by bit there had stolen into instrumental music the desire for more than this—the desire to follow out in tone not the changing aspects of a theme alone but the vicissitudes of a dramatic idea; and composers had long felt that the logic of the latter must be something other than the logic of the former, though as yet they did not quite know how to attain the structure they wanted. The purely thematic working-out aimed

[4] "On Franz Liszt's Symphonic Poems," in *G.S.*, v, 187.

mostly at alternation and contrast; the dramatic working-out must depend mostly on psychological development. "It is obvious," says Wagner, "that in the conflict of a dramatic idea with [symphonic] form, there must at once arise the necessity of either sacrificing the development (the idea) to the alternation (the form), or the latter to the former. . . . I once held up Gluck's Overture to *Iphigenia in Aulis* as a model, because the master, with the surest feeling for the nature of the problem we are now considering, had here so happily understood that he must open his drama with an alternation of moods and their antitheses, in keeping with the overture form, instead of with a development impossible in that form. That the great masters who came after him, however, felt themselves circumscribed by this, we may clearly see in Beethoven's overtures; the composer knew the infinitely richer delineations of which his music was capable; he felt equal to carrying out the idea of development; and nowhere do we realise this more distinctly than in the great *Leonora* Overture. But anyone with eyes can see precisely in this overture how prejudicial to Beethoven the retention of the transmitted form was bound to be; for who that is capable of understanding such a work will not agree with me that its weakness consists in the repetition of the first part after the middle section, whereby the idea of the work is marred almost to the point of making it unintelligible; and that the more as in all the other parts, and especially at the end, Beethoven is obviously governed simply by the dramatic development? But whoever is intelligent and unprejudiced enough to see this must also admit that this mishap could only have been avoided by forswearing the repetition altogether—which, however, would mean the abrogation of the overture form, *i.e.* the original symphonic dance form with its mere play of motives [*nur motivirte*], and the first step towards the shaping of a new form." [5]

[5] "On Franz Liszt's Symphonic Poems," in *G.S.*, v, 109.

XVI · *Wagner's Symphonic Lineage*

Beethoven, in fact, had brought a new spirit into the symphony and the overture without being able to discover a new and inevitable form in which this spirit could express itself. Wagner from his earliest years must have felt that he too had a dim perception of a new world of expression, if only he could discover the form for it. That form clearly did not exist in the symphony even as Beethoven had left it, for Wagner's vision was ready to take a bolder poetic flight even than Beethoven's, and it would have been as sadly hampered by the more freely symphonic but still largely formal method of Beethoven as the latter had been by the traditions of form he had taken over from his predecessors. It was still more useless for Wagner to seek the new logic of form in the other great art genre of his day—the opera—for here illogic reigned supreme. The opera not only did not achieve the unity it professed to aim at; it did not even let either of its two great and ever warring constituents tyrannize effectively over the other. Instead, each merely lamed the other; the average opera was neither a good play spoiled by music nor good music spoiled by a play, but merely a bad play and formless music adding each to the other's foolishness. How hopelessly impotent the current opera was to furnish a form that should be adequate for all that a modern musician might have to say was shown by the practice of Beethoven: the greatest musical brain of its epoch turned in anger and disappointment and disgust from the opera after one experiment with it, and concentrated more and more on the symphonic forms, endeavoring to make these more expansive and more flexible.

A hundred composers and theorists had for a century past realized the insufficiency of the opera. Gluck's manifestos are known to every student. More than a generation after Gluck, the same problems were still being discussed in virtually the same terms and with the same results.

Theory was evidently a long way ahead of practice; but even theory failed because it missed just the one seminal thing that it was Wagner's mission to bring to light. The excellencies and the final limitations of the theory of the time are best seen in a little known but rather remarkable work—Ignaz Franz Mosel's *Versuch einer Aesthetik des dramatischen Tonsatzes* (*Attempt at an Aesthetic of the Musical Drama*)—that, curiously enough, was published in the year of Wagner's birth.[6] Much in this book might have been written by Gluck; some of it might even have been written by Wagner himself. Mosel expresses more clearly perhaps than any previous writer that conception of the unified art work upon which Wagner so strongly insisted. For Mosel the ideal opera is a combination, on practically equal terms, of poetry, music, acting, singing, and the art of the stage; the plastic arts, however, play a smaller part in his theory than they do in Wagner's. He regards the drama as the basis of opera. He sees, as Wagner did, that the rules of procedure of pure music are not applicable in their entirety to the dramatic stage. Like Wagner, again, he holds that complicated subjects, founded on intrigue or political action, are unsuitable for opera. Music being a purely emotional art, addressing itself more to the heart than the head, the best subject is that that gives full play to the emotional power of tone. The best subjects are the mythological ones. The poet must so shape his text that it is "thoroughly musical, that is, not only containing nothing that is outside the possibility of musical expression, but also nothing to which music cannot give a heightened beauty and a strengthened effect." The verse should be of such a kind that the composer's melody can spring naturally out of it. As a rule one syllable should be set to one note only. The melody must rise or fall precisely at the point where a good declaimer of the verses who is not musical would

---

[6] It was republished a few years ago with an introduction and notes by Dr. Eugen Schmitz. (Verlag Dr. Heinrich Lewy, Munich.)

make them do so. Mosel sees that dramatic music frequently demands a different method of structure from that of pure music; as he puts it, the so-called musical period of two, four, or eight-bar melodies can often be departed from with advantage. The style of the music as a whole must vary with the quality of the poetic subject; and not only must the general nature of the theme be reproduced in music, but also the physical, moral, or conventional character of each person; and this adaptability of style to subject must be preserved in the orchestra as well as in the voice. The overture, having for its subject the preparation of the hearer for what is to come, must bear the same character as that which is dominant in the opera itself. There must be as little distinction as possible between recitative and aria. Form and expression must always follow the feeling. And so on and so on.

This was the sole result of a hundred years of keen theory and ardent practice. The form of opera remained virtually what it always had been; the most that anyone could suggest was a rationalizing of the form here and there, the ridding it of some excrescence or absurdity. And so, in all probability, it would have remained for another hundred years, had not Wagner come with the conception that the old form itself was not worth tinkering with but must be cast aside and a new one made, not out of Mozart, not out of Gluck, not, indeed, out of any opera whatever, but *out of the instrumental music of Beethoven*. And this was a marvelous perception for one man out of all Europe's music-making millions to have.

His own accounts of the dawning of this idea upon him betray a fundamental inconsistency. On the one hand he is always stoutly asserting that he only found his way to the new music at the impulse and under the guidance of the poet. On the other hand it is clearer to us than it was to him that the poet in him was allowed to co-operate with the musician only in much the same way that the poet is allowed to co-operate in the symphonic poem. The musician, that is to say, feels a vague desire to express certain emotions of love, of pity, of terror, of aspiration; and he calls in the poet to supply him with a framework that shall be able to give consistency to his emotions and make the sequence of them intelligible to his hearers. Wagner, in his analysis of his own psychological processes, inverted the real relations of them, misled by the fact that *as a musician he developed much later than as a poet*—the obvious reason for this being that in poetry he had not, as in music, to make a new instrument, a new vocabulary and a new technique for himself. But even from his own account it is evident that the new ideal of music drama arose in him through the convergence of two great impressions—the acting and singing of Schröder-Devrient, and the later sonatas, symphonies, and quartets of Beethoven. He was amazed to find how much Schröder-Devrient could do in the way of dramatic expression with the poor puppets and absurd situations of the Italian opera stage. "I said to myself, what an incomparable work must that be, that in all its parts should be worthy of the histrionic talent of such an artist, and still more, of a body of artists like her." Then, he says, he got the idea of what could be done with the operatic genre "by turning the whole rich stream of German music, that Beethoven had swelled to the full, into the bed of the musical drama." [7]

And the essence of Beethoven's achievement, at its best, as he saw, was that not only had all the earlier formalism become inevitable form, but that form itself was dissolved in the idea; the Beethoven symphony becomes in the end simply a continuous flood of meaningful melody. "For it is surprising," he says, "that this method of procedure, developed in the field of instrumental music, should have been employed to some degree in mixed choral and orchestral music, but as yet never properly in opera. . . . Yet the possibility must exist of obtaining in the dramatic poem itself a poetic counterpart to the

[7] "*Zukunftsmusik*," in G.S., vii, 97.

symphonic form, which, while it completely fills this copious form, should at the same time correspond to the inmost laws of dramatic form." [8]

The real ancestry of Wagner the opera writer is then clear enough; it is not an operatic but a symphonic ancestry. I therefore cannot wholly agree with Dr. Guido Adler that "as an opera composer Wagner stands in the frame of Renaissance art and culture. His fundamental aims coincide more or less with those of the founders of that culture epoch in general and of the representatives of the High Renaissance in the musical drama in particular. . . . The founders of the opera created the *stilo rappresentativo*, in which the musical expression was to follow the representations and the actions as closely as possible. . . . The true theatre style proceeds historically from Peri, Monteverdi and Cavalli to Wagner and Verdi. These are the representatives of emotionalism in music, of that fundamental æsthetic principle that recognises expression as the sole or main essence of music." [9] Resemblances between Wagner and the Renaissance founders of the opera there certainly are; but in comparison with the basic difference between him and them the resemblances are superficial. That basic difference is that while their reforms were born of the desire to model music upon and control it by speech,[1] Wagner's reform was born of the conception that the most copious and eloquent of musical instruments is the orchestra, to the emotions of which the voices, by means of words, can give direction and precision. Wagner's true lineage is that of instrumental music, the symphony and the symphonic poem.

[8] *"Zukunftsmusik,"* in G.S., vii, 127, 128.
[9] Guido Adler: *Richard Wagner: Vorlesungen gehalten an der Universität zu Wien*, pp. 3 ff.
[1] This is a broadly true statement of the historical facts, though it has to be remembered that the theory that the *first* Florentine reformers aimed at a *recitative-like* delivery of a dramatic idea is only one of the errors of the popular historian. Their earliest attempts were more in the arioso form. See Hugo Riemann's *Handbuch der Musikgeschichte*, ii, 2, chap. xxiii.

He is not the child either of the stage or of the song; the instrumental musician in him simply enters into an alliance with these for purposes of his own.

XVII · *Poetic Music and the Program*

Of this he was more than half conscious himself; and it was always clear to him that as he was in the great line of instrumental succession, and that what he was doing was to extend still further the expressive range of instrumental, endlessly melodic music, it might be urged against him that the logical outcome of all his theory and his practice was not the opera but the symphonic poem or the program symphony. But against that conclusion he always strenuously protested in advance. Something he saw there *must* be to make definite to the hearer the indefinite emotion of the music alone. He knew that the classical symphony was a work of composite origin, one movement of it—the Minuet or Scherzo—still maintaining almost unchanged its dancelike character, while in the others the composer aimed more and more at emotional expression. But the musician was hampered here by the fact that the expression of emotion could not rise above a certain intensity without bursting the symphonic mold, and indeed prompting in the hearer a question as to the source of that emotion. There was, as Wagner says, "a certain fear of overstepping the bounds of musical expression, and especially of pitching the passionate, tragic tendency too high, for that would arouse feelings and expectations that would awake in the hearer the disquieting question of 'Why,'—which the musician himself could not answer satisfactorily." [2] But Wagner would not admit that this something might be a mere program. "Not a programme, which rather provokes than silences the troublesome question of 'why,' can therefore express the meaning of the symphony, but only the scenically-represented dramatic action itself." [3] With the liberation

[2] "*Zukunftsmusik*," in *G.S.*, vii, 128.
[3] Ibid., vii, 129.

of musical expression from the stereotyped images set before it in the ordinary musical verse, and with the liberation of musical technique effected by the breaking down of the old operatic conventions of form, the power of music could be extended indefinitely. The poet would discover that "melodic form is capable of endlessly richer development than had previously been possible in the symphony itself, and, with a presentiment of this development, he will already project the poetical conception with perfect freedom. Thus where even the symphonist timidly reached back to the original dance-form—never daring, even for his expression, wholly to pass the boundaries that kept him in communication with this form—the poet will now cry to him: 'Throw yourself fearlessly into the full stream of the sea of music: hand in hand with me you can never lose touch with what is most comprehensible to all mankind; for through me you always stand on the ground of the dramatic action, and this action, in the moment of its representation on the stage, is the most immediately intelligible of all poems. Stretch your melody boldly out, that it may pour through the whole work like an endless flood: in it say what I have unsaid, since you can only say it, and in silence I will utter all, since it is I who lead you by the hand.' " [4]

Here he is expressing only a personal bias. His own imagination was somewhat timid; it preferred the seen to the unseen, and he was consequently quite unable to take up the point of view of people to whom a thing mentally conceived is as impressive as, or even more impressive than, the same thing set bodily before their eyes. Had he had any inkling of this, he would not have brought so many animals upon the scene. The most striking instance of his inability to trust to the spectator's imagination is his vacillation over the ending of *Tannhäuser*. In the first version of the final scene, the last attempt of Venus to win back her old lover was shown only as a struggle in the mind of the frenzied Tannhäuser, with a red glow in the direction of the distant Hörselberg to

[4] *"Zukunftsmusik,"* in *G.S.*, vii, 129.

make the cause of the madness clear. The death of Elisabeth was merely divined by the intuition of Wolfram, while the sound of far-off bells and the faint light of torches on the Wartburg gave the spectator the hint he needed for the full comprehension of the scene. But Wagner was uncomfortable until he had made everything visible that had formerly been left to the imagination; so Venus had to appear in person to Tannhäuser and to the spectators, and the bier of Elisabeth had to be carried across the stage. It would have been better, in this and in many other cases, had he reposed more faith in the imagination of his audience. But his theory and his practice were often inconsistent in this as in so many other matters. We have seen him objecting, à propos of Berlioz's *Romeo and Juliet*, to music that required an explanation outside itself to make it clear. But several of his own orchestral pieces are unintelligible without a verbal explanation or its equivalent. Who could make anything of the prelude to the third act of *Tannhäuser*, for example, in the absence of such an explanation? It cannot even be said that the dramatic play of the motives is clear to anyone who has listened carefully to the opera, for the theme of Tannhäuser's pilgrimage, which is of such importance in the prelude, does not occur till the third act; during the prelude to that act the hearer who is listening to it for the first time must be ignorant not merely of its meaning but of its very existence. How, again, can the audience be expected to know, the first time they hear it, that the opening theme of the prelude to the third act of *Die Meistersinger* symbolizes Sachs's renunciation of Eva? The theme has appeared in the second act as an orchestral counterpoint during one of the stanzas of the cobbling song. Even supposing the hearer to have any notion on that occasion that the theme is more than an ordinary counterpoint—that it has a psychological significance—how is he to know what this later significance is; and how is he to read this meaning into it when he hears it at the commencement of the third act? It all has to be made clear to him by a prose explanation, as Wagner himself recognized when he wrote his explanatory program note upon the prelude. In the light of this and other instances that could be cited, how can Wagner consistently deny to other composers the right to call in the aid of verbal explanations for their symphonic poems or program symphonies?

xviii · *Contradictions between Theory and Practice*

There are as many contradictions between Wagner's theory and practice, indeed, as between his life and his art. Without attempting the impossible task of trying to reconcile them all, let us cast a rapid glance over the main features of his practice, which are far more important than his theory. From every side we are driven to the conclusion that the dominating force in him was the instrumental musician who was born to continue Beethoven's work in another sphere. As his powers developed, his music becomes more symphonic,[5] and he intuitively shapes his poems so as to allow the freest possible play to the symphonic succession and interweaving of themes. The characters serve to make the course of the story clear, and to give precision to the emotions that are being expressed by the orchestra. He saw in Beethoven's later works a colossal effort to make music free. Logic of some kind there must be in every piece of music. This logic depends fundamentally upon showing the interrelation of each part of the music by the recurrence of significant themes; and broadly speaking, there are only two ways of achieving this—by way of pattern or by way of poetry. At bottom all form, all logic, in music, in fiction, in drama, in architecture, in sculpture, is one in object and

[5] I do not mean, of course, that it has anything to do with the symphony in the formal sense, but that the orchestra weaves a continuous tissue of its own, instead of merely accompanying the voices as in the earlier operas.

process; a coherent whole has to be made out of parts, and the parts have to justify their existence by showing themselves indispensable to the whole. Pattern form and poetic form embrace between them every mode of structure of which music is capable. Sometimes a piece of music leans markedly to the one or the other; but in the vast majority of cases the actual form is a union of the two, or a compromise between them. It was a compromise of this kind that Wagner detected in some of the greatest works of Beethoven; the form that had been evolved mainly with reference to pattern was being applied, with only partial success, to music the prime impulse of which was poetic—however vague this poetry might be, however incapable of expression in words. But while pattern form pure and simple tells its own story and is its own justification, poetic form needs to be explained and justified by the poetic idea that is at the root of it. Go beyond Beethoven, says Wagner, in the expression of poetic emotion, and your form will become so free that the hearer will no longer be able to see it in terms of the old pattern logic, and the music will seem to him formless and incoherent. You can only win the full freedom you need for the expression of definite as distinguished from indefinite emotion by telling the hearer the nature and the source of this emotion. As Wagner put it, poetic music in pattern form always prompts the question "Why?" The symphonic poem writer answers with his program: Wagner answered with the characters and the action of the program set visible before us on a stage. There is no such fundamental aesthetic difference between the two methods as Wagner imagined; the differences are only in detail.[6]

The curious thing is that for all his theories, Wagner himself now and then wrote instrumental pieces that prompt a "Why?" as emphatically as anything of Beethoven's. He despised what he called the "quadrature musicians"—the composers who take refuge in phrases cut to a regulation length and pattern and worked out in

[6] See Appendix B.

a stereotyped four-square form. Music meant little or nothing to him unless it spoke directly of humanity and to humanity. No theme must be invented for mere invention's sake, or worked out for the mere sake of working out; it must spring into being as the expression of an overwhelming human need or of some arousing vision, and must answer in all its changes to the changing life of the man or mood it painted. It was this inevitableness of idea and of form that he admired in Beethoven and missed in Brahms. His inability to compromise on the matter made him contemptuously sweep out of existence most of the music of his day. It was precisely in this broadening of the Beethovenian spirit and design, and the making them capable of expressing every emotion that mankind can feel, that he himself opened out such enormous possibilities in music.

The ordinary "abstract" composer's mind must have been a pure puzzle to a man like him, who could not understand how modern music could have any *raison d'être* apart from something definitely poetic or pictorial to be expressed. To invent a theme for its own abstract sake, to pare and shape it till it was "workable," and then to weave it along with others of the same kind into a pattern of which the main lines were predetermined for him by tradition—this was something he could not imagine himself doing, and that he scoffed at when he found the Conservatoire musician engaged in it. "I simply cannot compose at all," he said once, "when nothing occurs to me." [7] He must always have a definite subject, which was to determine the nature of the theme and control the whole course of the development. Looking back through the music of the generation that has followed him, we can see how penetrating his vision was in all questions of expression and form. Beethoven's innovations, he points out, were mostly in the field of rhythmic distribution, not that of harmonic modulation. Rhythmic changes of all kinds come naturally within the scope of the ordinary symphonic movement, which is in essence an ideal dance;

[7] "On Operatic Poetry and Composition," in *G.S.*, x, 172.

but startling melodic or harmonic changes, or attempted subtleties of form, generally prompt that awkward question "Why?" and leave it unanswered. Take, for example, the efforts that have been made in our own day to unify the four-movement sonata form by the carrying over of themes from one movement to another, as in César Franck's violin and pianoforte sonata. Attach a poetic significance to a theme, and its recurrence in another movement explains itself; but in a piece of ostensibly abstract music the recurrence simply puzzles us. No satisfactory answer can be given—except in terms of a program —to the question of why a theme that has apparently served its purpose should be resuscitated by the composer at a later stage, in preference to the invention of a fresh theme. For every effect the composer makes, the logician in us insists upon knowing the cause. Hence the soundness of Wagner's advice to the modern composer—Do not consciously aim at harmonic and instrumental effects, but wait till there is a sufficient cause for them.[8] His own practice was a model of restraint: not one modulation, not one subtilization of the harmony, not one addition to the orchestral weight without a thoroughly good reason, rooted in the nature of the idea itself. "In the instrumental prelude to the *Rhinegold*, for instance," he says, "it was impossible for me to quit the fundamental note, for there was no reason whatever for changing it. A great part of the not unanimated scene that follows between Alberich and the Rhine Maidens permitted of modulation only to the most closely related keys, since passion still expresses itself here in its most primitive *naïveté*." [9] The rule he would enforce upon pupils is this: "Never leave a key so long as what you have to say can still be said in it." And only when the emotion becomes more complex must the harmony be colored more subtly to correspond. This, he lays it down, constitutes the great difference between the symphonic and the dramatic devel-

[8] "On the Application of Music to the Drama," in *G.S.*, x, 186.
[9] Ibid., x, 186, 187.

opment of themes. In the former the effect is meant to be kaleidoscopic; and a real master can work wonders in the arabesque-like combination and transformation of simple material. But do what he will, he cannot venture upon the variety of the dramatic composer, for if he goes beyond a certain point of audacity or singularity, he ceases to be intelligible in terms of pure music. "Neither a mere play of counterpoint, nor the most fanciful devices of figuration or harmonic invention, either could or should transform a theme so characteristically and give it so many and so varied expressions—and yet keep it always recognisable—as true dramatic art can do quite naturally." Proof of this can be had by pursuing the simple theme of the Rhine Maidens—

Rhein - gold! Rhein - gold!

"through all the changing passions of the four-part drama, down to Hagen's watch song in the first Act of the *Götterdämmerung*, where it appears in a form that, to me at any rate, is simply unthinkable as the theme of a symphonic movement, albeit it still has its *raison d'être* in the laws of harmony and thematism, though only in their application to the drama. But to try to apply what is thus made possible to the symphony itself must necessarily lead to the complete ruin of the latter; for there it would be merely a deliberate 'effect,' while in the other case it has a motive." [1] And he ends with the theory that symphonic

[1] "On the Application of Music to the Drama," in *G.S.*, x, 189, 190. The variation of the theme to which Wagner refers is as follows:

music and dramatic music are two quite different modes of expression, and that only errors of practice and of judgment can come from the attempt to blend them. This dictum the musicians of a later day can accept only with reservations. We admit that he did well to draw a line of sharp distinction between the older symphonic moods and forms and those of musical drama. But he overlooked the fact that the basic distinction was not between symphony and drama, but between purely abstract music of all kinds and purely poetic music of all kinds. There are procedures open to the latter which are still not open to the former— virtually as many procedures, indeed, as are open to opera itself. For the principle of the symphonic poem is at bottom the same as that of the musical drama—to follow in music the vicissitudes of a poetic idea; and given a knowledge of this idea on our part, whether it be communicated to us by a stage action or by a prose or poetic explanation, the composer is at liberty to indulge in as many audacities of melody, of harmony, of modulation as may be justified by the nature of his subject. Wagner, as I have tried to show, was prevented from applying his own principles to purely instrumental poetic music by his inability to follow imaginatively the "moments" of an action that was merely suggested to him, instead of being actualized on the stage. But there is no reason why *we* should fail to draw the conclusion that is obviously implicit in Wagner's own argument as to the relations of music and poetic suggestion. The strange thing is that every now and then he himself made an excursion into the fields he attempted to close to others. His *Faust* Overture, for example, is a pure symphonic poem, the full meaning of which only becomes apparent to us when we know the poetic subject. The opening tuba theme is of a type that a composer would hesitate to use for the opening "subject" of a symphony; it receives both its explanation and its justification solely from our knowledge that it depicts the world-weary Faust. The case of the *Siegfried Idyl* is still more instructive. That exquisite piece of music puzzles us once or twice by the apparent abruptness of its transitions. We might have guessed, from our knowledge of Wagner's precepts and practice, that he is following a quasi-poetic scheme of his own, and that the music does not always tell a coherent story to us because he has seen fit to keep this scheme from us. We now know for certain, on the testimony of Glasenapp, that this is so. Here we have another instance of flat contradiction between Wagner's theory and his practice. But had he reflected that a knowledge of the poetic basis of the *Siegfried Idyl* is necessary to us if we are to see the same coherence in the music as he saw, he would have been bound to admit that the communication of the poetic basis of any symphonic poem will justify the composer in writing in a style that would be unsuitable to abstract music—a style differing very little in its fundamentals from that of the Wagnerian stage. No middle course is possible: whatever justifies the Wagnerian music drama justifies also *Till Eulenspiegel* and the *L'Après-midi d'un faune*—not for Wagner, perhaps, but certainly for us.

His intransigent attitude toward program music is all the stranger in view of the fact that he persistently read concrete meanings or events into the music that moved him. Everyone knows his interpretation of certain of Beethoven's symphonies and the C sharp minor quartet. He read quasi-pictures and even words into certain of Bach's fugues; for the seventeenth fugue and the twenty-fourth prelude he had half a mind to write appropriate words. He ought to have seen that if instrumental music could thus suggest concrete associations, *vice versa* similar associations could also suggest music to correspond with them, and that the logical and inevitable outcome of this alliance between music and poetic suggestion is program music. It is interesting to learn, however, that in his last days he often talked of writing a symphony. He had, he says, no lack of ideas; his difficulty was to stop inventing. His symphony would have been in one movement only; "the finales are the awkward things [*Klippe*]; I will steer clear of them; I will keep to one-movement symphonies." Nor would he base them on the old system of theme contrast. Beethoven had exhausted the possibilities of that form. His own style would be that of a continuous melodic web—the principle, indeed, that we can see at work in all the operas of his maturity. "Only," he added, "no drama"; evidently his prejudice against story music apart from the stage persisted to the end.[2] The projected symphonies would apparently have been on the lines of the *Siegfried Idyl* and the larger pianoforte works such as the *Albumblatt for Betty Schott* (1875), the *Albumblatt for the Princess Metternich* (1861), the *Album Sonata for Frau Wesendonck* (1853), and the *Ankunft bei den schwarzen Schwänen* (1861). If so, we should probably have been compelled to pass the same criticism upon the symphonies as we do upon these works—that in spite of their unquestionable beauty we are sometimes at a loss to see the same coherence in them that they must have had for him. In the lengthy *Album Sonata for Frau Wesendonck*, for example, we feel that he is all the while following the outlines of some unavowed poetic theme, slackening and tightening the expression, lightening and darkening it, hurrying and pausing, in conformity with the demands of that. A musical picture of this kind, which disdains formal development of the pattern order, and simply weaves its tissue out of moods, is much more difficult on a large scale than on a small one. The trouble begins when a transition has to be made from one mood to another. In his last days Wagner was capable of wonderful quasi-symphonic meditations on a given theme; nothing could surpass for pure beauty or for continuity of invention the long orchestral passage that accompanies Kundry's account of Parsifal's mother (vocal score, p. 187 *ff.*). We feel that Wagner could have indeed worked marvels in this way to the end: but, as he himself once said in a letter to Frau Wesendonck, the art of composition is really the art of transition; and one fears that his symphonic transitions would have failed to make their reasons clear to us. The astounding tissue of *Götterdäm-*

[2] For details of these and other speculations of his, see the sixth volume of Glasenapp's Life.

merung teems with transitions of the most abrupt kind; but they are all intelligible because the physiognomies of the leitmotivs are familiar to us, and every allusion is instantaneously clear. Their logic is only partly in themselves, and partly in the poetic ideas of which they are the symbols. It seems probable that his symphonies would have been Siegfried Idyls on a larger scale, possessing every virtue but that of self-explanatory continuity.

· 3 ·

The Artist in Practice

❧

1 · *The Early Miscellaneous Works*

According to Wagner's own account, he sketched tragedies in his childhood, and worked out one that was a sort of blend of *Hamlet* and *King Lear*; and, inspired by Beethoven's *Egmont*, he desired to adorn this grand tragedy with music of his own. A brief study of Logier's *Method of Thorough-Bass* did not provide him with the needed technique; however, convinced that he was born to be a musician, he wrote a sonata, a quartet, and an aria in secret. In his sixteenth year he placed himself under a teacher, who, however, could do nothing with him in the excessively febrile state in which he then was. His nervous excitement culminated in a round of the usual student excesses; and having calmed down again he set himself to study composition in earnest with Weinlig, the cantor of the Thomas School. Six months' work sufficed to satisfy Weinlig that his pupil was now competent to stand on his own legs. It is at this time (1831) that he produces the compositions that are the earliest we now possess of his.

At present he has apparently no inclination toward opera. The raw works of his adolescence had all been instrumental; among them was the Overture in B flat major (1830) which was performed in the Leipzig theater, and in which the drum beat every four bars ended by moving the audience to uncontrollable merriment. It is not till the summer of 1832 that he plans a first opera, *Die Hochzeit;* he writes the text, but composes no more than a fragment of the music. Meanwhile he produces, as the result of Weinlig's schooling, a number of instrumental works more or less in the conventional style. The pianoforte sonata in B flat major which was published by Breitkopf & Härtel as the composer's Op. 1 is dedicated to Weinlig, under whose eye the work was written. His teacher had evidently seen the need for curbing the exuberance of the boy's undisciplined mind. He made him write simply, in the set forms, and with regard to the clarities of the pure vocal style. For this first sonata, Wagner tells us, Weinlig induced him to take an early sonata by Pleyel as a model; the whole work was to be shaped on "strictly harmonic and thematic lines." Wagner himself never thought much of it. But if it is no more than an imitation of the current sonata style, it is an unmistakably capable imitation. Weinlig was right; he had given his pupil independence. In all these youthful works, indeed, we are struck by the unquestioning self-confidence of the manner, and by the boyish vigor that animates them. As a reward for his docility in the matter of the sonata, he was allowed by Weinlig to compose a pianoforte fantasia in F sharp minor. He treated this, he says, in a more informal style. It is really a quite powerful work for a boy of eighteen. It defines a mood, and maintains it with singular persistence; it expresses something truly f lt; it comes from the brooding absorption of spirit that was afterward to produce the *Faust* Overture. It is liberally sown with recitative passages that suggest some knowledge of Bach (the Chromatic Fantasia or the G minor Fantasia for the organ), or of Beethoven (pianoforte sonata in A flat, Op. 110, etc.). The manner and feeling of the adagio suggest the slow movement of Beethoven's Fifth Symphony, the later ornamentation of the main melodic idea being quite in the style of that movement. Altogether the Fantasia is by no means a work to be despised; it is the one composition of Wagner's of this period in which we catch a decided note of promise for the future.

The Polonaise in D major for four hands (1831) is more in the conventional manner, but quite interesting, and as original as we can expect from the average young composer of eighteen. The A major sonata (Op. 4, 1831) flows on in the glib, confident way that is characteristic of all his early instrumental works, and has many good points. The weakest movement is the third—a rather amateurish fugue. There is some expression in the slow movement, and a general freedom of style everywhere except in the fugue. The idiom as a whole is that of the early Beethoven, but occasionally the writing suggests a boy who knew something of Weber and of the later Beethoven, though his invention and his technique were as yet equal only to imitating the simpler models.

For its day the Symphony in C major (1832) is a very capable piece of student work; the interest slackens considerably in the finale, but the other movements are handled with the customary young-Wagnerian vigor and confidence. In spite of the ease and the cleverness of it, however, we can rarely feel that it is anything more than a piece of competent school work, though there is undeniable thoughtfulness in the andante.

The work of the next five years varies in quality and purpose in a most puzzling way. In 1832 he writes the *King Enzio* Overture, under the influence, as he tells us in *Mein Leben*, of Beethoven. It is plainly modeled on the dramatic overture of the *Egmont* and *Coriolan* type— a type that Mendelssohn, in the *Ruy Blas* and elsewhere, afterward cultivated, without, however, adding anything to it. The young Wagner has a thorough grasp of the form. The overture is concise and well balanced; all the details are clearly seen in relation to the dominant idea. The thematic invention is good, the themes being not only expressive in themselves but capable of bearing the weight of a certain amount of dramatic development. Yet after writing this fine overture, which really may point without presumption to Beethoven as its parent, he was capable of producing in 1836 the shapeless and frothy *Polonia* Overture, which is the oddest mixture of a pseudo Polish idiom and the cheap, assertive melody of *Rienzi*. Here and there it gives us a foretaste of his later power of climax building, but on the whole it is a feeble and amorphous work. The *Rule, Britannia* Overture (1836) is hardly any better; it is a long-winded and pointless dissertation on our patriotic song, the original tune being by far the best thing in it. The *Columbus* Overture of the preceding year is rather better. Its style is a curious blend of Beethoven, *Rienzi*, and the Italian opera; it is oddly anticipatory of Liszt in its repetitions and its make-believe development: but the work has a sort of strength. It is evidently the outcome of a vision clearly seen, and translated into as good music as Wagner's powers at that time permitted.

Meanwhile in 1832—the same year as the *King Enzio* Overture and the C major symphony—he had written *Seven Compositions to Goethe's Faust*—"The soldiers' song," the "Peasants under the linden," "The song of the rat," "The song of the flea," Mephistopheles' song ("*Was machst du mir vor Liebchens Tür*"), Margaret's song ("*Meine Ruh' ist hin*"), and a "melodrama" to accompany the recitation of Margaret's prayer to the Virgin.[1] Almost all of these have individuality, the least notable being Mephistopheles' song. The soldiers' song is breezy, with one or two crudities in the vocal part-writing. The "*Bauern unter der Linde*" is fresh and gay; the rat and flea songs are fairly humorous; it is rather curious that Wagner's rat song should begin with the full scale of D major in descending motion, while that of Berlioz commences with the same scale in ascent. Margaret's song is quite good, though it moves a little stiffly, and has neither the ardor of Schubert's setting nor the perfect mating

[1] Three years before this, Berlioz had written *Eight Scenes from Goethe's Faust*—the germ of his *Damnation of Faust*.

of idea and expression which we find in that masterpiece. Wagner, indeed, developed very slowly. For a long time his genius could only move heavily: there was no swiftness in him, either of idea or of form—no consuming heat. The melodrama is expressive, and the reiterated syncopations are effective. Wagner probably chose the melodrama form, rather than a purely lyrical setting of the words, because he felt that the former gave the dramatist in him more scope.

In 1832–3 the dramatic impulse became very strong in him. He had written the *Hochzeit* fragment and *Die Feen* by the end of 1833, and between 1834 and 1836 he finished *Das Liebesverbot*. Already he had a technique equal to the expression of all the dramatic thinking of which he was capable at the time. How dexterous his hand had become is shown incidentally in the aria he added to Marschner's *Der Vampyr* in 1833—a very vigorous and finished piece of work. There is the same skill in the "Romance of Max," which he added to the Singspiel *Marie, Max and Michel* (1837). There is piquancy in the scoring of the latter, and the vocal part has a rhythmic variety that we do not often find in *Tannhäuser* and *Lohengrin*. Apparently the only nondramatic work he wrote at this time was the *New Year Cantata*, which is one of the freshest and most pleasing works of his youth. It consists of an overture and four other movements; the chorus takes part in the second and fourth of these, but in the latter the vocal parts are merely sketched in, and the words are lacking. In the slow opening section of the overture he introduces in the violas and cellos, with excellent effect, the theme of the andante of his C major symphony; it is apparently intended to symbolize the sadness of the departing year. It is impossible not to be captivated by the sincerity and the transparent simplicity of this little work.

During 1838 and 1839 his time was fully taken up with his theatrical duties at Königsberg and Riga, the composition of *Rienzi*, and the working out of other dramatic ideas; so that from 1837 to 1840 what may be called the occasional compositions are few in number. With the exception of the aria for *Marie, Max and Michel,* and the *Faust* compositions, his vocal works had so far all been settings of words of his own. Between 1837 and 1844 the texts of almost all his songs and choral works were by other people. At Riga, in 1837, he set a poem by Harald von Brackel in praise of the Tsar Nicholas, for soprano or tenor solo, chorus, and orchestra. The piece is appropriately broad and massive, and imposing enough in mere volume; but it is impossible to believe that Wagner's heart was in a work of this kind.

Of much more interest is "*Der Tannenbaum,*" a setting of a poem by Scheuerlein (end of 1838). The song is expressive, though the effect lies more in the general color, the harmony, and the pictorial realization of the scene— the brooding tree, the river, and the boy are all differentiated—than in any particularly striking quality in the melody. The vocal line has more flexibility than is usual with the young Wagner. In July 1839 he entered upon his Paris adventure. For a while he eagerly pursues his fortune among the theatrical directors; then, as his hopes fail him and need gnaws at his heart, he produces a number of vocal works that he trusts may appeal to the French singers and the French public. Some of these are potboilers pure and simple, the writing of which must have been gall and bitterness to the young composer who had by now begun to realize the wonderful music there was in him. The lowest depth is touched in the vaudeville chorus "*La Descente de la Courtille*" (1840)—a frank prostitution of his genius to the most superficial French taste of the time. Almost as bad is the song *Les Adieux de Marie Stuart.*" A bar or two here and there bears the signature of the true Wagner—he cannot quite keep his real self out of it; but on the whole the song is a desperate, pitiful attempt to manufacture something in the conventional French and Italian operatic idiom of the day. Wagner's tongue must have been in his cheek when he penned such passages as these:

To the same period and the same catchpenny mood belongs the *Aria of Orovisto*, which he wrote in the hope that Lablache would sing it in Bellini's *Norma*. It is an amusingly absurd but skillful imitation of all the tricks-of-the-trade of the Italian opera of the thirties.

Other works of this time are more sincere, and most of them have a decided charm. The Albumblatt in E major, written for his friend Kietz, is a simple but engaging piece, with a touch or two of melodic commonplace —the occasional insertion, for example, of a triplet group in a duple-time phrase. The little work is curiously like the *Lohengrin* of seven years later in general texture, in melodic and harmonic build, and in the peculiar white light in which it is bathed. The songs to French words, written at Paris in 1839–40, vary greatly in quality. The *"Tout n'est qu'images fugitives"* never descends to the depth of banality reached in the *"Les Adieux de Marie Stuart,"* but the effort to be ingratiatingly French is plainly evident. *"Dors, mon enfant,"* *"Mignonne,"* and *"Attente"* are all charming; he thinks of the French style and the French public no more than is necessary to lighten the heaviness of his native German manner, and the results are sometimes surprising, particularly in the matter of rhythm. For many years to come, as he admits in a well-known letter to Uhlig, he was obsessed by a vocal rhythm of this type:

—a type upon which hundreds of phrases in *The Flying Dutchman*, *Tannhäuser*, and *Lohengrin* are constructed. The best of these French songs have a rhythmic freedom and flexibility that he rarely attained in his later operas. Look, for example, at the following delightfully elastic vocal line from "*Attente*":

Assez vite

Ci - cogne, aux vieil - les tours fi - dè - le, ô—

vo - le et— mon - te à ti - re d'ai - le de l'é -

glise à la ci - ta - del - le, du— haut clo - cher, du

haut clo - cher au grand— don - jon.

It has always been evident that the rhythmic sameness of the earlier operas was mainly due to the monotonously regular recurrence of accents in the German verse he wrote at that time. These French songs make it clear—as, by the way, does the aria for *Marie*, *Max and Michel*—that when a more varied metrical scheme was given him, his music spontaneously varied with it. One cannot help feeling that in some ways it is a pity he did not meet with more success at Paris—that he was not allowed, in fact, to write some large work with the deliberate intention of appealing to the French taste by an exploitation of the styles and the formulas the Parisian public loved most. Such a work would not have represented the real Wagner, and in the end would probably have been negligible; but it would have given a much needed lightness and elasticity to his imagination, without harming him in any way. He would have benefited by such an experience as surely as Handel and Mozart benefited by their experiences with Italian opera. As it was, a certain slowness and ponderousness remain characteristic of Wagner to the end of his days. This inability to concentrate rapidly is instinctively shown in his French setting of Heine's *"Les Deux Grenadiers"* (1839–40). In general expressiveness the song need not fear comparison with Schumann's: perhaps Wagner's treatment of the *"Marseillaise"* at the end is even better. But the work has nothing of Schumann's terseness, ease, and lyric spontaneity; the whole thing moves a little stiff-jointedly.

The Paris period is a curious one in Wagner's artistic history. He wrote some very good songs, and one or two deplorable things like the *"Les Adieux de Marie Stuart"* and *"La Descente de la Courtille"*; at the same time, he was finishing *Rienzi* and working at *The Flying Dutchman,* and the *Faust* Overture assumed its first form. In April 1842 he settled at Dresden. Between then and 1848 he composed *Tannhäuser* and *Lohengrin,* and conceived the first idea of the *Ring* and other works. During this period he wrote no songs or pianoforte pieces: the occasional compositions are all choral works, which is sufficiently accounted for by the fact that Wagner had a good male-voice choir at his disposal. The most considerable of these works is *The Love Feast of the Apostles* (1843). Toward the end it has a touch of the melodic commonplace that Wagner found it so hard to avoid at this time; but the earlier choral portions are impressive in their simplicity and sincerity, and the whole thing is admirably stage-managed, so to speak. The effect of the voices from on high and of the first entry of the orchestra at the descent of the Spirit must have been very striking in the Dresden church.

The other choral works of this period are on a smaller

scale. For the unveiling of a memorial to King Friedrich August I Wagner wrote in 1843 a *Weihegruss* for male voices and brass orchestra, to words by Otto Hohlfeld. The choral portion of this work was published in 1906; the whole version is now published in Breitkopf & Härtel's *Gesamtausgabe*, and shows how indispensable is the orchestral part—the long-held vocal notes, for example, being helped out by trumpet, trombone, and horn fanfares, and the whole thing gaining enormously in richness by the discreet occasional entries of the brass. The general style of this work, as of the *Greeting of Friedrich August the Beloved by his Faithful Subjects* (August 1844), is that of the *Tannhäuser-Lohengrin* epoch; some passages in the *Greeting*, indeed, are extraordinarily suggestive of the "Hall of Song" chorus. For the reinterment of Weber's remains at Dresden, in December 1844, Wagner wrote a four-part male chorus that again recalls the operatic works of this time. It is the most expressive of Wagner's works of this class, but on the whole a little disappointing; his heart was so thoroughly with Weber that one would have thought the occasion would have wrung some music of the first class out of him.

II · *The Earliest Operas*

Wagner worked out the drama of his first opera, *Die Hochzeit (The Wedding)*, in 1833, but his sister Rosalie's antipathy to the gory and gruesome subject turned him against the work after he had written only some thirty or forty pages of the score—an Introduction, chorus, and septet. The style has little individuality, though the chorus of female voices is not without charm. The septet, however, is an excellent piece of work for a boy of nineteen—lucid, freely written, and with a certain amount of dramatic differentiation in some of the vocal parts.

His first complete opera, *Die Feen (The Fairies)*, was written during his stay at Würzburg in 1833. The story, which may be read in *Mein Leben* or any of the biographies of Wagner, has long lost any interest it may once have possessed.[2] In psychology and in structure alike the drama is very primitive. The magic element in it is fit only for the nursery, though it has to be observed that here we have for the first time that notion of "redemption" that plays so large a part in Wagner's thinking to the very end of his life. The construction is formal and cumbersome: the two chief lovers have as a foil two subordinate lovers, while set off against these couples is a third pair, who provide a sort of comic interest; the whole past, present, and future are explained in recitatives; everybody of any importance has his aria or his share in a concerted piece, and each act ends with an imposing *ensemble*. The stage apparatus is romantic to the last degree.

The music, however, is decidedly interesting. The third act, in spite of a few strokes that get home, is much inferior to the other two, for which the fact that it was written in a month may be answerable. But the first two acts and the overture are full of striking things. There is no question as to the thorough competence of Wagner's technique at this time: everything flows with the utmost ease and clearness from his pen. The opera has indeed a poise of manner and a unity of style which we do not find in some of the more mature works of his first period. In *The Flying Dutchman*, for example, there is a good deal of almost hobbledehoy awkwardness—a sort of cubbish clumsiness, though any discerning observer could have seen even in those days that this was a cub of the leonine breed, which would someday swallow up most of the other animals in the menagerie. There is nothing of this cubbishness, this stumbling over his own good intentions, in *Die Feen*. Such as the ideas are—and of course they never rise to anything like the height of the best things in *The Flying Dutchman*—they are expressed without effort, in an idiom and with a technique perfectly congruous with them. Aria, duet, ensemble, dramatic contrast, dramatic transition—the young composer is equal to whatever problem may be set him. The musical style as a whole reminds us of Weber and Marschner, but there is plenty of un-

[2] The text is published in the eleventh volume of the G.S.

mistakable Wagner in it. We are constantly meeting with progressions, turns of phrase, and devices that have been made familiar to us by the later operas. How like a score of melodies in *Tannhäuser* and *Lohengrin* is the following, for example:

No. 1.

When he wants to work up the excitement at the entry of Arindal, he does it precisely in the way he whips up our interest in the coming of the hero in the second act of *Tristan und Isolde*—by a series of breathless reiterations of the same figure:

No. 2.

When he has joy to express, he does so by means of the same ascending, bubbling phrases that he uses in the duet between Tannhäuser and Elisabeth (vocal score, p. 157, etc.).[3]

No. 3.

And although the duet between Drolla and her lover Gernot is subcomic in intention, their manner of rushing into each other's arms is precisely that of Tristan and Isolde:

No. 4.

[3] All references to the operas are to the new editions of Breitkopf and Härtel.

The style is frequently mature beyond the composer's actual years—the admirable finish to the scene between Arindal and the others, for example (full score, p. 111), where the vocal themes are taken up by the orchestra and played out in a beautifully managed diminuendo; or the perfect little picture of the fairy garden at the commencement of the first act (I question whether so imaginatively conceived and skillfully colored a garden scene is to be found anywhere in previous or contemporary opera); or the expressive scoring of Ada's cavatina (full score, pp. 114 *ff.*); or the septet at the end of the first act; or the fine management of the chorus of beaten warriors at the beginning of the second act, with the reiterated calls in the bass horn and trumpet; or the fine *Schwung* of the trio between Lora, Arindal, and Morald (pp. 219 *ff.*); or the big aria of Ada in the second act (pp. 251 *ff.*); or the charming theme that is used when the children are introduced. The born musical dramatist is seen in the variety of expression he can command even at this age; and one is struck by the first signs of the faculty that is so noticeable in the later Wagner—that of always having something in reserve when a new and cumulative effect is needed. The larger the canvas to be covered, as in the final *ensembles*, the more resource does he show himself to possess. There is a good deal in *Die Feen* that is quite boyish—much that is conventional, many things to provoke a smile. But it is equally certain that there was not another young man in Europe capable of writing such a work at that time. The overture, which was written a few days before the last touches were put to the third act, is excellently handled throughout; the invention never flags, the technique never fails; it is his best work of this order until we come to the overture to *The Flying Dutchman*—finer in idea, closer in texture, and surer in touch than the *King Enzio* Overture of 1832, and far beyond the *Columbus*, the *Polonia*, or the *Rule, Britannia*. Altogether one imagines that in spite of the old-fashioned quality of the libretto of *Die Feen*, one could listen to a stage performance of the opera with at least as much interest as to

Rienzi. It was given for the first time in Munich under Hermann Levi in 1888, and between then and 1895 it ran to over fifty performances.

As we have seen, *Das Liebesverbot* (*The Ban on Love*) was a product of the wild days of 1834–5, when he had momentarily turned against sobriety both in life and in art. In framing his libretto, he passed over everything in Shakespeare's *Measure for Measure* which had a touch of moral gravity in it: he transports the action from Vienna to Sicily, brings the straitlaced viceroy Friedrich into the same focus as the other amorists, and makes the whole play an attack on "puritanical hypocrisy" and a laudation of "unrestrained physicalism." In the music he does his best to forget that "German style" in which, as he says, *Die Feen* had been written, and copies to the best of his ability the more sparkling style of the lighter Italian and French opera. The work is in two acts—the only opera of Wagner's in this form—and in its structure follows the ordinary pattern of the day. Occasionally the spoken word takes the place of recitative.

In 1866 Wagner gave the score of the opera to King Ludwig, prefacing it with a stanza in which he spoke of it as a sin of his youth, for which he hoped to find pardon in his protector's grace. Apparently he always adopted this depreciatory attitude toward the work in later life. Glasenapp tells us that Wagner liked the overture to *Das Liebesverbot* better than that to Die Feen, but thought the rest of *Das Liebesverbot* "horrible," except the "Salve regina cœli." [4] A perusal of the score, however, will convince most people that he underrated the interest and the value of it. It almost invariably fails when it aims at expressing serious feeling; but the gay and humorous scenes are admirable, and the youthful gusto of the whole thing is irresistible. The general idiom may be a borrowed one, but for the most part Wagner uses it very skillfully, making at least as good a show with it as the ordinary French or Italian opera writer of the time. He has every trick of the trade at his finger-tips, every recipe for froth and

[4] Glasenapp, vi, 187.

foam and sparkle. He is as expert as any of them at lashing up the interest by the device of repeating a piquant figure a score of times: this, for example, from the overture—

No. 5.

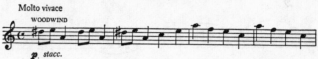

It is given first of all mainly to the strings, with a little harmonic thickening in bassoons and horns. Then, as the melody goes an octave higher in the strings, it is doubled in the oboes and clarinets, with added harmonic enrichment in the wood wind and brass. At the next repeat—an octave higher again—the melody is given out by piccolo, flutes, oboes, clarinets, and violins in octaves, while trombones are added to the harmony. All the while the tone is growing louder and louder, with a crescendo roll in the tympani. One has to listen, whether one wants to or not; and it is impossible to keep the blood from tingling under the whip. The whole overture is very effective in this noisy, rather empty way; there is much use of castagnets, tambourine, triangle, and cymbals. The general style of the writing may be gathered from a couple of examples—

No. 6.

No. 7.

and so on as before

either of which will serve to show the gulf that separates *Das Liebesverbot* from *Die Feen*.

The opening scene is very animated, the chorus of the people being full of *entrain*; the whole manner is thoroughly Italian, the orchestra chattering away more or less irrelevantly, and the voices interjecting their remarks in a facile, half-melodic sort of way. How careless Wagner was with regard to deeper musical characterization may be seen from the theme that accompanies the entry of Claudio—one of those typical Italian operatic themes of which we can never be quite sure whether they are meant to be tragic or comic, though here it is apparently meant to be serious—

No. 8.

Nor in any other work but this would Wagner have accompanied with so irresponsible a theme the appeal of Claudio (sentenced to death) to his friend Luzio to seek the aid of Isabella—

No. 9.

The melody runs a thoroughly Italian course—

No. 10.

with liberal opportunities for the tenor to poise himself
on a high note and deploy his resonance—

No. 11.

The chorus that follows is also quite in the Italian stage
style, the excitement being worked up according to the
established recipes; and of course the purely musical
stream flows on without the least regard to dramatic sense,
Luzio saying every other minute "I hasten, friend," but
without the slightest intention of hastening till the chorus
is finished. But, as almost always happens even when
Wagner is trying to be least like himself, a characteristic
little touch cannot be prevented from stealing in: after
the voices have ceased, the long-drawn theme of Claudio
sings on in the cellos, set against the noisy chattering of
the wood wind and brass. It makes a most effective ending
to the scene.

In the third scene appears a theme

No. 12.

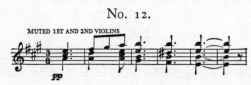

that was afterward expanded and put to splendid use in
Tannhäuser. Here the nuns sing it behind the scenes to
the words *"Salve regina cœli."*

The florid duet between the two novices, Mariana and
Isabella, is thoroughly Italian. Again one sees, by com-

parison of this music with any of that of *Die Feen*, how determined Wagner was to write down to the comprehension of the Italian-opera public: he evidently has his eye on the singers and the audience rather than on the psychology of the characters or the atmosphere of the scene. But in the admirable duologue that follows between Luzio and Isabella, the touch is again that of the born musical dramatist. It is all irresistibly animated: the music is psychologically characteristic, the blend of passion and irresponsibility in Luzio being particularly well suggested; and there are some striking pieces of orchestral color.

The court scene—the mock trial in which Brighella, the viceroy's servant, poses as the judge—is carried through excellently, with an abundance of light Italian-opera humor; the roguishly knowing theme to which Brighella sings his passion for the pretty Dorella may be taken as typical—

No. 13.

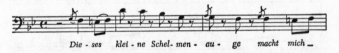

There are one or two happy instances of the tentative employment of the leading-motive system. The theme representative of Friedrich and his law against love (No. 18 below), for example, is parodied in this way when Brighella begins to try Pontio[5]—

No. 14.

[5] Cf. the parody of the theme of the Mastersingers in that of the apprentices.

and when Friedrich enters and asks Brighella what has
been going on, the latter replies apologetically and eva-
sively to the accompaniment of the previous theme of the
mock court, the orchestra, quite in the later Wagnerian
manner, being more truthful than he—

No. 15.

Isabella's aria of intercession to Friedrich is rather poor,
but the subsequent excitement is cleverly worked up, and
there is some dramatic characterization in the command-
ing phrases that are given to the viceroy. The finale is
excellent: it has amazing fire, is full of quick resource, and,
like the finales in *Die Feen*, shows how much reserve
Wagner had to draw upon when an extra effort was required.

In the opening scene of the second act—the garden of
the prison in which Claudio is awaiting death—we have
another employment of the leitmotiv, the oboe giving out

softly the theme to which Claudio had previously urged
Luzio to implore the help of Isabella, but now with appropriately altered harmonies—

No. 16.

The orchestral prelude to the scene is expressive, Wagner
putting off his Italian mask for the moment and speaking
in his natural voice: the sense of gloom and impending
tragedy is very well conveyed—

No. 17.

But the strains in which Claudio addresses Isabella are again conventional: it was not easy at this time for Wagner to find original accents for grief and passion. He is best all through the opera in scenes of humor, of comedy, of raillery. There is a charming, sunny trio later between Luzio, Isabella, and Dorella; the whole of this scene, in fact, is one of the happiest in the opera. Friedrich's soliloquy in his room has a good deal of strength in it, an impressive effect being made by the frequent recurrence in the orchestra of the motive that symbolizes the sternness of the attitude he has taken up toward the people's pleasures—

No. 18.

When he utters the words

"Doch als mir Isabella die Erdenliebe erschloss,
Da schmolz das Eis in tausend Liebesthränen."

("But when Isabella revealed earthly love to me, the ice was melted into a thousand tears of love"), the orchestra completes his thought with a reminiscence of the theme of Isabella's enchantment of him in the court (see No. 7, from the overture)—

No. 19.

The finale to the second act is as admirably animated as its predecessor; Luzio's carnival song, the dance, and the chorus have a truly southern warmth in them; and there is a lively quartet between Isabella, Dorella, Luzio, and Brighella.

Altogether *Das Liebesverbot*, like *Die Feen*, is a work upon which Wagnerian criticism will always look with an affectionate eye. If it contains much that Wagner did right to decline to take seriously in later life, there is also much in it that is eloquent of the coming dramatist in music—a surprising quickness of apprehension, a faculty for big picture-building, and above all an irresistible ardor. Like all Wagner's music of this time, the score anticipates many of the mannerisms of the later operas. It is unusually generous with the typical Wagnerian "turn"; at one point what must be a rather comic effect in performance is made by a series of these turns being executed in octaves by piccolo, flutes, oboes, clarinets, bassoons, violins, and cellos—

No. 20.

The later Wagnerian method of piling up excitement, which we have seen anticipated in *Die Feen*, is employed also in *Das Liebesverbot*, as in the following passage, which, like the one previously quoted, gives us a decided foretaste of the meeting of Tristan and Isolde—

No. 21.

And if for nothing else, *Das Liebesverbot* would be interesting for its use of the leitmotiv. There was virtually none
of it in *Die Feen*.

III · *The Operas of the Second Period*

Rienzi will always be something of a puzzle to the student.
Wagner's own accounts of it in later years show that he
too was a little uncertain as to the reasons for its obvious
defects. He had tired of his life among little theatrical
people in minor provincial towns, so he deliberately
planned *Rienzi* on an imposing scale in order that it might
be impossible except in one of the larger opera houses.
He had "grand opera" in his mind throughout, he tells us;
he intended not merely to imitate the showiest works of
this genre but to surpass them in prodigality. Yet to suppose, he adds, that this was all that was in his mind would
be to do him an injustice. He was "really inspired" by the
subject, and especially by the character of Rienzi. First and
foremost he had *Rienzi* in view, grand opera being only a
secondary consideration; yet grand opera was "only the
spectacles through which he saw the subject." He always
saw it, he goes on to say, on its own merits, and never
aimed consciously at merely musical effects; yet he could
never see the material except in terms of the merely musical effects—the arias, choruses, finales, processions, and
so on—of grand opera. "Thus on the one hand I was
always influenced by my subject in working out the details
of the work, while on the other hand I governed my subject entirely in accordance with the 'grand opera' form that
was in my mind." It is pretty evident that he found it as
difficult to come to any settled conclusion with regard to
Rienzi as we do. There is truth in the view that many
of the banalities of it are due to his having the Paris Opéra
and the Paris public in view. But we have only to study
the score in conjunction with those of *Die Feen* and *Das
Liebesverbot* to see that many of these same banalities are
the logical outcome of his cast of mind and his musical

attainments at that epoch, and would certainly have appeared in his music even if the idea of Paris had never occurred to him.

To put it familiarly, the youthful Wagner had been obviously shaping for some years for a bad attack of musical measles; he had to get it out of his system, and *Rienzi* was the illness that enabled him to do so. To me it is the least satisfactory of all his works—far less enjoyable than *Die Feen* or *Das Liebesverbot*. One can forgive the eager young-mannishness of these very youthful works: but one expects a composer to show more indubitable signs of originality at twenty-six or twenty-seven. The commonplace of *Rienzi* is different from that of the preceding operas; it is almost an offensive commonplace; the outlines of the objectionable phrases have all been thickened and the body of them puffed out till they positively irritate us by their grossness and fatuousness. It is astounding how few phrases there are in all these six hundred pages[6] which really seize upon us: we could probably count them all on the fingers of one hand. On its harmonic side the opera gives us a strange impression of pretentious poverty. All through *Rienzi* Wagner's mind seems to be struggling to fight its way through vapor and murk to the light. His dramatic intentions are evident enough, but he can rarely realize them. It is in vain that he exploits all the formulas for dramatic expression as they were understood at that time—diminished sevenths for horror, syncopations for agitation, and all the rest of it; in vain that he languishes or threatens, warbles unctuously or declaims aggressively, lets loose his noisy orchestra and piles up massive choral effects; they all fail to move us because there is hardly ever any bite in the phrases themselves. The obvious faults of the work are due not so much to technical inexperience or limitations of vocabulary as to a sheer failure of the

[6] The opera should be studied in Breitkopf and Härtel's new edition. Former editions have been printed from the curtailed score that was generally used for performances. The Breitkopf edition reproduces the original manuscript in full.

imagination; with the possible exception of Rienzi himself, not one of the characters has been seen with vividness enough to wring a really characteristic musical symbol out of the composer. No one lives except Rienzi; and he, as far as his music is concerned, is little more than half alive. Any critical-minded contemporary friend of Wagner's who happened to know all his work up to that time might have been pardoned for thinking, on the basis of *Rienzi*, that the composer was deteriorating, that on the whole his imagination had hardly grown at all during the past couple of years, and that while none of the earlier defects of style had been corrected, half a dozen new ones had been added —an intolerable prolixity, a tendency to rely on elephantine effects to the neglect of finely wrought detail, and to trust to stage mechanism to eke out the weaknesses of the musical invention. The only improvement on the earlier Wagner which the friend would have been able to observe in *Rienzi* would be that in spite of all its absurdities and infelicities, its commonness and elephantiasis, there is a new strength in the work. It is a strength clumsily used; the youthful hobbledehoy's limbs have hardened without his acquiring much more command over them than he had before, the boyish voice has gained in volume without much improvement in quality: but the general signs of muscular growth are unmistakable. Crude as the overture is, no one can deny its rampant, horse-power vigor. But the final convincing proof that though Wagner's voice was abnormally energetic in *Rienzi*, his imagination was virtually at a standstill is the fact that the opera has no color, no atmosphere of its own. Every other work of Wagner has. In *Die Feen*, as Mr. Runciman acutely points out, there is a strange new feeling for light; in *The Flying Dutchman* we are always conscious of the sea, in *Tannhäuser* of a world of sensuous heat set over against a world of moral coolness and rather anemic aspiration, in *Lohengrin* of the gleaming river and the tenuous air of Monsalvat. *Rienzi* conveys no pictorial or atmospheric suggestions of any kind.

But the opera was only a *reculer pour mieux sauter*. He needed a text that should be more purely musical in its essence than this; and when he found it, in *The Flying Dutchman*—the idea of which came to him shortly after he had commenced work on *Rienzi*—his genius took its first decisive leap forward. For some years he had been strangely undecided as to a suitable subject for an opera. He had experimented, and was still to experiment, in several fields. In 1836 he had turned König's novel *Die hohe Braut* into a libretto, making quite a good romantic opera in four acts out of it.[7] (It was afterward set by Joseph Kittl, in 1853, under the title of *Bianca und Giuseppe, oder die Franzosen vor Nizza*.) In 1837 he made a comic opera out of a story in the *Arabian Nights*, entitling it *Die glückliche Bärenfamilie, oder Männerlist grösser als Frauenlist* (*The Happy Bear Family, or Woman Outwitted by Man*). This is a delightfully vivacious little libretto, which might well be set by some modern composer. Wagner wrote some fragments of the music for it, but quickly became disgusted with the style and turned his back on the piece. In Paris in 1841 he made a preliminary prose sketch for a libretto on a gloomy and rather striking subject of Hoffmann's, *Die Bergwerke zu Falun* (*The Mines of Falun*), which one is sorry he did not set to music, for it has color and a certain individuality: he would probably have made more of it than he did of *Rienzi*. But perhaps he felt the somber vein he would have had to pursue in *Die Bergwerke zu Falun* had been worked out to the full extent of which he was capable in *The Flying Dutchman*. In the same winter of 1842 he made a first sketch of *Die Sarazenin* (*The Saracen Woman*), expanding it in Dresden two years later.[8]

It was after all a sound instinct, no doubt, that made

[7] In *Mein Leben* he speaks of it being in five acts, but in the form in which we have it, it has only four.

[8] Accounts of most of these experiments will be found in *Mein Leben* and elsewhere. The libretti and sketches are printed in the new eleventh volume of the *G.S.*

him concentrate on *The Flying Dutchman* and let the other schemes drop, for *The Flying Dutchman* gave him just what *Rienzi* did not—a concentrated dramatic theme, and one with a very individual atmosphere. Had his dramatic and musical technique been more advanced than they were at that time, he would probably have condensed the story still further. He saw clearly enough that the whole essence of the legend—or at any rate the whole of the musical essence of it—lay in the Dutchman and Senta, and that all the rest was mere scaffolding or trimming. "I condensed the material into a single Act, being chiefly moved to do this by the subject itself, since in this way I could compress it into the simple dramatic interaction of the principal characters, and ignore the musical accessories that had now become repellent to me." [9] But his musical faculties, which developed with a strange slowness, were still lagging a good deal behind his dramatic perceptions; and the result is that to us today there seem to be a good many superfluous "musical accessories" in *The Flying Dutchman*, owing to the fact that Wagner has not been able to give complete musical life to such characters as Daland and Erik. He himself has described for us very lucidly in "A Communication to My Friends" the diverging impulses in him that gave *The Flying Dutchman* its present only partly satisfactory form. He was wholly possessed by his subject, saw that it was necessary to allow it to dictate its own musical form and method of treatment, and honestly thought that he had let it do so; but the traditional operatic form was more potent within him than he imagined at the time. As in *Rienzi*, aria, duet, trio, and the other established forms somehow "found their way into" the opera without his consciously willing them.

Still the structure of *The Flying Dutchman* is a great

[9] *Mein Leben*, p. 220. Wagner always intended that *The Flying Dutchman* should be given in one act. It was played in this way for the first time at Bayreuth in 1901. The necessary skips in the ordinary three-act score are indicated in Breitkopf's edition, pp. 76 and 180.

advance on that of *Rienzi*: what was really happening was that the musician in Wagner was beginning to see that the whole drama must be *musical* drama, the poet not being allowed to insert anything that was inconsistent with the spirit of music. He himself persisted in putting it the other way—that the poet in him gradually took over the guidance of the musician. But we can see now that he misread his own evolution. The poet in him undoubtedly outgrew, bit by bit, the musical forms that had become stereotyped in the opera of the day; but the poet's growth only became possible when the musician, beginning to feel his own strength, gave the poet more and more imperative orders to shape his "stuff" in a form that would afford the musician the freest course. Wagner in later years insisted that after he had elaborated Senta's ballad in the second act, he found that he had unconsciously hit upon the thematic kernel of the whole, and that this thematic idea then spread itself naturally over the whole drama like a network. That is not quite true if we take his words literally, for of course a good deal of the thematic material of *The Flying Dutchman* has no affiliation with Senta's ballad. But in the broad sense, and with regard more to his intentions than his achievements, we can see that he was right. The whole drama really emanates from Senta; the Dutchman himself, as Mr. Runciman puts it, is merely Senta's opportunity personified; the remaining characters are only there to make the before and after of the central episode clear. With more experience and a surer technique he could have cut away more of the excrescences of the libretto and concentrated the action still further, making it yet more purely musical, as he did with *Tristan*. But for the day he had done marvelously well. With *The Flying Dutchman* was born the modern musical drama.

There is no mistaking the intensity and certainty of his vision now. He no longer describes his characters from the outside: they are within him, making their own language and using him as their unconscious instrument. The portrait painter and the pictorial artist in him are both coming to maturity. The Dutchman and Senta are both drawn completely in the round; we feel, for the first time with any of Wagner's characters, that we might meet them any day and that they would be solid to the touch. Even Daland and Erik, though not as real as the other two —for Wagner had not yet the art of breathing life into every one of his subordinate characters—have a certain substantiality. And roaring and whistling and surging round them all is the sea—not so much the mere background of the drama as the element that has given it birth. Stylistically and technically the new work is leagues beyond *Rienzi*. There is still something of the old melodic mannerism—which, indeed, he was not to lose for many years yet—but in many of the melodies there is a new leap, a new pulse, a new articulation; harmonically the work is richer; it often attains a rhythmic freedom beyond anything that Wagner had been capable of before; he is learning to concentrate his expression, and to beat out pregnant little figures that limn a character or depict a natural force once for all; there is a new psychological as well as a musical logic, binding the whole scheme together and working up from the beginning to the end in one steady crescendo. Wherever the score is tested, it shows something not to be met with hitherto either in Wagner's previous work or in that of his contemporaries. His imagination is at last unlocked.

After this he develops steadily and rapidly until a fresh check is given him, it being borne in upon him that neither his imagination nor his technique is equal to the creation of the new world that he feels stirring vaguely within him. But for a time all goes well. *The Flying Dutchman* had been finished in the winter of 1841. *Tannhäuser* was fully ready by April 1845, and *Lohengrin* by March 1848—just after he had completed his thirty-fifth year. In these seven years he exhausted all the possibilities of the style he had thus far made his own; after *Lohengrin* he instinctively feels that he is at the end of the old path and the beginning of a new one, though where this is to lead him he has as yet hardly an inkling. Both the later operas represent a gradual clarification and intensification of the style he had tentatively used in *The Flying Dutchman*. The breach with the older opera is even yet not complete; disguise the conventional features of it as he will, they are still recognizable; aria and duet and *ensemble* are still there, though they merge almost imperceptibly into each other. But if *Tannhäuser* and *Lohengrin* are in large part still the old opera, they are the old opera transfigured. The musical web spreads itself more and more broadly over the whole poetic material. Recitative virtually disappears; the text still retains a number of nonemotional moments for which no really lyrical equivalent can be found, but what would have been recitative naked and unashamed in *Rienzi* is now almost fully clothed song— the address of the Landgrave to the Knights in the Hall of Song scene is an excellent illustration. The choral writing attains an unaccustomed breadth and sonority, and at the same time the chorus becomes a more efficient psychological instrument. The harmonic tissue becomes fuller. The melodic line becomes more and more expressive and sensitive. The orchestration begins to give a distinctive color to both personages and scenes. A very ardent and penetrating imagination, the imagination of the born dramatist, seeing all his characters as creatures of flesh and blood, is now playing upon the material offered to the musician by the poet. Each scene suggests by its coloring its own indoor or outdoor setting, the hour of the day, the time of the year; yet each opera as a whole has a different light and is set in a different atmosphere from the others. The Wagner of this period reaches the supreme height of his powers in *Lohengrin*; and as one watches that diaphanous and finely spun melodic web unfold itself, one is almost tempted for the moment to regret that the daemon within him drove him on so relentlessly to another style. No one, of course, can be anything but thankful that Wagner evolved the splendid symphonic-operatic style of the second half of his life—the most serviceable operatic instrument that any musician

has yet hit upon. But the more purely lyrical style of
Lohengrin is so exquisitely satisfying in itself that one
would have been grateful had he turned back to it for a
moment in later days, when his melodic invention was in
its fullest glory. The main burden of the expression, in
the latest work, shifts more and more to the side of the
orchestra. In Lohengrin the voice is still the statue and the
orchestra the pedestal. The whole work is the product of
that equipoise of all the faculties which is often observable
in composers at the end of their second period, a serenity
resting upon their music which it never wins again in the
more troubled afteryears, when the soul is more at war
with itself, and the lips can hardly find language for the
pregnant images that crowd to them.

But vast as the imaginative growth had been from
Rienzi to Lohengrin, it seems almost like a mere marking
time in comparison with the subsequent development.
Most instructive in this respect are the alterations Wagner
made in his earlier works in later life. The Flying Dutchman ends with the destruction of the Dutchman's ship
as Senta leaps into the sea. The stage directions in the first
edition run thus: "In the glow of the setting sun the
glorified forms of the Dutchman and Senta are seen rising
above the wreck, clasped in each other's arms, soaring
heavenward"; and the final page of the opera in its original
form consisted of the "Redemption" motive followed by
the motive of the Dutchman, the opera ending with the
latter. When Wagner revised the work some years later,
he was conscious of the abruptness and inconclusiveness
of this ending. His pictorial imagination saw the transfigured forms of Senta and the Dutchman more vividly,
and the more luminous vision found expression in the
great stroke of genius with which the opera as we now
have it ends. The thundering theme of the Dutchman no
longer has the last word; the fortissimo swell of the full
orchestra suddenly breaks, and in a slower tempo there
steals out in the soft, pure tones of the wood wind and
harps the theme of "Redemption" in the form it first

assumes in Senta's ballad, but with an unexpected heavenward ascent in the violins at the finish—

No. 22.

p dolce

The effect is precisely as if the clouds had parted, and the
figures of the Dutchman and Senta were seen soaring aloft
in their purified and transfigured form.[1]

As the first version of the *Faust* Overture (1840) has
not been published, it is impossible to compare it with
the version we now have, which was made in 1855; but
we may be certain that the comparison would prove as
interesting as that between the earlier and the later versions of *The Flying Dutchman* finale. But the new Venus-
berg music that he wrote for the Paris production of *Tannhäuser* (1861) shows as emphatically as the altered *Flying
Dutchman* ending how immeasurably greater than all his
development from *Die Feen* to *Lohengrin* was the development from *Lohengrin* to *Tristan*—for it was in the *Tristan* period that he made this wonderful addition to *Tannhäuser*, the effect of which is to make the remainder of
the score seem almost cold in comparison, a pale moon
against a fiery sun. Had Wagner died after *Lohengrin* he
would still have been the greatest operatic composer of
his time. But the work of the later years is so stupendous
in every respect, imaginative, inventive, and technical, that

[1] The overture was altered to correspond with the altered
ending of the opera. Our concert audiences need to remember
that the electrifying effect of this wood wind entry in the overture is an afterthought on Wagner's part. At some time or other
he added to the score the following stage directions at the point
in the final scene where the passage just quoted enters: "A dazzling glory illumines the group in the background; Senta raises
the Dutchman, presses him to her breast, and points him towards heaven with hand and glance." This note is given in the
Fürstner score, but not in that of Breitkopf and Härtel.

even *Lohengrin* seems hardly to be the product of the same mind.

IV · *The Mature Artist*

1

The years 1848 and 1849 saw the climax of a great crisis both in Wagner's life and in his art; it had been developing for two or three years before, and its reverberations did not wholly die away for some years after. All his life and his work at this time were, as I have already said, simply a violent purgation of the spirit—a nightmare agony from which he wakened with a cry of relief. He shakes off the theater, and faces the world on a new footing as a man. And in silence, unknown to everybody and almost to himself, he develops into a new musician. For the moment his mind is a jumble of art, ethics, politics, and sociology. But as usual his artistic instincts guide him surely in the end. After many gropings in this direction and that, he settles down to the *Ring* drama, which he first of all plans, in 1848, in the form of a three-act opera with the title of *Siegfried's Death*. He falters a little even then, being obsessed by the two other subjects, *Jesus of Nazareth* and *Friedrich Barbarossa*; but finally he rejects them both, the greater adaptability of the Siegfried drama for music being intuitively evident to him. The next twenty-six years are to be taken up with the working out of this gigantic theme, with *Tristan* and *Die Meistersinger* as a colossal diversion in the middle of it; then comes the quiet end with *Parsifal*. I do not propose to discuss the philosophical—or pseudo-philosophical—ideas of any of these works. It is only as a musician that Wagner will live, and to a musician the particular philosophy or philosophies that he preached in the *Ring* and *Tristan* and *Parsifal* are matters of very small concern. Wagner himself was always inclined to overestimate the importance of his own philosophizing, and his vehement garrulity has betrayed both partisans and opponents into taking him too seriously as a thinker. Had he not left us his voluminous prose works and letters, indeed, we should never have suspected the hundredth part of the portentous meanings that he and his disciples have read into his operatic libretti. To those who still see profound metaphysical revelations in the later works, it may be well to point out that Wagner saw revelations equally inspired and inspiring in the earlier ones, which no one takes with excessive seriousness today on their dramatic side.[2] The philosophizing all smacks too much, for our taste, of the sentimental Germany of the mid-nineteenth century. For Wagner, Senta is "the quintessence of Woman [*das Weib überhaupt*], yet the still to-be-sought-for, the longed-for, the dreamed-of, the infinitely womanly Woman—let me out with it in one word: the *Woman of the Future*." [3] Tannhäuser was "the spirit of the whole Ghibelline race for every age, comprehended in a single, definite, infinitely moving form; but at the same time a human being right down to our own day, right into the heart of an artist full of life's longing." [4] "Lohengrin sought the woman who should have faith in him; who should not ask who he was and whence he came, but should love him as he was, and because he was what he appeared to himself to be. He sought the woman to whom he should not have to explain or justify himself, but who would *love* him unconditionally. Therefore he had to conceal his higher nature, for only in the non-revealing of this higher—or more correctly heightened—essence could he find surety that he was not wondered at for this alone, or humbly worshipped as something incomprehensible,—whereas his longing was *not* for wonder or adoration, but for the only thing that could redeem him from his loneliness and still his yearning—for *Love, for being loved, for being understood through Love*. . . . The character and the situation of this Lohengrin I now recognise

---

[2] Except, perhaps, Mr. Houston Stewart Chamberlain. See his *Das Drama Richard Wagners: Eine Anregung*. (In English [1923] as *The Wagnerian Drama*.)

[3] "*Eine Mittheilung an meine Freunde*," in G.S., iv, 266.

[4] Ibid., iv, 272.

with the clearest conviction as the *type of the only really tragic material, of the tragic element of our modern life*; of the same significance, indeed, for the *Present* as was the *Antigone*, in another relation, for the life of the Greek state. . . . Elsa is the unconscious, the un-volitional, into which Lohengrin's conscious, volitional being yearns to be redeemed; but that yearning is itself the unconscious, un-volitional in Lohengrin, through which he feels himself akin in being to Elsa. Through the capacity of this 'unconscious consciousness' as I myself experienced it in common with Lohengrin, the nature of Woman . . . became more and more intimately revealed to me . . . that *true Womanhood* that should bring to me and all the world redemption, after man's egoism, even in its noblest form, had voluntarily broken itself before her. Elsa, the Woman . . . made me a full-fledged revolutionary. She was the spirit of the folk, for redemption by whom I too, as artist-man, was yearning." [5]

This seems all very remote from us now; one wonders how anyone, even Wagner himself, could ever have taken these operatic puppets with such appalling seriousness. The *Ring* stands a little nearer to us; but no longer can we follow Wagner in his philosophizing even there. For Wagner, Siegfried was "the human being in the most natural and gayest fulness of his physical manifestation. . . . It was Elsa who had taught me to discover this man: to me he was the male-embodied [*der männlich-verkörperte*] spirit of the eternal and only involuntarily creative force [*Geist der ewig und einzig zeugenden Unwillkür*], of the doer of true deeds, of Man in the fulness of his most native strength and his most undoubted love-worthiness." [6] We can hardly regard Siegfried in that light today. As we meet with him in the libretto, he is, as Mr. Runciman says, rather an objectionable young person; we cannot quite reconcile ourselves to his ingratitude and his

[5] "*Eine Mittheilung an meine Freunde*," in *G.S.*, iv, 295, 297, 298, 301, 302.
[6] Ibid., iv, 328.

superathletic fatuousness; he reminds us too much of Anatole France's description of the burly, bullet-headed general in *Les Dieux ont soif*—the sparrow's brain in the ox's skull. As we see him on the stage, he is, under the best conditions, slightly ridiculous, a sort of overgrown Boy Scout. It is only in his music that he is so magnificently alive, so sure of our sympathy. Sensible musicians, indeed, do not trouble very much in these days about the metaphysics or the esoteric implications of the Wagnerian dramas. Wotan must stand or fall by his own dramatic grandeur and by the quality of the music that is given to him to sing, not by the degree of success with which he illustrates a particular theory of the Will. *Tristan* is none the better for all its Schopenhauerisms, natural or acquired; we may be thankful that it is none the worse for them.

Wagner's philosophical stock, indeed, was never a very large one. The "problems" of his operas are generally problems of his own personality and circumstances. His art, like his life, is all unconscious egoism. *His* problems are always to be the world's problems, *his* needs the world's needs. Woman obsessed him in art as in life: she kindled fiery passion in man, or she "redeemed" him from passion, or she set a sorrow's crown of sorrows on his head by failing to redeem him. Passion, redemption, renunciation—these are the three dominant motives of Wagner's work; and wherever we look in that work, we find himself. Indulgence—revulsion; hope—frustration; passion—renunciation; these are the antitheses that are constantly confronting us. In *The Flying Dutchman*, Vanderdecken-Wagner is redeemed by the woman who loves and trusts him unto death. Tannhäuser-Wagner fluctuates between the temptress and the saint. Lohengrin-Wagner seeks in vain the woman who shall love him unquestioningly. Wieland the Smith, the hero of a libretto he sketched in 1849, is again Wagner, lamed by life, but healed at last by another "redeeming" woman. Wotan-Wagner, finding the world going another way than his, wills his own destruction and that of the world. Tristan-Wagner finds love insatiable, and death the only end of all our loving. Sachs-Wagner renounces love. Parsifal-Wagner finds salvation in flight from sensual love. Always there is this oscillation between desire and the slaying of desire, between hope for the world and despair for the world. In 1848, in an hour of physical and mental joy in life, he conceives a blithe and exuberant Siegfried, the superman of the future, striding joyously and victoriously through life. But the revulsion comes almost in a moment. He realizes his solitariness as man and artist. "I was irresistibly driven to write something that should communicate this grievous consciousness of mine in an intelligible form to the life of the present. Just as with my *Siegfried* the strength of my yearning had borne me to the primal fount of the eternal purely-human; so now, when I found this yearning could never be stilled by modern life, and realised once again that redemption was to be had only in flight from this life, in escaping from its claims upon me by self-destruction, I came to the primal fount of every modern rendering of this situation—to the Man *Jesus of Nazareth*." Like Jesus, confronted with the materialism of the world, he longs for death, and straightway reads a similar longing into all humanity.

So the oscillation goes on to the very end of his days. There is no need, no reason, to discuss the "philosophy" of such a mind. He is no philosopher: he is simply a perplexed and tortured human soul and a magnificent musical instrument. All that concerns us today is the quality of the music which was wrung from the instrument under the torture.

2

The most astounding fact in all Wagner's career was probably the writing of the text of *Siegfried's Death* in 1848. That drama is practically identical with the present *Götterdämmerung*; and we can only stand amazed at the audacity of the conception, the imaginative power the work displays, the artistic growth it reveals since *Lohengrin* was written, and the total breach it indicates with the whole of the operatic art of his time. But *Siegfried's Death* was impossible in the musical idiom of *Lohengrin*; and Wagner must have known this intuitively. This is no doubt the real reason for his writing no music for six years, from the completion of *Lohengrin* in August 1847 to the commencement of work on *Das Rheingold* at the end of 1853. His artistic instincts always led him infallibly, no matter what confusion might reign in the rest of his thinking. He conceives the idea of *Die Meistersinger*, for instance, in 1845, just after finishing *Tannhäuser*. But a wise and kindly fate intervenes and turns him aside from the project. He was not ripe for *Die Meistersinger*, either poetically or musically, as we can see not only by a comparison of his later musical style with that of *Tannhäuser*, but by comparing the sketch of the drama that he wrote in 1845 with the revised drafts of 1861. It was his original intention, again, to introduce Parsifal into the third act of *Tristan*; but his purely artistic instincts were too sound to permit him to adhere to that plan. How unripe he was in 1848 for a musical setting of *Siegfried's Death* hardly needs demonstration now. The swift and infallibly telling strokes with which he has drawn Hagen and Gutrune in *Götterdämmerung*, for example, were utterly beyond him then; it took twenty years' evolution before he could attain to that luminousness and penetration of vision, that rapidity and certainty of touch. So much, again, of the tragic atmosphere in which *Götterdämmerung* is enveloped comes from the subtle harmonic idiom that Wagner had evolved by that time, that it is hard to imagine the extent of his probable failure had he persisted in setting the text to music in 1848. The lyrical style of *Lohengrin*, the leisurely spun tissue of that lovely work, were neither drastic enough, close enough, nor elastic enough for *Siegfried's Death*. And of this he must have had a dim consciousness.

So he puts the musical part of his task on one side for six years, broods continually over the subject, finds it growing within him, and at last shapes it into not one opera but four. When at last he begins work upon the music of *Das Rheingold*, he is a new being. His imagination has developed to an extent that is without a parallel in the case of any other musician. The characters and the *milieu* of *Das Rheingold* are themselves evidence of the audacious sweep of his vision: he undertakes to re-create in music gods and men and giants, creatures of the waters and creatures of the bowels of the earth; the music has to flood the scene now with water, now with fire, with the murky vapors of the underworld and the serene air of the heights over against Valhalla. Never before had any composer dreamed of an opera so rich in all varieties of emotion, of action, of atmosphere. The practice he had in *Das Rheingold* developed his powers still further: in *Die Walküre* the painting grows surer and surer, the imagination sweeps on to conceptions beyond anything that any musician before him would have thought possible: in *Siegfried* there is an absolute exultation of style; the music seems to dance and cry aloud out of pure joy in its own strength and beauty. His melody has already become terser and more suggestive in *Das Rheingold*, and has lost much of its earlier rhythmic formality. His harmonic range, while as yet narrow enough compared with that of *Tristan* and of *Götterdämmerung*, has yet developed greatly. He dares anything in pursuit of his ideal of finding in music the full and perfect counterpart of the characters and the scenes; that persistent E flat chord at the commencement of the *Rheingold* prelude is an innovation the audacity of which we can hardly estimate today.

It has been objected that the melody of *Das Rheingold* is on the miniature side, and that the score has little of the grand surge and sweep of the later operas. It may be so, but the style of the music seems admirably suited to the broad and simple outlines of this drama and the relatively simple psychology of the beings who take part in it

—beings who are now taking only the first step along the path that is to lead them all into such tragic complications. But in any case Wagner was obeying a sound instinct when he abandoned the broader, more flowing style of *Lohengrin* in favor of the seemingly shorter-breathed style of the *Das Rheingold*. It was the consequence of his intuition that his new dramatic ideas demanded a new musical form; we have to remember that everything he says on this topic in *Opera and Drama* is the outcome of his reflection upon *Siegfried's Death* and the best manner of its setting. The older forms of opera being inapplicable here, he had to devise a new method of unifying his vast design. He found the solution of his problem in an application to opera of the symphonic web-weaving of Beethoven; but for this he needed, like Beethoven, short and very plastic motives. That as yet he cannot weave these motives, and the episodical matter between them, into so continuous a tissue as that of the later works is only natural; to expect him to have done so would be as unreasonable as to expect the texture of Beethoven's second symphony to be as closely woven as that of his fifth. But Wagner knew he had a wonderful new instrument in his grasp, and he did well to learn the full use of it by cautious practice.

3

The leitmotiv, of course, is not Wagner's invention. Other operatic composers had tentatively handled the device before him; and in his own day Schumann had seen the possibilities of such a method being applied to the song. In his *Frühlingsfahrt*, for example, the joyous major melody that accompanies the bright youths on their first setting out in life changes to the clouded minor as the poet tells of the ruin that came upon one of them; and everyone knows the poignant effect of the winding up of the *Woman's Life and Love* cycle with a reminiscence of the melody of the opening song. The device of reminis-

cence in poetic or dramatic music is indeed so obviously
a natural one that we can only wonder that the pre-
Wagnerian composers did not make more use of it than
they did. But Wagner did more than employ it as a sort
of index or label; he turned it into the seminal principle
of musical form for perhaps three fourths of the music
of our time. He made it not merely a dramatic but a
symphonic-dramatic instrument. He had experimented
with the device from his youth, but until now without
perceiving its symphonic possibilities. We have seen him
carrying forward a significant theme from one scene to
another in *Das Liebesverbot*. In *Rienzi* there is very little
real use of the leitmotiv. He will adopt a characteristic
orchestral figure for a person or a situation at the commencement of a scene or "number," and play with it all
through that particular set piece; but it is very rarely that
he will remind us of a previous situation by importing the
theme that symbolizes it into a later situation. He does
this, for example, with the "Oath" motive, which first
accompanies Rienzi's story of his own vow to avenge his
murdered brother (vocal score, pp. 77, 78), and is afterward employed to accompany Colonna's threat of vengeance if Rienzi dooms him and his fellow conspirators to
death (p. 266), Rienzi's rejection of Adriano's plea for
mercy (p. 337), and finally Adriano's own resolve to be
avenged upon Rienzi (p. 416). In *The Flying Dutchman*
the tissue is largely unified by typical themes, which, however, are as a rule merely repeated without substantial
modification, though now and then a motive is melodically
transformed to suggest a psychological variation, as when
the "Redemption" theme from Senta's ballad—

No. 23.

afterward becomes the motive of "Love unto death"—

No. 24.

In *Tannhäuser* there is a good deal of recurrent material
—the Bacchanale and the Pilgrims' Chorus, for instance
—but the leitmotiv can hardly be said to be used at all
in the later sense. *Lohengrin* is strewn with leitmotivs that
are marvels of characterization; but here too they recur in
their original form time after time. For the most part they
merely label the character: they do not change as he
changes, nor do they spread themselves over the score with
the persistence of the motives of the later works.

4

The leitmotiv in the *Ring* is quite another matter. Most
of the motives in the earlier operas were vocal in origin,
and their relatively great length—which makes them as a
rule unsuitable for a flexible symphonic treatment—is the
direct consequence of the length of Wagner's poetic lines
at that time. In *Rienzi*, for example, the motive of Rienzi's
prayer, the *"Sancto spirito cavaliere"* motive, the "Freedom" motive, the motive of the "Messengers of Peace,"
and others, are all of this type. In *The Flying Dutchman*
the motive of "Longing for death," the two "Redemption" motives, the "Daland" motive, the "Festivity" motive, the "Rejoicing" motive, the "Longing for redemption" motive, and several others are all vocal melodies in
the first place; of the same kind are the motives of "Repentance," of "Love's magic," of "Love's renunciation,"
and others in *Tannhäuser*; and in *Lohengrin*, the "Grail"
motive, the "Farewell" motive, the "Elsa's prayer" motive,
the "Knight of the Grail" motive, the "Warning" motive,
the "Doubt" motive, and others. All of these are fully
developed, self-existent melodies, not germ figures destined
for the weaving of a quasi-symphonic web. And though
some of the less important motives in the early operas are

short, they were not made so with any intention of using them plastically. The first things that strike us in connection with the motives of the *Ring* are their general shortness, their very plastic nature, and the sense they convey of not having been conceived primarily in a vocal form. It is true that some of them *are* vocal in origin, but that fact does not stare us so aggressively in the face as it does in the previous works; while the lines of the *Ring* are themselves so short that even when a phrase is modeled on one or two of them it never spreads itself out so extensively as the typical phrases of *The Flying Dutchman, Tannhäuser,* and *Lohengrin* do.

This at first sight seems to imply that the poetic form of the *Ring* exercised a powerful influence on the musical form. It is permissible for us today to invert that proposition. Wagner, writing in 1851, maintained that he had discarded the older form of verse, with its long lines and its terminal rhymes, because of his conviction that this was too conventional a garment to throw over the sturdy limbs of Siegfried, the untutored child of nature, and that he was therefore led to adopt the *Stabreim* of the Folk. Consistently with the theory I have already advanced in these pages, I prefer to believe—guided, as of course Wagner himself could not be guided at that time, by the evidence of the function the music performs in his later works—that the new orchestral musician that was coming to birth within him felt the necessity of shorter and more plastic germ themes, and instinctively urged the poet to cast *his* material into a form that would place no obstacle in the musician's way. But explain it as we will, the fact remains that now he is coming to maturity, his leitmotivs are on the whole both more concentrated and more purely instrumental than they had been hitherto; as I have said, even when they come to us in the first place from the mouths of the characters, they assume quite naturally the quality of instrumental themes in the subsequent course of the opera, whereas a purely orchestral rendering of the themes of *Tannhäuser* and *Lohengrin* can never quite disguise their vocal origin. It is comparatively rarely that the *Ring* motives extend beyond two bars, or at the most three. The "Servitude" motive is virtually only one bar in length; so are the "Rhine Maidens' song," the "Smithing" motive, and the "Reflection" motive; the "Waves" motive, the "Ring" motive, the "Valhalla" motive, the "Might of youth" motive, the "Twilight" motive, the "Norns" motive, the "Dusk of the gods" motive, are all comprised within a couple of bars; several others run to three bars, and only one or two run to four.

In this respect, as in some others, *Die Meistersinger* stands in a class apart from the other works of Wagner's maturity. It is the most purely vocal of all his later works, in the sense that while the orchestral tissue is superbly full and unceasing in its flow, the voice parts have an independence that is rare in the later Wagner. The style is in a way almost a reversion to that of *Lohengrin*, allowance being made, of course, for the more symphonic nature of the orchestral portion, and the more continuous nature of the whole. *Die Meistersinger* is full of "set" pieces—arias, duets, trios, a quintet, choruses, *ensembles*, and so on. The necessity for all these lay in the nature of the subject; and Wagner, at that time at the very height of his powers, has so cunningly mortized all the components of the opera that not a join is observable anywhere. A superficial glance at a table of *Die Meistersinger* motives would be enough to convince us, without any knowledge of the opera, that a great many of the themes have had a vocal origin, either solo or choral. Others owe their length to the fact that Wagner is painting masses and types rather than individuals; only a fairly extended theme could depict, for instance, the sturdy, pompous old Mastersingers and their stately processions. Where he is not following a vocal line or painting with broad sweeps of the brush, and is free to invent motives for purely orchestral symphonic use, he generally throws them into the same concise form as those of the *Ring*—the "Wooing" motive, for example—

No. 25.

which, by reason of its brevity, is one of the most plastic motives in the score. But as a whole, *Die Meistersinger* lives in a different world from the *Ring* or *Tristan*. There is no great fateful principle running through it, which can be symbolized in a short orchestral figure and flashed across the picture at any desired moment, after the manner of the "Curse" or the "Hagen" motive in the *Ring*, or the "Death" motive in *Tristan*. The people in *Die Meistersinger* carry hardly any shadows about with them. Their natures are mostly ingenuous, transparent, unsubtle: such as we see them on the stage at any given moment, such are they to themselves and others in every hour of their lives. It was natural then that they should take upon themselves more of the burden of the drama than the characters of the *Ring* as a whole—for these are only instruments in the hand of a fate that is best symbolized by the ever present orchestra—and that the instrumental voices should co-operate joyously with them, rather than dog them and lie in wait for them, as in the *Ring*, with symbols of reminiscence and foreboding. That the whole essence of *Die Meistersinger* lies in its simple human characterization and simple storytelling is shown again by Wagner's reverting in the Prelude to the *potpourri feuilleton* form of the *Tannhäuser* Overture—a form he never used again after 1845, except here.

5

As he proceeds with the *Ring* his leitmotivs in general become more and more concentrated. Now and then he will employ a fairly extended theme, but never without a good psychological reason. One of the longest motives in the whole tetralogy is that of the "Volsung race." Its length is justified by the duty it has to perform: to concentrate the nobility and the suffering of that race into a chord or two would be beyond the powers of any musician; none but Wagner, indeed, could have expressed such an infinity of elevated grief within the compass of seven or eight bars. Some of the other motives are astounding in their brevity and eloquence. Not till after his work on *Das Rheingold* had unsealed his imagination and perfected his technique could he have hoped to hit off the wild, half-animal energy of the Valkyries in some four or five notes that are merely the expansion of a single chord, or have dared to trust to what is virtually only a series of syncopations to symbolize Alberich's work of destruction (the *Vernichtungsarbeit* motive). Never before could he have written anything so eloquent of death as the "Announcement of death" motive in *Die Walküre*. In *Siegfried*, though the number of new motives is comparatively small, the same process of concentration is observable. The godlike nature and the stately gait of the Wanderer are suggested to us in three or four chords. And in *Götterdämmerung* the concentration is amazing. In that stupendous work he is, in my opinion, at the very summit of his powers. He never wastes a note now: every new stroke he deals is incredibly swift, direct, and telling. Absolutely sure of himself, he dispenses with a prelude—for the few bars of orchestral writing before the voices enter can hardly be called one—and trusts to the color of a mere couple of chords to tune the audience's imagination to the atmosphere of the opening scene. One short characteristic figure suffices for the motive of Hagen, and nowhere in the whole of Wagner's or anyone else's work is a figure of two notes used so multifariously and with such far-reaching suggestion. It is evident that he now feels the harmonic instrument to be the most serviceable and flexible of all; and hundreds of his most overpowering effects in *Götterdämmerung* are achieved by harmonic invention or harmonic transformation. The grisliness of the Hagen theme comes in large part—putting aside the question of orchestral color—from the sort of dour, irreconcilable element it seems to introduce into certain chords—though in reality the harmony has nothing essentially far-fetched in it—as

in that tremendous passage near the end of the first act of
Götterdämmerung—

No. 26.

The new themes, too, rely for a great deal of their poignancy upon some subtle and fleeting taste of sweetness or
some swift suggestion of darkness and mystery in the
harmony, as in the exquisite motive that is associated with
the wedding of Gutrune—

No. 27.

or in the motive of "Magic deceit"—

No. 28.

while others make their effect by means of the utmost concentration of melodic meaning, like the "Blood-brotherhood" motive, or by an epigrammatic condensation of rhythm, like the "Oath of fidelity" motive, which only Wagner could have invented, and which no other composer but Beethoven would have dared to use if it had been offered to him—

No. 29.

It is on harmonic alteration that he chiefly relies again, in the latter stages of the *Ring*, to suggest the fateful gloom that is gradually closing in upon the drama; much of the tense and tragic and oppressive atmosphere of *Götterdämmerung* comes from this clouding of the simpler texture of the motives of the earlier operas. One of the most remarkable instances of this is his treatment of the "Servitude" motive, which is generally associated with Alberich. In *Das Rheingold* it appears in a variety of simple forms, such as this—

No. 30.

and this—

No. 31.

In *Götterdämmerung* a sense of almost intolerable strain, of a great tragedy sweeping to its inevitable end, is conveyed by various subtilizations of the harmony, of which the following may stand as a type—

No. 32.

When Siegfried appears on Brünnhilde's rock, disguised as Gunther, the theme of the latter is metamorphosed from—

No. 33.

into—

No. 34.

Here everything is exquisitely calculated—the harmonic alteration, the orchestral coloring (the soft mysterious tones of trumpet and trombones), the interrupted ending, and the long, fateful silence that follows.

When Alberich, in his colloquy with Hagen at the
commencement of the second act of *Götterdämmerung*,
looks forward to the approaching destruction of the gods,
the "Valhalla" motive becomes altered from the familiar—

No. 35.

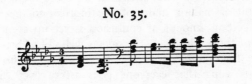

to—

No. 36.

Many other illustrations might be given of this harmonic
intensification of themes.

6

It has to be admitted, however, that Wagner's use of
the leitmotiv presents some singularities, and is at times
open to criticism. He undoubtedly introduces the motives
more frequently than they are really needed; there is no
necessity, for example, for the "Siegfried's horn" motive
to be sounded at almost every appearance of Siegfried or
every mention of his name. Debussy has made merry over
this superfluity of reference, comparing it to a lunatic
presenting his card to you in person. But we can easily
forgive Wagner this little excess of zeal. He was doing
something absolutely new for his time. He had a gigantic

mass of material to unify, and this incessant recurrence of significant themes seemed to him the only way to do it. He could not foresee how familiar the operas and their motives would be to the whole musical world half a century later. In any case this peculiarity of his style can be passed over with a mere mention. Of more importance is his habit of making many of the motives so much alike that a certain amount of confusion is set up even in the minds of those who know the operas well. The "Servitude" motive, for example, is so like the opening of the Rhine Maidens' song that everyone goes astray over the two themes now and then in the first stages of his acquaintance with the *Ring*. Still more confusing is his habit of taking a motive that at first has only a particular meaning, and making it express a general concept, the result being that we frequently associate it with the wrong character. His mind was curiously like Bach's in this respect, that having fixed upon a figure that seemed to him an adequate symbol for an action, a person, an animal, or a material object, he would use it for all future phenomena of the same kind. But Bach's procedure is rather more logical, for his typical themes have as a rule a pictorial or semipictorial character, and so they can be applied without incongruity to a number of pictures of the same general order. A phrase that symbolizes waves, for example, in one work may be legitimately employed to symbolize waves in another, for the theme itself is so constructed as to suggest the motion of waves: at least that is the intention. But Wagner necessarily has to find musical symbols for all kinds of things in his operas for which it is quite impossible to discover an unmistakable, self-explanatory musical equivalent. The symbol has therefore to be an arbitrary one; it has no claim to pictorial veracity, but we agree to accept it because it fulfils a useful musical purpose. The "Fire" motive conveys a real suggestion of fire; the *Rhinegold* prelude has certain qualities that make us willing to associate it with a mighty rolling river. But the "Ring" motive does not convey the slightest suggestion of a ring, nor has the "Gold" motive any resemblance to gold.

Wagner runs, then, a risk of being misunderstood, or not understood at all, when he takes an arbitrary symbol that we are willing to concede him in one case, and applies it to another. It would tax all the ingenuity of the thorough-going Wagnerian to justify, for instance, in the scene of the Norns in *Götterdämmerung*, the employment of the "Sleep" motive that is inevitably associated in our minds with Wotan's parting from Brünnhilde at the end of *Die Walküre*. When Brünnhilde is taking leave of Siegfried, in the second scene of *Götterdämmerung*, and giving him Grane as a perpetual reminder of herself, the orchestra accompanies his words with the "Love" motive from the duet between Siegmund and Sieglinde in the first act of *Die Walküre*. So profound and so personal has been the impression we have received from it there that it is impossible for us to associate it with any other pair of lovers; and we cannot help wondering what Siegmund and Sieglinde have to do with Siegfried and Brünnhilde and Grane. When Hagen describes the coming of Siegfried down the Rhine, it is quite right that the orchestra should give out the typical Siegfried theme, but quite wrong, surely, that this theme should be combined with that of the Rhine Maidens from *Das Rheingold*. The intention presumably is that from the Rhine Maidens we are to infer the Rhine;[7] but the musical intelligence does not like having to diverge into deductive reasoning of this kind. Anyone who has learned to associate the theme with the Rhine Maidens will naturally suppose either that they are to appear in person or that some allusion is to be made to them, neither of which things happens. The "Treaty" motive of *Das Rheingold*, again, has become so firmly associated in our minds with the agreement between Wotan and the giants that we involuntarily think of them when we hear it again in the orchestra during the swearing of

[7] It is possible, of course, for any Wagnerian commentator to give another reason for the introduction of the motive here; but the mere fact that more than one explanation can be given is itself a proof that Wagner has miscalculated.

Blood-brotherhood by Siegfried and Gunther (*Götterdäm-merung*, vocal score, p. 92).

One of the most curious uses of the leitmotiv is to be found in *Siegfried* (V. S. p. 35). Siegfried, pouring contempt on the idea that Mime can be his father, is telling him how he once saw the reflection of his own face in the brook:

> Unlike unto thee
> there did I seem:
> as like as a toad
> to a glittering fish.

There is excellent reason for accompanying the third line with the "Smithing" motive that so often characterizes Mime; but what reason can there be for accompanying the fourth line with the "Waves" motive from the prelude to *Das Rheingold*? As it is not in the Rhine but in a brook that Siegmund has seen his reflection, the motive here can only be taken as symbolizing not the waves of a particular and already familiar river—a procedure for which there might be some excuse—but waves in general, which is quite illegitimate. Wagner goes too far, as Bach used to go too far, in importing into the line a pictorial allusion that is not already there, and that we can only put there by an effort. For Bach also was in the habit of making his music argue, as it were, from one external fact to another. We can permit this within certain limits, but both Bach and Wagner sometimes go beyond all limits. When Bach has to set to music a stanza in which the faithful are spoken of as Christ's sheep (*Beglückte Herde, Jesu Schafe*, in the cantata *Du Hirte Israel*), he obviously aims at creating a pastoral atmosphere by the use of the oboes; and our imagination here is quite willing to accept the naïve translation of the religious idea into a pictorial image. But when Bach, possessed by the image of Jesus calling His disciples to be fishers of men (in the cantata *Siehe, ich will viel Fischer aussenden*), makes use of a motive of a type that he always employs to symbolize waves, we can only say, with all respect, that we had rather he did not ask us to deduce the necessity of waves from the fact that there is mention of fish. So with this passage from *Siegfried*: we would be quite satisfied with the mere comparison between the toad and the fish; to lay it down with such portentous gravity that where there are fish there must necessarily be water is to reduce pictorialism to an absurdity.

There is no lack of examples of this process of illegitimate inference and illegitimate association. After Mime has answered the first of the Wanderer's three questions, the latter congratulates him in this wise (*Siegfried*, vocal score, p. 74):

> Right well the name
> of the race dost thou know:
> sly, thou rascal, thou seemest!

—to the same phrase that is often used in *Das Rheingold* to suggest the trickiness of Loge in particular, but also, apparently, to suggest deceit in general. It accompanies, for example, Fafner's remark to Fasolt, *à propos* of the attempt of Wotan to evade the promised payment for Valhalla—

> My trusty brother,
> seest thou, fool, his deceit?

(V. S. 89, 90); and again the words in which Wotan tries to calm the apprehensions of Fricka—

> Where simple strength serves,
> of none ask I assistance:
> but to force the hate
> of foes to help me,
> needs such craft and deceit
> as Loge the artful employs.

(V. S. 82, 83.) That is to say, a purely arbitrary musical figure is to be taken as symbolizing not merely the slyness of a particular person, but slyness in the abstract—a length to which we must decline to go with Wagner.

And as with his waves and his moral qualities, so with his animals; they too try to be both particular and universal. When Alberich, at the urging of Loge, turns himself into a serpent (*Rheingold*, p. 182), it is to the accompaniment of a motive that is itself admirably pictorial. But in *Siegfried* (p. 7, etc.) and in *Götterdämmerung* (p. 34, etc.), the same motive is always used to characterize Fafner, after he has turned himself into a dragon. One need not enlarge upon the confusion this is bound to create.

We are willing, again, to accept the "Swan" motive in *Lohengrin* as a purely conventional symbol for that particular work; but the same motive strikes rather oddly on our ears when it is used to suggest the swan in *Parsifal*. If in *Lohengrin* it typifies that particular swan, it is obviously not right to employ it for a totally different bird in another opera; for there is nothing in the outline of the theme which can be said to bear the remotest resemblance to a swan in the way that an arpeggio theme may be said to resemble waves, or a crepitating theme to suggest fire. Again, Wagner merely confuses us when he uses the motive that accompanies Kundry's ride in the first scene of *Parsifal* to accompany Parsifal's description of the horsemen he had once seen in the wood:

> And once upon the fringe of the wood,
> on glorious creatures mounted,
> men all glittering went by me;
> fain had I been like them:
> with laughter they swept on their way.
> And then I ran,
> but never again I saw them;
> through deserts wide I wandered,
> o'er hill and dale;
> oft fell the night,
> then followed day: etc.

(vocal score, p. 54); afterward to accompany Kundry's account of the death of Herzeleide:

As I rode by I saw her dying,
and, Fool, she sent thee her greeting;

(V. S. p. 57); after that, again, to accompany Kundry as
she hastens to the spring in the wood to get water for the
fainting Parsifal (V. S. p. 58); after that to describe the
rush of Klingsor's warriors to the ramparts (V. S. p. 120);
after that to accompany the thronging of the Flower
Maidens to the scene (V. S. p. 156); again to give point
to Parsifal's words:

And I, the fool, the coward,
to deeds of boyish wildness hither fled—

(V. S. p. 203); and to accompany—for what reason it is
difficult to say—Kundry's threat that she will call the spear
against Parsifal if he continues to repulse her (V. S. p.
222); and finally, as an accompaniment to her last words
to Parsifal:

For fleddest thou from here,
and foundest all the ways of the world,
the one that thou seek'st,
that path thy foot shall find never;

(V. S. p. 225). No ingenuity can justify the employment
of the same motive for so many different purposes. As a
matter of fact, after we have once become conscious of
it as accompanying Kundry's ride in the first scene of the
opera, it is inevitable that we should associate it with her
at each subsequent recurrence of it.

Another peculiarity of Wagner's use of the leitmotiv
may be noted; once or twice he gives a meaning to a theme
in the later stages of the *Ring* that we cannot be sure
it possesses at first. The most striking instance of this is
the "Reflection" motive. In *Siegfried* it is exclusively
employed in connection with Mime, and the manner of its
employment leaves no room for doubt that the commenta-
tors are right in giving it this title. The prelude to *Siegfried*
commences with it; it is used there to suggest to us Mime

pondering over the problem of the forging of the sword.
It frequently recurs with the same significance in the
scene that follows. It is used again all through the scene
of questions and answers between the Wanderer and
Mime, to suggest the dwarf putting his considering cap on
after or during each of the Wanderer's posers. Yet on its
first appearance in *Das Rheingold* (vocal score, p. 151)
there is nothing whatever to indicate that the theme is to
be taken as symbolical of reflection. It accompanies Mime's
plaint to Wotan and Loge—

> What help for me?
> I must obey
> the commands of my brother,
> who holds me bondsman to him.
>
> .　.　.　.　.　.
>
> By evil craft fashioned Alberich
> from the ravished Rhinegold a yellow ring: etc.

(Vocal score, p. 151.) From the words one would be *a
priori* inclined to associate the music with Alberich rather
than with Mime; and as it is not employed again in *Das
Rheingold*, the meaning we are suddenly asked to attach
to it at the opening of *Siegfried* seems a little far-fetched.

7

Wagner was not long in realizing that however thrilling
the timbre of the human voice may be, and useful as it
is for making clear the course of the action and the sentiments of the characters, the orchestra is the most powerful
and most resourceful of all the instruments at the disposal
of the operatic composer. More and more the main current of his thinking goes into this. In *Das Rheingold* the
orchestral texture is by no means continuous; frequently
it merely punctuates or supports the vocal declamation
by means of a detached chord or two, much in the way
that it used to sustain the older recitative. As the *Ring*

proceeds pages of this kind become rarer: the orchestra thrusts itself more and more to the centre of the picture. It would be impossible to make the tissue of *Das Rheingold* intelligible without the voices: but the orchestral part of *Götterdämmerung* would flow on with hardly a break if the vocal part were omitted; so also would large sections of *Tristan* and *Die Meistersinger*. It was inevitable that under these circumstances the vocal writing should occasionally become a little perfunctory. It is frequently said that the balance between the vocal and orchestral parts is most perfectly maintained in *Tristan*; but the most cursory examination of the score shows that even there Wagner could not always find, or would not take the trouble to find, a vocal line of equal melodic interest with that of the orchestra. In the opening scene, for instance, it is transparently clear that the really expressive voice is the orchestra, and that the vocal parts have been inserted, sometimes rather carelessly and unskilfully, after the orchestral tissue has been completed. The vocal writing in *Tristan* falls into four main categories. The first is that to which I have already referred; wholly absorbed in the orchestral working out of a theme, Wagner seems to pay the minimum of attention to the vocal line, which sometimes has as little real relevance to the music as a whole as if it had been added by another person. As a specimen of this kind of writing we may cite the music to the words of Brangäne at the commencement of the opera—

> Bluish strips
> are stretching along the west;
> swiftly the ship
> sails to the shore:
> if restful the sea by eve
> we shall readily set foot on land.

(Vocal score, pp. 7, 8.)

To the second category belong passages in which the voice is frankly in the forefront of the picture and the

orchestra is merely a background—as in the colloquy between Tristan and Brangäne (vocal score, pp. 18 *ff.*), or
in the music to Isolde's words shortly after the beginning
of the second act—

BRANGÄNE   I still hear the sound of horns.
ISOLDE   No sound of horns
were so sweet;
yon fountain's soft
murmuring current
moves so quietly hence;
if horns yet brayed
how could I hear that?

(Vocal score, pp. 90, 91.)

To the third category belong the passages in which
the voice simply sings the same melody as the orchestra,
as on p. 177 of the vocal score ("Thy kingdom thou art
showing" etc.); and to the fourth, those in which it
sings a real counterpoint to the orchestra—not a mere
piece of padding like the passage I have cited from pp. 7, 8
of the score, but a vocal line of genuine melodic interest—
as in a good deal of that scene of the third act through
which there runs the melancholy *cor anglais* melody.

Tristan, in fact, in spite of the splendour of its orchestral
polyphony, by no means exhibits Wagner's symphonic
powers in their full evolution. The most wonderful of his
works in this respect is *Götterdämmerung*, the stupendous
strength of which is beyond words and almost beyond
belief. The world had not seen a musical brain working
at such tremendous and long-sustained pressure since
the days when the B minor Mass and the "Matthew Passion" were written; and even those masterpieces have not
the continuity of texture of *Götterdämmerung*, nor do they
show so giant a hand at its work of unification. Turn
almost where you will, the course of the drama is told
with absolute clearness in the orchestra itself. Yet in
spite of his concentrating so largely on the orchestra, the

vocal parts have an extraordinary aptness; it would be hard to find a passage in the score as perfunctory as some that might be quoted from *Tristan*. The voice, it is true, is often used simply as another counterpoint among those of the orchestra; but as a counterpoint it generally has both dramatic appositeness and a melodic beauty of its own.

In *Parsifal* this tendency to make the orchestra the principal dramatic speaker goes so far that very frequently the vocal writing is thoroughly bad. Some writers have attributed this to a decline of mental power in Wagner's old age. I do not think that this is the correct explanation. I can see no general decadence of musical invention in the music of *Parsifal*: I am willing to believe that the peculiar emotional and intellectual world of the opera makes no appeal to many people; but the style as a whole is as admirably suited to that world as the styles of *Tristan* and *Die Meistersinger* are to their respective subjects, and I for one see no failure of inspiration except in some of the choral writing in the first act, where there is occasionally an undeniable touch of commonplace. Part of the admitted colorlessness of some of the vocal passages is to be accounted for, I think, by the utterly unmusical quality of the words. The defect is not in Wagner the musician but in Wagner the poet, who has forgotten for the moment several of the principles he had laid down in his prose works and put into successful practice in the six operas of his prime. The text of *Parsifal* contains a large amount of quite unmusical matter, especially at the commencement. Many of the lines have evidently not roused the slightest interest in the composer. He knew that the orchestral part was alive, and always developing the emotional possibilities of the situation; and when he comes to an obviously impossible verbal patch,—necessary for the telling of the story, but containing no stimulus for the musician— he simply refuses to waste time or trouble upon it. Take as an example one of the very worst passages for the voice in the whole opera—the words of Parsifal just before the beginning of the transformation music in the first act—

No. 37.

I hard- ly stir, and yet I move a - pace.

Granting that the words are unfit for music, it is incredible that Wagner could not have found a more interesting musical outline for them than this, if it had occurred to him to try. But I take it that he would not try, or saw no necessity for trying; his mind was wholly bent on working out his orchestral picture, which, after all, is the only thing that really matters here as in so many other places. In other passages, such as the long recital of Kundry to Parsifal commencing "I saw the babe upon its mother's breast" (vocal score, p. 187), the orchestral part is a sort of small symphonic movement in itself, in which the voice mostly sings the same melody as the orchestra. Where it does not do this in the symphonic passages the vocal writing again becomes a trifle careless, as here and there in the Good Friday music. The self-contained completeness of the orchestral part here is conclusively shown by its perfect adaptability to the concert room; and I take it that, feeling that virtually all he had to say had been said by the orchestra, Wagner worked out the mood of the scene with complete satisfaction to himself in that medium, and then added the vocal part as best he could—sometimes very well, sometimes by no means well. He had largely given up, indeed, thinking simultaneously in terms of both voice and orchestra, as he had done in the best parts of *Tristan*, *Die Meistersinger*, and *Götterdämmerung*. Those who will may put this down to a decline of his musical powers. To me it seems more probable that as a musician he came to rely more and more on his most eloquent instrument, the orchestra. It may even be that his carelessness with regard to the text of *Parsifal*, his inclusion of a number of episodes that he must have known were essentially foreign to his own ideal of music, can be accounted for by his belief that he could rely on the expressiveness and the continuity of the orchestral web to see him through all the inevitable difficulties. As one looks at the score of *Parsifal*, in truth, one can readily understand his desire to try his hand at a symphony in the last years of his life.

8

It is open to doubt, indeed, whether Wagner ever attained the homogeneity of form that was his ideal. His most homogeneous work is probably *Lohengrin*; after his developing imagination and technique had made him dissatisfied with the style of that opera, and pointed him on to more difficult achievements, he does indeed paint pictures of magnificent scope and exquisite fineness of detail, but he hardly attains the perfect balance of all the factors and the perfect consistency of style that make *Lohengrin* flow so smoothly. The reason, I think, is that while he was urged on to this reform and that by the logical quality of his mind, he was never quite logical enough—which is only another way of saying that even the greatest minds cannot create a wholly new form of their own in art. All they can do is to add something to the structure they have inherited from their predecessors, and pass the transformed product on to their successors as something to be transformed still further. An ideal like that of Wagner—to create an art form that should be musical through and through, a continuous, endlessly varied web of melody— is realizable in instrumental music pure and simple, but hardly in connection with the stage. Concentrate the dramatic action as he would, so as to provide the musician with a framework that should be musical in every fiber, the poet was still compelled to retain a certain amount of non-musical matter in order to tell his story clearly to the audience. The concision of *Tristan* is wonderful; but even in the first act of *Tristan* there are verse-passages the pedestrian quality of which the composer has not been able to disguise. The style of all his later works fluctuates in character because he is divided between a desire to keep the actors in the forefront and the necessity for relegating them to the background in order to give the orchestra an absolutely free course. We feel with Wagner, as we do with certain others of the most fertile minds in art—with Goethe, with Leonardo, with Hokusai—that one human lifetime was too pitifully short for the realization of everything of which the great brain was capable; that the body broke down while the mind was still capable of adding to its store of knowledge and feeling. All Wagner's greatest works, regarded from the standpoint of the twentieth century, are hardly more than magnificent attempts to find a compromise between drama and music. At times the compromise worked admirably; at others there is perceptible friction. His dilemma was the one that has confronted every composer of opera since the day when opera was invented. Poetry and music are not the loving sisters that the fancy of the literary man would make them out to be; they are rival goddesses, very jealous and intolerant of each other. The poet, in proportion as his work is genuine, faultless poetry, has no need of the musician. Music is cruel, ravenous, selfish, overbearing with poetry; it deprives it, for its own ends, of almost everything that makes it poetry, altering its verbal values, disregarding its rhymes, substituting another rhythm for that of the poet. It has no need of anything but the poetic idea, and to get at that kernel it ruthlessly tears away all the delicacies of tissue that enclose it. Wagner himself, however much he might theorize about poetry, was never a poet; he was simply a versifier who wrote words for music, words sometimes admirably adapted for this purpose, sometimes exceedingly ill-adapted. In *Tristan*, which he himself regarded as the one of all his poems that was best suited for music, what he writes is generally not poetry at all. Who would give that title to lines that scorn all grace of rhythm, all variety of cadence, all the magic that comes of the perfect fusion of speech and expression: lines like those of the final page, for example:

> *Heller schallend*
> *mich umwallend,*
> *sind es Wellen*
> *sanfter Lüfte?*
> *Sind es Wogen*
> *wonniger Düfte?*
> *Wie sie schwellen*
> *mich umrauschen,*
> *soll ich atmen,*
> *soll ich lauschen?*
> *Soll ich schlürfen,*
> *untertauchen?*
> *Süss in Düften*
> *mich verhauchen?*
> *In dem wogenden Schwall,*
> *in dem tönenden Schall,*
> *in des Welt-Atems*
> *wehendem All,—*
> *ertrinken,—*
> *versinken,—*
> *unbewusst,—*
> *höchste Lust!*

or those at the meeting of Tristan and Isolde in the second act—

> TRISTAN *Isolde! Geliebte!*
> ISOLDE *Tristan! Geliebter!*
> *Bist du mein?*
> TRISTAN *Hab' ich dich wieder?*
> ISOLDE *Darf ich dich fassen?*
> TRISTAN *Kann ich mir trauen?*
> ISOLDE *Endlich! Endlich!*
> TRISTAN *An meine Brust!*
> ISOLDE *Fühl' ich dich wirklich?*

TRISTAN	*Seh' ich dich selber?*
ISOLDE	*Dies deine Augen?*
TRISTAN	*Dies dein Mund?*
ISOLDE	*Hier deine Hand?*
TRISTAN	*Hier dein Herz?*
ISOLDE	*Bin ich's? Bist du's?*
	Halt' ich dich fest?
TRISTAN	*Bin ich's? Bist du's?*
	Ist es kein Trug?
BOTH	*Ist es kein Traum?*
	O Wonne der Seele,
	o süsse, hehrste,
	kühnste, schönste,
	seligste Lust!
TRISTAN	*Ohne Gleiche!*
ISOLDE	*Überreiche!*
TRISTAN	*Überselig!*
ISOLDE	*Ewig!*

If this telegraphic style, as Emil Ludwig calls it, is poetry, then we shall have to give that word a meaning it has never yet had.

But if the *Tristan* order of verse is not poetry, it is magnificently adapted to the needs of the symphonic musician. It is unobtrusive; it is pliant; it serves to *préciser* the musical emotion without fettering the orchestral composer either melodically or rhythmically. Compare now with the previous extracts one or two from *Parsifal*—

> *Denn ihm, da wilder Feinde List und Macht*
> *des reinen Glaubens Reich bedrohten,*
> *ihm neigten sich in heilig ernster Nacht*
> *dereinst des Heilands sel'ge Boten:*

> (To him, when 'gainst the savage foeman's might
> this realm of faith he had defended,
> oh wonder rare! in solemn, holy night
> from heaven the Saviour's messengers descended.)

Des eig'nen sündigen Blutes Gewell'
in wahnsinniger Flucht
muss mir zurück dann fliessen,
in die Welt der Sündensucht
mit wilder Scheu sich ergiessen:
von neuem sprengt es das Tor,
daraus es nun strömt hervor,
hier durch die Wunde, der seinen gleich,
geschlagen von desselben Speeres Streich,
der dort dem Erlöser die Wunde stach,
aus der mit blut'gen Tränen
der Göttliche weint' ob der Menschheit Schmach
in Mitleid's heiligem Sehnen,—
und aus der nun mir, an heiligster Stelle,
dem Pfleger göttlichster Güter,
des Erlösungsbalsams Hüter,
das heisse Sündenblut entquillt,
ewig erneut aus des Sehnens Quelle,
das, ach! keine Büssung je mir stillt!

(In maddest tumult, by sin defiled,
   my blood back on itself
   doth turn and rage within me;
to the world where sin is lord
in frenzied fear is it surging;
again it forces the door,
in torrents it poureth forth,
here through the spear-wound, alike to His,
and dealt me by the self-same deadly spear
that once the Redeemer pierced with pain,
   and, tears of blood outpouring,
the Holy One wept for the shame of man,
   in pity's godlike yearning,—
and from this my wound, the Grail's own chosen,
   the holy relics' guardian,
   of redemption's balm the warder,
the sinful fiery flood wells forth,
ever renewed from the fount of longing
that, ah! never penance more may still!)

So hofft sein sündenreu'ger Hüter,
   da er nicht sterben kann,
   wann je er ihn erschaut,
   sein Ende zu erzwingen,
und mit dem Leben seine Qual zu enden.

(Thus hopes its sin-repentant guardian,
   since he can perish not
   while on it he doth gaze,
   by force to draw death to him,
and with his life to end his cruel torment.)

How incredibly careless is the construction here—the long, involved sentences, the parentheses, the separation of substantive and verb by several lines! It is this absence of poetic concentration that makes *Parsifal* a trifle *langweilig* at times; for no matter how expressive Wagner may make the orchestral music, he cannot quite reconcile us to the frequent flatness of the vocal writing and the difficulty we often have in getting the sense, or even the grammatical construction, of the words.

That Wagner at the end of his life could put together a text like *Parsifal* after having made the poems of *Tristan* and the *Ring* is not in the least a proof of mental collapse, but only of the almost insuperable difficulties in the way of finding a perfect compromise between music and dramatic poetry. He was fortunate enough, in the case of *Tristan*, to hit upon a subject that was comparatively easy to concentrate. Two duties, it must be remembered, an operatic poem has to perform: it has to provide the composer with opportunities for emotional expression, and it has to make a story clear to the spectator. The ideal text would be that in which the action was implicit in the emotion, that is to say, one in which there was no need for any explanation, through the mouth of this or that actor, of events that were happening off the stage or that had occurred before the drama began. It is when the composer has to interrupt his purely emotional outpouring in order to allow the poet to become explanatory that he realizes the difficulty of making his opera musical throughout. Even in *Tristan* Wagner could not wholly dispense with a certain amount of explanation, in the first act, of the events in Ireland and Cornwall which have led up to the situation in which Tristan and Isolde now find themselves. The music in consequence halts decidedly at times; all the art of the composer cannot disguise the fact that he is momentarily being held up by the exigencies of the stage poet. In the *Ring*, as it was first drafted, Wagner was faced with the same problem, but he solved it in another way. *Siegfried's Death* was to be merely the climax of a long sequence of tragic events. Without some knowledge of these events, however, the spectator would be unable to understand the final tragedy. So Wagner resorted to the device of making the characters themselves recapitulate the earlier stages of the story, in much the same way that Isolde, in the first act of *Tristan*, tells Brangäne—for the benefit of the audience, of course—all about the coming of Tristan to Ireland, his slaying of Morold, her nursing of the wounded Cornish hero, his wooing her as bride for King Marke, and so on. In the opening scene of *Siegfried's Death* the Norns tell each other—again for the benefit of the audience—how Alberich ravished the gold from the Rhine, made a ring from it, and enslaved the Nibelung race; how the ring was stolen, and Alberich himself became a thrall; how the giants built Valhalla for the gods, and, denied their promised reward, got possession of the ring that the gods had stolen from Alberich; how there was born a free hero, destined to redeem the gods from *their* bondage; how Siegfried slew the dragon and wakened Brünnhilde from her sleep. Having made all this clear in an introductory scene, Wagner raises the curtain upon Siegfried and Brünnhilde. Later Hagen tells Gunther—all for the sake of the audience—how Wotan begot the Volsung race; how the twin-born Volsung pair Siegmund and Sieglinde had for son the mighty hero, Siegfried, who "closed the ravenous maw" of the dragon with his "conquering sword." In the next scene Siegfried explains to the audience—via Hagen and Gunther—how he came into possession of the tarnhelm and the ring, whereupon

Hagen describes the virtues of the former. In the third scene the Valkyries[8] fly to the solitary Brünnhilde and learn of her awakening by Siegfried, and of the intervention of Wotan in the combat between Siegmund and Hunding. In the first scene of the second act Alberich tells Hagen how he won the gold and forged the ring, and compelled Mime to make the tarnhelm for him; how the ring was ravished from him by the gods and given to the giants; how one of the latter guarded it in the form of a dragon; how Siegfried slew the latter and Mime. In the second scene of the third act Siegfried tells the Gibichungs—the audience overhearing—how Mime tended the dying Sieglinde in the wood, saved her child, and brought him up to his own craft of smith; how he (Siegfried) forged his father's sword anew and did the dragon to death; how the bird warned him of Mime's plot against his life, told him of the powers of the ring and tarnhelm, and sent him to rouse Brünnhilde from her sleep on the fire-girt rock.

Wagner must have felt the clumsiness of this method of constant explanation, and anticipated that it would impede the free flow of his music; while in any case the audience would probably still not be quite clear as to certain points. So, as all the world knows, he first of all prefixed to *Siegfried's Death* another drama—*The Young Siegfried*—designed to put the bearing of all the stages of the action beyond the possibility of misunderstanding. But again the fear haunts him that there may still be some things insufficiently accounted for; so even *The Young Siegfried* has to have a certain number of pages of explanation. The fact of Siegfried being there at all has to be explained by Mime, as well as the further fact of the death of Siegmund in battle and the perishing of Sieglinde in giving birth to Siegfried. In the next scene, almost the whole story of what afterward became *Das Rheingold* and *Die Walküre* is told afresh in the competition of questions and answers between the Wanderer and Mime. In the first scene of the third act, we have the completion of

[8] In *Götterdämmerung* Wagner sends only one Valkyrie, Waltraute.

the story of *Die Walküre* given to the audience in the dialogue between the Wanderer and Erda—how the earth goddess bore a daughter, Brünnhilde, to Wotan, how she flouted the god's will, and for punishment was doomed to sleep on the fiery fell. Not content with all this, Wagner afterward stages, in a third opera, *Die Walküre*, the whole of the action that has been told and told again in *Siegfried* and *Götterdämmerung*, from the love of Siegmund and Sieglinde down to the punishment of Brünnhilde. Even here he has to find room for explanations; in the first scene of the second act Wotan tells the audience—via Brünnhilde—the whole story of the rape of the gold by Alberich and all the events that followed from it. Finally Wagner comes to the conclusion that this whole action, from its beginning in the depths of the Rhine, had better be put visibly upon the stage; and so *Das Rheingold*, the story of which has been already told more than once, is prefixed to *Die Walküre*. But in spite of his having shown everything so completely that nothing remains to be explained by word of mouth, he still retains all the explanations he had inserted in the three later dramas of the tetralogy. No doubt he was aware of their superfluity, but shrank, as he might well do, from the enormous task of reconstructing the whole work yet again. He may have argued, too, that as each of the operas would have to stand by itself on the particular occasion of its performance, it would be no disadvantage to have the events of the preceding evening fully explained, even at the cost of some otherwise needless repetition.

I have not gone over this long familiar ground merely to tell again a thrice-told tale, but to bring into high relief the fundamental difficulty of the musical dramatist who is working along the Wagnerian lines—the difficulty of taking up the whole of the poet's work into the being of music, when the poet, in order to leave no room for misunderstanding on the part of the audience of the reason for the visible actions and the audible sentiments of the actors, has to pad out his poem with a certain amount of matter that is explanatory of the past rather than emotional

in the present. So desperate a device as the visible representation in three or four evenings of every stage of a
dramatic action was obviously, he must have felt, not to
be resorted to again. It was equally impossible to reduce
the story of *Parsifal* to the highly concentrated form into
which he had managed to cast *Tristan*. So he had to do
what it had been his first impulse to do in the *Ring*—
elucidate the visible action of the moment by a narrative
of all that had happened before the action, or that
particular stage of the action, began, and trust to the
orchestra to maintain the musical interest by means of the
interplay of leitmotivs. Hence the lumbering stage technique of the first act of *Parsifal*, and the *raison d'être* for
the endless garrulity of Gurnemanz. That venerable worthy
is not a character; he is merely a walking and talking guide
book; he stands outside the real drama, somewhat in the
style of the *compère* in a revue; and the proof of his almost
complete nullity is that Wagner has been utterly unable
to characterize him musically. Every other character in
his operas—even the minor personages, such as Kurvenal
and David and Gutrune—exists for us as a definite personality, someone drawn in the round in music as effectively as
a painter or sculptor could have shown him forth. But even
Wagner has been unable to invent a single phrase that
shall be characteristic of Gurnemanz and Gurnemanz
alone. He is the one Wagnerian character who simply
does not exist for musicians. As far as his music is concerned, he has neither mental characteristics nor bodily
form; we remember him solely for his interminable talk.

9

If Wagner failed in his struggle with the musical-dramatic
form, it was the failure of a Titan in a struggle that only a
Titan would have ventured upon. Form and the perfection
of form are simple enough matters for the smaller musical
intelligences, for whom form means merely a symmetrical
mold to be filled. It is for the greater minds that the problem of form is always a torture, for their ideas are perpetually outgrowing the mold. In sheer fertility of idea Wagner

was probably the greatest musician the world has ever seen. It was of the very essence of his work that there should be no repetition either of mood or of procedure. Without, indeed, making the necessarily futile attempt to decide which is per se the finer order of musical mind, the dramatic or the symphonic, it may be confidently said that to a dramatist—or at all events a dramatist like Wagner—there is permitted no such easy returning upon his own tracks, no half-mechanical manipulation of the same order of ideas time after time, as is possible to the worker in the stereotyped instrumental forms. Great as is the inventive power of a Bach, a Beethoven, or a Brahms, it cannot be denied that much of their work is simply a varied exploitation of a relatively small number of formulas—that a very small amount of thematic invention can be made to go a very long way under the guidance of an established pattern. Nor, broadly speaking, is the same intensity of imagination or the same scope of imagination required to invent a hundred ordinary fugal or symphonic themes as to find a hundred themes that are the veritable musical counterparts of as many human beings. The family resemblance between "subjects" which is permitted to a Bach or a Beethoven is not permitted to a Wagner: the dramatist's work must be a perpetual re-creation—and a definite, unmistakable re-creation—of the life around him in all its multiformity. In this sense Wagner is without an equal among composers; never has there been a brain so apt at limning character and suggesting the *milieu* in music. We can speak of the Wagnerian imagination as we can speak of the Shakespearean imagination; Wagner's is the only imagination in music which can be compared with Shakespeare's in dramatic fertility and comprehensiveness. It pours itself over the whole surface of a work, into every nook and cranny of it. It is a vast mind, infinite in its sympathies, protean in its creative power. For drastic incisiveness of theme he has not his equal in all music; each vision instinctively, without an effort, finds its own inevitable utterance. In the works of his great period every motive has a physiognomy as distinct from all others as

the face of any human being is distinct from all other
faces. The motives are unforgettable once we have heard
them. They depict their subject once for all: who today,
enormously as the apparatus of musical expression has developed since Wagner's time, would dare to try to find
better symbols than these he has invented for the tarnhelm, the fire, the Rhine, the sword, the dragon, the potion
that brings oblivion to Siegfried; or for any of the men
and women of the operas—for Wotan, for Siegfried, for
Mime, for the "*reine* Thor," for Herzeleide, for Hagen,
for Gutrune, for Brünnhilde, and for a dozen others? To
hear any of these themes today, after a generation or more
of daily familiarity with them, is like looking at a medal-
lion of a hundred years ago in which not a point of the
outline or a single plane of the relief has been blurred,
or a single grain of the first sharp milling been lost. They
are what they are because they combine in the fullest
measure and in impeccable proportion the two great preser-
vatives of all artistic work—a piercing personal vision and
consummate style.

10

In the operas of his prime, every one of his characters is
musically alive, down to the smallest. Tristan is not more
real to us than Kurvenal, or Walther more real than David,
or Brünnhilde than Gutrune. His fiery imagination saw
over the whole field of the drama with the same intensity.
In this respect, as in so many others, not one of his successors can compare with him. Strauss, for instance, has
always failed to give reality to any but the leading characters of his operas. His Faninal in *Der Rosenkavalier* is
decidedly not alive, nor is his Chrysothemis in *Elektra*.
There is not a single truly characteristic phrase by which
the musician can recall the former to his memory in the
way that he can recall David or Kurvenal or Mime; the
only piece of music by which he can recall Chrysothemis is
an atrocious waltz that he would prefer to forget. Strauss's
minor characters are known to us through the poem rather
than the music; while Wagner's minor characters are

clear-cut personalities to thousands of opera-goers who have never read the poem. And like the true dramatist, Wagner has no moral prejudices; for the time being he puts himself into the skin of each of his characters and looks at the world solely through his eyes. Nowhere is the author to be detected in the work, just as Shakespeare is nowhere to be detected in his; each of the characters sees the world from his own standpoint, and while he is talking, we are for the moment bound to see the world precisely as he sees it. In anyone else's hands Alberich would have been a mere conventional villain of melodrama. As Wagner draws him he is as real as Iago—an enemy of the light and all that live in the light, but their enemy by reason of the very nature of his being, following his own instincts with perfect naturalness and perfect consistency. So it comes about that we invariably believe in Alberich and the justice of his cause when he is speaking for himself; nowhere is he a mere foil or relief to characters with whom we may have more moral sympathy. No one can fail to be moved, for instance, by his appeal to Hagen in the second act of *Götterdämmerung*—the genuine heart-hunger of this repulsive gnome, lusting for power with all the passion and all the sincerity of his narrow soul. How vast and terrible a force of evil, again, is Hagen, but at the same time how natural, how inevitable. Even Mime is always right from Mime's point of view: the spectator can for the moment no more turn against him than against Alberich.

It is one of the mysteries of human psychology, indeed, how the mind that could be so incurably egoistic in the ordinary affairs of life, so incapable of seeing people as they really were, not merely as they were in relation to the gratification or frustration of his own desires, should be capable of such universal sympathy in his artistic creation. The crowning wonder of Wagner's artistic psychology is his treatment of Beckmesser. We have seen what a deadly and unreasoning hatred he had for Hanslick, and that it was Hanslick he had in view in the later poetical drafts of the character. Yet in the opera, though Beckmesser is made appropriately ridiculous, he is handled almost throughout without a touch of the malice one might have expected when one knows that the character is meant as a satire upon a detested enemy. I say "almost throughout," for it has always seemed to me that there is just a shade of unnecessary harshness, and therefore of dramatic inconsistency, in Sachs's words after Beckmesser has left the house with the manuscript of Walther's song in his pocket:

> A heart more base I never have known,
>   Ere long he'll be paid for his spite:
> Though men cast reason down from its throne
>   They cannot deny it quite:
> Some day the net is spread before them:
> In it they fall, and we triumph o'er them.

Beckmesser, for all his wiles, has not hitherto struck us as being base (*boshaft*). We laugh at him, but we love him, as we love all the fools and rogues of pure comedy. I fancy I can detect in this passage the last angry flash of the eye and the snap of the jaw as Wagner thought of Hanslick. Apart from this little lapse, it is wonderful with what detachment the composer has been able to see his personal enemy. The artist in him was too strong, too infallible, to permit of his fouling the ideal world of his art with any breath from the bitter, muddy world of real life. Mr. Bernard Shaw is of the opinion that Strauss, in *Ein Heldenleben*, gives "an orchestral caricature of his enemies which comes much closer home than Wagner's mediævally disguised Beckmesser." I hardly think the musical world as a whole will agree with Mr. Shaw. The "Adversaries" section of *Ein Heldenleben* always strikes me as a mere outburst of rather stupid bad temper: the humor is as ill-conditioned as the psychology is crude and the expression commonplace. We have long since ceased to bestow on it the compliment of even as much thin laughter as we gave it when it was quite new. It is bad art for this reason if for no other—that the petty, snappy hero shown in this section is inconsistent with the sort of superman who figures in the rest of the work; who can believe that the hero of the noble ending, set high above earth and all its littlenesses, is the same individual as the small bundle of wounded vanity and irritated nerves whose reply to his critics takes the form of putting out his tongue and "talking back" like a street urchin? Wagner's caricature is at once deeper, truer, kindlier, more universal, and more enduring. He could be little enough in his life: in his art the gods took care that he should never be anything but magnanimity itself.

And if there has never been a brain in music which saw so deeply into the springs of character, there has never been a musical brain with such a grasp of a drama as a whole. It was the mighty, tireless synthetic engine that we meet with only some score of times, perhaps, in the whole history of human thought—in two or three great military commanders, a few great architects, and half a dozen philosophers. It is becoming more and more evident each year that since his death, there has been no single composer of anything like his bigness, no single composer capable of work at once so new and so coherently wrought. His was the last truly great mind to find expression in music. That statement is not at all inconsistent with the admission that modern composers have said many hundreds of things Wagner could never have thought of: I simply mean that the brains of Strauss and Debussy or any two others put together would not equal Wagner's in range, in depth, in staying power. There has not been a musician since his time who can "think in continents" as he did. The more we study him, indeed, the more wonderful does this sweep of vision and tenacity of hold become to us. There is nothing in all other men's music comparable to Wagner's feat of keeping the vast scheme of the *Ring* in his head for more than a quarter of a century, and actually laying it aside completely for eleven years during that time, without his grip upon the smallest limb of the great drama relaxing for a moment. It is in virtue of this fiery and unceasing play of the imagination and this stupendous

364] WAGNER AS MAN AND ARTIST

synthetic power that he takes his place among the half-
dozen most comprehensive minds that have ever worked
in art.

In music there are only two brains—those of Bach and
Beethoven—to compare with his in breadth of span.
Say what we will about the repetitions and the *longueurs*
of the *Ring*, there is nothing in all music, and very little
else in any other art, to compare with that wonderful work
for combined scope and concentration of design. Wagner
had in abundance the rarest of all artistic gifts—the faculty, as a great critic has put it, of seeing the last line
in the first, of never losing sight of the whole through
all the tangle of detail. Wagner forgot nothing in his
work: at any stage of it he could summon up at a moment's
notice not only any figure he wanted, in all its natural
warmth of life, but the very atmosphere that surrounded
it, the very mood it induced in others. To me one of the
most marvelous instances of this has always been the
passage in Waltraute's recital in the third scene of *Götterdämmerung*, in which, in the midst of that extraordinary
picture of the frustrated Wotan brooding among the
joyless gods in Valhalla, she speaks of the god remembering
his favorite and banished child:

> Then soft grew his look:
> He remembered, Brynhilde, thee!

It is a far cry at this stage from the parting of the god
and his daughter in *Die Walküre*; but at the mere mention of it there wells up in Wagner, after twelve years or
more, all the emotion of the wonderful union between
them, and the gloomy, careworn music melts for a bar
or two into a tear-compelling tenderness. Another magnificent illustration of this gift of his of looking before and
after may be had in the third act of *Die Meistersinger*,
just after the greeting of Sachs by the populace of Nurem-
berg. That reception is surely the most overwhelming thing
of its kind the earth has ever seen or heard; it has always
been a mystery to me how any merely human singer can
find a voice in which to respond to it. But it is precisely

here that we realize the subtlety of Wagner's conception of Sachs, the profoundly imaginative way in which he saw him, and his ever present sense of the fundamentals of the character through apparently the most distracting vicissitudes. Any other operatic librettist and composer, after that million-throated outburst, would have set a strutting Sachs on his feet, smilingly and condescendingly accepting the homage of the multitude. Wagner makes *his* Sachs realize nothing but his own unworthiness and the sense of something hollow and fleeting in all this acclamation; and there is hardly an effect in all music to compare for subtlety, for poetry, for the profundity of its humanity, with the instantaneous melting of the crimson and purple strains of the folk into the quiet gray theme of Sachs's sorrow in the strings. It was the only possible outlet from what any other sincere composer would have instinctively felt to be an emotional impasse; and it was only Wagner who could have found the outlet. He is great in many ways, but in no way greater than in this faculty of keeping the vision of the moment always in touch with those that have passed and those that are to come; in all contemporary music there is not to be found a brain with a third of his power in this respect. In the operas of Strauss, strewn with fine things as they are, there is no such unity of style, no such ardor of conception, no such unrelaxing hold upon every character in every phase of it; and of course no purely orchestral modern work can compare with even a single opera of Wagner's for combined sweep of design and closeness of texture.

11

The clarity and unity of Wagner's vision are evident again in the pictorial element that plays so large a part in his works. He was often pictorial without intending it, and was himself probably unconscious of many of the effects of light, color, and atmosphere which delight us in his music. Mr. Runciman has done well to insist upon the gift, exhibited as early as *Die Feen*, for not only visualizing a scene or a character for us but giving it us in its natural tints. We have happily got past the day when old-fashioned theorists used to lay it down that "pure" music was "concerned with nothing but itself," and that whoever makes it concern itself with appearances of the visible world is at the best no more than half a musician. As I have argued in an earlier chapter of this book, we cannot parcel off the human consciousness into psychology-tight bulkheads in this way. The various faculties are always crossing over into each other's territories for a moment, and coming back with spoils that they refuse to surrender for the rest of their days. The theorists have always been telling us that music cannot "paint." The composers, knowing much more about the matter than the theorists, have always gone on painting to their heart's content—Bach, for example, being incorrigibly realistic. The three minds with the most pronounced bias toward tone painting were probably those of Bach, Schubert (in his songs), and Wagner. But between the musician painters there are as many differences of vision and of manner as there are between "pure" musicians or "pure" painters; and Wagner, in this regard as in every other, brought certain new elements into music, and still stands in a class by himself.

The curious thing about him is that while no other man's music gives us such an impression of being bound up at almost every point with the visible world in which we live and move, actual realism of the ordinary kind is comparatively rare with him, and it is certainly the least important factor in this impression. Now and again, of course, he does "paint" the concrete in the realistic way made familiar to us by the modern symphonic poem writers. But this way was not at all a new way. The music of Schubert and that of Bach, as has been said, is full of realism of this order—Schubert's spinning wheel and Bach's serpents, to give merely two well-known instances. To this category belong Wagner's Rhine, and his fire music, and the whinnying of the Valkyries' horses. But there is really not much realism of that sort in Wagner's music. He objected to it in Berlioz and others unless there was a very good reason for it, and never employed it himself except where it complied with the dual condition of being thoroughly justified by the scene and unquestionably within the scope of musical expression. Wagner does comparatively little tone painting of the purely realistic kind, but of course he does it always with superb certainty, profiting by a hundred years of evolution of technique since Bach, and by the gorgeous instrument that the modern orchestra places at his disposal.

A subtler sort of pictorialism—subtler because it is unpremeditated and unconscious—is that to which Mr. Runciman has drawn attention. No one except Hugo Wolf has ever approached Wagner in the capacity for bathing each scene, each character, in a light and an atmosphere of its own. (Wolf's achievements in this line were of course on a much smaller scale than Wagner's, but some of them are hardly less wonderful if we take into consideration the limitations of the black-and-white medium in which he worked.) This is surely one of the most baffling mysteries in music—how the same few dozen tones and colors can be made to suggest such differently colored aspects of the visible world, a world, we must remember, from which music is utterly cut off by the very nature of its medium. But whatever the explanation, the fact is indubitable; though it is a comparatively new thing in music, and indeed would not be possible without our modern developments of harmony, color, and technique. It is virtually unknown in pre-Wagnerian music. I do not mean that no previous composer ever gave a specially appropriate tint to a particular scene. That was frequently done; but it was done more or less by a convention, by the use of instruments having a particular association in the minds of the audience, as when the oboe or the *cor anglais* would be used for suggesting a pastoral scene, or the horns,—as in the beautiful passage at the commencement of the *Freischütz* overture—for suggesting a wood. The Wagnerian and Wolfian method to which I am now referring is something quite different from this. The term "method," indeed, is inappropriate, for it is impossible to reduce it to any rules or to trace the secret of its effect, as we can in the two more general instances I have just cited. It is possible to say that the cold, bare effect of Wolf's *Das verlassene Mägdlein* comes from the peculiar harmonies he uses, and the pitch at which they are used—just as the pastoral effect of the *"Scène aux champs"* in Berlioz's *Symphonie fantastique* comes from the use of the *cor anglais*. But the difference is this—that you can standardize, as it were, the pastoral effects of the oboe or the *cor anglais*, whereas you cannot standardize the effects of *Das verlassene Mägdlein*. Even in the hands of a fifth-rate composer the oboe may be made to suggest a shepherd: but give Wolf's harmonies to a second-rate musician and tell him to "paint" with them as Wolf has done, and he will soon realize that the "painting" is really not separable from *the music as a whole*, even though we may be able to say analytically that it is due to one factor more than another. The truth is that the scene has been perceived with such intensity of vision by the composer that, unknown to him, and without any volition on his part, the vision has made its own idiom for itself, incarnated itself in lines and colors that are expressive of it and it alone.

It is this subtle faculty that is always unconsciously operative in Wagner. It first comes to light in *Die Feen*. It gave parts of *The Flying Dutchman* their strange salt tang. It makes the peculiar white light of *Lohengrin*. And after that opera, when Wagner had attained full command of his powers, it did astounding things for him. There is a different light, a different air, in each of the four dramas of the *Ring*; and this broad difference between any two of the four is maintained in spite of there being minor differences of color between the various scenes of each of them. How mysterious and infallible this faculty is in its workings is best seen from the fact that when Wagner took up the second half of *Siegfried* in 1869, after having suspended work upon it in 1857, he did what no other musician before him or since could have done— spontaneously, unconsciously reverted to the idiom of twelve years before. Between those two dates he had traveled an incredibly long path as a musician; he had written *Tristan* and *Die Meistersinger,* two works with as many differences of idiom between themselves as there are between either of them and the *Ring.* Yet the wonderful brain could sweep itself clear of all the new impressions that had fed it during those twelve years, and though the new acquisitions of technique of course remained, he thinks himself back in a flash to the very center of the souls of the *Ring* characters and the very color and temperature of the scenes he had parted from so long ago.

This is the pictorial instinct of Wagner seen in its totality. In its detail it is equally marvelous. Each scene is so bathed in its own appropriate light and color, and strewn with its own peculiar shadows, that the music itself, apart from the scenic setting, is eloquent of the place and the hour of the action. In Wagner's music, as in Wolf's, one is conscious not only of the locality and the person and the race: one can almost tell the time of day. Music like that at the awakening of Brünnhilde would go with nothing but a mountain height in blinding sunlight. Hunding is not physically darker to the eye than he is to the ear in that marvelous tuba motive that accompanies his first entry in *Die Walküre.* The gait of Siegfried's music is as rapid as Mime's; but the differing stature of the two men is unmistakable from the music alone. One might multiply instances by the hundred of effects of realistic differentiation obtained not merely by orchestral color, but by something subtly interwrought into the very texture of the music. (The Hunding theme, for example, is "black" and sinister even on the pianoforte.) It is just this faculty of seeing everything with the most precise of painter's eyes, and then finding the infallibly right musical correlative of it, that enables Wagner to achieve such variety among pictures that are in essence the same. How many and how different woodlands there are in his music, how many degrees of sunlight, how many shades and qualities of darkness! The storm that maddens Mime after the exit of Siegfried is a very different storm from the one through which Siegmund rushes to the house of Hunding. What other man could have written *two* Rhine Maidens' trios like those in *Das Rheingold* and *Götterdämmerung*, each so liquid, so mobile, so sweet with the primal innocence of the world, and therefore so alike in some respects, yet so absolutely different?

So it comes about that without any tone painting in the ordinary acceptation of the word, Wagner succeeds in bringing the visible universe before our eyes in a way and to an extent that no other musician has done. Of tone painting pure and simple there is practically none in *Tristan*. Wagner is here concerned solely with a man and woman; yet how actual he makes every scene in which they move, and this without a single realistic stroke. In the garden scene he uses none of the conventional musical recipes—there is no obvious rustling of leaves, no sighing of the breeze, no purling of the brooks—yet how the magic of the garden and of the hour steals through us and intoxicates us! How hot and dry the air has become in the third act—as dry to us as to the parched tongue of the wounded man alone on the castle walls, with the mid-day sun turning the blue sea beyond to a vibrating, blinding haze. And—to me the most wonderful of all—how sinister is the atmosphere he creates through virtually the whole of *Götterdämmerung*; how, though indeed it is mostly set in the daylight, one feels that here among these Gibichungs, with gaunt, grim Hagen for weaver of the web of fate, the very earth has lost the radiant smile it had in Siegfried's forest and on Brünnhilde's mountain top. The sun no longer warms, the Rhine no longer laughs and glints and gladdens. And finally, how exquisitely adapted is the melodic and harmonic idiom of *Parsifal*—so smoothly flowing, so full of melting and caressing tenderness—to that static world from which, with the purging from it of so much human passion, so much even of the ordinary physical energy of humanity too has gone. For this, as for everything else, he found the right, the only musical equivalent, without seeking for it. His visions painted themselves.

12

Even the best of Wagnerians today become a little impatient at the occasional *longueurs* in his operas. Not merely does he plan his works on a scale that makes it almost impossible to give some of them in their entirety under ordinary conditions, but he sometimes lapses into a prolixity that is saddening or maddening according to the frame of mind we happen to be in at the moment. Most of his prolixity is to be accounted for by that bad text construction to which I have drawn attention. Music, let it be said again and again, is primarily an emotional art, and the less it has to do with mere dramatic explanation, the better. We can never tire of Wotan pouring out his heart in loving farewell to his child; but we can hear Wotan tell the long story of his financial and matrimonial troubles once too often. We could listen as often to Kundry's story of Herzeleide as to the slow movement of the Ninth Symphony or the *"Kleine Nacht-Musik"* of Mozart; but wild horses would not drag us to the theater merely to listen to old Gurnemanz's too-often-told tale of Amfortas and Klingsor, and how the sacred spear was lost. Yet though the poet Wagner is generally answerable for the occasional tedious quarters of an hour in the operas, the musician Wagner is not wholly free from blame. He never managed to get quite rid of the slow-footedness that was characteristic of his music from the first; to the very end he sometimes takes rather longer to drive his points home than is absolutely necessary; and in these more rapid and impatient days that goes against him sorely. He is often reproached with rhythmical monotony. There is some truth in the charge, which as a whole he himself would probably not have taken the trouble to repel. There is a passage in one of his letters in which he recognizes that his music is not so rhythmical as it might be, but he holds that some lack of rhythmical variety is inseparable from an ideal of dramatic music such as his. As I have attempted to show, he relied much more on harmonic effect than on rhythm, the latter being more peculiarly the instrument of the symphonic composer, while harmonic change is more suited to depict the varying aspects of a dramatic action. But against the comparative regularity of his rhythms is to be set his sense of style. He had an intuitive knowledge of how and when to break up a melodic line that was in danger of becoming too uniform. One of the simplest illustrations of this may be seen in the *Parsifal* Prelude (vocal score, p. 5, lines 1 and 2); just at the moment when we are beginning to suspect that the theme of "Faith" has been repeated quite often enough and to dread the further repetition that has already got under weigh, he alters the signature from $\frac{6}{4}$ to $\frac{9}{4}$, and gives a new rhetorical turn to the familiar melody. In Wotan's *Abschied*, again, we are unconscious of the uniformity of the rhythm in phrase after phrase, so consummate is the art with which the interest is always being transferred from one part of the combined vocal and orchestral tissue to another, and so beautifully planned is not only each section in itself but what may be called the exposition and development and cadence of the whole scene. Wagner could afford to dispense with the smaller rhythmical maneuvering of individual musical phrases; he had the much greater faculty of endowing long scenes and even whole operas with a vast dramatic rhythm of their own. Hundreds of smaller composers can give this page or that of their music a rhythmic piquancy that Wagner could never have attained on the same small scale; but not one of them could achieve such a rhythm as that of the second act of *Tristan*, with its slow, steady, imperceptible transition from night and its rapture to daylight and its cruel disillusioning glare.

Wagner's prolixity, again, is not the flabby dullness of a mind that is merely maundering on and on from sheer incompetence to get to grips with the essentials of an emotion, but the overcopiousness of an inexhaustibly rich brain. And if this quality of his has its occasional bad side, we do well to remember that it is accountable also for some of his most gigantic achievements in expression. Were it not for the endless inventive power and the never failing sense of beauty in it, a work like *Tristan*, which never pauses till the last drop of bitter-sweet juice has been squeezed out of the theme, would be hardly bearable. Like Bach, Wagner could never conceive any emotion without intensifying it to the utmost. The barest hint of joy in one of Bach's texts will set him caroling like a lark; the barest hint of mortality will bedim his music with all the tears of all the universe for its dead. Wagner has the same insatiable hunger for expression. In *Tristan* in particular every emotion is developed to its furthest limit of poignancy. The passion of love becomes almost delirium; when Tristan, in the third act, sings of the thirst caused by his wound, our very mouths, our very bones, seem dried as if by some burning sirocco blowing from the desert; when the sick man praises Kurvenal for his devotion, it is a cosmic paean to friendship that he sings.

In hundreds of other cases it is not by elaboration of speech that he makes his overwhelming effect, but by a sort of volcanic concentration. Mingled rage and grief and despair have never found such colossal expression anywhere, in any art, as in those few bars given to the frustrated and maddened Wotan after Fricka has foiled his plan for the protection of Siegmund in the fight (*Die Walküre*, vocal score, pp. 118, 119). Pathos will never find more touching accents than those of Brünnhilde in her last great scene with Wotan (*Die Walküre*, pp. 292, 293); few things in all music convey such a sense of tears as the strange salt tones of the oboe and *cor anglais* here. For concentrated fury there is nothing to compare with the outburst of the bound and impotent Alberich as he dismisses the Nibelungs who have witnessed his shame (*Das Rheingold*, pp. 199–201); technically this is one of the most effective crescendi in all Wagner's works. His imagination always takes fire at a single touch, a single suggestion, and there is no staying it until the fire has burned itself completely out. In the *Siegfried Idyl* he has only to think of the child whose coming meant so much to him, and all the fountains of human tenderness are unsealed; this is not an individual father musing over his child's cradle, but all nature crooning a song of love for its little

WAGNER AS MAN AND ARTIST

ones. It is this intensification of every emotion he has to
express that makes each of his characters, like Shakespeare's, seem the epitome of that particular phase of
human nature. Tristan and Isolde are the world's most
passionate and most tragic lovers: the opera is the very
quintessence of the egoism of love. So with a score of
other characters. The last word—for our own day at any
rate—in godlike majesty has been uttered in Wotan; the
last word of womanly gentleness and sweetness in Eva and
Gutrune; the last word of tragic womanhood in Sieglinde;
the last word of superb womanhood in Brünnhilde; the
last word of mellow and kindly middle age in Hans Sachs;
the last word of scheming feebleness in Mime; the last
word of elemental savagery in the Valkyries; the last word
of youthful irresponsibility in the *Mastersinger* apprentices; the last word of human grimness in Hagen; the last
word of doglike devotion in Kurvenal. The character drawing is endless in its variety and infallible in its touch.

13

Parsifal stands in a class apart from all the other works of
Wagner. Its characterization is not individual but symbolic; Amfortas and Parsifal and Kundry and Klingsor are
not men and women whom we might meet any day in the
flesh, but simply types of human aspiration or failure. We
have outgrown the mental world of the work; the religious
symbolism of it, *qua* religious symbolism, leaves many of
us unimpressed; yet the basic emotional stuff of it all is
enduring, and we must not allow ourselves to be set
against the opera because the forms in which Wagner has
embodied a durable philosophy are themselves of a time
instead of all time. Evidently the symphonist in him was
at this stage overpowering the dramatist. The symphonist
can safely deal with types or abstractions; the dramatist
can only deal with individuals. Wagner has made the
blunder of trying to translate the most delicate, the most
esoteric perceptions into the language of the theater, of
setting symbols upon the stage. The force of a poetic symbol lies wholly in the imagination: as soon as a dramatist

or a painter tries to set it visibly before us, the free flight of the imagination is curbed by the physical obviousness, the physical limitations, of the figure that is put before the eye; the universal cannot be perceived for the particular. Wagner's root idea in *Parsifal* was to show us, in Kundry, a living symbol of the dual nature of woman, half-angel and half-beast, in turns sensual and repentant, the destroyer and the savior of man. But it is precisely symbols of this kind, cutting down to the obscurest depths of human psychology, that cannot retain their vast suggestiveness after they have been narrowed down to the personality of a single actor. We no longer see the eternal and infernal womanly; it is only a prima donna, stout of build and heavy of movement, that we see upon the stage. So with Parsifal himself. Mr. Huneker has called him "that formidable imbecile." So might we style St. Francis of Assisi, or the Buddha, or any other of the simple wise ones of the world, if we persist in looking at them through unsympathetic and unimaginative eyes. The conception of Parsifal is fine enough in itself—as unstained soul made divinely wise by its very simplicity, its love, its pity. But a character of this kind should be left to the imagination, or to music to suggest to the imagination: it is impossible to realize it behind the footlights in the person of an actor. A Parsifal is a figure for the quiet of one's chamber, not for a crowded theater lying the other side of the box office. Hundreds of people must have felt, as I have done for many years, that a good deal of *Parsifal* affects us more deeply at home than it ever does in the theater, the loss of the orchestral color being more than made up for by the gain in imaginative intensity. And the difficulty of making such a character vital and credible upon the stage is increased when he becomes the center of a quasi-religious ritual that has long ceased to have a meaning for many people.

But in spite of it all, *Parsifal* is a masterpiece. The story of it seems to arouse a violent antipathy in some people, who apparently regard it as an immoral work. The pleasant little game of *Parsifal*-baiting began with Nietzsche, who said that he despised everyone who did not regard the opera as an outrage on morals.

Like most philosophers, Nietzsche had the charming failing of imagining that the only right way for the world to go was his way. He was singularly taken with that notion of his of the superman—a mythical and unidentifiable mammal about which we have never been able to get any definite information, either from Nietzsche or from any of his disciples. Now Nietzsche found this ideal of his in Siegfried, and he loathed *Parsifal* because it preached the negation of life, the denial of the Will to Power. Later writers, like Mr. Runciman and Mr. Huneker, who are not, I think, Nietzscheans, agree with him in seeing something peculiarly weak in the philosophy—to call it by that name—of *Parsifal*. They see in the opera not merely moral weakness but moral nastiness. I remember one of the simpler adherents of this theory telling me, in awe-stricken tones, that this "sexless" opera was the resort of a set of men who were mixed up in a German scandal of a few years ago which sent its unwholesome odor through the civilized world: and he obviously thought that this discredited Wagner's *Parsifal*, whereas it struck me as being very like asking us to give up having breakfast because some horrible murderer or other liked bacon and eggs.

Nor can any moral flabbiness, I think, be discovered in *Parsifal* except by people who make the mistake of thinking that the "philosophy" of any musical work matters very much. Mr. Runciman detests Parsifal and calls him a perfect idiot—that epithet being Mr. Runciman's playful intensification of Wagner's "pure [i.e., stainless] fool" —"fool" being unfortunately the only monosyllable we have in English for the translation of "Thor." But even supposing Parsifal were an idiot—which I dispute—would it greatly matter? Mr. Runciman has launched his full battery against the Siegfried of Wagner's poem—a swaggering, quarrelsome, ungrateful young noodle; but, as Mr. Runciman's own eloquent description of the opera shows, the Siegfried of Wagner's music is a vastly more interesting and sympathetic person than the Siegfried of Wagner's verse. Similarly, even if I could think, when reading the libretto, that Parsifal is an idiot, I could never think so when listening to his music. The truth is that a good many of Wagner's characters and dramatic motives seem rather foolish to us nowadays. For my part I do not know or care whether or how Parsifal is to "redeem" the world. The word "redemption" has no meaning for me in the sense in which Wagner and the theologians use it. I can believe that redemption is a reality in the pawnbroking business; but if anyone tells me that men's souls are to be bought and sold, or lost and found again, without any volition of their own, I can only say that all this conveys about as much to my intelligence as talk about a quadrilateral triangle would do. But to appreciate a work of art it is not in the least necessary to subscribe to its author's philosophical or religious opinions; a rationalist can be as deeply thrilled by the *Matthew Passion* as any Christian can be. The "thesis" of a work of art is the one thing in it that does not concern us as artists. Who is to decide between rival philosophies or sociologies? Personally I believe that one philosophy is about as good as another, and worse, as the Irishman would say; but if an artist chooses to set forward a character as the embodiment of some philosophy that possesses him at the moment, I am willing to listen to him so long as he can talk interestingly about it, without my wishing either to subscribe to the philosophy or to dissent from it. Mr. Runciman thinks there is something frightful in the thesis—let us call it that—of *Parsifal.* I do not see anything frightful in it. I do not believe in it as the only rule of life; but then I do not believe—in *that* sense—in Senta's "redemption" of the Dutchman, or Elisabeth's "redemption" of Tannhäuser, or that Lohengrin was right in withholding his name from Elsa and then going off in a huff when she asked for it. But all these fantastic motives in which I have no belief no more affect my appreciation of the operas than my disbelief in ghosts affects my appreciation of *Hamlet.* I do not want any of my friends to be like Parsifal, Amfortas, or Klingsor—especially poor Klingsor: but neither do I want any of them to be like Lohengrin or Elsa or Senta or the Dutchman. A real world run on the lines of *Parsifal* would probably drive normal men mad in a month: but then who could live in a world in which Senta-sentimental maidens insisted on jumping into the sea to "redeem" master mariners, callously taking no account of the able seamen and the stokers and the stewards, who, from anything I can gather to the contrary in the text of *The Flying Dutchman*, all go to Davy Jones's locker in a state of pure damnation, while the captain and the girl ascend to glory? No, we had better leave alone the question of what the world would be like if we were to try to model it on *Parsifal*. We know very well that nothing of the sort will ever happen, just as we know that Little Red Riding Hood's wolf will not gobble up our little Phyllis on her way to the high school next week, or the door of the banker's safe fly open when the burglar says "*Sesame*." These be but fairytales. We can still sleep in our beds o' nights: and we can still go to *Parsifal* without either having our morals corrupted or feeling that we are encouraging race suicide.

I listen to *Parsifal*, then—and I imagine most other people do the same—as I would to any other outpouring of a great man's spirit on a world of ideas which fascinated him for the moment, and without any more impulse to translate it all into terms of reality than when I am listening to *The Flying Dutchman* or *Lohengrin*. The opera is in no sense the work of an exhausted old man. It has been alleged that the plot is "the work of Wagner's tired-out old age." But *Parsifal* was sketched as early as 1857, worked out in detail in 1864 (when Wagner was only fifty-one), and turned into verse in 1877. Further, the central ideas of the drama are to be found both in the sketches of *Jesus of Nazareth* (1848) and *The Victors* (1856); while in 1855 it was Wagner's intention to bring Parsifal on the stage in the final scene of *Tristan*, opposing him, as a symbol of renunciation, to Tristan as a symbol of passion. At almost any time of Wagner's life, indeed, he might have written a *Parsifal*. All his life through he fluctuated between intense eroticism and an equally intense revulsion from the erotic. One may say, in truth, that such a man *had* to write a *Parsifal* before he died. "*Il est à remarquer, mon fils,*" says the excellent Abbé Coignard in Anatole France's *La Rôtisserie de la reine pédauque,* "*que les plus grands saints sont des pénitents, et, comme le repentir se proportionne à la faute, c'est dans les plus grands pêcheurs que se trouve l'étoffe des plus grands saints. La matière première de la sainteté est la concupiscence, l'incontinence, toutes les impuretés de la chair et de l'esprit. Il importe seulement, après avoir amassé cette matière, de la travailler selon l'art théologique et de la modeler, pour ainsi dire, en figure de pénitence, ce qui est l'affaire de quelques années, de quelques jours et parfois d'un seul instant, comme il se voit dans le cas de la contrition parfaite.*"

In the great book of sex there are many chapters, and *Parsifal* is simply the last of them for some people. For others it is a chapter that they turn to again and again in moments of revulsion from the illusions of passion. Wagner's insight was clear enough: the Parsifals are no more denials of the Life-Force than the Tristans are; they are simply another phase of the Life-Force. When we disengage the central idea of *Parsifal* from its rather unskillful operatic setting, the work is simply an artist's dream of an ideally innocent world, purged of the lust, the hatred, the cruelty that deface the world we live and groan in. This is the world the *music* paints for us—

Summers of the snakeless meadow, unlaborious earth
   an oarless sea;

and the cumbrous, old-fashioned stage framework upon which the drama is constructed means no more to me than a clumsily drafted program to a great symphonic poem—it detracts no more from my musical enjoyment than that would do. The music itself, apart from a few commonplaces in the first act, is marvelous. It is indeed an old man's music, but only in the sense that it opens windows for us upon regions of the soul to which only the old and emotionally wise have access. Swinburne some-where speaks of Blake's face having the look of being lit up from the inside. I see a similar luminous transfigura-tion in the later portraits of Wagner[9]—they have the look of a man who has penetrated to the great underlying sim-plicities of things; and I find in the music of *Parsifal* the same subtle, searching simplicity, the same almost un-earthly illumination. Nowhere does the great master seem to me more truly powerful than in these quiet strains, whose suggestiveness, as is the case with the last Italian songs of Hugo Wolf, is inexplicably out of proportion to the quiet economy of their tissue. To the last the wonder-ful brain kept growing. Wagner makes a new musical idiom, a new texture, for *Parsifal* as he had done for every other of his works—above all, a harmonic language of incomparable subtlety, a gliding, melting chromaticism that searches us through and through. It is from this novel chromaticism—a very different one from that of *Tristan*—that the harmony of César Franck has come, and all the modern harmony that builds upon Franck.

14

Wagner saw his own work as a transmutation and amplifi-cation of the speech of Beethoven—infinitely changeful, but controlled in every bar by a never sleeping sense of the organic unity of the whole; but it is clear to us now that some features in his work derive from Bach, or are a re-

[9] The anti-Wagnerians take a malicious delight in pointing to the old-age portrait of Wagner by Renoir (it is reproduced in Emil Ludwig's diatribe *Wagner, oder die Entzauberten*). This shows as a rather flabby and senile face, with a pronounced re-laxation of the mouth. But Renoir was an impressionist, and inclined to take the usual impressionist's liberty with his subject. Moreover, the portrait was the product of no more than half an hour's sitting, given much against Wagner's will one afternoon after he had tired himself with talking to this new visitor, who saw him on that occasion for the first and, I think, the last time in his life. To ask us to believe that this slap-dash thing is the only veracious portrait of Wagner is making too great a demand on our credulity.

discovery of certain principles of form that Bach affected. It is from Bach, rather than from Beethoven, that such things as the *Tristan* Prelude come, with their incessant evolution of new life out of a single thematic germ, and their adoption of a comical form of slow ascent to a climax and descent from it, in place of the square symphonic form of return and re-start. In Bach, again, will be found the basis both of Wagner's realism and of the Wagnerian system of allusive "motives." The towering greatness of Wagner is nowhere more strikingly shown than in the failure of all his successors to handle his form—or, indeed, any other—with anything like the same power, freedom, and consistency; both the opera and symphonic music are waiting for someone big enough to build afresh upon the foundations Wagner has laid, and with the materials he has left. At present the most that any of his successors can do is to fit a few of the more manageable of the stones together, with a deplorable quantity of waste and confusion all around and in between. *Salome* and *Elektra* may be taken as instructive examples. There is not a living man big enough to occupy more than a room or two at a time of the vast house that Wagner reared about him. It is true that in certain details—in the furnishing and decoration of one or two of the rooms, let us say— modern music has gone beyond him. Strauss's orchestration has an eloquence—not merely a color, but a soul and a voice—of which Wagner probably never suspected the possibility. Strauss, Wolf, and others have shaken off the rhythmic fetters that sometimes hampered the movement both of Wagner's poetry and of his music. Wolf and Strauss have shown us the possibilities of what may be called a prose style in music—a more continuous and less formal style than that of verse, with the rhythmic joints and pivots more skillfully concealed. Superb examples of it are to be found in the later scene between Octavian and the Princess in the first act of *Der Rosenkavalier*, and in the great trio in the third act. Wagner, it is safe to say, would have flatly pronounced it impossible to make rhythmic music of a piece of frank prose like the latter, in which there is not a suspicion of a pretext for any of the staple rhythmic formulas.

But though the Wagnerian apparatus has been improved upon at these and other points—Strauss, for example, has subtilized the employment of the leitmotiv—no one has been great enough to manipulate the apparatus as a whole with anything like Wagner's power, scope, and freedom, and opera is still waiting for its new redeemer. Even an anti-Wagnerian work like *Pelléas et Mélisande* is, in a sense, a tribute to the Titan: the very sharpness and thoroughness of its recoil from everything that hints at Wagner is an admission of the impossibility of continuing his work on its own lines. And after all, *Pelléas et Mélisande* is only a beautiful and wonderful *tour de force*—a sort of glorified musical mule, without pride of ancestry or hope of posterity. Its idiom is too small for the expression of great things; we might as well try to build a city out of nothing but mother-of-pearl and opals.

Like Bach and like Beethoven, Wagner closes a period and exhausts a form. And as with Bach and Beethoven today, it is indirectly rather than directly that his best influence is being exerted; there is no room for imitation of him, but his speech and his vision are eternal stimuli to our imaginations. It is inevitable that in some quarters a reaction should have set in against his music and his influence. He has been too overpowering a force. His music has been performed with such fatal frequency that the merest amateur can hardly remain unconscious of the weak points in it; and for more than a generation he made all but the very strongest minds among composers a mere shadow and echo of himself. Music, as was only to be expected, has now gone beyond him in certain respects, and the erstwhile anarch is now one of the greatest of the forces that conservatism claims for its own. The French and some of the Russians have revolted against what is less a Wagnerian than a German domination of all European music. A number of our very newest young men are delightfully contemptuous of him: every puny whipster now raises his little hand to deal the reeling colossus another blow. But the colossus will easily right himself. There are moments when one is tempted to say that he and Bach and Beethoven have expressed between them almost all that is essentially original and great in the music of the last two centuries. When a composer is so mighty of body as this, he can well afford to lose a drop or two of blood on his pilgrimage through the ages.

"In music, as in nature," says Vincent d'Indy, "there are mountains and valleys; there are artists of genius who raise their art to such heights that the herd of second-rank creators, unable to breathe in these altitudes, is forced to descend again to more temperate levels (which, however, are often sown with charming flowers), until the eruption of a new genius heaves up a new mountain peak.

"Such were Bach, Haydn, Beethoven and César Franck in the symphonic order; and in the dramatic order, Monteverdi, Rameau, Gluck and Wagner. At the present moment we are descending the slope created by the Wagnerian upheaval, and we are hastening gently towards the hopeful presage of a new summit. But all our drama—even that of the composers who most energetically deny the imputation—comes from the spring which rises at the feet of the titanic Wagner.

"Richard Wagner still casts his great shadow over all our musico-dramatic production. But it is certain that the latent work that is going on in the souls of creative artists is to favour the ascent towards a distant height, of which we cannot yet foresee either the glaciers or the precipices."

His work, in truth, will flower afresh some day in some great composer who will sum up in himself, as Wagner did, all the finest impulses of the music of his day—who will have absorbed the essential, durable part of the spirit of his predecessors, and who will have at his command an idiom, a vocabulary, and a technique competent to express every variety of human emotion. But we may hazard the conjecture that the new flowering will be in instrumental music rather than in the opera. It seems to be a law of musical evolution that at the end of a period of crisis the seminal force that has exhausted itself in one genre passes over to, and finds a new life in, a wholly different genre. Beethoven left no real successors in the classical symphony—for great as Schumann and Brahms are, they are in this field no more than epigones of Beethoven. It is in the Wagnerian opera that the new expressive, half-poetic power of Beethoven's music finds its further logical development. All the opera writers who have followed in Wagner's tracks—Strauss included—are to Wagner simply what Brahms was to Beethoven. As Beethoven fertilized not the symphony but the music-drama, so Wagner has fertilized not the music-drama but poetic instrumental music—the innumerable symphonic poems and program symphonies of the last fifty years. The idea of the new form may have been Liszt's as much as Wagner's, or even more; but Liszt's music was not rich enough to do the full work of fertilization. Now, apparently, we are nearing the end of a period of transition. Already there are signs that the formal program was little more than a crutch for poetic music in the days of its hesitating growth. Composers are beginning to master the art of suggesting the dramatic inner conflicts of the soul without needing to rely on any outer apparatus of suggestion. We are probably developing toward a form of symphonic music that shall be to the art of its own day what the Beethoven symphony of the middle period was to the art of his time —a musical drama-without-words, and perfectly lucid without words. When the new instrumental music has assimilated all the finest spirit and mastered the full harmonic and rhythmic vocabulary and the best technique of the new day, some future Wagner will perhaps turn the mighty stream into a fresh dramatic channel, the nature of which it is impossible to anticipate. So the great series of cross-cycles will no doubt go on and on, into a day when dramatic music shall no more resemble Wagner's than Wagner's music resembles that of Palestrina. In that distant day he may be no more to mankind than Monteverdi is to us; but music will still be something different from what it would have been had he never been born; and of only some half-dozen composers in the whole history of the art can that be said.

The Racial Origin of Wagner

Wagner's Autobiography has thrown a good deal of light on certain obscure episodes in his career, but it has signally failed to satisfy the world's curiosity on perhaps the most interesting point of all—the question as to who was Wagner's father. Was it the Leipzig police actuary, Karl Friedrich Wilhelm Wagner, or the actor, painter, poet, singer, dramatist, and what not, Ludwig Heinrich Christian Geyer, who married Frau Wagner after the death of her first husband? Under normal circumstances the question would have little or no interest except for the sort of people who dearly love a scandal, even if it be a century and a quarter old. What gives the question its piquancy today is the fact that Geyer was a Jew—or at least has always been held to have been one. Now Wagner hated Jews all his life with an insensate hatred, and to have it proved that the composer himself was a Jew on his father's side would give a malicious pleasure to many people to whom Wagner's whole character is a trifle repugnant. Moreover, Wagner was always insisting on the specially German quality of his life's work; and again it would be amusing if it should turn out that the greatest "national" art work of modern Germany was the creation of a Jew. As might be expected, those who have a bone to pick with Wagner on any subject under the sun are delighted to point at this supposed bar sinister in his escutcheon. Wagner did not like Brahms, and so he accused poor Johannes of being a Jew. It was therefore natural that the out-and-out Brahms partisans should hail with glee any opportunity of making a retort in kind upon Wagner. This is attempted by Sir Charles Stanford in a preface to a volume of Brahms's compositions issued by Messrs. T. C. & E. C. Jack. He affirms afresh—what we all knew quite well—that Brahms was of the purest Teutonic blood; and, in his opinion, "the humour of the situation reaches its climax when it is discovered that the very man who attacked any music or musician of Jewish connection was himself tarred with the brush with which he had been endeavouring to orientalise his blue-eyed, fair-haired, and high-instepped German contemporary." So confident, it will be seen, in this statement of the Hebraic origin of Wagner that any plain man, unversed in these matters, who happened to read Sir Charles Stanford's preface, would naturally assume that Wagner's Hebraism is as universally admitted as the death of Queen Anne. Yet Sir Charles offers no evidence as to Wagner being a Jew; he simply tells us that the fact has been "discovered."

Where and when, we may ask, was this "discovery" made? We know that there has long been tittle-tattle current to the effect that Wagner's real father was not the police official whose name he bears, but the brilliant man of many parts who came to the rescue of Wagner's mother in the early days of her widowhood, and married her some nine months afterward. For the last generation or two a certain number of people have been going about the world shaking their heads mysteriously and darkly hinting at what they could tell if their lips were not sealed. The root of the legend is a notorious remark of Nietzsche's. That philosopher had seen one of the privately printed copies of the Autobiography about 1870, and his query in the postscript to *Der Fall Wagner*, "was Wagner a

German at all?" and his point-blank statement that "his father was an actor of the name of Geyer," were supposed to have their justification in the Autobiography. It was confidently asserted that when *that* appeared, the truth would be made known to all the world in Wagner's own confession. Well, the Autobiography *has* appeared, and what Wagner says there is that Friedrich Wagner was his father. There is not the shadow of a hint in the book that Geyer was anything more than a friend of the family. (Mr. James Huneker, who discusses the subject in an essay in his book *The Pathos of Distance* (1913) thinks he sees such a hint, and a pretty broad one, in one passage that he quotes; but the wish, I imagine, is father to the thought: few people would care to put the construction upon it that he does.) Mr. Huneker as good as asserts that the commencement of the Autobiography has been tampered with. The reputation of Villa Wahnfried in editorial matters is certainly not of the best; but after the express assurance that has been given the world that the Autobiography has been printed just as Wagner left it, something more than mere suspicion is required to bolster up a charge of such atrocious bad faith. Mr. Huneker tells us that "the late Felix Mottl [the conductor], in the presence of several well-known musical critics of New York City, declared in 1904 that he had read the above statement" (i.e., "I am the son of Ludwig Geyer"). That is a little staggering: but again one prefers to think that Mottl or someone else was mistaken, rather than that Cosima and Siegfried Wagner have been guilty of an incredible piece of literary dishonesty. As for Mr. Huneker's further "fact" —that there are portraits of Wagner's mother and of Geyer at Wahnfried, and none of Friedrich Wagner— that is easily accounted for; no portrait of the latter has ever been traced, with the exception of a small pastel, while Geyer was an artist and fond of painting himself.

Sir Charles Stanford attempts to support his very dubious thesis by some show of musical argument. He alleges that the most marked characteristic in such little Jewish music as still exists is the continual repetition of short

phrases—a method, he says, which Mendelssohn "uses to
the verge of monotony" in his later works, and which is
visible again in Wagner's employment of leading motives.
Note, to begin with, the restriction of the use of this
method to Mendelssohn's *later* works. Being a Jew, Mendelssohn surely would have betrayed this characteristic in
the work of his whole life, if it really be a characteristic
rooted in the Hebrew nature. It looks as though the ingenuous argument were that there is no Jew like an old
Jew. But it is of even less applicability to Wagner than to
Mendelssohn. It is true that in the *Ring* Wagner worked
to a great extent upon short leading motives; but the employment of these was due to the special problems of structure which he was then engaged in working out. Sir
Charles Stanford, with his extensive knowledge of Wagner's music, must know that the short phrase is not a characteristic of Wagner's style as a whole. The phrases in
Rienzi, The Flying Dutchman, Tannhäuser, Lohengrin,
the youthful Symphony, the *Faust* Overture, and half a
dozen other works, are as long-breathed as any of Brahms's.
Moreover, Sir Charles Stanford admits that in at least
half of his work Wagner was a typical Teuton. He speaks
of Brahms's melodies as being "long, developed, diatonic,
and replete with a quality which may, for lack of a better
term, be called 'swing.'" We get precisely the same qualities in *Die Meistersinger*. Sir Charles Stanford can hardly
be serious when he lays it down that Wagner was a typical
Teuton when he wrote *Meistersinger* and a typical Jew
when he wrote the *Ring*. But further, *is* the short thematic
phrase a characteristic of the Hebrew composer? Will Sir
Charles be good enough to illustrate this point for us from
the work of Jewish composers like Mahler and Max Bruch?
If, indeed, we are to attribute Hebraic ancestry to a composer on the strength merely or mainly of a certain shortness of melodic breath, there are dozens of composers who
would have difficulty in repelling the imputation. Was
there ever a composer who habitually worked upon such
short phrases as Grieg, for example? Is there anything to

equal for brevity some of the themes with which Beethoven worked such wonders? And what precisely *is* a short phrase? Will someone provide us with a sort of inch rule and table of measurements, by the application of which we shall be able to say precisely where musical Judaism ends and Gentilism begins?

These are surely very flimsy foundations on which to erect a theory that Wagner was a Jew. It is, of course, not impossible that he was: nothing is impossible in this world. One of the rumors afloat is that Wagner himself, in private, spoke of Geyer as being his father. Again proof or disproof is impossible; though Mrs. Burrell gives a facsimile of a letter from Wagner of October 23, 1872 (sending Feustel a certificate of baptism), in which he goes out of his way to call himself "Polizei-Amts-Actuarius-Sohn" (Police-actuary's son).

Another branch of the argument is that Wagner was typically Jewish in appearance. I question whether that theory would ever have gained currency except for the back-stairs gossip with regard to his supposed paternity. It has long been a puzzle to the present writer to discover what there is particularly Jewish in Wagner's face. It is true that his nose was large and to some extent aquiline; but it is certainly not the nose that we are accustomed to regard as typically Jewish. The portraits of Geyer which we possess do not show a physiognomy that anybody would call peculiarly Hebraic. On the other hand, Wagner's mother had a nose not only very prominent and curved like Wagner's, but suggesting a Jewish origin far more than either his or Geyer's. For the rest there is nothing whatever in Wagner's face that could lead anyone to think he was a Jew. Let us take Sir Charles Stanford's own test. He remarks that "no one who had known Brahms, especially in his later years, when the Jewish type, if it exists in the blood, is most accentuated, could fail to see that in face, in complexion, in hair and in gait he was a pure Teuton, without a trace of Eastern relationship or characteristics." Let us admit, for the sake of argument, that it is in a man's later years that Jewish characteristics in the blood show themselves most markedly in the face. Now Wagner, so far from looking more Jewish in his maturity and old age, looked decidedly less Jewish. In some of the later full-faced portraits, indeed, the face bears an extraordinary resemblance to the Mr. Asquith of about ten years ago. Some people would call it a very English face. And what of the other members of the Wagner family? We have portraits of his uncle Adolf (1774–1835) and his brother Albert (the latter was born fourteen years before Wagner, and long before Geyer comes into the story). These faces are unmistakably of the same general cast as Wagner's: that of Albert, indeed, is almost exactly the face of Wagner, but without the genius. The bust of Adolf Wagner shows a nose, forehead, and other features very like those of Richard. The chin is not so pronounced, but the two faces are incontestably of the same type. According to Frau Rose, the daughter of Carl Friedrich Wagner's friend, Gustav Zocher, Wagner's father "was small and slightly crooked, but had a fine face." "I have often thought," says Mrs. Burrell, to whom Frau Rose made this communication, "in looking at Wagner, that he had a narrow escape of deformity; he was not in the least deformed, yet the immense head was poised on the shoulders at the angle peculiar to hunchbacks." The mother also was tiny and eccentric, with "an electric disposition." No judge and jury would say on this evidence that there was any reason whatever to doubt the German paternity of Wagner and assume the Jewish.

There are one or two facts, however, that must be taken into consideration on the other side. Why should Geyer, a struggling artist, be so willing to assume the burden of the widow Wagner and her seven young children? A man of the highest character and the warmest heart he certainly was: are these sufficient explanations of his chivalrous conduct? We have letters of his to Frau Wagner during the weeks that immediately followed the husband's death. The tone of them is warm, but friendly and sympathetic rather than loving. He generally addresses her simply as "Friend," or "Dear Friend." His goodness of heart is shown by such remarks as that *à propos* of the recovery of the little Albert from illness: "I have indeed felt sincerely with you in your terrible experience, for if Albert were my own son he could not be nearer to my heart." There is not a line in the letters which shows any more affection for Richard than for Albert; the latter, indeed, is mentioned the more frequently. Yet some suspicion clusters around a fact that cannot be discovered from the ordinary biographies of Wagner. The date of the marriage of Johanna Wagner and Geyer is not generally known; it cannot be found, for example, in Glasenapp's big official life of Wagner; while in other biographies the date is variously given as from one month to two or three years after Carl Friedrich's death. The marriage is now known to have taken place in August 1814—on the 14th according to Otto Bournot, on the 28th according to Mrs. Burrell;[1] and a daughter, Cäcilie, was born to them on February 26, 1815—i.e., six months later. This fact must necessarily count somewhat in our estimate of the nature of the earlier relations between Geyer and Frau Wagner.

On the whole the weight of external evidence is against the theory that Geyer was Wagner's father: the facial resemblances between Richard, his brother Albert, his sister Ottilie (born March 14, 1811), and his uncle Adolf, and Frau Rose's testimony as to the size and appearance of the police actuary, Carl Friedrich, make it more than probable that the last was the composer's father. But the explicit statements of Nietzsche and Mottl cannot be disregarded. The question of their veracity, however, could very easily be settled. There must be more than a dozen of the early copies of *Mein Leben* in existence. Mrs.

[1] Mrs. Burrell tells us that the Saxon law forbade a woman to marry again until ten months after the death of her husband. This apparently means "in the tenth month," for only nine full months had elapsed between November 22, 1813, and August 28, 1814.

394]   Wagner as Man and Artist

Burrell, who seems to have spent a lifetime and a fortune in accumulating Wagner letters and documents,[2] actually managed to buy a copy of this privately printed edition. One gathers that she knew Wagner and Cosima, and had evidently small liking for the latter. She appears to have been horrified by the picture Wagner gives of himself and his friends, and at the many evasions, suppressions, and distortions of the truth in the work. "This unmentionable book," she calls it in one place. She doubts whether Wagner wrote it, and hints that it has really been pieced together—presumably by Cosima. "To the well-informed and candid mind the book cannot fail to give the impression of being written up after conversations; the exact words are not remembered, and the writer unconsciously imparts another stamp to the language; it is not the German of a German," which is an obvious side blow at the Franco-Hungarian-Jewish Cosima. "The easily proved inaccuracies are legion. . . ." "The unmistakable purpose of the book is to ruin the reputation of everyone connected with Wagner. . . . I maintain that Wagner consented under pressure to the book being put together, that he yielded to the temptation of allowing everyone else's character to be blackened in order to make his own great fault [apparently his conduct toward Von Bülow] pale before the iniquities, real or invented, of others. . . . The poet who wrote the pure and impassioned poems of which Senta and Elsa are the heroines could never have conceived so flat and prosaic a plan of revenge upon everyone that had ever annoyed or thwarted him, yes, and worse still, upon many who had benefited and befriended him." She concludes that "Richard Wagner is not responsible for the book."

These remarks are interesting as showing the disgust felt by one who knew something of Wagner at the many base-

[2] She compiled a biography of him covering the years 1813–34, which was published in sumptuous form in 1898, after her death. Only one hundred copies were printed, or rather engraved. The book may be seen in the British Museum. I learn from Mr. O. G. Sonneck's *Suum Cuique* that there is a copy in the Library of Congress.

nesses perpetrated in *Mein Leben*—a disgust that thousands of readers have felt since the publication of the book. There may be something in Mrs. Burrell's theory as to how the work was put together; but Wagner undoubtedly assumed full responsibility for it, as is shown by the letter of his to the printer, Bonfantini, Basel (July 1, 1870), of which Mrs. Burrell gives a facsimile: he is having fifteen copies printed "*dans le seul but d'éviter la perte possible du seul manuscrit, et de les remettre entre les mains d'amis fidèles et [conscientieux?] qui les doivent garder pour un avenir lointain*" ("with the object simply of guarding against the possible loss of the sole manuscript, and of placing the copies in the hands of faithful and [conscientious?] friends, who should keep them for a distant future"). But Mrs. Burrell is generally right in her facts, and there may be something more than mere conjecture in her hint that the book, so far as its actual composition is concerned, is Cosima's work at least as much as Wagner's. This would account, among other things, for the tone of enmity or contempt toward almost everyone who had come into his life before herself. But the point with which we are most closely concerned here is not how *Mein Leben* came to be written, but what it contains on the first page. The copies that Nietzsche and Mottl saw belonged to the same imprint as Mrs. Burrell's copy. This last must still be in existence somewhere. If the possessor would allow an inspection of it, it could be settled once for all whether the first page opens with the words "I am the son of Ludwig Geyer," or "My father, Friedrich Wagner. . . ." If Mottl was speaking the truth, there is an end of the matter—except that our last remaining shred of respect for the editorial probity of Wahnfried will be gone. If Mottl was deceiving himself and others, we can only fall back on a balance of the evidence I have tried to marshal in the preceding pages.

A touch of unconscious humor has been given to the situation by a recent book of Otto Bournot, *Ludwig Heinrich Christian* [strange name this for a Jew!] *Geyer, der Stiefvater Richard Wagners.* Bournot has delved with Teutonic thoroughness into the records of the Geyer family, has traced it back to 1700, in which year one Benjamin Geyer was a "town musician" in Eisleben, and has established the piquant facts that all the Geyers were of the evangelical faith, that most of them were Protestant church organists, and that all of them married maidens of unimpeachable German extraction. It makes one smile to find how many of these alleged Jews had "Christian" as one of their forenames, as Wagner's putative father had. Even, therefore, if it should be proved at some time or other that Geyer was Richard Wagner's real father, this can only bring with it the admission that the amount of Jewish blood in the composer's veins must have been negligibly small. At the worst he was much more of a German than, say, a semi-Dutchman like Beethoven; much more German than the present English royal family is English; and Bournot is therefore justified in holding that in the last resort the question of Wagner's paternity cannot affect the "national" quality of the work of Bayreuth.

*   *   *

I leave the foregoing as it stood in the first edition of this book, because the argument there set forth has a certain unity of its own, and because it represents fairly well, perhaps, the point of view of those who, on the whole, do not believe that Geyer was the father of Wagner. In the ten years since this was written, however, new light has been thrown on the matter from various quarters; and I am now unable to declare myself a convinced partisan on either side.

It was not until some time after the publication of the first edition of this book, in 1914, that I became acquainted with a valuable article by Mr. O. G. Sonneck, "Was Richard Wagner a Jew?" which first appeared in the Proceedings of the Music Teachers' National Association for 1911, and was later reprinted, with additions, in Mr. Sonneck's book Suum Cuique (1916). Mr. Sonneck, working, of course, quite independently of me, arrived at practically the same conclusion—that on the whole the evidence was against the Geyer paternity, and that even if Geyer were Wagner's father, the former's antecedents show him to have been much more of a Christian than a Jew. Mr. Sonneck, however, went into the matter more thoroughly than I had then done, and his article may be recommended to anybody who wants to have the whole evidence available up to that time marshaled in coherent and logical form.

In an appendix to the article (in *Suum Cuique*), written after the publication of the first edition of the present book, Mr. Sonneck disputes the validity of two of my remarks. The first is that in which I expressed the hope that someone would be able to settle the disputed question of the opening sentences of *Mein Leben* by obtaining access to Mrs. Burrell's copy of the autobiography. "This," says Mr. Sonneck, "is a rather unkind, though unintentional, slur on Mrs. Burrell's willingness to report and ability to notice, *if it were there*, an important and startling biographical line like 'I am the son of Ludwig Geyer,' in a book which she had studied and which she despised." I am inclined now to agree fully with Mr. Sonneck that "the very fact that Mrs. Burrell did not call our attention to such a line or a line of the same content is practically conclusive evidence in itself that it does not occur in her copy of the original issue of *Mein Leben*." I only expressed the doubt in 1914 because of the seemingly hopeless confusion in which the whole question was enveloped—on the one hand the categorical assurance of certain people that the autobiography begins with an avowal of Geyer's paternity, on the other hand the impossibility of our consulting the original.

It will be conceded, I think, that in the foregoing pages I have given proof enough that Wahnfried is not to be trusted unquestioningly in the matter of the Wagner documents. But the fact that Mrs. Burrell makes no reference to the line in question is probably proof sufficient that it does *not* exist in the original copies of *Mein Leben* which Wagner had privately printed in 1870. We have to decide between the likelihood of Mrs. Burrell willfully concealing so important a fact and the likelihood of Mottl (a) having been misreported, or (b) having deliberately told an untruth, or (c)—which is most probable of all—having heard the story, repeated it, and, as so frequently happens in these cases, become more and more persuaded of the truth of it the oftener he repeated it. It is anything but an uncommon occurrence for people of complete honesty in most matters to give currency to some fable that happens to be in the air, and to do so in, as far as we can see, perfect good faith. A generation or so ago there were many people who assured us that Charles Bradlaugh once, at a lecture, took out his watch and defied the Almighty to strike him dead in five minutes. That incident never happened—indeed, precisely the same story is told of various Freethinkers as far back as the eighteenth century; yet I myself have heard people swear that they had seen the Bradlaugh incident with their own eyes. It is quite credible, then, that Mottl deceived himself in the attempt to convince others. We may, I think, in the absence of any corroborative evidence, rule his statement out completely.

The other point on which Mr. Sonneck joins issue with me is the one with reference to the premarital relations of Geyer and Frau Wagner as revealed in the birth of their daughter, Cäcilie, six months after their marriage. On this I shall have something to say later. Meanwhile let us look at the other evidence, such as it is, pointing to Geyer's paternity.

There is no doubt that Wagner had a peculiarly warm and reverential affection for Geyer. Every memento of him calls from Wagner an expression of almost passionate feeling. He frequently refers to him in his letters as "my father," sometimes also as "my father Geyer"—which latter, of course, may be taken merely to indicate that he was distinguishing between his stepfather, who had acted as father to him, and his real father. He more than once speaks of Geyer as his father in his letters to Minna. In his Venice "diary" of 1858—really a series of letters to Frau Wesendonck—he says: "On the table before me lies a little picture. It is the portrait of my father[3] which I could no longer show you when it arrived. It shows a noble, gentle, suffering, thoughtful face, that moves me infinitely. It has become very dear to me. Whoever enters probably suspects at first the picture of a beloved woman." On the other hand, writing to Otto Wesendonck in 1870, speaking of his being able to get together some of his scattered possessions, he says: "I possess now the very good oil portraits of my mother, my uncle and my stepfather." No positive conclusion, then, can be drawn from the frequent occurrence of the expression "my father" in the letters. Of his love for Geyer there can be no question; he writes to Minna in 1843 that he has been out to Blasewitz, near Dresden, where he gave orders for the restoration of "my father's grave." There is a later letter, too, in which he speaks of another visit to the grave. I can find no references in any of his letters to visits to the grave of Friedrich Wagner.

On several important occasions in his life his first thought was of Geyer. On May 22, 1873, he arranged a performance, in the old opera house at Bayreuth, of Geyer's comedy "*Der Bethlehemitische Kinder-Mord.*" At the Christmas festivities at Wahnfried in 1878 he tells the eight-year-old Siegfried, with delight, that he resembles Geyer; and for the birthday celebrations of May 22, 1879, there was arranged a little *tableau vivant* to accentuate the resemblance. Lenbach's portrait of Cosima had just arrived. Siegfried is dressed up as Geyer, with the hat shown in the well-known Geyer portrait, with his hair arranged like Geyer's, and, with brush in hand, the boy pretends to be giving the last touches to the portrait.[4]

Everyone knows the story, told by Wagner himself in

[3] Here, it will be observed, it is not even "my father Geyer."
[4] Glasenapp, *Das Leben Richard Wagners*, vi, 203.

Mein Leben and elsewhere, that the night before Geyer's death he (Wagner) was picking out on the piano the folk song *"Ueb' immer Treu' und Redlichkeit,"* and that the dying man turned to the mother and said: "Is it possible he has a talent for music?" At the festival in the old Bayreuth theater in 1873, between the two acts of Geyer's comedy, Wagner had this folk song played by the orchestra.[5]

Again and again we find evidence of the deep affection of Wagner for Geyer, and of his devotion to his memory: it is one of the most moving traits in Wagner's character. It may be said that it was only natural that he should have no particular feeling for, because he could have no remembrance of, his real father, who died when he was six months old, and that he should remember with gratitude the stepfather who had done so much for him. The explanation cannot be ruled out; at the same time it must be remembered that Wagner's memories even of Geyer could not have been very copious or vivid, as the latter died when Richard was eight years old.

We have seen that Wagner frequently refers to Geyer in his letters as "my father." Did he ever refer to him in conversation in the same way? Glasenapp tells us categorically that he did. In the fourth edition of his biography he writes thus: "The idea that the deceased [i.e., Geyer] might even have been his real father he repeatedly expressed as a possibility in conversation with intimate friends, of whom we could name several." [6] (This passage does not appear in any edition before the fourth.) Mr. Sonneck rightly draws attention to the careful wording of this—"as a possibility"—and then throws doubt on the validity of the remark as evidence. He thinks the statement is not admissible as evidence unless we can get the names and the direct testimony of the people to whom Wagner is alleged to have said that Geyer might be his

[5] Glasenapp, v, 87, 88.
[6] Glasenapp, iv, 78. I am indebted to Mr. Sonneck's article for my introduction to this passage. I had till then known only the third edition of Glasenapp's first volume.

father. Naturally it is impossible now to get the direct evidence of such persons. Glasenapp, however, would be the last person in the world likely to repeat such a story without being perfectly sure of the truth of it. But we have what I think is quite unshakable indirect evidence in one case—that of Nietzsche.

And here, perhaps, we can get at last a little light upon one of the darkest of the older questions in connection with this matter. Mr. Sonneck asks: "As to Nietzsche, will those who operate with his name in this connection kindly step forward with a reference to when and where Nietzsche stated that Wagner's autobiography, which (we know) had passed through his hands, opened with or contained the line 'I am the son of Ludwig Geyer'? In 1888 he merely averred that Richard Wagner's father was a stage player named Geyer;—not a syllable to the effect of having seen this stated in Wagner's autobiography. Had he seen it there, he hardly would have hesitated to say so." The point is a good one, so far as it goes. The Geyer theory plainly became public in the first place through Nietzsche, but I myself do not know of any passages in his writings in which he expressly states that *the autobiography* began with an avowal of the Geyer paternity. But is it really necessary that Nietzsche should have said this? Would it not be sufficient if Wagner himself had told him that Geyer was his father? And this, it seems to be beyond all doubt, Wagner had done.

One fact of decided importance comes to light in the volume of Wagner-Nietzsche Letters published by Nietzsche's sister, Frau Elisabeth Förster-Nietzsche, in 1920. As we know, in December 1869 Wagner entrusted to Nietzsche the work of seeing the manuscript of *Mein Leben* through the press, and having some fifteen copies struck off for private purposes. At Wagner's request, Nietzsche had a vulture (*Geyer*) engraved to serve as a crest for the volume. "As it is of importance," Wagner writes on June 16, 1870, "on account of the associations, that the vulture be instantly and clearly recognisable [i.e., not to be mistaken for an eagle], we beg you to procure for the engraver

the best possible picture of such a beast, and instruct
him to hang the characteristic vulture ruff round the neck
of our bird. This of course cannot be done properly without making some changes in the neck, but perhaps it is
possible."

Frau Förster-Nietzsche, after quoting this letter, makes
it clear that the bird had already been adopted by Wagner
as his crest, though it was her brother's suggestion that it
should appear on the title page of the autobiography. She
gives a facsimile of the crest as it originally was—a ruff-less
bird. Julius Kapp, in his *Richard Wagner*, gives us a
facsimile of the title page of the privately printed edition
of *Mein Leben*.[7] The vulture shown there is unmistakably
that shown in Frau Förster-Nietzsche's book, plus a ruff:
all the engraver has done is to add this feature to the original Wagner crest, leaving it otherwise quite untouched.

"My brother asked me," Frau Förster-Nietzsche goes on
to say, "to look for a good picture of a vulture, and I
could not understand why an eagle would not do for the
crest." At this time Nietzsche had evidently not discussed
the Geyer matter with her. "Later," she continues, "my
brother told me that Wagner regarded his stepfather,
Geyer, as his real father. As this matter is now freely and
publicly discussed, I may repeat the remark, especially as
my brother himself alludes to it in his book *Der Fall
Wagner*. As for that matter, the stepfather was an excellent and gifted man. . . ."

I think Frau Förster-Nietzsche's testimony can be accepted without hesitation. She is a credible witness; in
spite of the later quarrel between her brother and Wagner,
she always writes of the latter calmly, justly, admiringly,
and even affectionately. When she tells us categorically
that Nietzsche had told her that Wagner regarded Geyer

[7] Kapp tells us that the imprint is in three volumes, dealing
respectively with the years 1813–42, 1842–50 and 1850–61.
Incidentally I may remark that had this private imprint opened
with the words "I am the son of Ludwig Geyer," Kapp would
surely have said so.

as his father, we are bound to believe her. There seems no need, then, to search Nietzsche's works for a statement that he had seen "I am the son of Ludwig Geyer" *at the commencement of the autobiography*. It is sufficient that Nietzsche told in private the story of Wagner's private confidence; however much we may regret the tone of some of his later references to Wagner, there is no reason to think him a liar. And if Wagner had thus expressed his views on the matter to Nietzsche, it is credible enough that, as Glasenapp says, he should have done so to other intimates.

We can drop then, perhaps, the theory of a falsification of the opening page of *Mein Leben*.

Let me now digress for a moment to the second of Mr. Sonneck's objections to my former statement of the case. He protests against my regarding with particular interest the fact that Cäcilie, the daughter of Ludwig Geyer, was born six months after his marriage with the widow Wagner. "This fact," I said, "necessarily counts somewhat in our estimate of the nature of the earlier relations between Geyer and Frau Wagner." On this Mr. Sonneck remarks: "Somewhat? Perhaps! Necessarily? No! 'Estimate' of the nature of the earlier relations? It is not a question of estimate—that is a matter of taste and inclination—it is a question of fact." I would not attach too much importance to the revelation with regard to Cäcilie; but I think most people will agree that it is not wholly without importance. It surely throws a little light, however little, and however dim, on the characters of both parties. Friedrich Wagner had died on November 22, 1813; Frau Wagner married Geyer on August 28, 1814 (this seems to be the correct date, not the 14th as was formerly supposed); and Cäcilie was born on February 26, 1815. (It must be admitted that in Geyer's published letters to the widow, dated December 22, 1813, January 14, January 28, and February 11, 1814, the tone is merely one of sympathetic friendliness; in fact, Geyer addresses the widow with the formal *Sie*, not the more intimate *du*.)

From *Mein Leben* we learn for the first time that the matrimonial situation in the Wagner house was a little strained at times by reason of the extra-domestic adventures of Friedrich. He was not altogether free, says Wagner, "from a gallant passion for actresses. My mother used to complain jokingly that she often had to keep lunch waiting a long time for him while he was paying ardent court to a certain famous actress of the day [Madame Hartwig]. When she scolded him, he said he had been delayed by business papers, and by way of proof pointed to his fingers, which were supposed to be stained with ink, but, when she insisted on examining them, were found to be perfectly clean." Later we get this:—"Even when the police actuary [Friedrich] was spending his evenings at the theatre, the worthy actor [Geyer] generally took his place in the family circle, and, it seems, had frequently to appease my mother, who, rightly or wrongly, complained of the inconstancy [*Flatterhaftigkeit*] of her husband."

It does not seem to have occurred to anybody to ask—though obviously the question is of some importance—*how* Wagner knew this. Precocious child as he was, it could hardly have been from personal observation, as he was only six months old when Friedrich Wagner died. It is hardly likely that Geyer took him into his confidence, if for no other reason than that Wagner was only eight years old when Geyer died. Who, then, was his informant, and when did this information reach him?

The most significant document of all, perhaps, is Wagner's letter to Cäcilie of January 14, 1870. She has sent him copies of a number of Geyer's letters to their mother. Wagner writes back in a way that shows him to have been profoundly affected. "The contents of these letters has not only moved me, but verily shaken me to the depths. The example of complete self-sacrifice for a noble purpose in private life has hardly ever presented itself so clearly as in this case. . . . Especially the delicate, fine, and highly cultured tone of these letters, particularly of those to our mother, moves me. . . . At the same time, it was possible for me, from these letters to Mother, to gain a deep insight into the relations of the two in difficult times. I believe I see now with absolute clearness, though I must consider it extremely difficult to express myself on these relations, as I see them. It impresses me as if our father Geyer, with his self-sacrifice for the whole family, believed to atone for a guilt" [*eine Schuld zu verbüssen*].

Mr. Sonneck truly says that this "is the only instance that Wagner in his writing ever permitted himself to use words concerning the relations between Geyer and his mother which might be construed by others to mean that he had conclusive doubts as to his paternal parentage." But even Mr. Sonneck, anxious as he is to discredit the Geyer theory, is compelled to admit that "these doubts he [Wagner] would seem to have entertained even before reading those letters on Christmas Day, 1869, for the first time." Wagner's letter to Cäcilie makes this, indeed, tolerably clear; and, as we have already seen from the Nietzsche correspondence, earlier in 1869 Wagner was writing to Nietzsche on the subject of the crest in a way that suggests that some confidences on the matter had already passed between the two.

Glasenapp's attitude is interesting and rather peculiar. *He* was the editor of these Family Letters of Wagner. The volume containing them appeared in 1907. The fourth edition of his Life of Wagner, in which, as we have seen, he deals for the first time with the possibility of Geyer having been Wagner's father, appeared in 1905. It is not unlikely, then, that his remarks in the fourth volume of the Life were partly motived by his knowledge of this letter to Cäcilie. Let me repeat Glasenapp's words: "the idea that the deceased [Geyer] might even have been his real father he repeatedly expressed as a possibility in conversation with intimate friends, of whom we could name several." Then he adds: "And yet, *if* there was a secret here to be preserved, then his mother took it with her into her grave and never confided it either to him [Wagner] or to any of the other grown children." From whom, we may pertinently ask, did Glasenapp get *this* information? Not, it is clear, from Wagner himself. Glasenapp could have known nothing more than the rest of the world about the Wagner-Geyer household when the first edition of his biography was issued in 1882 (i.e., a year before Wagner's death). He evidently did not at that time even know the correct date of the marriage of Geyer and the widow Wagner,[8] which seems to have been kept a secret by the Wagner family. It is only in 1905, about the time the Family Letters would be placed in his hands by Cosima, that he touches at all upon the matter of the Geyer paternity. We may reasonably assume, then, that it was from Cosima that he got the information that Wagner's mother had carried the secret, if there was a secret, with her to the grave.

To anybody who is familiar with Glasenapp's obsequious attitude toward Wagner and the Wagner family, the freedom of his comments in his fourth edition is surprising—on any supposition other than that these comments were authorized. After quoting the passage about Geyer's "atoning for a guilt," he says: "A guilt? What guilt? The guilt of having given a Wagner to the world? We go no further in our conjectures [*Vermutungen*] than this letter does, with its delicate hints" [*in zartester Andeutung*]. Then follows the passage, already quoted, to the effect that Wagner had confided to several intimate friends that Geyer may have been his father.

To appreciate the full significance of all this, we have to remember that it was in this third chapter of the fourth

---

[8] He says in his first edition that Geyer married the widow *two years* after the death of Friedrich Wagner. All the earlier biographers are at sea on the point. Mr. H. T. Finck, apparently following Glasenapp, tells us on p. 8 of his *Wagner and his Works* that Wagner received a stepfather "before his third birthday," and on p. 11 that the widow remarried "only nine months" after her husband's death. Wagner himself does not tell the strict truth in *Mein Leben*, though he must have known the facts: he says that Geyer married Frau Wagner "a year after the death of his friend."

edition of the Glasenapp Life that Wagner's letter to Cäcilie of January 14, 1870, was given to the world for the first time—for its publication in the *Familienbriefe* did not follow till some two years later. Why, we may ask, did Cosima allow Glasenapp to quote from this as yet unpublished letter and to make on it the very pointed comments he did, unless she had no objection now to the world knowing Wagner's opinion on the matter—nay, positively desired that the world should know it?

I cannot see what other interpretation can possibly be put on the letter to Cäcilie of January 14, 1870, than that both Wagner and Cäcilie believed that Geyer was the former's father. The plain sense of the letter is that the relations between Geyer and the widow have been difficult to explain hitherto; but now Wagner sees it all clearly. At the same time it is too delicate a matter for him to be able to put on paper precisely what he thinks, even in a letter to his sister. He explains Geyer's "self-sacrifice for the family" (meaning, evidently, the assumption by an impecunious actor and painter of the responsibility of a widow with seven young children), by the fact that he was atoning for a guilt. Mr. Sonneck himself seems hardly able to resist the conclusion that Wagner believed Geyer to be his father, but he makes a desperate attempt to show that *we* ought not to believe it without better reasons than Wagner had. "Is it not possible," he says, "that Wagner, for real or fancied reasons, having had previous doubts as to his origin, too willingly and too hastily saw in these letters a corroboration of his doubts, and that other, more unbiased readers, would decline to share his views? Nor will a cautious historian stop here. He will demand proof that Wagner continued to put the above—at best, probable—construction on the letters. How if Wagner in later years relinquished his first interpretation? How if it should turn out that this first interpretation was but temporary and not permanent with him? Would not then Wagner's supposedly implied testimony have lost most of, if not all, its force?" This, surely, is asking too much. Most people will agree that in a matter of this kind, where the *facts* are obviously inaccessible, we must go by the general trend of the evidence.

Mr. Sonneck stresses the fact that in 1872, when Feustel, of Bayreuth, asked Wagner for his baptismal record, Wagner sent it with "a humorously-worded note," signed "Richard Wagner, Polizeiamts-Actuarius-Sohn." Mr. Sonneck seems to think that this points to Wagner having abandoned in 1872 his belief of 1870. But it is not clear to me why Wagner, having confided his secret to a few intimates, should be held to be morally bound to shout it also from the housetops. As a matter of fact, this very letter to Feustel suggests either an understanding between Feustel and himself or a sly joke for his own delectation; his humorously solemn description of himself—a quite unnecessary piece of elaboration in a letter—as "Polizeiamts-Actuarius-Sohn" suggests, not a desire to insist on the truth of this description, but a desire to raise a smile over it, either in Feustel, or in himself, or in both. But perhaps the conclusive answer to Mr. Sonneck's surmise that Wagner may have changed his mind in later life is that passage on page 78 of the fourth edition of Glasenapp's Life which has already been so fully discussed both by him and by me. It is frankly incredible that Cosima would have given Glasenapp this letter for publication or allowed him to state categorically that Wagner had told various intimates that he was the son of Geyer, or sanctioned the comments Glasenapp permits himself on the subject, had Wagner's view of the matter changed in later life. Rather does it all suggest that the Wagner family itself has now no doubts on the matter, and no longer cares who knows the whole facts.

It seems to me now beyond question that whether Geyer was Wagner's father or not, Wagner himself believed that he was. Look at the evidence *en masse*. We have the statement of Frau Förster-Nietzsche that Wagner had confided in Nietzsche. We have the evidence of his anxiety to get the vulture crest upon the title page of *Mein Leben*. We have the assurance of Glasenapp that the same confidences that had been given to Nietzsche were given to other intimate friends. We have Glasenapp discussing quite calmly, in his fourth edition, the possibility of Geyer having been Wagner's father—a discussion which we may be sure he would not have permitted himself had there been any possibility of its being repugnant to Cosima and the Wagner family. We have the record of his being gratified to discover that the eight-year-old Siegfried resembled Geyer. We have the letter of January 1870 to Cäcilie, upon which only one construction can be put—that the letters of Geyer which Cäcilie had sent him have confirmed his previous surmises. At some time or other Wagner must have obtained, from sources that he felt to be reliable, the information as to the flightiness of Friedrich Wagner and the consequent strain upon the domestic relations of the latter and his wife; and in the light of all our other knowledge it is not a farfetched conclusion that this reference to Geyer in *Mein Leben* was a veiled hint that he had already surmised that the relations of the latter with Frau Wagner had been unusually intimate.

Mr. Sonneck quotes the four letters from Geyer to the widow Wagner which have been published, and asks, not unjustly: "Are these letters in address, signature, form, contents and tone the utterances of a man who has possessed a woman, soul and body, for several years?" [9] That indeed is a difficulty. I fully agree with Mr. Sonneck when he says: "I do not believe that the parties to a clandestine love-affair would go to that unnecessary trouble in confidential letters after the death of the husband." But I cannot agree with Mr. Sonneck in his further deductions. "Supposing this, for a moment, to be true," he says, "what would follow? That Richard Wagner must have seen less harmless and more incriminating letters which compelled

---

[9] The "several years," however, is an exaggeration. The letters all belong to the period from December 22, 1813, to February 11, 1814, and "possession" need not be assumed before the late summer of 1812.

him to infer, what we, if we are so inclined, may in turn infer from *his* letter to his sister Cecilia. These really incriminating letters would have been written during the lifetime of the husband, that is, when, as surmised above for the sake of argument, such extreme caution and concealment of the real status of affairs would actually have been necessary! Few will be willing to follow anybody into such an abyss of absurdity as that into which the dilemma would then force us. Most of us, I trust, will refuse to believe that the Avenarius archives contains two such diametrically opposed kinds of letters. But this forces us immediately to a further conclusion, namely, that Wagner had only such letters as quoted above before him, perhaps, indeed, these four letters only and no others. If that be the case, and unless the Avenarius archives have been tampered with, then two conclusions are inevitable. Either Wagner was not justified in drawing from the letters the inference of an illicit love-affair between his mother and Geyer of which he was the offspring, *or* we are not justified in reading this inference into his letter to his sister Cecilia."

These conjectures can hardly be made to square with the four letters. They are letters merely of kindness and sympathy, written within a period of four to twelve weeks after Friedrich Wagner's death. There is nothing whatever in them to call forth so grave a letter as that of Wagner's to Cäcilie, nothing whatever in them to have given him at last the needed light upon the relations of Geyer and his mother; nothing whatever in them to justify his saying that he believed Geyer to have sacrificed himself for the whole family in order to atone for a guilt. We are forced to the conclusion that he *must* have had other letters before him—letters not hitherto made public. Mr. Sonneck having persuaded himself that Wagner had no other Geyer letters but these four, on the basis of the quite unjustified assumption, asks: "May not the 'difficult times' be reasonably interpreted to refer to the time between his father's death and her so unconventionally, though in her desperate situation quite pardonably, rapid marriage to Geyer, which took place ten months after the father's death, the shortest period permissible under Saxony's laws? And Geyer's guilt (*Schuld*)? May there not be hidden here an allusion to something in Geyer's life quite different from adultery, some guilt of which the inquisitive world as yet knows nothing and may never know anything, a guilt of which, however, Friedrich Wagner had known and from the consequences of which he had rescued his friend Geyer, thereby earning the latter's undying gratitude?"

All this, of course, is not impossible; but that it is highly improbable will be clear, I think, to anybody who reads Wagner's letter carefully without having previously made up his mind either way. There is a law in logic known as the law of parsimony, which forbids us to go out of our way to find a remote explanation of the facts when an explanation that meets the facts lies close to our hand. Why should we so contemn this law as to conjecture some "guilt" in Geyer's life of which there is not the smallest hint anywhere, when a "guilt," of a kind that explains everything, actually stares us in the face? Cäcilie was born six months after the marriage: intimate relations between the pair, then, must have commenced not later than six months after the husband's death. By August 1814 they would both realize that the only way by which a scandal could be averted was the speedy remarriage of the widow. What more natural assumption could be made, then, than that *this* was the "guilt" for which Geyer thought he ought to atone by the "self-sacrifice" of taking on his impecunious shoulders the burden of the widow's seven young children?

Otto Bournot, who also is anxious we should believe that Wagner was mistaken in his conjecture, thinks that "atoning for a guilt" means merely "liquidating a financial debt." I myself cannot see anything in Wagner's letter to justify this interpretation of *"Mir ist es, unser Vater Geyer durch seine Aufopferung für die ganze Familie eine Schuld zu verbüssen glaubte."* Bournot shows that there were "misunderstandings" and "jealousies" between Geyer and Friedrich Wagner's brother Adolf, who lived in Leipzig. Apparently Adolf looked with no favorable eye on Geyer, whose youth had been a wild one. The letters to Frau Wagner indicate that Geyer felt Adolf to be standing between them. It is just possible that the use of *"Sie"* in the four letters printed by Mrs. Burrell may be accounted for by the fact that they might come under the eye of Adolf.

Mr. Sonneck's last card is this: "Geyer can possibly have been Wagner's father only if he is proved to have been in Leipzig from six months, at the very latest, to nine months before Wagner's birth on May 22nd, 1813. I know very well that the Seconda theatrical company usually played at Leipzig from the Oster-Messe until the Michaelis-Messe (that is, from spring to fall), but it must be proved, if the Geyer claim is to be operated in that orderly, methodical fashion which has been sadly lacking so far and which alone makes history sound, that this was true also of the year 1812." A partisan of the Geyer theory who has been worried by the pertinacity of Mr. Sonneck's demands for irrefragable proof of everything might reasonably ask Mr. Sonneck here why he in turn should not be called upon to give reasons for his doubt. We know that Geyer had been a friend of the Wagner family from about 1801. We know that after that he was away from Leipzig about five years, and that he returned in 1807. We know that in 1809 he joined the Seconda theatrical troupe, a member of which he remained till his death. We know that the troupe played every year in Leipzig from Easter to Michaelmas, and in Dresden during the winter. We know that this theatrical engagement was the backbone of Geyer's finances. We have no record of his having ceased to be a member of the company in 1812 and rejoined it later. If, then, Mr. Sonneck should, in the face of every probability, doubt that Geyer was a member of the Seconda troupe during the summer of that one year, he might quite fairly be asked to give some reason for his skepticism. If Geyer was not in Leipzig with the Seconda troupe in the summer of 1812, where was he? His biographers have traced his life in fair detail; there is no hint in them of any uncertainty as to his having played in Leipzig as usual in that summer. In the absence of any rebutting evidence from Mr. Sonneck, most people, I think, will take it for granted that he did.

Mention may be made of one or two minor matters, none of them of much evidential value in itself, but each of them, perhaps, able to play the part of a tiny link in the chain. Wagner seems to have been especially fond of his sister Cäcilie. So far as I have been able to discover, it is only with her that he discusses the Geyer question, and only in his letters to her, of all the family circle, that he speaks of Geyer as their father. There seems to be no doubt that he felt a particular kinship with Cäcilie. He invariably, I think, refers to Geyer as his father in his letters to Minna; and as we have seen, he speaks of Geyer as his father in one communication to Frau Wesendonck. These are practically all the references to Geyer one finds in the correspondence.

Evidence from physiognomy is notoriously dubious, and in the first part of this essay I have pointed out the resemblances between Wagner's face and those of his uncle Adolf and his brother Albert. It is worth noting, however, that these resemblances are more pronounced in Wagner's later years, when, with success, his face seems to have filled out somewhat. In the earlier pictures, where he wears a rather pinched look, the nose, mouth, and eyes have rather more suggestions of Geyer and Cäcilie about them. Some ingenious person might perhaps make a special study of the eyebrows of the three. Cäcilie's eyebrows have a pronounced upward turn about two thirds of the way from the center to the outer rim of the eye. I cannot find this shape of eyebrow in any other of the children of Frau Wagner except the composer. It is noticeable, however, in every early portrait of him that is clearly printed. I fancy I can detect this shape of eyebrow also in the three portraits of Geyer which we possess, but as they are not clearly printed I cannot be quite sure. There can be no mistaking, however, the resemblance between Cäcilie and the Wagner of the earlier years.

*   *   *

One last word on *Mein Leben*. Lilli Lehmann tells us that from the autobiography as we have it now "much has been omitted." She remembers Wagner's readings from the privately printed volumes to select circles of friends at Bayreuth in 1875 and 1876. "Just to please my mother, he read us, that evening, the portion about *Othello* at Magdeburg, where he had conducted, and a panic had arisen because the audience had understood 'fire' instead of 'further.' Then followed a scene from Königsberg,—or was it Riga?—where Wagner's creditors, late one evening, still pressed him hard, encircled his residence, forced their way in, and he had to escape somehow from it or save himself through the adjoining house. These two scenes, the descriptions of which we remember well, are wanting entirely in the book that has just appeared."

It is a pity that someone who has access to the original edition does not tell us in detail where and how it differs from the *Mein Leben* we possess.

Wagner and Super-Wagner

[This appendix is an expansion of an article that originally appeared in the *Musical Times* for February 1913. One or two points in it have already been dwelled upon in the foregoing pages, but I have ventured to reprint the article here, even at the cost of a little repetition, because in this form it presents concisely and compactly the argument as to the possibility of a further development from Wagner's own principles.]

I

It would be very interesting if some enterprising interviewer in the shades could procure for us Wagner's opinion upon the course of events in music in general and the opera in particular during the thirty years that have elapsed since his death. He would probably cling with his characteristic tenacity to the views he held in his lifetime; but if he were candid, he would have to admit that the old problems have latterly taken on a new aspect. The theories he expounded so eagerly in his prose works and illustrated so eloquently in his music dramas have not passed through the fire of thirty years' criticism without suffering some loss of vitality. Supposing a brain as comprehensive, as variously gifted, and as forceful as his were now to take up the problem of opera, seeing it all afresh as Wagner did, and combining, like him, all the potencies of the best instrumental and operatic music of his day into one vast synthesis, what would be the new form he would strike out—for that a new form is now a necessity is evident on *a priori* and *a posteriori* grounds. Music could no more stand still after Wagner than after Bach or Beethoven; a new humanity must find a new expression for its own reading of life. And a survey of the opera since Wagner's death leaves no room for doubt that the emotions and aspirations of the new humanity have not yet found the form most appropriate to them. Wagner has no more succeeded in making his special type of musical drama the norm for later generations than Bach succeeded in imposing the forms of *his* music upon the art of the epochs that have followed him. In each case the spirit endures, but not the form. Some elements of the Wagnerian form have of course become, as far as we can judge, permanent factors in opera in general—the use of leading themes, for example, and the system of entrusting a melodious, flowing, quasi-symphonic development to the orchestra. But not even these elements are recognized as indispensable constituents of opera everywhere: Debussy, for instance, discards both of them in the greater parts of his *Pelléas et Mélisande*. For the rest, the departures from Wagner's precepts are noticeable enough, especially as regards the poetic basis of opera. Putting aside the negligible work of second-rate imitators, it would be hard to point to a single opera by a man of original genius who follows Wagner in his reliance upon the primitive myth as the clearest and most fundamental expression of the "purely human," or in his planning of the subject so as to reduce to a minimum the less musical matter in the text, and make the whole opera, as far as may be, a pure expression of nothing but "soul-states."

II

Wagner's famous formula was that hitherto the means in opera (the music) had been taken for the end, and the end (the drama) for the means. His own avowed object was to restore to the drama the right of pre-eminence in opera. His claim to have done so is only valid if we define music and drama in the rather limited senses he had in view when framing his theory. His proposition is correct enough if we take it to mean that music must not, as in the Italian opera, occupy the ear to the exclusion of all worth in the story and all psychological interest in the characters. In the sense that he made opera acceptable to men's heads and hearts as well as their ears, Wagner certainly did make the drama the end, and music the means. But viewed more broadly, his work was really the greatest glorification of music which the theater had ever seen: for while he enormously increased the expressive scope of the music, he cut out of drama more than half the elements that give that word a meaning apart from music. Drama, with him, meant in the last analysis little more than the best possible text for theater music. He would have denied this interpretation of his theories and practice, but all the same that is the upshot of them. "Word-speech," he argues, is merely the organ of the intellect, and has therefore the right of entry into music— the emotional art *par excellence*—only so far as it is necessary to give coherence to the rich but indeterminate flood of feeling that music pours out; and music can, and ought to, ally herself only with words that have themselves an emotional content. It was for this reason that he rejected historical and political subjects, and found the ideal "stuff" for opera in the "purely human" legends of "the folk"; and in "A Communication to My Friends" he traces in close detail the gradual growth of his perceptions in this respect. What was hidden from him, what, indeed, he persistently denies, is now evident to everyone else—that the change in his theories and practice was due to the musician in him slowly asserting himself with greater and greater urgency, and finally demanding imperatively a form of text which would allow his gift of musical expression the utmost possible freedom. It must always be borne in mind that Wagner's theory of a unification of all the arts in the one art work was the product of a brain that had comparatively little sympathy with, or understanding of, any art but music. This may seem a hard saying, but the proof of it is to be found in many declarations in his prose works, his letters, and *Mein Leben*. He could never see in painting, in the prose drama, in poetry, and in sculpture, precisely what painters, dramatists, poets, and sculptors saw there. He seriously thought that "the spoken form of play" (*die Schauspielform*) must "necessarily vanish in the future"; and that painters would give up their "egoistic" decorating of little canvases and be content to devote their powers to contributing, along with the poet, the musician, and the rest of the theatrical forces, to the "united art-work of the future." Clearly it was Wagner the musician who dominated all the other Wagners, and determined both the choice of subject for his operas and the manner of their treatment. "What I saw," he says in "A Communication to My Friends," "I now looked at solely with the eyes of music." He is careful to add, not of the formal, cramping style of music, but of the kind that came straight from the heart and that he could pour out like a speech in a mother tongue. That is the whole secret; the "music" he wishes to see made subordinate to "drama" is merely the music that claims to pursue an egoistic existence, bound by its own arbitrary laws alone; but though *his* music must be natural and unfettered by conventional formulas, and must aim at giving heightened emotional expression to the feeling suggested by the verse and the action, it is still the predominant partner in the union, and only so much of the stuff of the verbal drama will be permitted in the art work as will give point to the vague musical emotion without hindering its full expression. Like a true musician, he saw drama from a purely musical angle.

III

But granting the premises implicit in Wagner's theory—that music is an art of intensely emotional expression, that it can only ally itself with poetry and drama on the condition that these allow themselves to be bent to its will, and that the ideal "stuff" for an opera is that which contains the minimum of matter that music cannot take up into itself and endow with its own loftier and warmer life—it surely becomes evident that the theory cannot be allowed to end there. In a long article on program music in my *Musical Studies* (1905), I have argued that the strictly logical conclusion of Wagner's own theory is not the music drama but the symphonic poem. He himself admitted that the more we can refine away from the music drama all the nonmusical matter—the matter that is required merely to make the nature of the characters and the thread of the story intelligible to an audience sitting on the other side of the footlights—the nearer we shall approach the ideal. It was for this reason that he was dissatisfied with his earlier works, and so proud—justifiably proud—of *Tristan*, where, as he said, he "immersed himself in the depths of soul-events pure and simple, and from out this innermost centre of the world fearlessly fashioned its outward form. A glance at the volumen of this poem will show you at once that the copious detail which an historical poet has to employ in order to make the outer connections of his plot evident, to the detriment of a clear exposition of its inner motives, I now trusted myself to apply to these latter alone. Life and death, the whole significance and existence of the external world, here turn on nothing but the inner movements of the soul." There is a touch of exaggeration in the claim, but in the main it holds good; *Tristan* comes nearer to being *all music and nothing else but music* than any other work of Wagner. I suggested that in the symphonic poem, rightly planned and rightly worked out, we had the nearest possible approach to this ideal, and I availed myself of a simile

Browning uses in *The Ring and the Book*—that of the
jeweler who finds it advantageous to mix a certain amount
of alloy with the gold while he is working at the ring, but
afterward burns it out with a spirt of acid, leaving simply
the circlet of pure gold. The practice of the composer of
the symphonic poem seems to me to be analogous to this:
he uses the poetic alloy in the conceptual stage of his
work to give coherence to the tissue of it, but leaves none
of the alloy visible in the completed work itself; to vary
the simile, he uses poetry as his scaffolding, but as his
scaffolding only. The trouble with opera—viewed from an
ideal standpoint—is that it too often shows the scaffolding
projecting at a score of points through the finished building. Even in *Tristan*—especially the earlier scenes—we are
too conscious at times of verbal matter that all the genius
of the musician has hardly been able to fuse into music.
We accept it, but we are not convinced of the absolute
necessity of it.

IV

Apart from theory, we have only to look at a few concrete
instances of both types of art to see that the ideal symphonic poem is the unalloyed quintessence of opera, and
that the average opera is merely a symphonic poem puffed
out to three acts, and made rather loose of tissue in the
process. What could be easier than to make a three-act
opera of *Ein Heldenleben*—and what more futile? Apart
from the Adversaries, there are only two characters in *Ein
Heldenleben*, and we cannot fill up a whole theatrical
evening with two characters alone. To have made an opera
of it Strauss would have had to get a librettist to surround
the only two persons who really matter with a number of
minor persons who would not matter in the least; and after
spending three of four hours in the theater, we should
come away with precisely the same fundamental impression
as *Ein Heldenleben* gives us in the concert room in about
forty minutes—that a hero has passed through sundry
spiritual crises and developments, and at last, after much
battling and much error, attained to a superearthly resigna-

tion. This is the ring; everything else we should see and hear in the theater would only be so much alloy, pleasurable or tiresome. Who does not feel, again, that all the essential emotions of the story of Francesca da Rimini are given us in Tchaikovsky's tone poem?[1] Who wants to see the merely historical and topographical details that would be inevitable in an opera on the subject? Who wants to see the furniture of the house of Malatesta, and the ladies and gentlemen moving about among it? Who wants to see and hear Giovanni? He interests us only as a fragment of the force of fate which drives Paolo and Francesca to love and death; surely we are content to accept his existence as assumed in the great central tragedy, without having him put before us in the flesh to sing a lot of words that do not matter?

Who does not feel that Strauss has given us the quintessence of *Macbeth* in his symphonic poem, and that no opera on that subject could hope to express the spiritual tragedy of Macbeth so swiftly and so drastically? Or, to look at the matter from the other side, take the case of Strauss's *Salome*. Does anything really count there but the train of moods in Salome's soul, and is not all this expressed fully and incomparably in the great final scene—with perhaps a little assistance from the music of the impassioned monologue of Salome to Jochanaan in the earlier part? What is all the rest of the opera but a mere recital or representation of a story the details of which everyone in the theater already knows quite well? How Herod was married to Herodias, the mother of Salome, how Herod gave a banquet and became enamored of his stepdaughter, how one Jochanaan, a Jewish prophet, had been imprisoned by order of Herod, how Salome conceived an unholy passion for Jochanaan, how she danced for Herod and won as her reward the head of Jochanaan on a charger—who needs to go to the theater to be told all this: who takes more than the most languid interest in the telling of it? Music has next to no concern with most of it, because

[1] It is not necessary for me to discuss in detail the various operas that have been written on the Francesca subject.

it is of a quality that prevents music attaining to its full emotional incandescence; and it is only when it is playing with ease and ardor around a subject fit to call out the best there is in it that music is really worth writing. If anyone doubts that it is only the final scene and the mono-logue of *Salome* which count for anything in the opera, let him ask himself how many people would stay away from the theater or the concert room because *only* these portions were being given, and how many people would go to the theater if it were known that these portions were to be omitted. Or again, does the whole opera of *Tann-häuser* tell us very much that is not already told us in the overture? I am not alleging, of course, that there is not a great deal of very interesting music in the opera. The question is whether the essence of the struggle in Tann-häuser's soul between spiritual and physical love is not fully given us in the overture, and whether, had this alone been written, we should have felt any more need for an opera upon the subject than we do for an opera on the subject of *Ein Heldenleben*. What is the opera of *Fidelio*, Wagner himself asked, but a mere lengthy watering down of the dramatic motives that have been painted so finely for us in the great *Leonora No. 3* Overture? May we not say as much of *Tannhäuser*? Is not a great deal of this also a mere padding-out of the subject to comply with the exigencies of a whole evening in the theater?

v

It is true that Wagner tried to demonstrate that the symphonic poem was a less perfect art form than the music drama, inasmuch as it left it to the imagination to supply the characters, the events, or the pictures upon which the music is founded, whereas these really ought to be shown to the eye upon the stage. But a twofold answer can be given to Wagner. In the first place, there are dozens of passages in his own works which depend for their effect upon precisely that visualizing power of the imagination the legitimacy of which he denied in the case of the symphonic poem. Is Siegfried's Rhine Journey, for example, intelligible on any other supposition than that with each change of theme in the music the hearer's imagination visualizes a fresh episode in the hero's course? How do we listen to the *Mastersinger* Overture except just in the way we listen to a symphonic poem—the imagination calling up before it the bodily presence of each of the characters in turn? In the second place, the evidence is overwhelming that Wagner's own imagination was much more restricted in this respect than that of other people; and it was precisely this inability to trust very much to the visualizing power of the imagination which made him fall into so many crude errors of realism. All his life through he was unable to see that the imagination has a much wider scope than the eye because, not being tied down to the mere spatial dimensions of an object, it can add enormously to it out of its own store of memory and vision. Vastness is a quality inseparable from any concept of a god; but can the grandest creation of sculpture or the most heroic of stage figures ever hope to give us such a sense of the illimitable power and beauty of godhead as the imagination can supply? Whose god comes nearest to filling the earth with his presence—the invisible one of Milton or Spinoza, or the visible Wotan of Wagner? Does not the least analytical spectator of a Wagnerian opera often feel that it would have been better if the composer had insisted less on material facts upon the stage and left our imagination a freer wing? How much of the exquisite poetry of the idea of the *Waldweben*—the natural, untainted boy at home in nature's heart, dowered by his native innocence with the gift of understanding the song of birds—is spoiled for us by the grossly unideal presence of the average actor, by the reduction of the wayward breath and infinite soul of nature to a few yards of painted pasteboard, and by the narrowing down of all our ideas of the lyric freedom of bird life to one poor piece of stuffed mechanism jerked at the end of a wire, and a tremulous soprano somewhere up

in the wings? Who would exchange the imagination's
vision of the glorious Valkyrie flight through the storm
and the cloud wrack for the actual visible equine Grane,
with his evident air of having been borrowed from the
mews, around the corner? Who that is moved by the Grail
music in *Parsifal* has not felt his heart sink within him at
the sight of the slow mechanical evolutions of the Knights
in the Grail scene? Who has not felt at the sight of the
"property" swan that the rarefied atmosphere of Monsalvat
has gone, and with it most of the remoteness, the shining
whiteness, of Lohengrin? Or, not to multiply instances of
this kind from the Wagnerian operas themselves, who
can doubt the general proposition that the more the
subject approaches the sublime, the more it demands purely
poetic or musical treatment, and the more lamentably it
suffers by being narrowed down to a canvas or a stage?
What painter could hope to suggest, even in the largest
picture, the vision of the vast evil form of Lucifer, the
mighty sweep of his fall, and the horror of the fiery underworld, that Milton can give us in a line or two;[2] and who,
in spite of all the splendor of the music of the *Ring*, does
not feel that the actual *spectacle* of gods and heroes that
has been put before our eyes on the stage cannot compare
in true sublimity with the picture given us in the great
opening lines of Morris's *Sigurd the Volsung*:

There was a dwelling of kings ere the world was waxen old;
Dukes were the door-wards there, and the roofs were
thatched with gold;
Earls were the wrights that wrought it, and silver nailed
its doors;

___

[2] See *Paradise Lost*, Book I, lines 44 *ff.* Compare the passage
in which Lessing (*Laokoön*, Chap. XII) is discussing the felling
of Mars by Minerva by means of a huge stone. The overthrown
god, according to Homer, "covered seven acres." "It is impossible," says Lessing, "that the painter could give this extraordinary
size to the god; but if he does not give it him, then Mars does
not lie upon the ground like the Homeric Mars, but like a
common warrior."

Earls' wives were the weaving-women, queens' daughters
  strewed its floors,
And the masters of its song-craft were the mightiest men
  that cast
The sails of the storm of battle adown the bickering blast.
There dwelt men merry-hearted, and in hope exceeding
  great
Met the good days and the evil as they went the way of
  fate:
There the gods were unforgotten, yea whiles they walked
  with men,
Though e'en in that world's beginning rose a murmur now
  and then
Of the midward time and the fading and the last of the
  latter days,
And the entering in of the terror, and the death of the
  People's Praise.

How the imagination fills out the ample spaces here left
to it to play among—how great and godlike and noble
and beautiful a world of men and women it is that the
poet evokes for us!

VI

The elimination from an opera text of everything that
is not suited to musical expression is perhaps an unattainable ideal. It is only the titanic *musical* genius of Wagner
that makes us more or less tolerant of what we may call the
baser metal in the structure of his music dramas. Since
his day the problem has proved so baffling a one that
composers have frankly given it up in despair. Wagner was
right: the simpler the story or legend on which we found
an opera—the more it can be trusted to make its own
motives and development clear—the less nonmusical matter shall we be burdened with, and the more chance we
shall have of being able to keep the musical tissue on a
consistently high level. The proof of this is to be found
not only in Wagner's own work but in that of his suc-

cessors. It is hardly possible to recall a modern opera in which, at some point or other, the composer has not tried to delude us into the belief that the music means something when it really means nothing. Take, for example, the opening scene of *Elektra*. The scene is *dramatically* necessary because it informs the spectator of the relations between Elektra and her mother, and explains the miserable servitude of the maiden in the house of her murdered father. But no man who ever lived could set such words as these to good music; and all that Strauss can do is to make a mere pretense of writing music, let the orchestra play almost anything and the voices shriek almost anything, and trust to the audience being carried blindly along, partly by the excitement of the noise, partly by the bustling stage movement. Wagner's superior artistic sense would have seen from the outset that this part of the libretto was outside the sphere of music, and, being his own librettist, he would, in obedience to the prompting of the musician in him, have so reshaped the opera that there would have been no need to communicate that particular piece of information to us in this particular form. The procedure of Strauss and Hofmannsthal is hardly less absurd than that of the old composers who used to set to music not only the actual words of the Bible but "Here beginneth the . . . chapter of the . . . book of . . ."

How much of the merest putty, again, is left visible in the libretti of Puccini, Charpentier, and others—passages that are essential if the story is to be made clear to the spectator, but absolutely defying musical treatment. There is scarcely a single opera of which the music gives one the impression of pure necessity from first to last; every now and then our teeth are set on edge by some pieces of grit left by the bad cooks in an otherwise good dish. The handling of passages of this kind has become the most stereotyped of formulas; the characters talk rather than sing, while the orchestra keeps the ear interested by playing pretty tunes on its own account, much as a nurse tells a child fairytales to keep it quiet during the ordeal of the bath. Only the easygoing attitude toward all questions of form which is bred in us by theatrical art could possibly blind us for a moment to the helplessness and ineptitude of a method of this kind. Debussy evades the difficulty in another way. He starts with a text that is already a complete, self-sufficing work of art, capable, without the assistance of music, of holding an audience interested in it by virtue of its own dramatic life and its fine literary quality. He is thus, to begin with, in a far stronger position than that of nineteen opera composers out of twenty, whose texts have no artistic quality of their own and have to receive the whole breath of their life from the music. Having the good fortune to be working upon a libretto that is itself moving and beautiful, Debussy can frequently afford to leave it to speak for itself, his own contribution to it being sometimes no more than a momentary heightening of the force of the words by means of a poignant harmony or a suggestive touch of color. I hope I shall not be held to be insensitive to the peculiar charm of Debussy's *Pelléas et Mélisande*, or to the rare musical invention of the more continuous portions of it, if I say that a good deal of the opera could have been written by a much less gifted man. Now that the novelty of it has passed off, it is seen to be not at all a difficult matter to subtilize a stage effect by the addition of a poignant chord here and there. *Pelléas et Mélisande* is mostly an extremely beautiful work, but it will probably have no posterity[3] because while the more musical portions of it depend less for their effect on any essential novelty of form than upon the very individual quality of Debussy's imagination, the style of the other—the merely atmospheric —portions is so easy to imitate that it is within the scope of dozens of composers with only a quarter of Debussy's genius. Debussy, then, has not, any more than his con-

[3] I leave this sentence as it stands, in spite of Ravel's *L'Heure Espagnole*. That charming little work does not succeed in convincing us that the *parlando* method in opera has much of a future.

temporaries, solved the problem of weaving the combined vocal and orchestral tissue of the opera into a continuous and homogeneous whole; for a great part of the time he simply evades the problem. *Pelléas et Mélisande* is a *tour de force* that will probably never be repeated; it depended for its success on the concurrence of a number of factors that are hardly likely to be met with in combination again.

VII

To recapitulate, then, for a moment: Wagner's theory of the ideal music drama is sound enough, but neither he nor any of his successors has been able to realize the theory in practice. In every combination of music with the other arts it must of necessity play the leading role because of the greater expansiveness and superior warmth of its expression.[4] As Wagner saw, it will tolerate no text but one that is thoroughly musical in essence—that is to say, one that is so purely emotional throughout that at no time can we feel that in order to associate with it music has had to descend from its ideal sphere. It is in the process of making the action clear to the spectator that opera generally has to admit certain elements that drag music down from its high estate. We have therefore at present two chief forms of the association of poetry and music—the opera, in which actual characters, using actual words, are shown to us in the actuality of the stage, and the symphonic poem, in which we are given not the characters but the emotions of the characters, and not the scene but an imaginative suggestion of the scene, while the general nature of the subject is communicated to us by means of a printed explanation or a title. This necessity of putting the hearer *en rapport* with the story by a device that stands outside the music seems to many people an ineradicable flaw in the symphonic poem; a work of art, they say, should be self-contained, and opera, with all its admitted faults,

[4] This is the explanation of the fact that good music often floats a poor poem, while the best of poems has never been able to float poor music.

has the virtue of being its own explanation. I do not think, however, that this matter is so simple as it looks.

Closer analysis will show first of all that many apparently self-contained musical works are as greatly in need of verbal explanation as a symphonic poem, and secondly, that in the full sense of the term hardly any opera or drama can be said to be wholly self-explanatory, inasmuch as, at every hearing of it except the first, we witness the unfolding of the earlier stages of the action with a knowledge of the later stages, and are thus as effectually adding something from an outside source to the visual and auditory impressions of the moment as when we follow a symphonic poem with the story in our minds which we have just read in the program book. What real difference, for example, is there between the frame of mind in which we listen to the *Tannhäuser* Overture and that in which we listen to *Ein Heldenleben?* In each case we are conscious that the music is not self-existent and self-explanatory, but depends for its full intelligibility on our knowledge of the characters and incidents upon which it is based. We get this knowledge in the case of *Ein Heldenleben* from a book; in the case of the *Tannhäuser* Overture we get it from our experience of the opera on the stage.[5] What essential difference is there between the two cases? In each of them we have to rely upon experience outside the work itself in order to grasp the full meaning of it. The *Tannhäuser* Overture and other works of that class are, in fact, artistic solecisms. No one, surely, will contend that at the *first* performance of *Tannhäuser* the overture conveyed its poetic meaning to the audience any more clearly than a performance of *Ein Heldenleben* would do without a literary explanation of its contents. The overture does not explain the opera, but is explained by it, and it is consequently absurd to play it first. It only happens to come first because the old practice of having an orchestral intro-

[5] We may, of course, get it from a program note, but this in turn must have been derived from some experience of the opera, either on the stage or in the printed score.

duction to an opera was unthinkingly retained long after the character of the introduction had so altered that there was no longer any sense in its use. The purpose of the overture originally was simply to play the audience into their seats. We see it performing this function in an overture like that to *The Messiah*: the music has nothing to do with the oratorio, and any one of a hundred other orchestral introductions would do just as well. But when opera composers began to make the overture a summary of the opera itself, they entered upon a course that utimately made it an absurdity. In so far as the overture sums up the opera, and therefore depends for its intelligibility on a knowledge of the opera, it ought logically to be played not at the commencement of the evening but at the end. Modern composers have instinctively recognized the truth of all this, and the operatic overture is now virtually abolished; there is none, for instance, to *Salome*, *Elektra*, or *Pelléas et Mélisande*.

All the overtures, then, that epitomize the opera with which they are connected are in the same category as the symphonic poem; for an understanding of the literary basis of them we have to go to a source outside themselves. The theory that a piece of music is bad music unless it is "self-sufficing" and "self-explanatory" is a mere fantasy of the armchair aesthetician. There are thousands of pages in Bach which only yield up their full secret to us when we get some outside light upon the sequence of poetic ideas in his mind at the time of writing. This is the case with many of the chorale preludes, for example. But Bach's music is often rich in a kind of allusive symbolism greatly resembling Wagner's use of the leading motive, though it is bolder than that, inasmuch as the musical symbol has not been made familiar to us by a previous definite use of it in the same work of art. In the *Christmas Oratorio* Bach sets the words of a chorale addressed to the infant Jesus to the music of another chorale that was already associated in the minds of the congregation with the Passion—thus in a flash bringing the death of the Savior into the same mental picture as the birth.[6] The chorale fantasia that the blind old man dictated to his pupil Altnikol a few days before his death united the music of the hymn "In our hour of direst need" with the words of "I come before thy throne." And who can forget the effect, comparable to some of the most thrilling of those that Wagner makes with his leading motives, of the trumpet pealing out with the melody of "Great God, what do I see and hear! The end of things created" in the midst of the bass recitative describing the terrors of the Day of Judgment (in the cantata *Wachet, betet*). Bach anticipated, as he did most things in modern music, the Wagnerian use of the leading motive, the function of which is to suggest to the hearer's imagination another idea simultaneously with the one the music is explicitly expressing. I think Bach would have smiled at anyone who chose to object that his chorale in the *Christmas Oratorio* was not self-sufficing, inasmuch as it depended for its affecting double meaning upon knowledge that the hearer had gathered elsewhere. He would probably have been satisfied with the unshakable fact that the hearer *had* this knowledge, and that it was therefore quite safe to rely on his making use of it. Surely the composer of the symphonic poem and allied forms is also justified in trusting occasionally to his auditors' outside knowledge of the subject of his work. Is there anything less legitimate in Strauss's trusting to our imagination to summon up at

[6] A correspondent of the *Musical Times* objected to this statement, alleging that the so-called Passion chorale is really the tune of the Communion chorale *Herzlich tut mich verlangen*, which is used for a variety of other hymns, including the *O Haupt voll Blut und Wunden*. "The result is," he said, "that to the German mind it conveys no particular association, just because it is so frequently used and at the most varied occasions." As a matter of fact, it is precisely to "the German mind" that it *does* convey the Passion association I suggested, as is shown by the remarks of such German writers as Spitta (*Life of Bach*, Eng. trans., ii, 579), Schweitzer (*J. S. Bach, le musicien-poète*, p. 281), Arnold Schering (*Bach's Textbehandlung*, p. 19), and Wolfrum (*Johann Sebastian Bach*, ii, 14, 15).

performance the scenes and the figures of *Don Quixote* than there is in Wagner's trusting to it, during the *Tannhäuser* or *Die Meistersinger* Overture, to summon up the scenes and figures of the opera? I have already pointed out that in his music dramas Wagner is continually asking us, by means of recurrent leading motives, to visualize more than is actually set before us on the stage—thus flying in the face of his own theoretical arguments. It only needs to be added that he also relied, at times, as much as the writer of symphonic poems does, upon the hearer's or spectator's knowing more about the course of the drama than has been revealed to him in the drama itself. How do we know, for example, that the "Sword" motive in the final scene of *Das Rheingold* is a "Sword" motive at all? How do we know the train of thought running through Wotan's mind at this point as he looks into the future? Simply by antedating the information we have gained from the later dramas of the *Ring*. At the time the "Sword" motive is first heard there has never been the slightest suggestion of the sword that is to help to lift the curse from the gods; not only Siegfried but Siegfried's parents are as yet unborn. Again, the phrase that Tannhäuser sings to the words *"Ha, jetzt erkenne ich sie wieder, die schöne Welt der ich entrückt"* in the first act of the opera is explained only by the association of it with Elisabeth and the Hall of Song in the second act. Anyone with a knowledge of the Wagnerian operas can multiply these instances for himself.

Does not everything, in fact, point to the impossibility of our listening to any performance of a drama or opera, *except the first one*, with a mind that is absolutely a clean slate? Are we not always drawing consciously or unconsciously upon our store of acquired knowledge of the work, and blending this with the visual or auditory impressions of the moment? Do we not all know, long before it happens, that the screen will fall down at a certain climactic point in the *School for Scandal* and show us Lady Teazle hiding behind it? Is not our appreciation of all the dialogue of this scene whetted by our knowledge—gained from "outside" sources—of what is going to happen at the end of it? The instructed spectator or reader invariably keeps looking ahead, his interest or delight in what is occurring at the moment being intensified by what may be called anticipatory memory. It is only at the first time of reading *Tom Jones* that we can be in the slightest doubt as to who is the hero's mother. The ever present clue to the solution of the mystery does not spoil our pleasure, however, in the second and subsequent readings; nay, it rather adds to it, for it makes us conscious of a number of cunning strokes of construction which we had not noticed at the first reading. At the second and every subsequent performance of Mr. John Galsworthy's *The Pigeon* a thrill of horror goes through us at the exit of Mrs. Megan in the second act, for we know—what we did not know at the first performance—that she means to throw herself into the river; and for this reason the second performance necessarily makes a profounder effect on us than the first.

I take it, then, that an exaggerated importance can be attached to the principle of art being "self-sufficing" and "self-explanatory" at the first time of hearing or seeing; the subject is a far more complex one than the amateur aestheticians have imagined. They had only to turn to the Greek drama to see a form of art in which deliberate advantage was taken by every author of the fact that the audience had an "outside" knowledge of the characters and events of the play. The Greek drama, broadly speaking, did not rely, as ours does, on the effect of a slow unfolding of a complicated plot—the main art of which consists in first of all giving the audience something to hunt for and then finding it for them. The Greek drama was based on a myth or a legend every detail of which was known to every member of the audience. *At a first performance*, therefore, the audience would be in precisely the same position as a modern audience is when it reads in its program book the analysis of a new symphonic poem that is about to be performed. And this knowledge, so far from diminishing the audience's enjoyment of the drama, actually intensified it, and permitted to the author an

amount of subtle psychological allusion that can only be
compared with the effects of the leading motive in modern
opera. When Clytemnestra, for instance, in Aeschylus's
drama, greets Agamemnon with falsely fawning words, the
thrill that ran through the Athenian audience came not
from any feeling of foreboding inspired by the visible
situation or the actual words, but from its *outside* knowledge that all this was feigning, and that the hounds of
death were already hot on the track of the unsuspecting
king. Wagner would have flashed the same light upon
Clytemnestra's words by means of an orchestral motive.
An Athenian, again, at the first performance of the *Oedipus
Rex*, must have known the whole of the story from the
beginning. There could be for him none of the cumulative
surprise at the slow unraveling of the web which we feel
at a first reading of the tragedy; rather did he accompany
the first blind steps of *Oedipus* with a pity born of the
knowledge—the *outside* knowledge—of the doom the gods
had woven for him.

VIII

If, then, there is no aesthetic falsity involved in assuming
some previous knowledge of the action or the motive
on the part of the spectator, or in communicating this
knowledge by other means than a stage presentation, why
should we not boldly recognize that the time is ripe for
a new form of art which shall carry the potency of music
a step further than it was carried by Wagner? After all,
it is the music that counts for ninety-five per cent of our
enjoyment of a Wagner opera. The "philosophy" of the
Ring may be something to write or read about in the study,
but in the theater it really goes for very little. It is interesting to talk about the Schopenhauerian or Hindu significance of the discourse of the lovers, in the second act of
Tristan, upon Love and Death, and Night and Day; but
again—for how much does this count in the theater?
Has there ever been a single spectator, since *Tristan* was
first given, who could make out from the performance

alone what philosophy it was the lovers were talking, or whether they were talking philosophy at all? And how many people who *do* know the text at this point—because they have read it—feel in the theater that very much of the essential emotion of the work would be lost if the characters sang Chinese words, or Choctaw words, or no words at all, so long as the music was left to tell its own tale? I must guard against possible misunderstanding here. I am not for a moment urging that speech should henceforth be banished from opera as a mere superfluity.[7] There are many subjects in which it will always be a necessity; the world of *Die Meistersinger*, for instance, could have been made real to us in no other medium than that of music with words. But I do contend that there are many poetic subjects in which virtually the whole of the expression could be entrusted with perfect safety to music alone —not necessarily in the form of a symphonic poem, but in a sort of drama without actors—if the paradox may be permitted—or with speechless actors. And could we not in this way approach a step nearer to the ideal musical art work, in which all the needful suggestiveness of poetry was retained without any admixture of the cruder non-musical elements that at present merely go to make plot and persons intelligible to the auditor?

IX

Maeterlinck and others have of late familiarized us with the idea of a "static" as distinguished from the older "dynamic" drama. It is highly probable that in the future, men will go to the theater craving the satisfaction of rather different desires from those they seek to satisfy there now. That "drama" is capable of more than one meaning is proved by the existence of dramatic forms so varied as those of the Greek drama, the Shakespearean drama, the Maeterlinckian drama, the *Atalanta in Calydon*

[7] Nor, I should think I scarcely need add, do I imagine that opera will die out in the near future, though some critics of the original article naïvely attributed this view to me!

of Swinburne, *The Dynasts* of Mr. Thomas Hardy, and the *Getting Married* of Mr. Bernard Shaw. It is quite reasonable to suppose, therefore, that a new generation may read another new meaning into the word. Among the finer minds of the present day there is a decided movement away from what seems to them the crudity of the old-style "well-constructed" drama of action. Maeterlinck, in one or two of his essays, has given eloquent expression to the feelings that inspire this movement of revolt. Many of the time-honored dramatic "motives" are already sadly discredited. The dagger and the poison bowl no longer play the part in tragedy which they used to play. Humanity has come to see that things of this kind are the mere excrescences of a dramatic action—the mere crude outward and visible signs of desires and passions working in secret in the souls of men—and their gaze is being turned more and more on the psychological springs of action rather than on the visible actions themselves. Drama, in the hands of thoughtful poetical writers, is becoming more and more an affair of the inner rather than the outer man; and it is probable that as time goes on, still less reliance will be placed on the crude stage effect of violent action. It need hardly be said that as drama dispenses with piece after piece of action and explanation, and comes deeper down to the essence of tragedy as a war of impulses in a man's soul or of the fates about his path, it approaches more nearly to the mood of music. We may look in the future to a yet further purging of poetic drama of many of the tedious conventional devices on which it is still dependent so long as it has to play off a number of characters against each other like chessmen on a few square yards of board in a theater. I think I can foresee the time when most of what now passes for "plot interest"—the pretense on the author's part of hiding something merely in order that it may in due time be triumphantly found again—will be regarded as something almost childish in the naïve quality of its appeal, and will be relegated to forms of art as much below the general intellectual level of the literature of the day as the detective story is below the intellectual level of our own better novels and dramas. The more artistic the race becomes, the less will it crave for mere facts and events in drama, and the more for an imaginative reading of the soul on which the facts and events have written their record. Again let me interpolate a word of warning against a misunderstanding of my thesis. I am not supposing that a time will ever come when the drama as we have it now will have disappeared from the stage. I fully recognize that there are certain dramatic concepts that can never be adequately expressed except by means of clashing and marching and countermarching characters, and action more or less violent or clockwork-like. But I fancy that in the not distant future the more poetic side of man will demand a form of art in which very little happens or is told, but in which the soul of the spectator is flooded by emotions of pity and sorrow and love which are all the more penetrating because they do not come to us through the relatively cold medium of words and the childish, creaking clockwork of exits and entrances and surprises and intrigue.

x

It is this attitude of the artistic mind of the future toward drama which will, I think, find utterance in a form of quasi-dramatic music in which we shall be rid of all or most of the mere scaffolding of narration or action which serves at present simply to give intellectual support to the music of opera. Even in Wagner are we not painfully conscious at times of the fact that the music, which matters a great deal, is being diluted and made turbid by a quantity of baser matter the only function which is to make it clear to us why these particular people are there at that particular moment, and what it is that they are doing? It cannot be reiterated too often that it is only the music that can keep alive any form of art into which music enters. The mere *facts* in an art work lose their force with repetition; it is only artistic emotion that can be born anew again

and again and yet again. Who feels anything but a glow
of rapturous anticipation when the first notes of the
Liebestod or of Wotan's *Abschied* are sounded? He may
have heard it all a hundred times before, and know every
note of it by heart; but it will all be as new and wonderful
and inevitable to him at the hundredth hearing as at the
first. But who does not involuntarily emit a groan from
the very depths of his being when Wagner's first care at
the moment is not to kindle us with great music but to
tell us through Wotan's lips at great length, and for the
hundredth time, certain mere facts that have long lost
their absorbing interest for us? And even in his most com-
pact work, *Tristan*, is there not a great deal that is, from
the highest point of view, superfluous? We can bear to
hear the same glorious music times without number; but
we will not bear being told times without number who
Tristan and Isolde and Marke and Morold are, and how
Tristan slew Morold, and how Isolde nursed Tristan back
to health, and all the rest of it. I can imagine a *Tristan*
in which things of this kind would be assumed to be matters of common knowledge on the part of the audience, as
the characters and motives of Tchaikovsky's *Romeo and
Juliet* or *Francesca da Rimini* are assumed to be common
knowledge, or those of Strauss's *Macbeth* or *Till Eulenspiegel*, or those of Beethoven's *Coriolan* and *Egmont*
Overtures or the *Leonora No. 3*, or those of Dukas's
L'Apprenti Sorcier. Then the whole of the composer's time
and the audience's attention could be devoted to that full
musical exposition of nothing else but the protagonists'
"soul-states" and "soul-events" which Wagner avowed
as the ideal of music drama, but which is virtually an
impossible ideal so long as opera is compelled to utilize
so many actors on so much and no more of a stage, and to
occupy precisely so many hours of an evening.

As it happens, we already have in the Greek drama—
especially that of the older type—a form of poetic art
strongly resembling that which I am here suggesting might
be now produced in music. Not only did the old Greek
dramatist, as we have seen, largely rely on the audience's

knowledge of the characters and events of his play, and so save himself the necessity of much action or much scene shifting, but he cast the drama into a concentrated form that enabled him to appeal rather to the spectator's sense of poetry than to the mere delight in external catastrophe and the unraveling of plot; while in the chorus he had under his hand an instrument capable of extraordinary emotional expression. The Greek drama, in fact, was singularly akin to the music drama of Wagner. As Wagner saw, the true modern equivalent of the Greek chorus is the orchestra; it is at once part of the action and aloof from it, an ideal spectator, sympathizing, commenting, correcting. The Greek drama resembles ideal opera, again, in that the ultimate sentiment disengaged from it is one not of facts shown, or of interest held by the mere interplay of intrigue, but of a high poetic spirit, purifying and transfiguring the common life of things.

Is not this form capable of further development? Is it not possible to construct an art form in which the mere facts that it is necessary for us to know are either assumed as known or set before us in the briefest possible way, so that music can take upon itself the whole burden of expression, and the whole work of art be nothing but an outpouring of lofty, quintessential emotion? Can we not imagine something like the second act of *Tristan* with silent and only dimly visible actors, the music, helped by their gestures, telling us all that is in their souls, while they are too remote from us for the crude personality of the actors and the theatrical artificiality of the stage setting to jar upon us as they do at present? Cannot some story be taken as so well known to everyone that only the shadowiest hints of the course of it need be given to the spectator, the real drama being in the music? Or, to go a step further, cannot we dispense altogether with the stage and the visible actor, such external coherence as the music needs being afforded by impersonal voices floating through a darkened auditorium? [8] The effect of disem-

[8] Mr. Rutland Boughton has already made a very suggestive beginning on this line.

bodied voices can be made extraordinarily moving; in all my experience of concert-going I can remember no sensations comparable to those I felt during the Grail scene from *Parsifal* at one of the Three Choirs Festivals; the exquisite beauty of the boys' voices floating down from one knew not where was something almost too much for mortal senses to endure. Here, in the concealed, impersonal choir, is an instrument, I think, the full emotional power of which is not yet suspected by composers. It lends itself admirably to just that desire for the exploration of the mysteries around us which music is always endeavoring to satisfy. As the cruder kind of action goes out of drama, the hovering Fates will come in. Mr. Hardy, in *The Dynasts*, has given us a hint of what may be done by a partial reversion to the Greek type of drama, the purblind, struggling human protagonists being surrounded by an invisible chorus of Fates that see to the hidden roots of things. A poetic scheme of this kind could be made extremely impressive by music—say a series of orchestral pictures of human desires and passions, having a simple intellectual co-ordination of their own, with an invisible chorus commenting upon it all now and then in the style of the Fates of Mr. Hardy or the chorus of Aeschylus. There are, I think, several possible new art forms open to us when we shall have learned to dispense, for certain purposes, with the actor and his speech, to rely upon the audience's previous knowledge of some story of universal interest and significance, and to leave it to music alone to express the whole of the dramatic or poetic implications of the story. But it is perhaps vain to try to forecast these future developments by means of reason. They will certainly come, but not by theorists taking thought of them; they will have to be born, as the Wagnerian drama was, out of the burning need of some great soul.

SYNTHETIC TABLE OF WAGNER'S LIFE AND WORKS AND SYNCHRONOUS EVENTS

YEAR	LIFE	MUSICAL WORKS	PROSE AND POETICAL WORKS	SYNCHRONOUS EVENTS
1813	May 22. Born at Leipzig. Nov. 22. His father dies.			Verdi born. Rossini's *Tancredi*.
1814	Aug. 14 [28?] His mother marries Ludwig Geyer. Aug. The family removes to Dresden.			
1815				Weber called to Dresden to found a German Opera.
1818				Spohr's *Faust*.
1819				Schopenhauer's *Die Welt als Wille und Vorstellung*.
1821				Weber's *Der Freischütz*.
1822	Sept. 30. Death of Geyer.			César Franck born.
1823				Weber's *Euryanthe*. Schubert's *Rosamunde*.
1824				Beethoven's Ninth Symphony. Bruckner born.

YEAR	LIFE	MUSICAL WORKS	PROSE AND POETICAL WORKS	SYNCHRONOUS EVENTS
1826				Weber's Oberon. Death of Weber.
1827	The family removes to Leipzig.			Death of Beethoven.
1828			"Leubald und Adelaide" (unpublished).	Death of Schubert. Marschner's Der Vampyr.
1829		1st Sonata in D minor. Quartet in D major.		Auber's Masaniello. Rossini's William Tell.
1830		Arrangement of Beethoven's Ninth Symphony for two hands. Overture in C major ($\frac{6}{8}$ time).		Berlioz's Symphonie Fantastique.
		Overture in B flat (performed at Leipzig, under H. Dorn, on Christmas Day).		Auber's Fra Diavolo.
1831	Feb. Studies music with Weinlig.	Pianoforte Sonata in B flat major (Op. 1). Polonaise in D major for four hands (Op. 2). (Both published by Breitkopf & Härtel, 1832). Pianoforte Fantasia in F sharp minor (not published in Wagner's lifetime: first		Bellini's Romeo and Juliet. Meyerbeer's Robert the Devil. Bellini's La Somnambula. Hérold's Zampa.

1832	issued by Kahnt, Leipzig, 1905). Overture to Raupach's *König Enzio* (finished Feb. 3, 1832. Performed in Leipzig theater, as prelude to the play, Mar. 16, 1832. Published by Breitkopf & Härtel, 1907). Concert Overture in D minor (never published; performed at a "Euterpe" Concert, Leipzig, Christmas 1831, and at a Gewandhaus Concert, Feb. 23, 1832). Concert Overture in C with fugue (never published: performed at a "Euterpe" Concert, Leipzig, winter 1831–2, and at a Gewandhaus Concert, Apr. 30, 1832). Symphony in C major (performed at Prague Conservatoire, under Dionys Weber, summer 1832, also at Leipzig, Christmas 1832 and Jan. 10, 1833). *Die Hochzeit* begun. Text completed, but music never finished. Setting of "Glockentöne" (poem by T. Apel).	Bellini's *Norma*. Death of Goethe.

SYNTHETIC TABLE OF WAGNER'S LIFE AND WORKS AND SYNCHRONOUS EVENTS—Continued

YEAR	LIFE	MUSICAL WORKS	PROSE AND POETICAL WORKS	SYNCHRONOUS EVENTS
1832		Seven compositions for Goethe's *Faust* (Op. 5). (Not published till 1914.)		
1833	Jan. At Würzburg. Returns to Leipzig at Christmas. Aug. 6. Finishes Act I of *Die Feen*. Dec. 1. Finishes Act II of *Die Feen*.	Sept. Allegro for Aubry's Aria in Marschner's *Der Vampyr*; text and music by Wagner (not published till 1914).		Marschner's *Hans Heiling*. Brahms born.
1834	Jan. 1. Finishes Act III of *Die Feen*. Jan. 6. Finishes Overture to *Die Feen*. (Opera first performed June 29, 1888, at Munich.) Jan. Returns to Leipzig. Writes text of *Das Liebesverbot*. July. Conductor at Magdeburg.	2nd Symphony in E major (unfinished).	Article, "The German Opera," published anonymously in the *Zeitung für die elegante Welt* of June 10, 1834. Article, "Pasticcio," published in the *Neue Zeitschrift für Musik*, Nov. 6–10, 1834 (signed "Canto Spianato").	Donizetti's *Lucrezia Borgia*. First number of the *Neue Zeitschrift für Musik* published.

Year				
1835	Mar. Finishes music of Das Liebesverbot.	Columbus Overture, performed at Leipzig, 1835, in Riga, Mar. 19, 1838, and at Paris, Feb. 4, 1841; published by Breitkopf & Härtel in 1907). Jan. New Year Cantata, "Beim Antritt des neuen Jahres" (published 1914).		Halévy's La Juive. Donizetti's Lucia di Lammermoor. Grimm's "German Mythology" published.
1836	Aug. Settles at Königsberg. Nov. 24. Marries Minna Planer.	Das Liebesverbot performed in Magdeburg, under Wagner, Mar. 29. "Rule, Britannia" Overture (published by Breitkopf & Härtel in 1907). "Polonia" Overture (begun in 1832; published by Breitkopf & Härtel in 1907).	Text of "Männerlist grösser als Frauenlist" (music never written). Article, "Aus Magdeburg," (published anonymously in the Neue Zeitschrift für Musik for April 19, 1836).	Meyerbeer's Les Huguenots.
1837	May. Leaves Königsberg. Aug. Settles in Riga.	Romance in G major, "Sanfte Wehmut will sich regen," (for insertion in Blum's Singspiel "Marie, Max and Michel").	Die hohe Braut (opera text, sketched in 1836 and sent to Scribe in 1837. Offered to Reissiger in 1842. Versified by Wagner in 1847, and composed by Johann Kittl under the title "Bianca und Giuseppa, oder die Franzosen vor Nizza").	Lortzing's Zar und Zimmermann.

SYNTHETIC TABLE OF WAGNER'S LIFE AND WORKS AND SYNCHRONOUS EVENTS—Continued

YEAR	LIFE	MUSICAL WORKS	PROSE AND POETICAL WORKS	SYNCHRONOUS EVENTS
1837			Articles, "Der dramatische Gesang," and "Die Norma von Bellini" (the latter lost). Article, "Bellini, Ein Wort zu seiner Zeit," published in the Rigaer Zuschauer, Dec. 7–19, 1837.	
1838	July. Begins Rienzi. Conceives idea of The Flying Dutchman.	"Der Tannenbaum" (song).	Die glückliche Bärenfamilie (comic opera in two acts, text only).	Berlioz's Benvenuto Cellini. Moussorgsky born.
1839	May. Completes first two acts of Rienzi. July. Leaves Riga. Sept. At Paris.	A Faust Overture (finished Feb. 1840, rehearsed by Habeneck at Paris, but not performed). Songs: "Dors, mon enfant." "Mignonne." "Attente." "Les Deux Grenadiers."		
1840	Sept. Finishes Rienzi. Sketches The Flying Dutchman. Meets Liszt for first time.			Schumann's Myrthen, Frauenliebe, and Dichterliebe. Donizetti's Favorita. Tchaikovsky born.

| 1840–? | Oct. Writes *Rienzi* overture.
Nov. Finishes scoring of *Rienzi*. | Articles written in Paris: "The Nature of German Music," (Gazette Musicale, Nos. 44–6, 1840). "Pergolesi's Stabat Mater," (G. M., No. 57, 1840). "The Virtuoso and the Artist," (G. M., No. 58, 1840). "A Pilgrimage to Beethoven," (G. M., Nos. 65, 66, 68, 69, 1840). "The Overture" (G. M., Nos. 3–5, 1841). "An End in Paris," (G. M., Nos. 9, 11, 12, 1841). "Report" for the Dresdener Abendzeitung (Feb. 23, 1841). "The Artist and Publicity," (G. M., No. 26, 1841). "Parisian Amusements" (Europa, Apr. 1841). "Report" for the Dresdener Abendzeitung (April 6, 1841). |

SYNTHETIC TABLE OF WAGNER'S LIFE AND WORKS AND SYNCHRONOUS EVENTS—Continued

YEAR	LIFE	MUSICAL WORKS	PROSE AND POETICAL WORKS	SYNCHRONOUS EVENTS
1840-2			"Report" for the Dresdener Abendzeitung, May 5, 1841. "Parisian Fatalities for Germans", (Europa, May 1841). "Der Freischütz" (G. M., Nos. 34–5, 1841). "Le Freischütz" (Dresdener Abendzeitung, June 20, 1841). "Report" for the Dresdener Abendzeitung, July 6, 1841). "Report" for the Dresdener Abendzeitung ("Impressions of a Parisian Sunday," Aug. 1, 1841). "Report" for the Dresdener Abendzeitung, Sept. 8, 1841. "A Happy Evening", (G. M., Nos. 56–8, 1841). "Report" for the Dresdener Abendzeitung, Nov. 5, 1841.	

1841	Engaged on *The Flying Dutchman*, music written in July and Aug.		"Report" for the Dresdener Abendzeitung, Dec. 1, 1841. "Rossini's *Stabat Mater*" (*Neue Zeitschrift für Musik*, Dec. 15, 1841). "Report" for the Dresdener Abendzeitung (Halévy's "*La Reine de Chypre*"), Dec. 23, 1841. "Report" for the Dresdener Abendzeitung ("On a New Paris Opera"), Dec. 31, 1841. "*Halévy, et La Reine de Chypre*" (G. M., Nos. 9, 11, 17, 18, 1842).	Feuerbach's *Wesen des Christenthums*.
1842	Apr. At Dresden. Plans *Tannhäuser* ("*Der Venusberg*").	Oct. 20. First performance of *Rienzi* at Dresden, under Reissiger.	*Die Bergwerke zu Falun*; opera in three acts (sketch only). *Die Sarazenin*; opera in five acts (sketched in Paris in 1841; text finished in Dresden in 1843; music never written). Nov. "Autobiographical Sketch."	Death of Cherubini.

YEAR	LIFE	MUSICAL WORKS	PROSE AND POETICAL WORKS	SYNCHRONOUS EVENTS
1843	Feb. Becomes a Court Kapellmeister at Dresden. May. Completes Tannhäuser poem. July. Begins composition of Tannhäuser.	Jan. 2. First performance of The Flying Dutchman at Dresden, under Wagner. May and June. The Love Feast of the Apostles. (Performed July 6). "Festgesang", for male chorus (published 1914).		Schumann's Paradise and the Peri. Robert Franz's first set of songs. Grieg born.
1844	Oct. Finishes Acts I and II of Tannhäuser. Dec. Finishes Act III of Tannhäuser.	Aug. "Gruss seiner Treuen an Friedrich August den Geliebten" for male chorus. Arrangement of the Triumphal March from Spontini's "La Vestale." Dec. Funeral music at Weber's grave (published 1914).	Accounts of the bringing home of Weber's remains from London to Dresden.	Verdi's Ernani.
1845	Apr. 13. Completes scoring of Tannhäuser. July. Sketches poem of Lohengrin. July. Idea of Die Meistersinger and Parsifal conceived but put aside. Nov. Poem of Lohengrin completed.	Oct. 19. First performance of Tannhäuser at Dresden, under Wagner.		

Year	Wagner's Works and Life	Arrangements	Writings	Contemporary Events
1846	Palm Sunday (Apr. 5). Produces Beethoven's Ninth Symphony at Dresden. Sept. 1846 to Mar. 1847. Writes Act III of Lohengrin.		Various articles on Beethoven's Ninth Symphony, a propos of his own performance of the work on Apr. 5. "Concerning the Royal Kapelle." "Artist and Critic. with respect to a particular case" (in Dresdener Anzeiger).	*Berlioz's Faust. Lortzing's Waffenschmied. Mendelssohn's Elijah.*
1847	May to June. Writes Act I of Lohengrin. June to Aug. Writes Act II of Lohengrin and Prelude.	Arrangement of Gluck's Iphigenia in Aulis.		**Death of Mendelssohn.**
1848	Jan. 9. His mother dies. Mar. Finishes scoring of Lohengrin. June 14. Makes political speech, to the "Vaterlandsverein." Nov. Writes poem of Siegfried's Death. Plans "Friedrich Barbarossa."	Arrangement of Palestrina's "Stabat Mater."	Summer. "The Wibelungen: World-history from the Saga" (not published till 1850). Autumn. "The Nibelungen Myth as sketch of a Drama." Speech at the 300th Anniversary of the Foundation of the Royal Musical Chapel in Dresden.	Feb. Revolution in Paris. Mar. Risings in Vienna and Berlin. *Schumann's Faust. Schumann's Manfred.*

YEAR	LIFE	MUSICAL WORKS	PROSE AND POETICAL WORKS	SYNCHRONOUS EVENTS
1849	Feb. 16. Liszt produces Tannhäuser in Weimar. May. Wagner flees from Dresden to Weimar and thence to Zurich; later to Paris; then returns to Zurich.		Dec., "Jesus von Nazareth." "What is the Relation of Republican Efforts to the Monarchy?" "Theatrical Reform." "A Project for the Organisation of a German National Theatre for the Kingdom of Saxony" (presented to the Ministry May 16, 1848). "Art and Revolution." Jan. "Edouard Devrient's Geschichte der deutschen Schauspielkunst." Apr. "Man and Existing Society." Apr. "The Revolution."	May. Risings in Dresden. Meyerbeer's Le Prophète. Death of Chopin.
1850	Jan. Goes to Paris, hoping to get an opera produced. Returns to Switzerland.	Aug. 26. First performance of Lohengrin at Weimar, under Liszt.	"The Art-Work of the Future" (written Nov. and Dec. 1849). "Wieland the Smith" (sketched as a drama end of 1849 or beginning of	Schumann's Genoveva.

1851	May to June. Writes poem of Young Siegfried.	1850; worked out more elaborately in 1850 in Paris). "Art and Climate." "Judaism and Music" (a pseudonymous article in the Neue Zeitschrift für Musik; expanded and re-published under his own name in 1869). Opera and Drama (written in winter 1850-1). "A Communication to My Friends." "On the Goethe Foundation." "A Letter to Franz Liszt." "A Theatre in Zürich." "Recollections of Spontini." "Explanatory Programme to Beethoven's 'Eroica' Symphony."	Schopenhauer's Parerga und Paralipomena. Verdi's Rigoletto.
1852	Meets the Wesendoncks. Writes poems of Die Walküre and Das Rheingold. Recasts Young Siegfried and Siegfried's Death, calling the		Death of Spontini.

YEAR	LIFE	MUSICAL WORKS	PROSE AND POETICAL WORKS	SYNCHRONOUS EVENTS
	former *Siegfried* and the latter *Götterdämmerung*. The text was privately printed as *Der Ring des Nibelungen* in 1853.		"On Musical Criticism." Explanatory programs to the "Coriolan" Overture, *The Flying Dutchman* Overture, and *Tannhäuser* Overture. "On the performing of *Tannhäuser*."	
1853	Oct. Working at music of *Das Rheingold*.	Album Sonata in E flat major (for Frau Wesendonck). "Züricher Vielliebchen" (Waltz in E flat major).	"Remarks on performing *The Flying Dutchman*." Explanatory program to the *Lohengrin* Prelude.	Jan. 3. Death of Uhlig. Verdi's *Il Trovatore*. Verdi's *La Traviata*
1854	Jan. Finishes *Das Rheingold* music. May. Finishes the scoring. June to Dec. Writes music of *Die Walküre*. Autumn. Conceives idea of *Tristan*. Reading Schopenhauer.		"Gluck's Overture to *Iphigenia in Aulis*." "A Letter to the Editor of the Neue Zeitschrift für Musik."	Hanslick's *Vom Musikalisch-Schönen*.

1855	In London and Zurich. Scoring Die Walküre.	A Faust Overture (second version).		
1856	Apr. Finishes scoring of Die Walküre. Autumn. Working at music of Siegfried.			Death of Schumann.
1857	Mar. Receives request for an opera for Rio de Janeiro. Apr. Settles in the "Asyl" by Wesendonck's house. July. Finishes Act I and part of Act II of Siegfried. Aug. Makes prose sketch of Tristan. Sept. 18. Finishes poem of Tristan. Idea of Parsifal revives. Dec. 31. Completes music of Act I of Tristan, also Prelude.		May. Die Sieger (sketch for a Buddhistic drama). "On Franz Liszt's Symphonic Poems."	Elgar born.
1857–8		Five Songs: "The Angel," "Be still," "In the Hothouse," "Grief," "Dreams."		
1858	In Paris and Switzerland. Apr. Scores Act I of Tristan. Summer. Writes Act II of Tristan.			Cornelius's Barber of Bagdad. Puccini born.

SYNTHETIC TABLE OF WAGNER'S LIFE AND WORKS AND SYNCHRONOUS EVENTS—Continued

YEAR	LIFE	MUSICAL WORKS	PROSE AND POETICAL WORKS	SYNCHRONOUS EVENTS
1859	April 9 to July 16. Writes Act III of *Tristan*. Aug. 8. Scoring of *Tristan* finished. Sept. 15. In Paris.		"Homage to Spohr and Fischer."	Gounod's *Faust*. Death of Spohr.
1860	At Brussels and Paris. Makes Paris version of *Tannhäuser*. Aug. Amnestied, except in Saxony.		"Letter to Hector Berlioz." "*Zukunftsmusik*."	Hugo Wolf born.
1861	Mar. 13, 18, and 24. *Tannhäuser* given in Paris. May. Hears *Lohengrin* for the first time, in Vienna. July 10. Minna leaves him finally, except for a visit to him in Biebrich in 1862. Dec. 1861 to Jan. 1862. Writes *Die Meistersinger* poem.	*Albumblatt* in A flat major. "*Ankunft bei den schwarzen Schwänen*." (An Albumblatt for Countess Pourtalès, based on Elisabeth's aria in Act II of *Tannhäuser*), Albumblatt in C major (for Princess Metternich).	"Account of the Production of *Tannhäuser* in Paris." Article, "On Rota's *Gräfin Egmont*," written for the Vienna *Oesterreichische Zeitung*, and signed "P. C." (Peter Cornelius).	

Year				
1862	Feb. At Biebrich. Commences composition of *Die Meistersinger.* Mar. Amnestied in Saxony. June 2. *Die Meistersinger* overture given in Liepzig. Nov. In Vienna.			Liszt's *St. Elisabeth.*
1863	At St. Petersburg, Moscow, &c., trying to raise money by concerts. May. In Penzing (Vienna).		"The Vienna Court Opera House." "Nibelungen" (poem published with a preface).	Debussy born.
1864	Mar. 10. Ludwig II ascends the Bavarian throne. Mar. 23. Wagner flies from his creditors to Mariafeld. May 3. Ludwig sends for him: Wagner settles at Starnberg. Oct. In Munich.	*Huldigungsmarsch.*	"To the Kingly Friend" (poem). "State and Religion" (not printed for public circulation till 1873).	Death of Meyerbeer.
1865	Apr. 10. Isolde, daughter of Wagner and Cosima von Bülow, born in Munich. July. Resumes composition of *Siegfried.*	June 10. First performance of *Tristan* at Munich, under Von Bülow.	"What is German?" (not published as a whole till 1878) "Report to His Majesty King Ludwig II of Bavaria upon a German Music-School to be founded in Munich."	Richard Strauss born.

SYNTHETIC TABLE OF WAGNER'S LIFE AND WORKS AND SYNCHRONOUS EVENTS—Continued

YEAR	LIFE	MUSICAL WORKS	PROSE AND POETICAL WORKS	SYNCHRONOUS EVENTS
1866	Aug. 27-30. Sketches Parsifal for King Ludwig. Dec. Leaves Munich; settles for a while in Switzerland. Jan. 25, Death of Minna. Apr. Settles at Tribschen (Lucerne). May. Cosima von Bülow leaves her husband and goes to live with Wagner at Tribschen. June. Composition of Act I of Die Meistersinger finished. Oct. Hans Richter sent to Wagner by Esser Act II of Die Meistersinger completed.			
1867	Feb. 18. Eva, daughter of Wagner and Cosima von Bülow, born in Tribschen. Oct. 20. Finishes Die Meistersinger.		Critiques: 1. W. H. Riehl. 2. Ferdinand Hiller "German Art and German Policy" (reprinted in book form in 1868).	Gounod's Romeo and Juliet.
1868	Nov. Makes Nietzsche's acquaintance.	June 21. First performance of Die Meistersinger at Munich, under Von Bülow.	"Recollections of Ludwig Schnorr von Carolsfeld."	Death of Rossini. Brahms's German Requiem.

1869	Feb. Finishes Act II of Siegfried. June 6. Siegfried Wagner born. Sept. Finishes Act III of Siegfried. Oct. Begins music of Götterdämmerung.	Sept. 22. First performance of Das Rheingold at Munich, under Wüllner.	Critiques: 3. Recollections of Rossini. 4. Edward Devrient. 5. Appendix to "Judaism in Music" (accompanying book-form edition).	Boïto's Mefistofele. Death of Berlioz.
1870	Jan. 11. Finishes Act I of Götterdämmerung. July 5. Finishes Act II of Götterdämmerung. July 18. Cosima divorced by Von Bülow. Aug. 25. Wagner marries Cosima von Bülow.	June 26. First performance of Die Walküre at Munich, under Wüllner. Siegfried Idyll (given at Tribschen, Dec. 25).	"On Conducting." Three poems: "Rheingold" (1868); "On the Completion of Siegfried" (1869); "25 Aug. 1870." "Beethoven." "Open Letter to Dr. F. Stade." Mein Leben (privately printed).	

YEAR	LIFE	MUSICAL WORKS	PROSE AND POETICAL WORKS	SYNCHRONOUS EVENTS
1871	Feb. Finishes scoring of Siegfried. May. Begins publication of his Collected Writings. June. Emil Heckel forms first Wagner Society at Mannheim.	Kaisermarsch.	Poem: "To the German Army before Paris." "A Capitulation" (not published until 1873). "Recollections of Auber." "On the Destiny of Opera." "Letter to an Italian Friend on the Production of Lohengrin at Bologna." "On the Production of the Stage-Festival-Drama The Ring of the Nibelung." Preface to the Collected Edition of his Prose and Poetical Works. "Report to the German Wagnerverein."	Death of Auber. Verdi's Aida. Death of Tausig.
1872	Feb. Finishes Act III of Götterdämmerung. Apr. Settles in Bayreuth. May 22. Foundation stone of the Bayreuth theater laid.		"Actors and Singers." "To the Burgomaster of Bologna." "To Friedrich Nietzsche."	Nietzsche's Geburt der Tragödie aus dem Geiste der Musik.

Year	Life	Prose Writings	Compositions	Contemporary Events
1873	Completes republication of nine volumes of works. May 22. Begins building of Wahnfried. May. Begins scoring Götterdämmerung.	"On the Name Music Drama." "Letter to an Actor." "Epilogue to the Ring." "A Glance at the German Operatic Stage of To-day." "The Rendering of Beethoven's 9th Symphony." "Prologue to a Reading of Götterdämmerung before a Select Audience at Berlin." "Bayreuth."—Final Report, &c. "The Festival Playhouse at Bayreuth."		Death of Peter Cornelius. Moussorgsky's *Boris Godounov*.
1874	Aug. 2. The Bayreuth theater finished in the rough. May. Enters into residence at Wahnfried. Nov. Finishes scoring of Götterdämmerung.	"On Spohr's *Jessonda*." "On an Operatic Performance in Leipzig."		Ravel born. Bizet's *Carmen*.
1875			Albumblatt in E flat major.	
1876			American Centennial March. Aug. 13-17. First performance of the Ring at Bayreuth, under Richter.	Goldmark's *Queen of Sheba*. Brahms's 1st Symphony.
1877	Jan. to Apr. Writes poem of Parsifal.	"To the Committee of the Wagnervereine."		Saint-Saëns' *Samson and Dalila*.

SYNTHETIC TABLE OF WAGNER'S LIFE AND WORKS AND SYNCHRONOUS EVENTS—Continued

Year	Life	Musical Works	Prose and Poetical Works	Synchronous Events
	Dec. Poem published. Autumn. Begins the music. May 7–29. Conducts eight concerts in Albert Hall, London.		"Sketch for a School for Style."	Massenet's Le Roi de Lahore.
1878	Jan. First number of "Bayreuther Blätter" issued. Apr. 20. Act I of Parsifal finished. Oct. Act II of Parsifal finished. Dec. Begins scoring of Parsifal. Apr. 28. Angelo Neumann gives (in Leipzig) first performance of the Ring after Bayreuth.		"What is German?" "Modern." "Public and Popularity." "The Public in Time and Space." "Retrospect of the Stage Festivals of 1876." "Introduction to the 'Bayreuther Blätter.'"	
1879	Jan. to Apr. Writes Act III of Parsifal.		"Shall We Hope?" "Open Letter to Herr E. von Weber." "On Poetry and Composition." "On Operatic Poetry and Composition." "On the Application of Music to the Drama."	

1880	In Italy.		"The Work and Mission of My Life." "Introductory Word" (to Hans von Wolzogen's "Über Errettung der deutschen Sprache"). "Religion and Art." "What Boots This Knowledge?" "Introduction to the Year 1880" ("Bayreuther Blätter"). "Communication to the Patrons of the Stage Drama."	Death of Moussorgsky.
1881	Jan. Angelo Neumann begins (in Berlin) his European tour with the Ring.		"Introduction to a Work of Count Gobineau." "Know Thyself." "Hero-dom and Christendom."	Stravinsky born.
1882	Jan. 13. Finishes scoring of Parsifal. Sept. Goes to Venice. Dec. Conducts his youthful symphony in C major in Venice.	July 26. First performance of Parsifal at Bayreuth, under Levi.	"Parsifal at Bayreuth." "On the Production of a Youthful Symphony." "Letter to Hans von Wolzogen." "Open Letter to Friedrich Schon."	
1883	Feb. 13. Dies at Venice. Feb. 18. Buried at Bayreuth.		"On the Human Womanly," (posthumous fragment). "Letter to Herr von Stein."	Saint-Saëns' Henry the Eighth. Dvorak's Stabat Mater.

INDEX